D1548201

LUDWIG BAMBERGER

UNIVERSITY OF PITTSBURGH PRESS

Ludwig Bamberger

German Liberal Politician
and Social Critic, 1823-1899

Stanley Zucker

Library of Congress Cataloging in Publication Data

Zucker, Stanley, birth date
  Ludwig Bamberger: German liberal politician and
social critic, 1823–1899.

  Bibliography: p. 315
  Includes index.
  1. Bamberger, Ludwig, 1823–1899. 2. Germany—
Politics and government—1848–1870. 3. Germany—
Politics and government—1871–1918.
DD219.B37Z92   943.08'092'4 [B]   74-17839
ISBN 0-8229-3298-9

For B.F.Z. who shared it all

Contents

Preface

Every country's history contains lost chances and might-have-beens, but in regard to no other country have missed opportunities been more greatly lamented than Germany. Friedrich Meinecke has identified three periods in the nineteenth century when the German people had an opportunity to embark on a political course which would have brought Germany closer to western European constitutional patterns. A. J. P. Taylor has written that Germany in 1848 reached a turning point but failed to turn. In the search for new paths for German political development, historians have fastened on liberalism as the major alternative in the nineteenth century. In the immediate aftermath of the Wars of Liberation, in 1848–49, and during the Prussian constitutional conflict of the 1860s, a liberal breakthrough was possible. The liberal forces failed to a lesser or greater degree each time, and Prusso-German development continued on its conservative, authoritarian way, although it was eventually covered by a veneer of constitutional life. Just why the liberal elements were unsuccessful has intrigued historians. Whether because of disunity within their own ranks, fear of democratic or socialistic groups on the left, an awareness that they lacked a strong popular base, or the brute fact of the military strength of the entrenched forces, the liberals failed to capitalize on the opportunities which offered themselves.

In the search for the supposed liberal failure in the nineteenth century, historical research has focused on the liberal spectrum spanned by the Progressive and National Liberal parties. The former, defeated in the Prussian constitutional conflict, was wracked by a secession which ultimately led to the creation of the National Liberal party. Although the policy of cooperation with Bismarck to which the National Liberals were committed apparently succeeded in the economic field, they split over this issue in 1880. Moving uneasily between the National Liberal and Progressive poles and united by a desire for a stronger dose of parliamentary government, a maximum degree of economic freedom, and an unwillingness to follow

ix

Bismarck blindly, a small group of liberals tried to walk the difficult path of accepting the realities of German life without denying liberal principles. At home in neither the Progressive party, which was too oppositional, nor the National Liberal party, which was too governmental, these Secessionists tried unsuccessfully to provide a rallying point for "healthy" liberal forces in Germany. One of the key figures in this group was Ludwig Bamberger.

Bamberger's political life spanned the last half of the nineteenth century. Starting in 1848 as a democrat, he moved to the Bismarckian camp in the 1860s only to break with the chancellor in the late 1870s. In the course of his life he joined five political groups in his fruitless attempt to reconcile personal ideals with German realities. Although his interests ranged far from the political arena his consuming passion was politics, and he was above all else a professional politician. His stances on various questions were subject to party considerations, and he was ready to compromise as long as he believed the agreement would result in a net advance toward his goal of a bona fide parliamentary system. This was the rationale for his actions from 1866 to 1878. When he no longer saw progress but only retrogression issuing from the compromises, he regarded opposition as the appropriate response.

His eventful life as a revolutionary democrat, a political exile, a successful Parisian banker, an influential journalistic advocate of Prussian-led German unification, a key figure in the National Liberal party and in the financial legislation of the 1870s, and a persistent critic of Bismarckian Germany from the late 1870s make Bamberger a significant figure in nineteenth-century German history. His extensive activities provide the observer with insights into the strength and weakness of German liberalism and offer a penetrating view of German society in the second half of the nineteenth century.

Bamberger left behind a large literary estate stretching over fifty-five years, including a sizable amount of unpublished material. The most important archival collection for a study of Bamberger and German liberalism is in the Deutsches Zentralarchiv in Potsdam and Merseburg. Bamberger's Nachlass in Potsdam was previously in the possession of Dr. Ernst Feder but was confiscated during the Nazi era and eventually found its way to the Deutsches Zentralarchiv in the late 1950s. Other significant collections of Bamberger's letters can be found in the Handschriftenabteilung of the Staatsbibliothek in Berlin-Dahlem, in Theodor Mommsen's Nachlass in the Handschriftenabteilung of the Deutsche Staatsbibliothek in Berlin, and in the Leo Baeck Institute in New York. The best collection of Bamberger's published works is in the Stadtbibiothek in Mainz. I wish to thank the appropriate people in these archives and libraries as well as in the others listed in the bibliography for being kind enough to make their possessions available to me. I am grateful for the financial assistance extended to me by Southern Illinois University at

Carbondale, and the American Philosophical Society. I would also like to express my gratitude to Theodore S. Hamerow for his encouragement and assistance during the various stages of the research and writing. Frau Gurtha Thomson is to be commended for typing the final version of the manuscript. And finally, to my wife for her continued understanding and help throughout this long project—thank you.

LUDWIG BAMBERGER

• 1 •
(Farly Life and Education

The Bambergers had been in the Mainz area for at least two generations prior to Ludwig's birth. His grandfather, Jakob, was a merchant in Bodenheim, a small town along the Rhine about eight miles south of Mainz. It was there in 1790 that Ludwig Bamberger's father, August, was born. The son, a merchant like his father, apparently traveled frequently but finally settled in Mainz, where he started a bank that lasted until the 1930s. On December 23, 1818, he married Amalia Bischoffsheim, a member of a prominent banking family. On July 22, 1823, in their house at Schusterstrasse 19, their second child and son, Ludwig Bamberger, was born. Besides his older brother, Rudolf, there were eventually a third son, Heinrich, and three sisters.[1]

The little we know about Ludwig Bamberger's childhood and adolescence indicates that they were happy years.[2] He was an unusually bright pupil and took private lessons in French and Italian. At the *gymnasium* which he attended he graduated first in a class of twelve in 1842. In German, Latin, Greek, French, Italian, history, and conduct he received grades of "excellent," while in mathematics and natural science he was merely "good."[3]

Since he "appeared to be cut out for study," upon completing his preparatory school work Bamberger began to study law at the Hessian state university at Giessen. Fifty years later he remembered this period as one of discussion and disputation and that several times after a heated debate he had a "slight discharge of blood. . . . But so great was the passion for discussion that I did not let myself be frightened away."[4] In the fall of 1843 the young student transferred to Heidelberg, where he was introduced to political economy, particularly the works of Adam Smith and Leon B. Say. He also struck up many lifelong friendships. There was Heinrich Bernhard Oppenheim, a lecturer on German constitutional law, who led him "into the world of political aspiration out of which 1848 was to arise and 1870 to be constructed." Through thirty-six years of university life, revolutionary turmoil, exile, and renewed political activity in Germany they remained close

3

friends and political allies. It was through Oppenheim that Bamberger met Friedrich Kapp, a fellow Heidelberg student, later a fellow exile, and still later a political ally in the Reichstag. At Heidelberg, Bamberger also tried unsuccessfully to organize a liberal student association called Valhalla.[5] With the end of the school year in July 1844, the young student traveled north to Göttingen University. He was of mixed emotions about his life there. "My life here goes on just so monotonously as it began," he wrote. "Each day passes like a clock which is wound up every morning for twenty-four hours. . . . I believe I could no longer work at any other chair, or after dinner go in any other direction around the wall [of the city] than I do now. A daily job is never as regular and uniform [as this]. If I had to look forward to a lifetime of this, perhaps I would no longer endure it; for a limited time however, it is very pleasant and satisfying." This was a time for serious study. With perhaps some exaggeration he claimed to spend ten hours a day immersed in books. He had given up attending lectures, discovering that they were only of use to "beginners." At Göttingen he briefly came under the spell of Friedrich List, whose main work, *Das nationale System der politischen Oekonomie (The National System of Political Economy)*, had recently appeared. It was only after the end of his university studies that he returned to the study of the classical economists.[6]

At the end of the winter semester, Bamberger returned to Giessen to study for his final law examination, which he passed in April 1845. Armed with his new degree, he returned to Mainz to prepare for the Hesse-Darmstadt bar examination. After serving as a law clerk in the Chancery of Appeals Court in Mainz and with an attorney, he passed the examination in the spring of 1847. This theoretically opened the door to a career in the bureaucracy or as a private lawyer. However, Bamberger was still undecided as to his future course. As a Jew he was excluded from a position in the Hessian civil service, and before he could assure himself of an independent existence as an attorney, a ten- to fifteen-year waiting period stretched out before him. The legal profession was licensed by the government, and lawyers moved ahead by virtue of seniority.[7]

His own inclination during these prerevolutionary years was toward further study. Finding himself not overworked as a law clerk, he carried on a wide range of literary activity, concentrating on the writings of major political economists and social theorists such as Adam Smith, Ricardo, Say, Bastiat, Saint-Simon, Blanqui, Blanc, Proudhon, and Fourier. He was also a member of a small literary circle that included clergymen, merchants, and even army officers. And as a politically conscious individual he zealously followed the debates in the French Chamber of Deputies. Into this externally placid world of discussion, the practical force of the revolution of 1848 would intrude.[8]

It is easiest to portray Bamberger's physical appearance during these stormy years. The warrant for his arrest drawn up by the Hesse-Darmstadt authorities after the collapse of the uprising of 1849 described him as follows: 5' 10" tall, red hair, high forehead, blond eyebrows, gray eyes, sharp nose, ordinary mouth, red beard, pale complexion, oval face, and slim, haggard stature.[9] More difficult to describe is his intellectual make-up. It is perhaps too easy to overemphasize Bamberger's Judaism or, more accurately, the fact that he came from a Jewish family. For the approximately two thousand Jews in Mainz, the years from 1815 to 1848 were unsettling. Although they were in an enviable position in comparison to their coreligionists in other German states, the post-Napoleonic period was one of retrogression. They had enjoyed complete civil rights under the French, but after 1815 the Jews of Mainz were excluded from the civil service, required to swear a special oath at trials, and governed by special laws regarding citizenship. While they were mainly small tradesmen and craftsmen, by 1848 there was evidence of dissatisfaction among young Jews who, upon returning from the university, could find no suitable occupation since state positions were closed to them. The social and economic advance of the Jews of Mainz also had a disintegrating effect upon the ghetto, which was dissolving by the mid-nineteenth century, and on traditional Jewish religious practices, which did not seem to meet the needs of the younger generation.[10]

Excluded from the state civil service and forced to suffer other indignities, Bamberger, as Gisbert Beyerhaus maintains, would have had little enthusiasm for the existing political system. Beyond this it is unsafe to go. What is certain is that even before 1848 he cut his ties to the Jewish religion and to any religious belief. As he wrote to his cousin and future wife, Anna Belmont: "If I ever again return to a belief in God, my path will go via the devil's bridge." This was not merely the raucous cry of youthful independence, but the decision of a lifetime. His close friend for over twenty years, Anna von Helmholtz, remarked upon hearing of Bamberger's death: "He was no longer a Jew and had never become a Christian. To him all religions meant the church and as such [were] incomprehensible." In his will, Bamberger expressly forbade any religious ceremony at his funeral. Perhaps, as Jacob Toury maintains, political involvement and political ideals became a substitute religion for Bamberger and other Jews who threw themselves with such abandon into the revolutionary turmoil. But the same should then be said about many politically involved non-Jews. In any event one cannot find a "Jewish" influence at work any more than a Christian. It seems correct to agree with his friend and obituary writer, Alexander Meyer, that Bamberger's Jewish origin did not exercise the least influence on his intellectual development.[11]

It was political events and intellectual currents that shaped Bamberger's world. Without question the impact of French rule deeply marked Bamberger's early life and his later career. Mainz had been part of France for almost twenty years before it was handed over to the small German state of Hesse-Darmstadt, and the memory of this attachment to a great nation remained indelible in the Mainz area as well as throughout the Rhineland. Bamberger's youthful recollections revolved around France and French events. His political memory began with the July Revolution of 1830. He remembered how veterans of Napoleon's army rejoiced in the streets when the news arrived and how they regaled their young admirers with tales from the Napoleonic age. In fact, the Veterans' Club in Mainz was composed of veterans of the French army. The Wars of Liberation seem to have left behind no heritage in the area. Prussia was remembered, not as the liberator or protector of Germany, but as the oppressor of 1793.[12]

Not merely the impressions of the past, but also the heritage of French institutions forced France upon the consciousness of the Mainzers. The civil code decreed by the French was the most treasured residue of their rule, and according to Bamberger this was the source of the attachment to France. It was a tangible point of contact with the former ruler, a progressive possession in a retrogressive period, and maintenance of this legal system became the loudest demand of the inhabitants of Rhenish Hesse after 1815.[13] France was also a source of political inspiration in the 1830s and 1840s. "All of Germany," he wrote in his seventies, "but particularly the west, drew its daily political nourishment from these regions." Bamberger followed with sympathy the struggles of the republican opposition in France. And he claimed that by 1840, rather than being satisfied with stories about the veterans' military exploits, he and his friends sought out those who remembered or participated in the brief republican period of the 1790s. In 1860, in "Die Französelei am Rhein" ("The Fawning for Everything French on the Rhine"), Bamberger treated favorably the "Clubist" period in Mainz history. This reliance on France for political inspiration fell into disrepute with the upsurge of German nationalism after unification, but Bamberger, nevertheless, had to confirm that French constitutionalism of the July monarchy was the formula which adapted the English system of government to continental conditions and traditions. "The liberals in the southwest of Germany followed the discussions of the French Chamber of Deputies and the party struggles with a feeling of solidarity. . . . It was in France that the liberal experiment was being made."[14]

While his attachment to or interest in French developments would no doubt have made it difficult for Bamberger to become a Hesse-Darmstadt loyalist, it did not prevent his emergence as a German patriot in 1848. This evolution, if there was one, is difficult to trace. The French impact would logically have turned Bamberger's thinking toward great nations rather than dwarf states. A German nation was the equivalent of France, but a Hessian state could never be. Karl-Georg Faber, in his excellent study of the Rhineland between 1815 and 1848, sees the crucial decade as 1830–40. After the July Revolution, Faber detects a mixed German reaction marked by a strong dose of cosmopolitanism. The eastern crisis of 1840 and the so-called war scare of that year, however, saw the formation of a German national consciousness on a scale broad enough to reach down to the mass of the population. This crisis demonstrated the Rhineland's national orientation and destroyed French dreams of a restored Rhine. In his memoirs, Bamberger remembered the war scare of 1840 and the literary exchange between Nicholas Becker and Alfred de Musset, but he noted that it was all over so quickly that there was no sustained excitement, "at least in my circles." He hurried on to tell of his interest in French politics.[15]

If heritage and geography inclined Bamberger to France, his university career made him a German. At Giessen, Heidelberg, and Göttingen, he came in contact with Germans from outside Rhenish Hesse, particularly from north Germany. His law studies introduced him to Germanic law, which he had to unlearn when he returned to Mainz, where French law still reigned. He also immersed himself (much too deeply, according to his future wife) in reading Kant, Hegel, and Schelling and studying the history of Germany rather than that of Hesse-Darmstadt. But more than becoming merely German, he was also becoming a German liberal democrat in the still vague way that German radicalism was emerging before 1848. As an old man he remembered the impact of the Hambach Festival, and at the university his knowledge of the new liberal democratic movement deepened. At Heidelberg he met H. B. Oppenheim, who had been witness to the expulsion of the "Göttingen Seven," listened to the lectures of the liberal professor and Badenese politician, Karl Mittermaier, and read speeches of the liberal deputies in Baden's legislature.[16]

One should not take this pre-1848 radicalism of the young student too seriously. Bamberger was the first to admit that he and his small circle of politically interested friends, who would not join the traditional student corps, were the exceptions. And there hovered over it all a philosophical innocence of the realities of politics. In 1846 or 1847 he wrote: "It is a custom of young people, in the sacred zeal for thought and truth, to struggle against empty forms of conventional life." "We did not stumble over practical attempts," he repeated in 1893, "and a childishly cheerful current of freedom blew platonically through our chests. Appropriate to the still life of the nation, [our efforts] turned out more literary than political." Bamberger would have agreed that German liberalism before 1848 was both an intellectual movement and a movement of intellectuals. His pre-1848 letters contain only isolated examples of his early liberalism or radicalism. He did refer to himself as a liberal, as a foe of despots and authority, and he once admonished Anna not to judge people too harshly since so much depended on education and on physical and social conditions. "The 'solvent morality' of the so-called respectable people," he told her, was the "dread of the hardness and atrocious injustice of our penal code."[17]

The years before 1848 mirror, not an emerging radical, but a young man who was uncertain of his future course. Like most university students he regretted the end of student life and disliked "burying" himself "among the philistines." He did not believe he was cut out for a lawyer's career because of physical limits (a weak chest) and intellectual inclinations (a preference for study). For a time he even considered going to Belgium or to Leipzig to work. He seemed unhappy among people of the everyday world and found solace in his books. "There is nothing better than a warm room and beautiful books," he wrote from Göttingen. He did not, however, incline to romanticism; he never wished to escape the civilized world, then or later. He could speak sarcastically of "J. J. Rousseau's people who run around on all fours," and he claimed that "an *Oberhofceremonienmeister* is far more natural than a Huron."[18]

It was an inwardly upsetting time for the young lawyer, who foresaw an endless and boring ten- to twelve-year period before he would achieve an independent position. It was further complicated by the unhappy position of his future wife, Anna, who had become a plaything between her warring parents. There seemed to be no way out of their dilemma. "When will the good time really begin?" he lamented in 1847:

> Understand that a life with great chances for fortune and misfortune is far preferable to a comfortable humdrum existence; but if one has set his whole life on thinking activity, on learning . . . , repose is everything. . . . For that reason . . . I can surrender myself to the status quo . . . for a time, for one year, one year I say, and after that?[19]

Bamberger had only a year to wait to find an apparent solution to his problems. When the bell of revolution sounded in February 1848 and "the most peaceful chapter which the annals of world history has to record, a time of despair for lieutenants and captains," came to a close, a new world opened to him.[20]

· 2 ·

𝕽𝖊𝖛𝖔𝖑𝖚𝖙𝖎𝖔𝖓 𝖔𝖋 1848

Ludwig Bamberger rarely disowned anything he had written earlier in his life. He liked to stress the continuity of his development from youth to old age. It was, he recalled in retirement, a quiet joy "to recognize on the whole the old Adam" in his youthful writings. For this reason alone his role in the revolution of 1848 is instructive. Involved in political action for the first time, he came face to face with emerging social and political problems that were to confront him and society for the rest of his life. His experiences in 1848 and 1849 also bring into sharp relief the dilemma of German democracy in the middle of the nineteenth century.[1]

"The French February Revolution occurred in an excited and politically tense time," wrote a Mainz historian. The Rhenish city had been anything but a satisfied community after 1815. After nearly twenty years of French rule, when it functioned as the capital of a department, the city and the adjacent territory on the left bank of the Rhine were awarded to the Grand Duchy of Hesse, a small state with no historic claims to Mainz. The lack of a common bond between Mainz and her new owners was mirrored in a number of political, social, and economic problems. The years of being part of a great nation had given the Mainzers a heightened sense of political awareness and importance which made it difficult for them to accept being an adjunct of an insignificant German state. Moreover, the Mainzers believed that their most treasured heritage of French rule, the Napoleonic code, was in danger of being replaced by the Germanic code in use in the rest of the grand duchy. Whatever else the Mainzers may have felt about the years of French occupation, they believed almost unanimously that the French code was far superior to the Germanic. Further complicating relations between Hessians on the right and left banks were economic grievances. The Mainzers believed, probably incorrectly, that they were being discriminated against in the construction of rail and bridge connections. Mainz had also lost its very profitable right to transship goods (*Stapelrecht*), and the advent of the steamboat had

10

hurt certain occupational groups severely. These points of friction were exacerbated by differences in the social structure. French control had effectively destroyed or severely weakened prerevolutionary conservative influences. A native aristocracy no longer existed; the few aristocrats in Mainz represented the occupying force of Austrians or Prussians, as Mainz was a federal fortress, or the ducal officials sent from Darmstadt. There was also a sharp decline in the conservative influence of the Catholic church as the old aristocratic control gave way to middle-class leadership. The Napoleonic period had permitted the lower church authorities to come to the fore, and these men sought to bind the church to the new age to make it more effective. With good reason did Treitschke call Mainz the most radical German city.

These developments funneled into the constitutional and national struggles which grew out of the hopes and subsequent disappointments of the Wars of Liberation. In December 1820, in order to bind his disparate territories together as well as to dampen dissatisfaction, Grand Duke Ludwig granted his subjects a constitution which provided for an elected assembly. The assembly became a source of opposition to the monarch, and in spite of repeated dissolutions, censorship, and extensive police interference, the political opposition was able to grow. In the election of 1847 the opposition, under the leadership of Heinrich von Gagern, won one-third of the seats in the lower chamber, and this was regarded as an overwhelming repudiation of the existing system. In the province of Rhenish Hesse not a single government candidate was elected. The forces around Gagern immediately demanded freedom of the press, an end to censorship, and a change in the system of government. And finally to the above circumstances must be added the impact throughout Europe of the depression of 1846 to 1848. Mainz suffered particularly from a lack of credit, and as a center of the grain trade it felt sharply the poor harvests of 1845 and 1846.[2]

The revolution in Mainz began at the end of February under the leadership of Franz Zitz, a forty-four-year-old lawyer. His presidency of the Carnival Association in 1843 and 1844 signified a position of political prominence, since the carnival was used as a means of expressing political dissent. This, plus his excellent speaking ability and physical presence, placed him in the revolutionary limelight, and he quickly became the favorite of the crowds at the public meetings. At a major assembly on February 28 it was decided to propose an address to the legislature in Darmstadt which demanded freedom of the press, the elimination of the standing army, the arming of the people, the removal of police restrictions, and the calling of a German parliament. The rejection of the petition in Darmstadt occasioned outbreaks of violence. A second rejection of the petition led to a decision by the Mainzers to march en masse to the capital to demand their rights. In the face of this threat, the grand ducal government capitulated. On March 5, the grand duke's son was named regent, and on the following day the hated minister of the interior, Baron Karl du Thil, was replaced by the opposition leader, Heinrich von Gagern. The press was freed immediately, and legislation was to be introduced to meet the other demands raised by the Mainzers. Those dealing with the right of petition and assembly, the removal of censorship, and the elimination of the most odious police regulations became law on March 16. That was the Hessian revolution, and March 8 was set aside for public festivities to celebrate it.[3]

It was not long before the young lawyer was swept up in these events. Bamberger was visiting friends in Heidelberg when he received news of the Parisian revolution. Filled with political enthusiasm and searching for revolutionary activity, he proceeded first to Strassburg, then Karlsruhe, back to Heidelberg, and finally to Mainz in time for the festivities of March 8. On that evening, in the midst of the fireworks, torchlight parades, and Zitz's eloquent oratory, Bamberger was still free of any participation in the new movement. But he did not consider the recently acquired and promised freedoms secure. "With all the enthusiasm for what one at that time in Germany called revolution, I felt still more acutely the urge to guard the naive blind faith of the liberals against the danger of self-deception." Believing that the "March achievements" rested on an insecure foundation, Bamberger did not remain an inactive spectator. "And the natural way to satisfy the irrepressible urge to action was the daily press."[4]

The daily press in Mainz consisted of one newspaper, the *Mainzer Zeitung,* founded in 1822. It was a four-page affair, liberal in outlook, consisting almost exclusively of reports from other newspapers, on the average a week old. The publisher and owner was Theodore von Zabern and the editor, Karl Bölsche. Bamberger proceeded to the offices of this modest daily on March 9 and offered his services, which were accepted with a salary of 400 gulden per year. So began a relationship which lasted until June 1849. From April 4 to May 6, 1848, and November 5, 1848, until January 11, 1849, Bamberger was joint editor. From January 11 until June 1849 he was sole editor. His feature articles and reports appeared almost every day and helped extend the reputation of the newspaper beyond the borders of Mainz and make it a pleasure to read even today.[5]

Years later Bamberger claimed that his articles in the *Mainzer Zeitung* contained three elements: a general democratic tendency, the special variety peculiar to the Rhineland, and his own intellectual make-up. "It was a first stormy eruption which, suddenly unchained, let the quietly gathered material stream out."[6] Bamberger's first article, "Die französische Revolution und die

Stimme in Deutschland" ("The French Revolution and the Mood in Germany"), appeared in the issue of March 10. It tried to counter fears that the revolution in France would lead to a French invasion of Germany, and on the contrary hinted that those who were spreading these tales were merely attempting to misdirect the aroused temper of the people away from the task of internal reform and toward an imaginary foreign danger. In his second article he pleaded for the acceptance of change as normal and told his readers not to be impressed by calls for "legal change." As he put it, "The law is the expression of the existing and the enemy of the becoming. . . . All reformers were criminals." The first article and those that followed made the former law clerk a prominent figure in Mainz. Not simply what he wrote, but also the freshness of his style attracted attention. His coeditor, Karl Bölsche, expressed it well: "The way he could blare a thought at the people, wedge an idea in their souls, the clever fashion in which he brought the light of day, the sharp look . . . to everything. They were offensive and defensive weapons like this age so much requires and are so little possessed by the German press." The immediate success of Bamberger's articles caused an enlargement of the paper, a doubling of his salary, and his appointment as joint editor in April. What this meant to the struggling and unsure university graduate can easily be imagined. "I live in a frenzy of work," he wrote to Anna. "But it is a great satisfaction to me that the first thing which I lightheartedly started on appears to succeed beyond all expectation. In fourteen days I have transformed a little obscure local rag into a general sensation. I, an unknown novice . . . have gotten the whole leadership in my hands. The publisher views me as an excellent acquisition. All this, as little as it really is, gives me confidence which I did not possess before." He had finally found a cause.[7]

These newspaper articles, supplemented by letters and speeches, offer an excellent insight into the young revolutionary's political, economic, and social thought. The total impression is one of groping, of ideological confusion or uncertainty. We are not certain whether we are facing a future liberal or future socialist politician. We do see the problems of German democracy, and we do know that we have come in contact with an exciting writer, an inspiring orator, and an exceptionally able organizer.

Although Bamberger claimed that with the February Revolution in France he saw a new world open, he first had to turn his attention to the death cries of the old. As in other German states, the first waves of revolution in Hesse-Darmstadt brought with them outbursts of Luddism centering around the steamships and railways. These new means of conveyance were inflicting serious hardships on those whose jobs were being made superfluous. In the days of the sailing ships, people had been employed to pull boats to higher ground, but by 1848 these *Voranzieher* were being replaced by steam-driven barges and tugs. The coachmen formed another dissatisfied group. They had formerly carried travelers from Mainz to Wiesbaden and Frankfurt, but the railroad was threatening their livelihood. A third group faced with occupational extinction was the draymen. They had short-hauled goods to and from ships and trains, but recently the merchants had begun to use their own horses and vehicles for the transportation of their wares and also to rent equipment to fellow merchants. To alleviate their distress these groups demanded a limitation on the use of the steamships for carrying goods and pulling barges, and a prohibition on the use by merchants of their own horses and carts. A petition was drawn up on March 18, 1848, which in addition to the above demands called for the reintroduction of the old requirement of transshipment of goods, thus re-creating jobs for those who had once done the unloading.[8]

To call attention to their plight they resorted to repeated outbreaks of violence against the steamers and railways during the spring of 1848. Several times tugs were halted, their barges cut loose and, to the cheers of the shore population, pulled manually upstream. Other times the tugs were simply prevented from operating. On the night of April 5 the violence spread to the railway in Kastel across the river from Mainz. A mob of coachmen, stevedores, and day laborers tore up a part of the track in Kastel and destroyed the station house.[9]

The problem was difficult to attack, not least of all because the plight of the *Voranzieher,* draymen, and coachmen evoked much sympathy from the population. In his memoirs Bamberger relates how one day the boatmen were in the midst of "capturing a barge" in order to pull it upstream. The city militia, which had been dispatched to the scene, did not seem inclined to intervene. Bamberger questioned several members of the militia, "all comfortable citizens." "How astonished I was when I heard from them that they supported the boatmen and declared that they were completely right. And this happened in a province which for a half century had known no trace of compulsory guilds, in which at that time much more occupational freedom ruled than in the present-day imperial industrial code."[10]

As soon as the disorder had begun, the new columnist of the *Mainzer Zeitung* made his position clear but also demonstrated his ability to straddle a potentially dangerous issue. Bamberger had already witnessed examples of violence similar to those perpetrated in Mainz, when the tailors of Heidelberg had attacked the shops of the cloth dealers. He was now determined that such "misunderstood applications of the new freedom" would not take root in Mainz. "Let us not forget," he wrote, "freedom is not possession of the . . . goods of life, it is the surest way that all will succeed to them; it is a means, but it does not heal ancient wounds in the course of a day. . . . It is foolish to demand ... the solution of these infinite problems in the course of an hour. ... The silliest, however, is to raise one's voice against the improvements of the tools through which energies are saved because for a moment a certain craft becomes superfluous. No society can thrive by squandering, and squandering exists when any industry expends more time or energies or capital than is necessary." The crisis which the obsolescent workers faced was not much different, Bamberger claimed, from the changes the privileged classes were being asked to accept. One could not make privileges out of old customs and rights. "Progress cannot go its way via the denial of reality and cannot wish away and destroy the decisions which make the force of the elements of use to mankind. ... That would not be freedom but barbarism." But of course there was still a "momentary" problem of unemployment and privation during the "transition period." Here the budding radical appeared to lean to the left. He counseled his readers to let the "unfalsified voice of the people" solve this problem and indicated that the press would no longer be hindered by the "fear of Communist bogeymen" from proving that so long as misery and degeneration affect even a small part of the population, true happiness would not be possible for anyone. "It will show that each state which does not make its first task the elimination of those evils races toward ruin." He called on "society to provide employment for those who were unemployed."[11]

Fifty years later Bamberger referred to the "well-meaning, moderately socialistic, pacifying phrases" which his articles contained. In 1848 they appear to have been something more. They form a constant theme in his writings and speeches for the next year and they prove, if not Bamberger's serious confrontation with these ideas, at least the importance of the ideas for the political situation in Mainz. Socialism and socialist ideas did have a significant weight in the events of 1848, and Bamberger recognized probably more clearly in 1848 than in 1898 his true relation to them.[12]

The shipping dispute dragged on until the summer, when steps were taken to ease the distress of the boatmen and draymen. The city council requested the *Voranzieher* not to increase their ranks and asked the merchants not to transport their wares on their own horses. It then turned to the ministry in Darmstadt for further assistance. The government prevailed upon the steamship companies to pay damages to the *Voranzieher,* while the owners of sailboats were pacified by a decision of the Central Commission for Rhine Shipping that until further notice only such steam-driven ships could travel on the Rhine as were engaged in shipping as of August 1, 1848.[13]

While the problems of progress were being ironed out, Ludwig Bamberger was becoming ever more involved in the revolutionary turmoil. Via a private conversation with Zitz and then by a lead article, he successfully toned down the reception accorded the son of the grand duke upon his visit to Mainz. He wanted the Mainzers to engage in "no act of subjection" to the dynasty, he wrote, and the subdued reception went off without incident. On March 16 he called for the transformation of Germany into a single national state, with the implication that only a republic was in accord with this goal. His article provoked a quick reply from the president of the Darmstadt ministry, Heinrich Jaup, who was also the father-in-law of the publisher of the *Mainzer Zeitung*. The exchange publicly broached the idea of a German republic for the first time. For the young journalist, a republic was not an end in itself, but the only means of destroying the particularism rooted in the German Confederation and the dynasties, and of creating a single united German state. His political education and involvement increased sharply at the end of March, when he was assigned as a correspondent to the preliminary parliament in Frankfurt. His first impressions strengthened his doubts about the permanence of the initial gains. He attended the meetings of the democrats and, disturbed by what he considered to be the too trusting speeches of Franz Raveaux and Robert Blum, he made his first public speeches on behalf of the republic. The stay in Frankfurt, coming after the tumultuous days in March, was a turning point in his life. "One lives in a completely different way than four weeks ago," he wrote. "Whatever may come, and much evil will still come, I am resigned and swim with the current which impels the age."[14]

Back in Mainz and officially made joint editor on April 4, and apparently radicalized by his stay in Frankfurt, Bamberger moved to give a new direction to the revolutionary momentum in the city. He began to attack the Citizens' Committee (Bürgercomité) which had been formed after the disturbances of early March. Similar committees were formed in various cities of Rhenish Hesse, and they seemed to be aiming at administrative control of the province. In Mainz it was a middle-class body dominated by merchants and other businessmen, and its various programs had a progressive ring. It proposed the replacement of all internal tariffs with a progressive income and inheritance tax; it also called for the improvement of the condition of the working classes and the establishment of a ministry of labor. It favored a general arming of the people and the organization of a central German government based on democratic principles.[15]

In spite of the democratic tone of the program, Bamberger became dissatisfied with the committee partly, he tells us in his memoirs, because it reacted too timidly to the railway destruction, but primarily because it seemed too loyal to the dynasty in Darmstadt. He feared that the latter tendency would weaken the revolutionary momentum. In his articles of April 11 and April 12, he attacked the moderates who claimed that everything had been accomplished with the March concessions, and he urged the citizens to seize the initiative. He focused his attack on the committee's support for a "division of Germany according to nature," which he interpreted as leaving the way open to maintaining the existing states with their dynasties. He charged that the committee had lost touch with the mood of the people and called for a public meeting to discuss the issue.[16] The Citizens' Committee agreed to a public assembly on April 16 in the former electoral palace, setting the stage for the young and still relatively unknown journalist's first public triumph. Speaking twice and literally swaying the crowd of two thousand away from the temporizing Zitz, Bamberger won approval for a rewording of the offensive article which now explicitly rejected a monarchy and called for a future national parliament without a chamber of princes. He also won acceptance of his demand that a new committee be elected, which he hoped would be controlled by republican elements. His triumph was complete one week later when he and fifteen supporters were elected to the new Citizens' Committee.[17]

This achievement marked one peak of Bamberger's revolutionary year. From April 16 on he counted as one of the leaders of the democratic movement in Mainz and one of the most prominent figures in the city. And he was still too young to vote in the elections for the National Assembly in Frankfurt. However, he was less than clear and consistent in his actions. Except that he favored a republic rather than a monarchy, his position is difficult to establish. He had no apparent quarrel with the social and economic proposals of the committee. Even his faith in the people was less than complete. As he confessed to Anna after being the recipient of a torchlight parade and serenade under his window: "Is it not a sad commentary on the whole affair that I have come to the top so quickly. . . . 'Le peuple n' est pas du tout sublimé.' So it looks to me from time to time when I view things and people individually; who wants to be effective in the world may take them . . . only as a collective idea."[18]

His articles during this period also reveal an uncertainty of ideas, an ideological juggling act until he could find a suitable place for all the pieces, and perhaps a fear of the Hessian government. In two articles on April 21 and 23, Bamberger attacked his more moderate and well-to-do opponents on the right for favoring a "constitutional democratic monarchy" and for their subservience to the ministry in Darmstadt. On the evening of April 23, a crowd of about a thousand from the artisanate honored him with a demonstration. When several speakers attacked the rich he cautioned, "Far be it from us to want to damn the propertied merely on account of their possessions; only if they prove themselves enemies of the people would they be our opponents." The banker's son perhaps recognized that he had gone too far in using his ability to evoke feeling.[19]

The same dualism is revealed in his article about the French socialist, Louis Blanc. Bamberger called him a very modest revolutionary and saw in his writings only thoughts, not a plan of action, which would have to develop out of the actual course of events. The journalist clearly indicated that his exposition of Blanc's version of socialism was designed to instruct rather than convince, but he added, "The impartial person will long have recognized that there is a truth in those theories and that a future is reserved for them."[20]

The discussion of Louis Blanc's ideas was soon followed by an essay on political economy, concentrating on the views of Adam Smith and Leon Say. It gives evidence that Bamberger was not the dogmatic liberal that he was to become later. He noted:

> The errors of the political economists lie perhaps in that they have proceeded with too great a feeling of security in calculating in advance what might occur. It is almost impossible to calculate theoretically in advance the course of causes and effects, which are living constellations. . . . For that reason the problem of protection of industry, the kind of taxation, or the choice of currency are always open questions which can never be solved on the basis of theory alone.

Equally at variance with his later views were his comments on social welfare. He attacked the notion that unrestricted competition and unconditional concern for the consumer would produce welfare for all. These were developments, he argued, which were outside the limits of a mere conceptual system. But in spite of the weaknesses, Bamberger concluded, the Smithians recognized the deficiencies of the old system and where it would lead, and "spoke out with clarity and strength of conviction as scarcely one of the newest socialists." He again disclaimed any partisan purpose; he merely wanted to acquaint the general public with the teachings of political economy. He seemed to be thinking out the problem in his own mind as well, still the seeker rather than the convinced liberal dogmatist of later years.[21]

Besides the more theoretical discussions, the radical columnist concerned himself with improving the current economic situation. He favored a progressive tax on capital and a rationalization of indirect taxes. But at the same time he recognized that business activity needed encouragement and this meant security. He saw a vital role for banks to play in the rebirth of confidence. Banks could stabilize the exchange; they could supply the credit necessary to mobilize the productive forces of the economy, in which he included factory owners, merchants, retailers, craftsmen, and peasants. He was cool to the idea of public works, like railroads, arguing correctly that excessive investment in them had helped cause the pre-March crisis.[22]

While the young journalist was sorting out his political, economic, and social ideas, his political standing deteriorated rapidly in the erratic swing of Mainz politics. His apparent triumph in the election to the Citizens' Committee proved to be a Pyrrhic victory. Eleven moderate members immediately resigned after the radical majority declared that the committee was an independent body in no way subordinate to the city council. The mayor, Nikolaus Nack, attacked the rump committee, accusing it of usurping power and trying to turn itself into a committee of public safety. He appealed to the population for support and forced the committee to resign. No new elections were held.[23]

Shortly after the collapse of the committee, Bamberger suffered a second blow. He was forced to resign his editorship of the paper. His caustic articles against the ministry in Darmstadt, whose chairman was the publisher's father-in-law, and against the prominent citizenry who did not see the world through Bamberger's radical eyes, led to pressure on Zabern for his young editor's dismissal. On May 5 Bamberger submitted his resignation.[24]

A third and far more serious setback not merely for Bamberger but for the whole democratic movement occurred on the night of May 21–22 in a clash with the Prussian garrison. In the early days of March, as a result of the Luddite disturbances, a citizen's militia had been organized and provided with weapons. With Zitz as commander, the militia began to train regularly. Since the Austro-Prussian garrison was loyal to the Hessian government and the militia counted as an arm of the democratic forces in Mainz, these two armed and potentially hostile groups created tension which the formation of a mixed civilian-military commission failed to reduce. Several tavern incidents between soldiers and civilians, sporadic shooting between the two, and finally some dead and wounded brought the two sides to the verge of open warfare. On May 21 the Prussian garrison, after several of its men had been killed in an exchange, ordered the militia to surrender its arms or face bombardment. Since the garrison dominated the city, its demands were met. The night of May 21–22 ended any chance of a seizure of power by the radicals and set the stage for a gradual conservative reaction.[25]

The turning point of May 21–22 was of course not immediately understood. After his resignation from the *Mainzer Zeitung,* Bamberger was nonetheless active, dividing his time between Frankfurt and Mainz. In the former he served as a reporter for the *Mainzer Zeitung* to the National Assembly. As the weakness of the left became apparent, Bamberger's interest in the proceedings correspondingly declined. With the election of Archduke John as imperial regent, he wrote off the assembly as an agency of change, returned to Mainz, and devoted his energies to his major accomplishment of 1848, the organization of the Democratic Association (Demokratische Verein).[26]

The origins of the Democratic Association went back to early April, when the democratic forces throughout Germany were beginning to organize. Similar associations were already in existence in Bonn, Berlin, Frankfurt, and Trier. In Frankfurt, out of the preliminary parliament, a democratic central committee had emerged which tried to coordinate left-wing forces. One of its members was Franz Zitz. In Mainz the direct spur to the association seems to have been the abortive uprisings in Baden in April. Bamberger discussed with some of his friends how they could build "a rallying point . . . for common action by the like-minded, a firm, comprehensive core of opposition against the enemy, a point from which the ideas of freedom could be planted in wider and wider circles." With Bamberger as one of the three signers of the petition calling for a constituent assembly, the Democratic Association was officially organized and the statutes accepted by May 16, 1848.[27]

The purpose of the association, in Bamberger's somewhat extravagant language, was the "complete transformation of political and social conditions." With all the impetuosity of a twenty-four-year-old, he rejected previous political and social forms as unsuited to the modern age. Action must be directed toward the realization of the good life not after death but during one's earthly existence. "We are ripe," he cried, "we do not want to wait any longer." More modestly the statutes spoke of realizing the principle of the sovereignty of the people by means of oral and written propaganda, although other means were not excluded.[28]

The success of the new organization was rapid, beyond even the expectations of the founders. It became the focus of all radical elements of the area. Seven months later Bamberger could claim with not too much exaggeration: "Our idea took root and the organization grew so quickly that we have established something that is rooted in the nature of people. It has become the highest regulator of the political life in our province. . . . Our whole province has become a single Democratic Association."[29] Meetings were held once a week in a well-situated tavern, and the attendance, at least according to newspaper reports, was excellent. A major innovation was the attendance of women, although when the crowds grew exceptionally large the number of female spectators was limited to one hundred. Different topics were discussed every week, and reports on the work of the National Assembly were given. By August, membership in Mainz was over six hundred; by October, fifteen hundred; and by May 1849 the figure was two thousand. Such was the impact of the organization that Bamberger claimed one went into a Democratic Association meeting as the pious entered the church.[30]

Not content with success in Mainz, Bamberger undertook to organize sister associations throughout the province of Rhenish Hesse. The inhabitants of the area proved to be excellent material for the purpose. By August there were twenty-two regional groups, by October, seventy, and by December, over one hundred. The population then and later was democratically inclined. It was an area of small but relatively prosperous wine and grain farms with a middle class composed of doctors, justices of the peace, notaries, pastors, judicial officials, and teachers. Both Protestant and Catholic communities were represented, although there were more of the former than the latter. It was also this area and these elements which were to provide support for Bamberger as a Reichstag deputy from 1874–93.[31]

Bamberger and his colleagues also tried to spread their influence into the military. On June 11, in a meeting in Hochheim, Bamberger called for fraternization of civilians with the military. Prussian soldiers were invited to attend meetings of the Democratic Association, and some did. Attempts were made to organize potential draftees for the Hessian army, but the rally was forbidden by the police.[32]

Greater success was achieved in obtaining support from nonpolitical organizations. The Democratic Association was able to join to it a part of the gymnastic society. With the outbreak of the revolution of 1848 in Germany the increasingly politicized gymnastic groups organized themselves on April 2, 1848, into the German Gymnastic League (Deutscher Turnerbund). The apparent unity concealed divisions over the future shape of a united Germany, whether a republic or a constitutional monarchy. These differences split the league in June 1848 at the second meeting in Hanau. Bamberger participated and was elected chairman, but after a debate with the aged Turnvater Jahn over the political goals of the gymnastic league, he led a secession of the democratic elements and formed the Democratic Gymnastic League (Demokratischer Turnerbund), whose program included support for a German republic. The Democratic Gymnastic League proved to be one of the strongest props for the democratic movement, and it played a prominent role in the revolutionary wave of May, June, and July 1849.[33]

The alliance with the gymnasts was supplemented by an alliance with the local Workingmen's Educational Club (Arbeiterbildungsverein), which was formed at the end of March 1848. The membership was mainly from the artisan class, both masters and journeymen. It had an official organ in Der Demokrat, founded by Ludwig Kalisch in April 1848. The club's chief aim was to raise the intellectual level and increase the material well-being of the worker. It held weekly meetings, gave lessons in school subjects, and discussed topical questions such as: What is the proletariat? Does the machine benefit or harm the worker? Why do the middle class and the propertyless want a republic and the nobility of birth and wealth no republic? Are workhouses useful or not to the worker? What tax system is most purposeful for the state and least oppressive for the people? The club became a regular fixture on the Mainz scene and impressed observers with the seriousness of its purpose. Although it was initially under the control of individuals who were secretly members of the Communist League, such as Karl Wallau, Adolf Cluss, and Gottfried Stumpf, it ultimately adopted a moderate approach to political and social problems.[34] Machines were praised, communism condemned, and separation of the working class from other social groups rejected. The club also criticized the manifesto of the artisan and handicrafts congress which was held in Frankfurt in July for demanding the reintroduction of the guild system.[35] Membership or participation in the Democratic Association and Workingmen's Educational Club overlapped. The Democratic Association supplied speakers to the workers' group, and one report spoke of a "true family celebration" when Zitz and other leaders of the Democratic Association attended a Saturday meeting of the workingmen's club. In July, reacting to the decisions of the artisan congress in Frankfurt, the democrats commissioned Bamberger and two others to contact the workers in order to agree on common measures. On August 13 a meeting of representatives of the Democratic Associations, the Democratic Gymnastic Associations, and the Workingmen's Clubs from Rhenish Hesse was held in Worms.[36]

The relationship between the two products of the revolutionary wave of 1848 points to one of the thorniest problems of the day, the social problem, which was the source of the ultimate failure of the democratic forces. Not that they were uninterested in the problem. In both the preliminary parliament and the Frankfurt National Assembly, the democratic forces had introduced various proposals including dividing up estates, taxing usury, establishing a labor ministry and a credit system for the poor, and equalizing the disproportion between capital and labor. At the level of the Democratic Association in Mainz, these issues were discussed even more intensely. Although we do not know the details, the newspaper reports indicate clearly what was discussed among the democrats. Social matters were high in priority although always connected with political and economic matters. Gottfried Stumpf called for comprehensive state social and economic programs. He proposed state aid to education that would be available to the lower classes, a government program of inner colonization, a state credit bank for business, a public works program, state ownership of railways, and finally an income tax. Someone else wanted to educate working youths at the cost of the factory owners and limit the size of large estates; another suggested that child labor be ended and that the state provide work for all who wanted it. Ludwig Bamberger's brother Rudolf discussed the question: "What is meant by the Red Republic?" At the end of October the following question was placed in discussion: "Which of the three directions of the German Revolution should receive the most accelerated development: the political (establishing civil freedom), the social (production of just and reasonable social conditions) or the national (establishment of national unity)?" The views reported reflect a variety of ideas, but Rudolf, perhaps speaking for his absent brother, claimed that political freedom must come first; only then would it be possible to unify Germany and improve social conditions.[37]

The membership of the Democratic Association cut across class lines, with shopkeepers, small businessmen, and artisans predominating and a leadership group made up of lawyers. Eight of the thirty members of the board of directors were "Doctors," although the chairman, P. J. Schöppler, apparently was an artisan. Included in the association were Theodore von Zabern, the publisher of the *Mainzer Zeitung,* who was married to the daughter of a high Hesse-Darmstadt official, and Germain Metternich, radical and revolutionary. How much general participation there was at the well-attended meeting is difficult to say. The *Mainzer Zeitung* felt it necessary to answer charges that only a few spoke while the great mass was passive. The newspaper reports, without mentioning names in most cases, did cite a variety of speakers.[38]

This, then, was the milieu in which Bamberger operated: a heterogeneity of opinions, a proper anvil on which the association's vice-president could hammer his thoughts into shape. Looking back on 1848 from the vantage point of the 1890s, Bamberger described himself and his friend Julius Fröbel as "convinced radicals but not fanatics." This will do as an apt characterization of Bamberger's beliefs during the revolutionary period. Politically all was clarity and precision. He favored unification, not so much he tells us in the 1890s because of the better "technical work" of the state machine, but rather because of the educational value of a great state. Particularism bred an "unpolitical spirit." In 1848 Bamberger did believe that the existence of a small state encouraged petty actions. The great moral tasks of a large state were impossible in small ones because of limited abilities and ideas. "They cannot solve great problems; their influence on world affairs is nil." Because of the existence of small states, Germany suffered from a lack of statesmanlike talent and of a "general political sense." This latter charge would be reechoed in the 1880s and 1890s at the same time that Bamberger admitted he had underestimated the strength of particularism in Germany. For the resident of French-influenced Rhenish Hesse without strong ties to any princely house, for the university graduate exposed to the most progressive ideas of the age at universities in three different states, for a young man whose own path to advancement seemed interminably slow under the old regime, the leap upward to new political forms was understandable.[39]

Bamberger was equally clear on the shape of the new Germany. It would be republican and unitary. He rejected as impossible a federation of the existing German states under a constitutional monarchy because he viewed the continued existence of the princely houses as a block to true national unity. Bamberger lumped the passing of the princes with the plight of those who had become unemployed through technological changes. It was simply impossible to visualize German unity without the dismissal of the princes, who symbolized disunity and repression. He did recognize the difficulties of his position and stressed the opposition to the idea of a republic that he encountered in Frankfurt during the meeting of the preliminary parliament. His lead articles in April and May seemed designed to insert into the minds of his readers the notion of a republic as a viable political alternative. By discussing the question of a republic openly, he could attack the moderates as too willing to be content with small gains which would leave the powers of the ruling dynasties relatively undisturbed. "No, these are not the people who can regenerate Germany," the young journalist wrote. "Our opinion is that it is a question of a revolution. The [moderate] opponents deny the necessity of the revolution; we are convinced of it. . . . We say it openly: we want a break with the past."[40]

Bamberger's democratic and republican beliefs led him to favor universal manhood suffrage, direct election of representatives and a responsible administration and ministry. Where the ministry is not strongly dependent on the legislative body, he wrote, "an enlightened constitution is a cipher. . . . The soul of a constitutional system is . . . that the majority of the representatives creates and destroys the ministry." Even bureaucrats must be removable. To the claim, explicit in the abortive constitution of 1849, that an independent legislature could exist along with a monarch, Bamberger retorted: "Every legislature under a monarch is a greater or lesser illusion. The power of the monarchs always finds the means, indirectly and through the natural power of attraction of an eternally enduring force, to ruin a legislature and to make it into the blind adherent of the monarchical will." Fifty years later Bamberger would have concluded that events in Germany confirmed his prophecy.[41] True to his democratic beliefs, he did not allow his German patriotism to be transformed into expansive nationalism. He opposed Germans' fighting in Italy and Poland and denounced such appeals as based on an outmoded aristocratic concept of national honor. They were, of course, anything but that. More expansion-minded Germans he denounced as cannibals.[42]

As clear as the political imperatives were, so cloudy were the social and economic requirements—not only for Bamberger but for the democratic left. Looking back on his activity in the Democratic Association, with the benefit of nearly fifty years of hindsight, Bamberger was forced to admit:

When I read once more the discussions which were carried on in our Mainz Democratic Association, I perceive that this [social] ferment, even at that time in the summer of 1848, made itself more clearly noticeable than one usually accepts, and than even hovered in my memory. Completely socialistically formulated proposals kept emerging, and fundamental rejections seldom occurred. . . . Clear ideas about the methods of execution were at that time naturally just as little at hand as they are today.[43]

One of the earliest indications of the dilemma in which Bamberger found himself occurred from June 14 to June 17 when, while covering the Frankfurt Assembly for the *Mainzer Zeitung,* he attended the first Democratic Congress. It was called by the Democratic Association of Marburg to bring unity and organization to the democratic forces in Germany. The response to the call for a congress was encouraging, producing 234 delegates from 89 clubs in 66 cities, including all of the major cities in north and south Germany. The political coloration of the group was decidedly leftist; as Bamberger explained, "The extreme right in this congress begins where the extreme left in the Assembly ceases." Its major decisions were to establish a central committee to work out a common policy for the local Democratic Clubs and to proclaim the democratic republic as the most suitable system of government for Germany.[44]

Bamberger's reports on the congress define more precisely the contours of his political beliefs. The tendency of the congress, according to Bamberger, was socialistic, and he was critical of the leader of the more radical elements, Andreas Gottschalk, whom he incorrectly regarded as an adherent of Karl Marx's. His criticism, however, centered not on an outright rejection of Gottschalk's principles, but on the question of tactics and style. Gottschalk's intemperate language, the democratic leader wrote, was conducive to weeding out weak sisters from a large amorphous party rather than nursing a tiny growth into political manhood. Such "straightforwardness," he argued, would decrease the groups' effectiveness, noting that many participants had already deserted the congress. "The more correct and inescapable the social views, the more moderately should they be put forth in awareness of their enormous practical incompleteness." On the basis of this dispute over tactics, Bamberger concluded that the congress would do more harm than good.[45]

Fifty years later Bamberger gave a somewhat sharper opinion of the proceedings in Frankfurt. "Here for the first time," he wrote, "I realized the sharp difference which separated the . . . radical republican views from the purely socialistic and was to continue to separate them for the future. . . . I still recall quite clearly the ill feeling with which it filled me." The "cold-bloodedness" with which Gottschalk expounded his "communistic" views as something self-evident was at that time new and "staggering" to Bamberger.[46]

A more staggering event occurred a few days after the Democratic Congress closed. From June 23 to June 26, Paris was the scene of a workers' insurrection which resulted in the bloodiest street fighting Europe had experienced. When the news of the "June Days" reached Frankfurt, Bamberger was sitting in a tavern with Ludwig Feuerbach and Friedrich Kapp. "We felt that a great decision would fall there," he remembered, "which had to change the course of the French revolution and with it the whole European situation. We had a clear premonition that a turning point had set in for the whole course of future political development. . . . The social question had thrown its sword into the turmoil of the political struggle, never again to disappear from the battle and to make more difficult if not impossible for all time the victory of . . . political freedom."[47]

Bamberger's initial reaction to the struggle between the bourgeoisie and the workers in the streets of Paris was not one-sided or even clear. Aware that his Democratic Association was composed of elements from both middle and lower classes, and also to avoid giving the Hesse-Darmstadt government an excuse for restricting his activities, he tried to steer a middle course in a speech he gave to the association. The Parisian events, he began, made clear that the "colossal thought of a complete transformation of all human relations, the thought of social revolution," had raised its threatening head. "The basic thought of the workers was social revolution, but the National Assembly, composed of the propertied and the educated, recoiled from grasping the social element and shrank from the necessary sacrifices. It was a mistake of the National Assembly that it wanted to treat the social question as equal to other problems. It is central to all human society and in order to make good a crying evil one may have to go far to the other side." The burden of responsibility for the June uprising, he went on, had to be shared. The bourgeoisie, "did not provoke the struggle because it did not help [the working class] —that would have been unthinkable so quickly—but because it threatened to deny the principle. Nevertheless the bourgeoisie triumphed and had to triumph because they knew what they wanted after the victory while the worker did not. The worker may have been right. The rightness of a principle, however, also means that it actually offers applicability, and this element was lacking in the will of the worker." There could be no doubt, the young democrat continued, that as soon as the proletariat stepped forward with a realizable plan, "its victory is certain. As long as it does not, it will have many of its supporters as opponents in the hand-to-hand fighting."[48] Dictated no doubt by the realities of the Mainz scene, the speech also reflected Bamberger's inner uncertainty regarding the emergent social movement. For the next several years he would fight out within himself the pros and cons of social change.

His continued dualism was evidenced several weeks later in a speech in Kostheim. He first rejected the charge that democracy signified sharing. "It strives only for such a state institution where each person is capable of acquiring the highest possible degree of education and welfare according to the measure of his physical and intellectual powers." He balanced this basically nineteenth-century liberal statement by concluding that the institutions of a society were worthless if the possibility existed that even a single individual could starve.[49]

As Bamberger searched for his political and social bearings, the course of revolution in Mainz was anything but favorable. Although crowned with apparent success in organizing a network of political clubs throughout the province, the democrats were faced with a rejuvenated and newly confident government in Darmstadt as well as competition from rival political groups. The growth of the Democratic Association in Mainz and the establishment of sister clubs in the province tended to obscure the fact that no breakthrough had been made into the old core of Hesse-Darmstadt on the right bank of the Rhine and north of the Main. The overwhelming majority of clubs were in the province acquired from the French in 1815. The turning point in the growth of the association outside Rhenish Hesse occurred on July 23, 1848, with the failure of a major democratic rally in Darmstadt. The geographic limits of the Democratic Association had been reached.[50]

More serious to the democrats in Mainz were the activities of the Darmstadt government. It enacted into law many of the promises made in March, and freedom of speech, religion, and the press became a reality. Even Bamberger was later astonished by the extent of free expression. The army was sworn to the constitution; fishing, hunting, and forest privileges were eliminated; strict budgetary economies were instituted. The government was also able to satisfy partially the protesting draymen, coachmen, and boat pullers whom Bamberger had castigated in April. Steps were taken to reorganize the provincial administrations in the direction of greater democracy, and the new head of the administrative commission for the Mainz area was the tough and capable Baron Karl von Dalwigk.[51]

With Dalwigk at the helm, the Hessian government began to reassert its authority in Rhenish Hesse and to take a harsher stand toward the democrats in Mainz. His recommendation of a general prohibition of the Democratic Association failed, but the Hessian government did enforce the press regulations with a new strictness and was able to restrict the association's placing of placards and spreading of pamphlets. Bamberger and several other young lawyers made themselves available for legal advice when an individual believed his rights were being threatened by the authorities. It cost him a reprimand by the district court, but as he wrote forty-five years later: "We were happy about the opportunity to show our lack of respect for the authorities."[52]

While the government was counterattacking, new competition for popular support appeared in Mainz. One result of Bamberger's advocacy of a republic in the columns of the *Mainzer Zeitung,* his swaying of the public meeting of April 15 to support a republic, and his engineering of the new elections to the citizens' committee, was to destroy what anticonservative unity had existed. Moderate elements organized a Citizens' Association (Bürgerverein) composed mainly of merchants, manufacturers, shopkeepers, and government officials. They gave their support to a competing newspaper, the *Rheinische Zeitung,* which was founded in April 1848 and edited by an old friend of Bamberger's, Julius Creizenach. It supported the revolution and German unity, but it proposed the establishment of a constitutional monarchy with democratic institutions and the preservation of the various German dynasties. By September, a network of Citizens' Associations had been formed throughout Hesse-Darmstadt with a coordinating central committee of fifteen. The Mainz branch had over five hundred members. Although the Citizens' Association could not match the Democratic Association in size and propaganda, it did signal the disintegration of the united front of March 1848.[53]

A further loss of potential support occurred with the organization of Catholic interests on March 23 in the Pius Association (Pius Verein). Mainz had long been the center of an active Catholic community, and over three-fourths of its population was Catholic. The Catholic church initially had welcomed the revolution of 1848 and supported separation of church and state and religious freedom. It was, however, disturbed by the secular and antireligious tendencies of many of the revolution's supporters. Bamberger himself had rejected the notion of a morality based on religious principles. In his words, "The religion of our time is called politics and our confession, freedom." Or he would see the Democratic Association as the new church. He denied strenuously that democracy contained hatred against religion as such but made it clear that he would always oppose a party whose primary motive was religious interest or the penetration of religion into secular fields such as education. This was hardly reassuring to Catholics. What disturbed them most was the fear that the revolution would mean the end of confessional schools. In the early days of the revolution the Citizens' Committee would not give sufficient assurances to the contrary. The formation of the Pius Association was followed in June by the establishment of the *Mainzer Journal,* which defended Catholic interests. Already in 1848 one saw the tripartite division of

Mainz society that would endure until the growing Social Democratic party forced a reshuffling.[54]

A further blow to the democratic cause came with the abortive uprising in Frankfurt on September 17, touched off by the Malmö cease-fire and its ultimate acceptance by the National Assembly. The revolt in Frankfurt, led by groups closely allied with the Democratic Association in Mainz, placed Bamberger in an awkward position. The conservative counterattack was gaining momentum, and support for a roundly condemned *putsch* could lead only to further governmental harassment in Mainz. In a speech to a Democratic Association meeting, Bamberger tried to forestall any secondary reactions from Darmstadt. He openly admitted that those who undertook rebellion in Frankfurt were supporters of the democratic party, but he nevertheless spared them no criticism. They acted without a plan, he admonished, having only political passion as their driving force. Thus they did a disservice to the cause. "The right of revolution," he reminded his listeners, "exists only in its success. There is no investigation into the justification of unborn revolutions." The September uprising was to mark the stemming of the revolutionary tide.[55]

Having condemned the Frankfurt rebels for their impulsiveness, Bamberger was soon off again, this time to Berlin to attend the second Democratic Congress which convened on October 26. The Frankfurt congress in June had established a central committee to coordinate the work of the local democratic clubs. It remained moribund until the September uprising in Frankfurt, when it bestirred itself to call a new meeting. Approximately 230 delegates appeared, representing 260 clubs from 140 cities, the majority from north Germany. The congress ran its course in four days of stormy debates marked by a large number of walkouts. Bamberger was elected chairman, but he resigned and left on October 29.[56]

Bamberger had gone north with no illusions. "From the Berlin mission I expect nothing," he wrote Anna. "To me it is a . . . pleasant trip because of the insight [it gives] into the world and politics." His reaction to the experience is clear in a letter to his future wife. "It [the congress] was the superlative of all wretchedness, and I was at times so filled with loathing for the stupid fellows who mouthed the fine words that I began to doubt myself and the cause. The congress was miserable, but I have learned a lot in Berlin, and what I have taken along as consolation is the experience that the abler persons of the party in all parts of Germany agree exactly, and that to belong to the party one need not be jointly responsible with the stupid boys."[57]

When he returned to Mainz, Bamberger wrote a series of articles for the *Mainzer Zeitung* in which he depicted the course of the congress and tried to salvage something from its shipwreck. The issue which really divided the congress, he claimed, was the social question, and it is here that Bamberger strove to maintain his radical credentials while drawing a line between himself and the "fanatics." What separated the opposing groups, he maintained, was method, not purpose. "All genuine democrats want the republic; all genuine republicans want a republic which rests not on the appearance of justice and freedom but on its true core, on the deliverance from social evil." But he viewed the differences in means as indicative of a larger conflict over the principle for which the method was to be used. A believer in democracy, he argued, could not deny the principles on which it rested—"freedom from prejudice and pure humanity." He did not see how devotion to these ideals could be squared with slogans about class war. "We must view it as a fundamental opposition to democracy itself that hate, abhorrence, and contempt are preached against whole large classes of society."[58]

Once again in his criticism of the extremist elements he was forced to return to the issue of practicality: "Social reform is an infinitely just claim on society but also a colossal claim on the capital of human creativity, and nothing can be more foolish, nothing can awaken more mistrust in the intelligence and the honor of the party leaders than if they demand that one deliver over the world to them without further ado in order to remold it according to their ready-made system."

His own supporters, Bamberger declared, drew the consequences of the democratic principles and were not satisfied merely with democratic forms. But they rejected the idea that there was no difference between democracy and military rule. They were motivated by the conviction that the social question could only be solved in "an already created state with democratic institutions ... and the democratic republic will not be able to evade for a moment its first and last responsibility, the founding of social freedom. Any other method can only be the result of complete idiocy or frivolity and can only lead to the complete ruin of all democratic strivings."[59] Fifty years later Bamberger still saw the basic issue as whether the social problem should be regarded as concerning all society or narrowly as a struggle of the worker against the bourgeoisie.[60]

Back from Berlin in early November, he once again became a coeditor of the *Mainzer Zeitung,* and in the next six months over one hundred of his articles and speeches filled the pages of the newspaper. His editorials called for a responsible ministry, removability of officials, the dismantling of the military system, and of course the republic, becoming shriller as the hopes for a democratic German state faded. He also attempted, with limited success, to set up a "people's goverment"—a commission of the Democratic Association which would advise people, primarily country folk, about civil, political, and communal affairs.[61]

But in the midst of the political agitation and organizational work, Bamberger never lost sight of the social issue. In fact his speeches and writings demonstrate a greater commitment to social change and socialism. In early December he told his audience that the people must rise up and tear everything down. Later in the same month he announced that what he and his supporters wanted to make was "not only a political revolution but also a social revolution." He also attacked the military system as "unconditional slavery of the poor for the advantages of the rich and the ruling families." In February, during the Frankfurt Assembly's debate on the imperial voting law, he attacked the proposals which would have disfranchised lower-class elements. He argued as before that political power was the road to raising the "worker at the expense of the privileged." The following month he admitted to his readers: "There was a time, right at the beginning, when many believed that one could hold back the social tendency for a time and fight solely for political freedom. The course of this year will have taught them how impossible this is; they perceive how the social direction of the revolution stepped forward ever more clearly and more strongly." By April he was speaking in the first-person singular: "Until not too long ago I too believed in a philosophical humane revolution. Our opponents have torn away this childish illusion. They fight theoretical liberation attempts with the sword. They also want to root out even the innocent core of the development. With that they teach us that they themselves must be eliminated root and branch."[62]

His growing radicalism seemed to be matched by the discovery of a workable variety of socialism, that of Pierre-Joseph Proudhon. Bamberger had concerned himself with the French socialist's writings for several years before 1848, and he did not cut his ties to him until at least 1850. What particularly attracted Bamberger to Proudhon's plans was their apparent practicality. In March and April, 1849, he ran a series of articles on Proudhon's plan for a "people's bank." Bamberger praised him as one of the few social theorists who was willing to descend into the real world and make concrete proposals. The scheme for a "people's bank" seemed to offer him a way out of his philosophical dilemma, to enable a sympathizer to become a convinced believer. He saw the foundation of Proudhon's bank resting on the demand that instead of the accident of privilege only the earnings from work deserved acknowledgment. He was attracted by the French socialist's acceptance of property coupled with the idea of nonpayment of interest to unusued capital. "He who lets others work the property can get no payment from those who do work. The fundamental idea . . . when carried through by the state would avoid the whole ill-reputed distribution of goods and the maintenance of the idle at the cost of the diligent. Each would merit only what he achieves by work." Each one, the future coupon clipper concluded, would receive from the state, the general credit giver, only so much material as he could guarantee to work. Whether the bank succeeded or failed, Bamberger announced, it would in any event be of significant use as a practical attempt at a system of state-directed social reorganization. When the bank failed a short time later, he warned that "the renunciation of the people's bank is the renunciation of the peaceful development of socialism."[63]

Years later the old liberal seemed almost amazed that he had seen so much promise in the bank. He dismissed it as a chimera but admitted that Proudhon, "with all his socialistic conceptions, was a positive spirit who could clothe his proposals in concrete form and who guarded himself against the suspicion of a hazy utopia."[64] The search for practical means to implement socialist ideas was the key issue which Bamberger faced in 1848–49 and for a time thereafter. The inability to discover any workable schemes contributed to his later disenchantment with socialism.[65]

Bamberger's intellectual struggle gave way in the spring of 1849 to armed insurrection when the Prussian king, Frederick William IV, refused the National Assembly's offer of the crown of a united Germany. In Saxony, the Rhineland, and southwestern Germany, rebellions broke out with the avowed purpose of carrying through the new constitution. In Rhenish Hesse, Bamberger became a member of a provincial committee charged with organizing support for the insurgents in the Palatinate, and on May 9 as a leader of the Rhenish Hessian contingent he left Mainz for Kirchheimbolanden. The intervention of the force was short, futile, and tragic. From the outset it was clear that there was a serious shortage of arms and money, and many of the volunteer groups arrived unarmed. Moreover, Bamberger and the other two members of the provincial committee, Franz Zitz and Karl Wallau, lacked any military experience that would be of use against well-trained professional soldiers. Most serious of all was the lack of cooperation between the Rhenish contingent and the revolutionary leadership in the Palatinate and in Baden. The apparent jealousy and unwillingness to share weapons and other material or effectively coordinate operations indicated in microcosm the difficulties in creating a united German state. At the head of a rapidly disintegrating and increasingly demoralized force, Bamberger on June 2 tried unsuccessfully to have his corps absorbed into the Palatinate army. This was rejected as an example of defeatism. The end came on June 18 at Kirchheimbolanden as the Prussians took the town with a loss of seventeen insurgents killed and ten wounded. The remnants of the Rhenish Hessian contingent made their way to Karlsruhe, where they disbanded. On June 22, Bamberger crossed the border into Switzerland to begin a fourteen-year exile from German soil.[66] Several prison sentences meted out by the courts of Hesse Darmstadt and Bavaria followed him into exile. In November 1849, he was sentenced to two years' imprisonment for insulting the by then defunct National Assembly. The following September he received an additional four months for offending the honor of the Hessian army. In May 1851, Bamberger was sentenced to eight years for his participation in the insurgency in the Palatinate. Finally in 1852 the Bavarian authorities in whose territory Kirchheimbolanden lay sentenced him to death for high treason.[67]

Coming out of the turmoil of 1848 and 1849 as a loser, an exile, and a criminal, Bamberger did not try to escape into the realm of revolutionary mythology. He was disappointed by the failure but not blinded by the defeat. He retained the capacity to analyze and learn from the reasons for the collapse, and he never viewed the failure of the German revolution as simply a "trick of fate." In his *Erlebnisse aus der pfälzischen Erhebung (Experiences from the Palatinate Revolt),* which he wrote shortly after arriving in Switzerland, he unmercifully described the confusion, incompetence, lack of preparation, and selfishness which made a difficult struggle an impossible one. He even rejected pleas not to print the essay. "If it is worthwhile," he wrote, "to believe in the future victory of democracy . . . it would be more beneficial to believe that this victory is to be achieved with caution and open eyes rather than merely with blind and crazy risks." His conclusions focused on two major deficiencies: a lack of military experience and the absence of a revolutionary mass. Enthusiasm could not, in Bamberger's view, replace military training. "The art of war," he wrote, "is one of the most difficult in the world, and where the capacity for genius does not intervene it will be learned neither more nor less than shoe-making in which one must be an apprentice for three years or longer." He also expressed his disillusionment with the weak revolutionary élan which he found among his troops, primarily peasants or small towners. These "dull, narrow-minded citizens" were not the stuff from which revolutions were made. "Our experience up to now has revealed the elements and means for a struggle only in the large cities."[68]

• 3 •

Exile and Unification

The four years after Bamberger's flight from Germany led him to many cities—Basel, Zürich, Geneva, Bern, London, Antwerp, Amsterdam, Rotterdam, and finally Paris in October 1853. With poor prospects of an early return to Germany, Bamberger and his fellow exiles were forced to survive in an alien environment and to find a new place and purpose in life.

Initially Bamberger, along with Franz Zitz and Friedrich Kapp, devised a plan to establish a law firm in New York, and the latter two went ahead to test the terrain. While waiting for word from his two friends, Bamberger received an invitation from his younger brother, Heinrich, to visit him in London, where he had a position in a bank owned by relatives. Since England was on the way to America, Bamberger accepted the invitation, arriving in London in October 1849. Still occupied with his plan to practice law in America, Bamberger used his stay in London to acquaint himself with Anglo-Saxon jurisprudence. He found it quite different from French and German law and realized that it would require far more effort than he had imagined to master the "unsystematic" Anglo-Saxon law code. The prospect of further struggle with law books, coupled with the strain and depression caused by his enforced separation from his fiancée, Anna Belmont, made him receptive to the offer he received to enter his relatives' banking firm in London.[1]

The decision to embark upon a banking career was probably the most difficult of his life. Bamberger had grown up in a banking milieu, and he had decided well before 1848 to avoid that kind of career. In 1846 a family crisis had seemed resolved by Ludwig's taking over the family banking business. He was the epitome of despair: "A life without import, . . . an activity which is alien and disagreeable to me, which smothers all of my innermost wishes, the path of ambition cut off, . . . my whole existence given up." So a banking career appeared to the recent university graduate.[2]

His opinion of the world of finance had not changed by 1849. When he entered the banking profession he believed he had climbed down from his academic heights. It was difficult to begin again when one had the "pride of the German scholar." But climb down he did, because a banking position seemed the surest and shortest way to end an unbearable existence. The offer of a job had come from his mother's brothers, the Bischoffsheims, who operated a chain of banks in Amsterdam, Antwerp, Paris, and London. He joined the London firm of Bischoffsheim, Goldschmidt and Avigdor. The law career in the new world was given up, and Bamberger was on his way to becoming a millionaire.[3]

His apprenticeship in London was followed by additional training in Antwerp, where his brother had taken over the direction of the Bischoffsheim bank. In Belgium he was in contact with his old mentor and friend, H. B. Oppenheim, who was in Brussels, but his attempt to divide his time between Brussels and Antwerp put a severe strain on his work in the counting house. "The friends in Brussels sound their siren song," he wrote his aunt. "The dawdling did not want to end until it became too much, and I had to exert myself seriously to save my business reputation by the skin of my teeth at the last moment." From then on he apparently worked in earnest. Perhaps with some exaggeration he described his day: "I have literally no unfilled minute; I work in the bank normally from 9 A.M. until 11 P.M., less the hour at the exchange and time for lunch and a digestive pause."[4]

In spite of his devotion to work, Bamberger still was haunted by the fear that he had made a wrong choice in entering upon a banking career. He felt apart from the people with whom he consorted during business hours and thought that his new profession would force him to acclimate himself to an atmosphere that oppressed him. He particularly disliked the required trips to the stock exchange. His depression was deepened by the troubled relationship with his fiancée's father, who still refused to permit his marriage to Anna.[5]

After a year in Antwerp, Bamberger's protectors decided that the time had come to establish him in his own bank in Rotterdam. Still gnawed by a fear of sacrificing his whole personality without even the assurance that it would bring external success, he proceeded to Rotterdam in September 1851 and established the firm of L. A. Bamberger and Co. Gradually he met with success, and his income reached such a respectable figure that he was able to seal his ten-year courtship of Anna Belmont on May 5, 1852. His Rotterdam days, although happy, were short. In October 1853 he accepted an offer to join the Bischoffsheims' Paris bank. A more stable and immensely successful period in his life had begun.[6] The four years from 1849 to 1853 represented a time of doubt and desperation. Looking back on this period and on his banking career, however, an older Bamberger saw it in a different light. He called it "a gain." "It is my final conviction . . . that I learned more about the world and people in this career than if I had been able to realize my original ideal."[7]

Besides finding financial security during these first four years of exile, Bamberger for a time continued his political activity. In an article about the Erfurt Parliament in Proudhon's *La Voix du Peuple,* he defended the democrats' decision not to participate in the election. He viewed the Erfurt Assembly as a fraud because it preached a false unity. The meeting at Erfurt, according to Bamberger, was an appeal to romanticism and nationality rather than unity. To the democrat, unity signified a revolutionary undertaking in order to carry out political and administrative reform. The Erfurt Assembly on the contrary would merely patch together a national rather than a constitutional regime and would be based on the old order. "Nationality" in his words signified a "constitutional regime," not a "sentiment." Although Bamberger's political ideals would change by the 1860s, his path to Bismarck was already marked out by 1850. The goal of a new political and administrative order would eventually find its apparent executor in Bismarck's policy of the late 1860s.[8]

Besides finding financial security during these first four years of exile, correspondent for Adolf Kolatschek's *Deutsche Monatsschrift für Politik, Wissenschaft, Kunst und Leben,* which was published in Switzerland. The periodical, which served as the voice of the German democratic exiles, contained articles by H. B. Oppenheim, Carl Vogt, Ludwig Simon, Franz Raveaux, Richard Wagner, and Heinrich Heine. It lasted less than two years, collapsing as a result of the censorship policies of the larger German states. Bamberger's reports still reflect an individual who had not made his commitment to the social and economic ideals of nineteenth-century liberalism. He did continue to advocate centralization as the necessary way to individualism and freedom. He called attention, however, to the poverty and suffering in England, especially Ireland, suffering which seemed to have no relation to the debates in Parliament. His harshest criticism was directed toward the Manchester school of economics, the "fanatical free traders." He attacked their opposition to factory legislation and traced the weakness of the English educational system to them. He suggested that the state would have to intervene and not be scared off by cries of socialism. He did not think that nonintervention would be tenable and predicted accurately, for Germany, that ultimately the Manchesterians would split, one segment marching leftward toward democracy and the other in the direction of conservatism.[9] Bamberger indeed foresaw the ultimate instability of a rigid laissez-faire system, although he did not suspect that in the 1860s he would try to marry nonintervention to a conservative political structure.

Bamberger's political activity ceased after he left London for Antwerp in

July 1850. He was the subject of a number of police reports which suggested continued political involvement, primarily with the European Democratic Central Committee organized by Alexandre Ledru-Rollin and unnamed workers' organizations. Much of the factual information contained in the reports was incorrect, and the rest cannot be corroborated. The 1850s were a decade of political abstinence as well as political maturation, most of it coming from his years in Paris.[10]

Ludwig Bamberger made it through his apprentice years in the banking profession, but without enthusiasm. Only his feeling of obligation and sense of duty enabled him to overcome the first painful years. It was the fifteen years in France (1853–68), however, which effected significant changes in Bamberger's life and outlook. Both he and his wife were fluent in French and moved with ease in French social circles. A two-hundred-page section in his memoirs recounts his experiences with the social, political, and intellectual elite of Bonapartist France. He described one such salon: "Here I found past and present, old and new world, literature, art, politics, serious and frivolous life, the Faubourg St. Germain, the republican opposition, and even a piece of the Napoleonic court, all pressed together in the narrow room of a small salon."[11]

Not only were the cultural attractions of Paris endless, but even Bamberger's daily work routine became more palatable in such surroundings. His office, he tells us, lacked the imprint of a "dry narrow trade" but had a "salonlike atmosphere." He also had the enviable ability to break off his work and pick it up again at any time. He started out at 12,000 francs per year and a 1 percent interest in the business, but his earnings did not increase markedly until the 1860s, when they grew rapidly. He attributed his slow advance to the Crimean War, which dampened business activity, and to his perhaps excessive caution in making investments. Besides the acceptable income, he was further comforted by being part of an established banking house. "I did not depend any longer on my own still precarious business ability but on a larger, strong undertaking led by tested leaders." His business activity, which concerned itself with railroad and mining ventures, not only deepened his understanding of the world of business, but also broadened his horizons. His bank's investments reached into Luxemburg, northwestern Germany, Italy, Spain, North Africa, South America, and East Asia. They also sharpened his judgment. Mining investments, in particular, he believed, tested all of an individual's ability to distinguish good from bad risks. "There is scarcely an industrial area in which unpleasant surprises so frequently lie in wait and in which the danger, after one has once said A, to become trapped into the whole ABC of unfruitful sacrifice, threatens so fatefully."[12]

The young banker's fifteen years in the French capital not only broadened and deepened his knowledge of the worlds of business investments and international finance; they also left a marked imprint on his socioeconomic ideas. He had come out of the revolutionary period as a convinced democrat sympathetic to socialism or social reform. He was still the seeker who had closed off few paths to human improvement, but by the 1860s he had lost all tolerance for socialistic experiments and had burst forth as a proponent of individualism. His own personal triumph over adversity, his ability to distinguish a good risk from a poor one, and his success in a highly competitive and personal banking system made him unsympathetic to those who were unable or refused to rely on their individual talents. In his memoirs, the descriptions of his mining and railroad experiences are usually followed by axioms on the superiority of individualism: "It is always an individual who accomplishes something, never collectives. . . . Each opponent of individualism . . . should involve himself in enterprises with his own weal and woe to cure himself of abstraction." Only when "each error cuts immediately into the flesh can one learn how only an able mind accustomed to an infinite variety of cases and no mechanism can" carry on a business. Even a corporation, he believed, did not need a board of directors. "At the side of an able director they [the board] are superfluous, at the side of an incompetent one, helpless." Having attached such importance to leadership, Bamberger called the employees who were provided with work by the entrepeneur only functioning items and implied that their labor was a ware. "Socialism was indeed the war of the arm against the head."[13]

Summing up his first five years in Paris, Bamberger wrote that it offered "a beneficial contrast to what had gone before. First of all I was rid of all oscillations about my course of action. Also the business activity had turned out to be more appealing than in London, Antwerp, and Holland. . . . Daily contact with pleasant and educated people of the most varied professions freed my mind from all the pressure which the prose of everyday routine of the trade had exerted. To that was added the fact that the great financial operations . . . stood in close connection with high European policy and at that time Paris was the center of policy."[14]

But in spite of his general contentment with the course of his life, he could not rid himself of an undercurrent of dissatisfaction. He was removed from his political and cultural foundations, which no fluency in the French language or contacts with Frenchmen could remedy. He did not possess the right of domicile which gave one guarantees against expulsion, and his request for it was denied. As a former revolutionary and one who socialized with anti-Bonapartist elements Bamberger was no doubt under suspicion. During the temporary police crackdown following Felice Orsini's attempt to assassinate Napoleon in 1858, Bamberger was harassed by the French police. He also continually felt an inner alienation, that his "way of thinking" was different from that of his French friends. And finally there was no chance for an active political life.[15]

Bamberger's inability to feel at home in France presented him with what seemed to be an insoluble problem. The chances for an early return to Germany were slight, and a hopeless mood ruled in the refugee world. Political activity from afar seemed fruitless. Even the change of rulers in Prussia in 1858 brought little enthusiasm. Bamberger remembered King William as the suppressor of the uprising of 1849 in southwestern Germany, and he was considered the personification of militarism. "The pitiless executions which were carried out in Baden under his commands lived in fresh loathsome memory," Bamberger noted.[16]

With the outbreak of the French-Austrian war in May 1859 the situation was suddenly transformed. Immediately Bamberger was convinced that a major turning point was at hand, which could have a wholesome effect on Germany. As little confidence as the Prussian government inspired, Austria was still considered the major source of opposition to German unification, and to strike down this arch evil was the primary task. But Bamberger's approach was not shared by major elements within the German states, where sympathy for a fellow German land was strong and anti-French feeling always present. Many also saw the attack on Austria as the first stage of a French onslaught against Germany. Undeterred by the sympathy for Austria—almost maddened by it since it was so against Germany's true interests and smacked of emotionalism rather than realism—Bamberger penned his *Juchhe nach Italia (Hurrah for Italy!)*. It stressed the necessity of destroying Austria's power in Italy to further the cause of German unity. This was an old idea of Bamberger's, going back to 1848 and 1849, when he had stressed the connection between Italy's independence and Germany's freedom.[17]

With this first literary effort since 1850, Bamberger had reentered the German political scene, even if from afar. But in order to maintain the connection with Germany, a more permanent political and literary vehicle was necessary. He canvassed his comrades-in-exile about issuing a periodical to deal with current events. The reception was favorable, and *Demokratische Studien (Democratic Studies)* was born in June 1860 to bring some unity into the 1848 democratic camp. The two issues of the journal contained articles by Friedrich Kapp, Ferdinand Lassalle, Ludwig Simon, Arnold Ruge, H. B. Oppenheim, and Carl Vogt. Difficulties with the editor, Ludwig Walesrode, who was in Hamburg, plus the return of Oppenheim to Berlin, led to a new periodical, *Deutsche Jahrbücher für Politik und Literatur (German Yearbooks for Politics and Literature)*, which the latter edited. This second journalistic venture lasted from September 1861 to December 1864.[18]

Besides bringing him closer toward the mainstream of German political life, the early 1860s also saw Bamberger achieve his much desired financial independence. The accumulation of sufficient riches to become a *Rentier* was a slow process. The first eight years were lean. Only with 1861 did the good years begin and Bamberger achieve a greater percentage of the profits. By 1866 he was wealthy enough to live off his investments. Bamberger considered this personal independence necessary to carry on an active political life.[19]

These years also brought with them an open door to Germany. Beginning in 1861 he put out feelers to the Badenese, Württemberger, and Prussian governments for a return to Germany. In September 1862, his family in Mainz arranged for an eight-day amnesty so that he could visit his ailing mother, on condition that he not engage in political activity. This was done without his knowledge, and Bamberger feared that he would be compromised with his democratic friends. He refused it, and to make clear his rejection he accepted an invitation to participate in the unveiling of a statue of the 1848 democrat, Heinrich Simon, who had recently drowned in Lake Wallen in Switzerland. On October 5, 1862, some three hundred old friends took part in the ceremony, and Bamberger's speech, the most compelling of many, contrasted the advanced intellectual life of Germany with its retarded political development. In evocative phrases he also portrayed the sadness of the exiles' lives but announced that they would return to Germany for the hour of victory unbowed and uncompromised.[20]

The door to Germany opened for Bamberger only in July 1863, with a vacation in Baden. To oversee mining operations in Westphalia, he then undertook a tour of northern Germany via Giessen, Gotha, Dresden, Leipzig, and Berlin. The net impact of the trip was to stimulate even more his desire to return permanently to Germany. The forty-year-old felt young and was ready for a new life. He was buoyed by the liberal opposition to Bismarck, but even more by the "enlightened" direction in commercial policy which moved toward free trade. His own impressions coincided with those of Friedrich Kapp, who toured Germany in 1862. Kapp believed a new Germany, more self-reliant and energetic, was being created by the economic transformation. The concrete foundations for a new era in German history were being laid. It was, in Bamberger's own words, "the time of development, which so often is more beautiful than that of fulfillment."[21] Not only did these years reopen the channels to Germany, but they were a time when Bamberger hammered out many of the ideas which he would carry over to the Bismarckian camp after the civil war of 1866.

In the foreword to the first issue of *Demokratische Studien* he wrote: "Here is now space for each of us to show what the bitter experiences of a decade have made out of him." The years of exile seemed to make a "realist" of Bamberger. The former republican had become a monarchist primarily because of his contact with the real world. In the words of Bussman, he learned to distinguish a good investment from a poor one.[22] Of course this realistic streak had shown itself as early as the morrow of the collapse of the uprisings of 1849 in his *Erlebnisse aus der pfälzischen Erhebung.* Nevertheless, there is in Bamberger's writings of the early 1860s a new appreciation for realistic or material factors in political life. Writing in 1863, he noted that "each liberation process falls of necessity into two parts. The first concerns the struggle for inner enlightenment. . . . The second chapter is devoted to the elimination of the hostile forces who, themselves remnants of unfreer beginnings and because of egoistic caste interest, still try to keep their hold on people. . . . Germany, in the last decades, has reached the second . . . stage." The kind of effort needed in the second stage also differed from the first. The earlier stage was an intellectual process, the latter a "more or less material struggle." His new realism also came through in his essay about the French impact on the Rhineland in the 1790s. The pro-French movement in Mainz he characterized as "theoretically pure and purely theoretical," led by "scholars of every stripe" and marked by "speeches without end." The successful businessman had little patience for those who expected a messianic deliverance into the realm of freedom or who tried to avoid the "raw winds" of the political world. Words alone would not unify Germany.[23] Corollaries of his concern for what seemed to be real and practical were an appreciation of activism and determination and a need for positive commitment. "Strength . . . of will," he wrote, "is capable of more than understanding, or reflection." He was also critical of those, mostly 1848 democrats, who refused to search for what was positive in events but remained rooted in a negative pessimism. For Bamberger this was sterile labor.[24]

What changed least during his years of exile was his desire for German unity, but even here he stressed the transition from the "empire of thought" to the realm of material facts. "Every nation," the new pragmatist wrote, "wants to have not merely a spirit but also a body," and the purpose of this body was not to be merely technical but, even more, moral and educational. To belong to a "great, that is united and respected country" was a moral possession which ennobled and uplifted the individual. In Bamberger's eyes, the future belonged to great states. Only they could maintain an independent existence, while the smaller states existed only by political dexterity or through the sufferance of a large state. Moreover, great states would carry out rational or progressive policies if only in order to maintain themselves as great powers. Even absolutist Prussia, according to Bamberger, was forced by reasons of state to prevent the hiring of mercenaries in its territories during the eighteenth century and to institute the Customs Union. International developments seemed to confirm his predilection for a unified and centralized state. Particularism was the bridge for French intervention and aggrandizement in Germany. Even a federal solution to the German question held little appeal for him. Federalism, he claimed, had never stood the test. It was a hybrid form of government which contained lower and higher forms of life, and any such system had to sink to the lowest common denominator. Confirming or creating this belief was the American Civil War. The German Confederation reminded Bamberger of the United States under the Articles of Confederation. Because of the success of the constitution, America had prospered for ninety years; but because that success was not more complete, the present tragedy was occurring.[25]

If one accepted the basic premise of a unified German state, and if one foresaw the new Germany as a monarchy, then for Bamberger one had to climb aboard the Prussian bandwagon. No other state in Germany had advanced the cause of unity as much as Prussia via the Customs Union, and no other German state was capable of absorbing the others. Bamberger singled out Austria as the center of feudalism and reaction in Germany. He saw the danger to German unity not on the Seine but on the Danube. Austria was the personification of the police state, of the Jesuit state, of antinational and particularist sentiment. Germany's unity, Bamberger wrote, would be possible only when Austria was expelled from Germany, and when Prussia "as completely as possible absorbs the robber states." This sentiment for Prussia marks perhaps the sharpest departure for the one-time south German democrat. He had given up hoping for or even desiring a movement from below, and of the three remaining options—Prusso-Austrian dualism, continued particularism, or Prussian-led unity—the last was the most desirable. Not that he was emotionally enthusiastic about Prussia. He became a supporter of Prussia by reason of his desire for a unified German state. "When I hear the name of Prussia," he wrote in 1859, "I feel neither trust nor love nor hope rise up in my bosom. I only say that a large state can never be so miserable as a small one, and according to the law of gravity I know that the smaller masses are attracted by the larger ones, not the reverse. If there is any chance of uniting Germany by monarchical means, only Prussia can be the engine. . . . I know no state but the large state, I know no German state but the Prussian." He hoped that Prussia, freed from the "vices of the deep-rooted feudal system" and transformed into a modern constitutional state, would exercise an irresistible magnetism on the adjacent lands. He paid little attention to the warning of his imaginary antagonist, "Thomas Contra," that he was constructing a "Prussian state as it could or should be but not as it is." He never regretted the choice. Even thirty-five years later, Bamberger saw no other route to unity. "It is exceedingly illuminating for the basis of German development," he wrote in the 1890s, "that the necessity of attaching oneself to Prussia" crossed with "the repeated experience of the repulsiveness of the Junker-dominated government."[26]

This necessity of attaching oneself to Prussia led him in the early 1860s to play down the significance of Otto von Bismarck's accession to power in September 1862. Although the chancellor would fascinate Bamberger and provide the inspiration for several articles and one book, at the end of 1862 Bamberger refused to attach any particular significance to his prime minister-ship. He called on his fellow Germans to place the event in the proper perspective. From Paris it seemed preferable to tolerate the unhappy situation than to try to change it by force. "The higher life of nations begins," noted the chastened ex-revolutionary, "when their weal and woe are no longer won and lost in the game of revolution." The era of revolution was over, and those who refused to see it were romanticists. The Prussian parliament, he maintained, by its responsible behavior, was making moral conquests in the south. In fact he considered the whole constitutional crisis as merely part of the German question. It was an unhappy but necessary process.[27]

The polemics of the early 1860s were merely preparatory for the bitter exchanges of the years after the civil war. Until 1866, Bamberger still counted as a democrat and also considered himself one.[28] With the civil war he, in part involuntarily, found himself in the enemy camp and in a formal sense became one of those converted to the logic of the facts.[29]

But how was one to take advantage of the new situation in Germany? After seventeen years outside the country, he wrote, it was "difficult to weigh anchor again and to search out a harbor in the fog of Germany's future." "No reward stimulated our labors," he called out, "no parliamentary seat summoned us to rest. Without a homeland at home, never having attempted to be at home abroad, German citizens *in partibus infidelium* and corresponding honorary members of several native prisons, inclining to the south through the senses, to the north through reflection, we set out on our travels in order to preach the badly received word 'unification.'" As a first step to reentering the German political arena he resigned from his bank, having reached a position of financial independence.[30]

The meaning of the civil war to Bamberger was most vigorously expressed in a series of articles written for the *Rheinische Zeitung* in which he tried to give the "accomplished facts" their due but at the same time keep in mind the immutable goals of liberalism. He attempted to square the circle of realism and idealism and demonstrated how difficult it was. He stressed the moral impossibilities which would open up if belief in the accomplished fact were raised to an official religion; yet the goal of national unity must go forward with events. He also emphasized that Prussian authoritarianism was still the enemy and warned that political realism (*Realpolitik*) could be a euphemism for continued servility. Nevertheless, "between the denial of the events and the lackey philosophy, which finds all events reasonable and honorable, lies a whole universe." The solution, according to Bamberger, was to be found in an appreciation of the principles which made up the substance of the facts, "in the separation of that which we cannot help adopting" from that which, "uncorrupted by all success, we have to reject forever and ever as eternally inadmissible and reprehensible." Precisely what out of the substance of events was eternally unacceptable? The "idolatry" of the army and of war. What must be firmly grasped? The connection to the Prussian state until the final fusion. For Bamberger no other solution was possible. Federalism had no future in Germany. An independent south German state would only mean the reemergence of dualism and the reentry of Austria into Germany. He also dismissed the fear that Germany would be conquered by Prussia as unworthy of a great nation. (Thirty years later he would admit that precisely this had occurred.) "So let unity, as bad as it is, have room to earn its place in the sun."[31]

Prussia's victory was the inescapable fact of 1866, and Bamberger drew the necessary conclusions. He praised the indemnity compromise as one which enabled the Prussian chamber, by accepting the government's offer, to avoid the greater defeat of being deserted by its voters. The government provided the chamber with a graceful escape route, and by taking it the majority preserved the legal continuity of the pre– and post–civil war periods.[32]

The most difficult aspect of Bamberger's attempt to ease himself into the new situation was to answer the charge that he had ignored freedom for the sake of unity. His record before 1866 was ambivalent. He referred to freedom as a precondition for a feeling of nationality, as favorable to the principle of nationality, but not equally significant, and he called freedom and nationality two forms of one and the same essence.[33] After the civil war there was no such ambivalence. We treasure unity, he wrote, "because we see in it the cardinal condition for the achievement of freedom." But it was unity, the creation of a united state, which was the primary task before Germans. "Unity is not a piece of madness. It is the existence, the essence, the foundation of a people, . . . the current of its life, . . . the connection between head and body, between arm and brain. . . . A people which is not one is a crippled people." He did not deny the ultimate goal of freedom, but to the realist of 1866 new goals were needed to proceed with immediate tasks. The old slogans would not do for the Germany or Europe that had been transformed since 1848. "Principles," he noted, "are not invented but deduced from the needs and experiences of mankind," and Bamberger's most telling argument against his former democratic friends was the reality of Prussian power. He was not blind to the retrogressive nature of the Prussian political and social system, and he was not proud of it. He recognized that Prussian domination might gradually "lace up the nation into a uniform" and that Germany might not succeed to freedom through unity. "We know the pitfalls but yet we say: By this path or no other! Now or never." Prussia, in Bamberger's mind, was called upon to unify Germany as Piedmont was Italy. He reminded his readers that in 1849 a smaller and relatively weaker Prussia had made it impossible for any German state to gain its freedom. "It was Prussia's will that no free state emerge in Germany and that will was unfortunately irresistible." And now that Prussia was stronger, it was a dream to think that one could establish freedom anywhere in Germany while freedom was lacking in Berlin. All talk of a republic under such conditions was idle chatter. To Bamberger the conclusion was clear: "If you want to be free, help make Prussia free. All else is wasted effort. . . . Through unity to freedom."[34]

Not everyone found the prospect of helping to build freedom in the north very appealing. Many were unconvinced by Bamberger's attempt to explain away Prussia's militarism as a general European phenomenon, or her lack of freedom as an extension of the absence of truly free or constitutional states in Germany. Nor were they convinced by his argument that the independence of small states was due solely to the intervention of foreign powers. He became the focus of countless attacks from former democratic friends both inside and outside Germany, led internally by Karl Mayer and his *Stuttgarter Beobachter* and externally by Ludwig Simon in Paris. Old friendships broke, many never to be repaired, and on his seventieth birthday and retirement from parliamentary activity, the denunciations continued. Even on the occasion of his death, the *Frankfurter Zeitung* made the story of Bamberger's great betrayal the theme of its bitter obituary.[35]

With few exceptions, Bamberger had little patience with his denouncers. His sharpest statements were reserved for Ludwig Simon, who in his words, had not proceeded beyond the "babble" of 1848. "I must often ask myself," the new realist wrote to Oppenheim, "what was 1848, where [Simon] was considered number one?" The Trier democrat was a "chaste Joseph who damns himself to external sterility." He was placed in the same boat as the Swabian democrats around Karl Mayer, this "republican Vatican, the only guardians of the genuine faith . . . these purists to whom all are impure who do not belong to their congregation."[36]

Bamberger's defection from the democratic ranks was deeply felt. His articles had a wide audience in both the north and south. When he died in 1899 his old enemy, the *Frankfurter Zeitung,* noted:

One can imagine with what hopes the democracy looked forward to Bamberger's return to the long denied homeland after the amnesty of 1866. These hopes were miserably disgraced; Bamberger's defection brought not only sadness but also confusion into the ranks of the freedom lovers and led countless elements, who had become uncertain, into the camp of National Liberalism, in which Bamberger had planted his standard. . . . the blow which Bamberger inflicted by his desertion, one felt from the Main to Lake Constance. And where the loyalists gathered one constantly heard: We are sorry about that one.[37]

Bamberger was conscious of his ties to and influence on south German democrats. He judged Oppenheim's decision to return to Berlin and collaborate with the liberal *National Zeitung* in the following way: "Oppenheim, who like a smitten boar rushed to Berlin as soon as Bismarck opened the stall doors, clothes himself in the loyalist black and white. . . . That is not suitable for one of us, is offensive to me, and cuts off the connection to the south." He asked Oppenheim not to print any of his material in the *National Zeitung* since it would compromise him with his south German public. "The area of my effectiveness is south of the Main, and [if] I go another inch to the right I will cut myself off from any effectivenes."[38]

As a Bismarckian in the south, Bamberger was favorably placed to further the national cause as he defined it, both in Mainz and in Germany. He had returned to Mainz shortly before the civil war after an absence of seventeen years. The war, however, transformed the Mainz political scene. Hesse-Darmstadt was in the anomalous position of having part of its territory inside the new North German Confederation and the rest outside. Moreover, the dominant political party, the Progressives, who had won thirty-eight of fifty seats in the election of 1862, broke apart as a result of the War of 1866, with the anti-Prussian left wing forming the Democratic party. The proponents of union with the North German Confederation retained control of the party organization, but except for the name had little in common with their North German namesake. Shortly after the war Hesse-Darmstadt held its state elections. Into this heated atmosphere Bamberger entered with two essays which called for an acceptance of the new situation in Germany. His intervention into the Mainz political scene raised a storm around him. With his known journalistic and oratorical talent, he was beseeched to enter the political fray, if not as a candidate, at least as a speaker at election rallies. Bamberger contented himself with an election manifesto designed to win over wavering democrats.[39]

Bamberger's reluctance to get entrapped into Hessian state politics stemmed from his indecision regarding a political career as well as his desire to perform on the national political stage. From January 1867 on, he was in contact with his brother Rudolf, a Mainz banker who also was a member of the state legislature, about the availability of a Customs Parliament seat. For a whole year Bamberger hesitated to commit himself openly to a campaign for the first German parliament. He was hoping for a safe district in the countryside, particularly in the Bingen-Alzey area west and south of Mainz. He wished to avoid the Mainz district because the opposition from the Catholics as well as democrats appeared impressive and made victory uncertain at best. His brother continued to push his candidacy with the party organization while the banker-turned-politican remained for the most part in Paris. When finally the election assignments were made and Bamberger, because of his supposed strength, was accorded the task of keeping Mainz within the national fold, he wanted to quit. This last doubt passed, however, and by the first of the year (1868) he was in the midst of a vicious political campaign. He had to "make the best of a bad job."[40]

Mainz represented a political microcosm of Germany in 1866. Besides the liberal-democratic split, there also appeared an increasingly well-organized Catholic movement which had several newspapers at its disposal and a leader of national stature in Bishop Emmanuel von Ketteler. Also making its appearance was the emerging socialist movement, but divided into Lassallean and Eisenacher wings. And hovering over the local affairs of Mainz was the semiauthoritarian Hessian government under the leadership of Baron von Dalwigk zu Lichtenfels. Political passions were intense, and a three- or four-way division of the votes made a first-round victory unlikely. But at the outset the Catholics and democrats united behind Konrad Alexis Dumont, the democratic candidate, who was also supported by the Eisenacher socialists.[41]

Having made up his mind to accept the nomination, Bamberger threw himself into the campaign. In a series of articles and public speeches between December 1867 and March 1868 he focused on several issues. He tried to educate the voters regarding the significance of the Customs Union and stressed the necessity for tax reform. He also called attention to the impracticality of Hesse-Darmstadt's staying outside the North German Confederation or a newly constituted united Germany since the area north of the Main River was already incorporated into the confederation. The fact that Catholics were supporting the democratic candidate worsened his chances but sharpened the issues and lightened his heart. He was tarred by his enemies with being responsible in 1849 for leading many young men to their deaths at the battle of Kirchheimbolanden, and he had to produce statements from survivors exonerating him. He also had to demonstrate that although he no longer was in the democratic camp he still adhered to democratic principles. Bamberger himself best caught the spirit of the campaign as seen through the eyes of a liberal. "The last three weeks I have spent in Mainz and environs," he wrote to Arnold Ruge. "I found . . . a soil which was possessed by the charming trio: brother democrats, papists, and Dalwigk in heavenly harmony against us nationals. In these three weeks I have worked like a dog, and inch by inch I ploughed up the weed-covered ground. I could write volumes about the story of the alliance between the frivolous dumb democrats on one side and all the dark powers on the other. . . . In spite of everything I hope to be elected." Two weeks later he was less certain. "The more energy and activity I generate on our side, the more frenzied become the clericals and officials. The preacher and the district councilor go to the villages from house to house—all for the democrat Dumont."[42]

The election was close. Bamberger's margin of victory was seventy-three votes over his combined opposition out of a total of some twelve thousand cast. It was, as his brother wrote "a narrow escape." Bamberger agreed, but he was immensely proud of the triumph which, he claimed, only he could have accomplished.[43] His victory was one of the few bright spots on the south German horizon for the Prussian cause.

Although now catapulted to the national stage, Bamberger was forced by the narrowness of his victory to devote some attention to strengthening his position in Mainz. His election victory also promised to cost him dearly in terms of his personal freedom. He was charged with defaming the Hessian government and faced a prison sentence of up to nine months.[44] The latter development stemmed from an election broadside which appeared on March 17, 1868. It accused the Dalwigk ministry of having come to an understanding with "clerical intolerance" to the detriment of the schools and the administration. The purpose of the statement was to discredit the democratic opposition which was backed by Catholic elements and given tacit support by the Darmstadt government. The government responded by charging Bamberger and several colleagues with slander, which he considered equivalent to a conviction. The trial took place on November 11, 1868, with Bamberger acting as one of his own lawyers. He used the occasion, not merely to defend himself, but to attack the Hessian government as being in alliance with the extreme left and right against the group which desired legal, parliamentary, and free development. His defense collapsed when the judge ruled that the question of the truth of the contested statements was not at issue and refused to permit the defendants to follow this line of argument. The defendants left the chamber in protest. The verdict came on November 27, and Bamberger was sentenced to two months' imprisonment and a fine.[45] The verdict confirmed what Bamberger had expected and provided added evidence that the much proclaimed south German freedom was a myth. He and his colleagues appealed the decision, which was then overturned in the appeals court.[46]

But Bamberger had little interest in local affairs, his attention was fixed on the national scene. His efforts were concentrated on Franco-German relations and the formation of an all-German political organization. With the German civil war and the consequent increase in Prussian power, Franco-Prussian relations became very tense toward the end of 1866 and the early part of 1867. Napoleon III's desire for some tangible gain to match Prussia's winnings created an unstable situation which finally came to a crisis over Luxemburg in April and May, 1867. Napoleon's attempt to detach the Grand Duchy of Luxemburg from Holland proceeded smoothly until the end of March, when Bismarck began to have second thoughts. He encouraged Rudolf von Bennigsen, the National Liberal party leader, to interpellate about the issue, and the subsequent storm of national indignation in Germany plus the belief by the French that they were being played for fools threatened to drive the two countries to war.[47] As a fifteen-year resident of France, Bamberger considered himself a sharp observer of the Parisian scene. He had friends and contacts among most of the political groupings as well as confidants at court. Even after his reentry into German political life, he continued to live and spend most of his time in Paris until 1870.[48] He saw himself as an agent of Franco-German understanding. At home in both worlds, he hoped to make both countries at home in a reorganized Europe that he believed was emerging. In his very sympathetic treatment of Adam Lux, the Mainz republican who lost his life during the Reign of Terror, Bamberger portrayed him as a cosmopolitan citizen of the two worlds and found this a welcome contrast to his own age of emerging nationalism where people were learning to hate each other "because their rulers require it."[49]

Nevertheless, the year before the civil war he sought to explain German nationalism to the French through the example of Mainz. While he called the French renovation of Germany under Napoleon I an "excusable" error, paid his respects to the civil code, and admitted the strength of the Napoleonic cult in Mainz after 1815, he warned the French against misunderstanding the German scene. Sympathy for the French in the 1790s was due to the feudal regime, the lack of liberty, and the local people's dislike for the Austrian and Prussian occupying force. However, the revolution of 1848 cleared the air. It demonstrated that liberty would activate the latent nationalism of the German people. By the 1860s, he advised his French readers, the Germans, even those in the Rhineland, wished to move from platonic unity to physical unity.[50] However, he dismissed as nonsense German claims to Alsace-Lorraine, and he exchanged letters with the French historian Edgar Quinet, rejecting Quinet's claim that 1866 represented the victory of force. It was

Germany's destiny to go forward with the mainstream of the age, he maintained, even if the methods were not always ideal.

But it was the Luxemburg crisis that aroused him to excited activity. He was extremely pessimistic during the crisis, believing that hostilities were certain. He reasoned, however, that the war would hasten the unification of Germany, but at the price of further erosion of freedom. It was a price he seemed unwilling to pay. He admitted to Oppenheim that he would rather see Luxemburg lost than go to war against France. Publicly he argued against war and tried to explain the reasonableness of the French claim for compensation after the partial unification of Germany. He pointed out that neither Bismarck nor Napoleon III wanted war, attributing much of the war fever to the French opposition to Napoleon and south German particularists who were bent on using the Luxemburg affair to embarrass Prussia. He organized a formal letter from Germans residing in Paris protesting against a Franco-Prussian war, apparently with the cooperation of Jules Favre. When the crisis was defused at the London Conference on May 11, 1867, Bamberger breathed freely. "I am not one of those strong spirits," he wrote Arnold Ruge, "who can look *sub specie aeterni* at the slaughter of 200,000 persons and the misery of a great war."[51]

Besides trying to use his influence and experience to preserve the peace between France and Germany, Bamberger had to find his political niche in the emerging German party system, particularly with regard to the Progressive–National Liberal party split. Until 1866 Bamberger counted himself a member of the democratic camp. All his essays in the *Demokratische Studien* and the *Deutsche Jahrbücher,* although stressing a new note of realism and friendliness for Prussia, were directed toward his democratic colleagues. On February 14, 1860, he had turned down an invitation to join the recently organized National Association, in part because he was suspicious of its too close identification with the existing Prussian state. Shortly before the civil war he still retained his negative attitude toward the National Association, this time stressing the leadership of the Hanoverian Rudolf von Bennigsen. In a censored letter written in 1866 and published in the 1880s, Bamberger referred to the leader of the National Association and future leader of the National Liberal party as one of the "survivors of the race of 1848ers who have risen to a statesmanlike height and whose problem consists of swallowing . . . [censored] with high spiritual bearing and never leaving a position of tact and moderation."[52]

Prussia's victory in 1866 won Bamberger unreservedly to her side but still did not make easier the decision regarding political alignments on the national level. In Paris he had met many Prussian and other German liberals and was particularly close to Hans Viktor von Unruh. Unruh had been the president of the Prussian National Assembly in 1848, and in 1859 he was one of the founders of the National Association and later of the Progressive party. In 1866 he left the Progressives and signed up with the emerging National Liberal party. Bamberger also met and was favorably impressed by Karl Twesten, who likewise had made the switch from Progressive to National Liberal in 1866.[53]

Bamberger's first task was to sort out right from wrong in the Progressive–National Liberal conflict, which came in the wake of civil war. It took almost two years before he formally committed himself to the National Liberal party in April 1868. His hesitation and ultimate decision sprang from several considerations. As a southern German he wished to maintain ties to his geographic constituency, which he believed would be compromised by the excessively Prussian coloration of the National Liberals. He also did not want to be a southern dog on the back of a north German tiger. However, he sincerely regretted the split between the Progressives and the National Liberals, and he continued to hope as late as June 1867 that the wound in the liberal ranks could be healed. For these reasons he refused to sign the National Liberal program of June 6, 1867.[54]

Furthermore, he had serious reservations about the political stance of the National Liberal party and, foreshadowing later developments, tried to find a middle way between the National Liberals with their too compliant nature and the Progressives with their too oppositional posture. In April 1867 he was writing to Oppenheim about the necessity of establishing a newspaper for "one of us" along with an "opposition" party, but it had to be "impartial" and "not against Prussia." Several months later he took Oppenheim to task for going so far to the right, that is, signing the National Liberal party program, and added, "That is not my taste." The National Liberals were too "governmental." He did not believe Oppenheim's claim that the National Liberals could be a "governmental opposition" party. "I do not believe that it would be possible, and I am an ungovernmental being," he retorted. His pessimistic view was confirmed by a trip to Berlin in May 1867. "All in all," he summed up, "Prussia is still completely stuck in the personal monarchical regime. The king is everything and can do everything."[55]

He was finally brought around to the National Liberals by two considerations. His attempt to find some middle ground between the warring parties in Berlin failed. His explanation to Ruge in 1867 could serve as well for the 1880s. "For our point of view to which we would like to make the sacrifice of [founding] a great newspaper, there now exists only a quite small church in the north. I believe that earlier there would have been room in south Germany.... The nuance which we represent, further to the left [of the National Liberals], somewhat more idealistic, without getting into the Progressives, has no place in the momentary party structure." This lack of an alternative went hand in hand with a growing disenchantment with the Progressives. Already in May 1867, during his trip to Berlin, he had concluded that the National Liberals were moved more by "objective" considerations, the Progressives by the "subjective." "I concede," he wrote to Ruge, "that my instinct inclines me rather to the Nationals than the Progressives; however, my wife claims that I have become a reactionary." He criticized the Progressives for their unnecessary dogmatism and lack of awareness of the realities of German political life, and for not recognizing that one lived in an era of political compromise. As he denounced his opponents in the election of March 1868, "We have to deal with practical problems—it is not a question of theory but of the fatherland, and to further this [cause] is preferable to us than all the brilliant justification of theories." He was further upset by the behavior of the Progressives in the so-called Twesten Affair. For a parliamentary speech in which he attacked the Prussian government and administration on May 20, 1865, the National Liberal politician and former Progressive was persecuted by the Prussian government. It culminated on November 11, 1867, with a punishment of two years' imprisonment, the maximum permissible, and loss of his bureaucratic position. Eduard Lasker introduced a bill on November 27 which would clearly state that article 84 of the Prussian constitution permitted unlimited freedom of speech in the legislature. The Progressives opposed Lasker's motion on the grounds that article 84 already provided for freedom of speech and the motion would call in question this guarantee. For Bamberger that was "dogmatism." By April 1868, on the eve of the first meeting of the Customs Parliament, he had made his decision: "National Liberal ... there is no other party for me. For all other liberals, politics is *subjective.* "[56]

If reentering national politics finally meant attaching oneself to the National Liberals, being effective on the national level meant coming to terms with Otto von Bismarck, the Prussian minister president. The deputy from Mainz, like so many others, was fascinated by the Prussian leader. Between 1867 and 1898, Bamberger made Bismarck the focus of numerous essays, and references to him appear in almost everything he wrote over a thirty-five-year period. In his essay *Juchhe nach Italia,* his anti-Austrian stance paralleled Bismarck's. And his writings of the 1860s, even during the constitutional conflict, avoided criticism of Bismarck. After 1866 the returned exile was concerned about the unsavory reputation Prussia and Bismarck had received, particularly in France, as a result of the constitutional conflict and the Danish and Austrian wars. Bamberger was convinced that "international enlightenment" was required. Between September and November he wrote, in French,

"Monsieur de Bismarck," which appeared in the *Revue moderne* in February and March, 1868. It was quickly translated into German and English.[57]

Bamberger's aim in writing his first study of the chancellor of the North German Confederation was to explain Bismarck to the French, and in many ways it represents his most dexterous piece of writing. To make Bismarck palatable to the French, he portrayed the chancellor as a revolutionary ("He is a born revolutionist") replacing the masses, who in Germany proved to be so unrevolutionary. In September 1867, Bamberger had confessed to Oppenheim that given the fact of a "paralyzed people," the emphasis on Bismarck was justified. He claimed further that Bismarck had matured greatly since 1849 and was now aware of the political and economic requirements of the German people. In the decisive moment of 1866 the Prussian leader found his "moral" support in the nation. Moreover, Bismarck represented the moderate or enlightened wing of the Prussian autocracy and was relatively open to progressive ideas. "In the midst of a reactionary court and under a more or less despotic government, Count Bismarck represented justice and liberty." Bamberger's discussion of the constitutional conflict also showed Bismarck in the best possible light. He suggested that the most arbitrary measures of the government were not the minister president's doing, but rather the other ministers'. He characterized the indemnity as a "compromise between the mistakes of yesterday and the interests of tomorrow."[58]

It is difficult to disagree with the reaction of the *Frankfurter Zeitung* that the work was nothing less than an "apologia." Bamberger, the newspaper continued, "had constructed in his mind a Bismarck who, supported by the liberals [and] by the strength of the national idea, would now fulfill the demands of liberalism and rescue Germany from the bonds of feudalism and bureaucratic privilege." The liberal *Berliner Tageblatt,* of course, saw it differently. "Here for the first time," it noted, "an authentic democrat did justice to the statesmanlike genius of the . . . chancellor." Bamberger wanted to see in the chancellor a fulfiller of liberal demands. But if he did conjure up a gilded Bismarck, he never was swept into the sea of worshipers the German leader acquired after 1866. Even in his Bismarck study, Bamberger predicted very accurately what was at stake in the marriage of Bismarck and parliament. "Granted that the victory-laden commander saw in the acceptance of the parliamentary constitution only a marriage to his maid who was to serve him modestly in little things at home so that he could play a great role outside. He should not forget, however, that whoever marries his maid vows . . . to treat her as an equal and that the common progeny can only be brutalized and depraved if the mother is not honored at home." Bamberger realized that Bismarck despised parliamentarianism and was not concerned with the rights of the individual, but he hoped that the chancellor's "political instinct," his recognition of what was "capable of giving life to a nation," would lead him in the right direction, that is, toward liberalism.[59]

The reservations seemed insignificant at the time. Bismarck was "still a man of life and spirit with whom one ultimately is again reconciled," and Bamberger basked in the general approval with which the book was met. Bismarck read it and announced that Bamberger had treated him as well as could be expected from a liberal. At the meeting of the Customs Parliament in 1869, Bamberger announced that every delegate had read it and all praised it. Even as late as 1873 he wrote with unrestrained joy of a meeting he had with Bismarck's sister, who complimented him on his ability to depict the chancellor so accurately without even having met him.[60]

His study of Bismarck aided Bamberger's entry into national politics in 1868 with the opening of the Customs Parliament. He felt himself swept up in the tempo of events and looked hopefully to the future. In his diary he agreed with a French acquaintance who said: *" 'Le monde appartient aux optimistes, les pessimistes ne sont que des spectateurs.' "*[61] The Customs Parliament opened amid great fanfare on April 27, 1868. Protestant services were held in the palace chapel and Catholic services in St. Hedwig's Church; the opening sitting took place in the White Hall of the Royal Palace. But to remind everyone that an entirely new age had not dawned, the deputies were placed furthest away from the king. The parliament had competence over tariff matters, trade treaties, and a variety of consumer taxes. It contained representatives from the North German Confederation as well as the south German states of Baden, Bavaria, Hesse-Darmstadt and Württemberg.[62]

Although Bamberger claimed that he wanted to be prepared for the Customs Parliament and not appear a dilettante, his activity touched on all the important issues of the day: German unity, voting regulations, taxation, tariffs, and currency reform. He joined in the protest against Württemberg's government because its narrow interpretation of the term "residency" threatened to exclude large numbers of workers from the right to vote. The recently returned Mainzer believed that Württemberg's regulation infringed on the principle of freedom of movement. He also participated in the abortive negotiation to unite liberal and national forces of the north and south and was one of the sponsors of a rejected address to the Prussian king which spoke of the desire for the completion of German unity. He called attention to the need for tax reform and for a more rational and equitable tax system to replace the money lost through a reduction in tariffs. He favored an income tax rather than the tax on petroleum desired by Bismarck. He also spoke in support of lower tariffs and emphasized the need for a unified monetary system.[63]

Bamberger's activity in the Customs Parliament reached its high point in 1868 in connection with the reduction of the tariff on imported wine. Mainz was the center of a major wine-producing area of Germany, and Bamberger was sensitive to wine issues. He did not oppose the reduction of the tariff on wine, but he argued that it would leave the wine producers of Rhenish Hesse at a disadvantage since they still had to pay the high state taxes of Hesse-Darmstadt. Bamberger's target was not simply the tax system of Hesse-Darmstadt; he saw an opportunity to strike a blow for economic unity. Since one could not expect Hesse-Darmstadt to change its laws, Bamberger called for a general law which would provide a uniform wine tax throughout the customs area. His proposal, which threatened the financial sovereignty of the Darmstadt government, sparked the famous Customs Parliament debate of May 18, 1868. It included Bismarck's statement that "an appeal to fear [of French intervention hinted at by some south Germans] finds no echo in German hearts" and Joseph Völk's that "spring has now broken out in Germany." Bamberger's motion was passed by the Customs Parliament but rejected by the Federal Council (Bundesrat).[64]

Bamberger not only actively participated in the Customs Parliament discussions but also helped to publicize its work in a series of "Vertrauliche Briefe aus dem Zollparlament" ("Confidential Letters from the Customs Parliament") written during and immediately after the sessions. The letters tried to guide the reader through the intricacies of the parliamentary disputes, but more importantly they were a source of support for Prussia and propagated the message that the Customs Parliament was merely a transitional stage which would have to lead to greater unity. His letters received wide publicity in south Germany and even in France.[65] In other ways, too, Bamberger did what he could to advance the cause of German unity. He collected signatures for petitions in Mainz requesting entry into the North German Confederation. He was involved, to what extent is not clear, in the negotiations which led to Eduard Lasker's unsuccessful motion of February 24, 1870, to admit Baden into the North German Confederation.[66]

All of this, however, could not prevent him from becoming disillusioned with the Customs Parliament and the prospects for German unity. The parliament had failed to evolve into something more politically substantial, and the drive toward national unity seemed stalled. The failure was not merely institutional, he believed, but reflected a basic weakness within the German body politic. The German people seemed to lack the will to unification. Bismarck could not be blamed for moving slowly, given the mood in the south where, he claimed, "the Jesuits and democratic phrasemongers have the upper hand. With this pack in the rear," he wrote to Oppenheim prophetically, "how can one uphold German autonomy *vis à vis* France, as long as one is not actually determined to make war." After a trip to Worms in November 1869 he wrote that he "once more had an opportunity to observe the German philistine in his original wrapping. I do not know what has led to the thought that this people demands self rule. . . . Tobacco, and beer or wine— the rest leaves them cold." By March 1870 the recent successes for particularist elements in both Württemberg and Bavaria caused him to remark that unity could be achieved only with a "bold stroke." He still had faith in Bismarck and hoped that the latter would realize that "who does not go forward goes backward." He was more optimistic about developments in the North German Confederation, and this led to his next move. If there is a main theme running through Bamberger's career in the 1860s it is the desire to participate in the task of German unification and escape from parochial considerations. When the route via the Customs Parliament seemed blocked, Bamberger drew the necessary conclusions and announced that he was establishing residency in Kastel, across the river from Mainz, but in the confederation. After one year's residency he would be eligible for election to the North German Reichstag and participation in the writing of national legislation.[67]

This backdoor approach to the center of the German political stage was obviated by the outbreak of the Franco-German war in July 1870, which immediately placed Bamberger into the middle of the unification process. Although he felt that war between the two nations should be avoided, Bamberger immediately concluded that war was certain upon hearing the announcement that the house of Hohenzollern-Sigmaringen had accepted the Spanish throne.[68] He was in no doubt about the correct course. His diary records the war fever he encountered in France during the early weeks of July, and believing that he recognized more clearly than others the trend of events, he tried to warn Germany of the impending danger from France through letters to friends and through newspaper articles. He finally left Paris for Germany on July 13, arriving in Mainz via Cologne on July 15. The French declaration of war of July 19 he regarded as merely a postscript.[69]

The next three weeks in Mainz were bittersweet. On Sunday, July 24, listening to the peaceful ring of the church bells, he noted: "Nature at peace, and in a few days two worlds collide, a sea of blood spreading out." Bamberger experienced difficulty in generating patriotic enthusiasm in the area as attempts to unite the democratic and liberal forces in Mainz behind a common proclamation failed. He was unconvinced that the Mainzers had the proper attitude toward the war, and even his party colleagues in Mainz seemed petty and ungenerous. Financial contributions by notables to families of soldiers were low, and there were difficulties in regard to the quartering of troops. These attitudes were confirmed by other reports of secret pro-French feelings in the Hesse-Darmstadt judiciary, of Württemberger peasants who regarded the Prussians rather than the French as enemies, and of particularism in the army.[70]

These disturbing reports, however, could not permanently becloud the dawning day in Germany. As he wrote to Oppenheim: "A kind of confidence in Germany's rising and France's sinking star animates everyone and also me. And this war, victory or defeat, will penetrate deeply into all our personal fates, without even mentioning that it will make us all 30–40% poorer, to which I am indifferent." The emotional peak of this period probably came on September 4 when Bamberger, upon receipt of the news of the decisive German victory at Sedan, addressed a huge crowd from the balcony of the Gutenberg Theater in Mainz. He spoke of national unity crowning the great victory and obliterating the failure of 1848; the German people at that time thought they could achieve unity with noble feelings and without a "strong engine." That engine was now overrunning the external enemy.[71]

The one-time revolutionary and condemned man had come a long way in a relatively few years, and the dramatic occasion of September 4 highlighted Bamberger's major activity during 1871—cooperating with Bismarck in the work of German unification. The paths of the two men crossed on August 2, 1870, when the German army established its first headquarters in Mainz, and Bamberger was in Bismarck's retinue from August 2 to August 23 and November 1 to December 5. During these months the liberal politician, because of his contacts in northern and southern Germany, his connections with the press, and his knowledge of French affairs, was used by the chancellor for a variety of tasks. Bamberger was one of the government's conduits to the press, and his articles found their way into the *National Zeitung, Elberfelder Zeitung, Allgemeine Zeitung* (Augsburg), *Kölnische Zeitung,* and *Mainzer Zeitung.*[72]

Bamberger's primary concern during August and September was Alsace and Lorraine. There was never any doubt in his mind, then or later, that the two areas had to be taken. He regarded annexation as a military necessity that no leader of Germany could ignore, and he rejected the argument that renunciation of the two provinces would have dissipated French hostility. His attitude was strengthened in 1870 by disturbing reports from France of outrages against Germans. The French newspaper *Figaro* spoke of a racial war, and by the end of August, Germans were being expelled from France.[73] Bamberger thus needed no encouragement when Bismarck suggested on August 26 that he attach himself to the staff of the new military governor of Alsace, Count von Bismarck-Bohlen, and edit the government newspaper for the new province, the *Amtlichen Nachrichten für das General Gouvernement Elsass.* Initially the newspaper was printed in French and German and referred to Alsace-Lorraine as an occupied district. By September 15 the tone had changed, and in a lead article Bamberger argued strongly in favor of annexation of the "thoroughly" German territory of Alsace and Lorraine. Six days later the use of French was severely restricted.[74]

The connection with the *Amtlichen Nachrichten* lasted about three weeks. By the end of September, Bamberger had had enough of bureaucratic involvement, complaining that as an independent man who volunteered his services, he could not tolerate officials who treated him like a subordinate. "After three weeks in the bureaucratic circle," he wrote to Busch, "I have paid my obligation to the fatherland more than in a bivouac." Nevertheless, he continued his press efforts in favor of the annexation of Alsace-Lorraine.[75]

In addition to his press work, Bamberger hoped to move Bismarck along the proper, that is, liberal and national path. Close exposure to the Prussian military had given rise to doubt about the consequences of the war for German constitutionalism. On August 6 he noted that he surrendered himself for the moment to the fact that the "red collars [army] are master." Yet two weeks later he wrote Jacob Finger, a party colleague from Alzey and later minister of the Hesse-Darmstadt government, to encourage "pressure from below so that the German people profit from the victories on the battlefield. It half appears to me that we are threatened with a disappointment as after 1815." It has been suggested that Bamberger's letter to Finger, which was forwarded to Bennigsen and Lasker, played a role in triggering their trip to southern Germany to line up support for the impending reorganization of Germany. A similar call for popular agitation was dispatched to Oppenheim.[76] Bamberger also wrote Bismarck that public opinion in Germany would let him "do what he wanted" if only he carried on a "healthy German policy." Although Bismarck noted "nonsense" in the margin, he asked that Bamberger come to Versailles, since a personal contact would answer many questions that the latter might have. At the end of October he was on his way to Versailles to be there when "Germany is regenerated at the seat of Louis XIV."[77]

At Versailles, Bamberger's role was minor. He argued in vain against bombarding Paris and more successfully against calling the Reichstag to Versailles, which he regarded as a sign of Bismarck's disrespect. He was briefly involved in the negotiations regarding Bavaria's entry into the German Empire when Bismarck complained that Lasker had conceded more special privileges to the Bavarians than was necessary. Bamberger, acting as an intermediary, discovered that the key differences were over military matters and granted that Lasker might have been too obliging, but he claimed that Bismarck was exaggerating the difficulties in order to discredit the liberals.[78] His last act for German unity was fittingly as Bismarck's "imperial messenger." The chancellor was concerned that the concessions granted Bavaria might make the treaty bringing in the south German state unacceptable to the Reichstag of the North German Confederation. In order to impress upon the deputies the necessity of accepting the treaty unchanged, Bismarck dispatched Bamberger to Berlin, along with Franz von Roggenbach, the Badenese politician. Before leaving Versailles on December 5, Bamberger telegraphed Bennigsen, strongly warning against amending the treaties since it was "equivalent to rejection, that is, new chaos." Although Bismarck was sincerely concerned, the treaties were on their way to a bitter but easy passage when Bamberger arrived. The final vote was 195 32.[79]

With the passage of the treaties in December 1870 and the formal princely proclamation of the German Empire on January 18, 1871, Bamberger's dream of a quarter-century had been realized. Moreover, he had played a role in the councils of the mighty in bringing about German unity. That the structure of the empire was not entirely to his liking, that the role of parliament was hardly impressive, that the chancellor was too irresponsible, all these shortcomings could be corrected in the future. Surely, Bamberger claimed, Bismarck would have to realize what was "life-giving" to a nation.[80]

Participating in the exciting events of the war no doubt satisfied Bamberger's desire to be as close as possible to the center of German affairs. If he wished to continue to play a major role in building a powerful and respected German state there was only one path open—that of a parliamentary deputy. Accordingly, Bamberger returned to Mainz in January 1871 for the difficult election campaign for the new German Reichstag.[81] He faced strong opposition from Catholic and democratic forces who this time ran separate candidates against him, hoping to force a run-off, for which they would unite. His party was tainted by a scandal involving the embezzlement of tax monies. Moreover, the election was almost lost even before the campaign had seriously begun as a result of a proposed gerrymander. Bamberger's electoral district, the ninth, was composed of Mainz and a rural area to the south. While he ran behind his opponents in the city he was able to make up the deficit with overwhelming support in towns such as Oppenheim, Nierstein, Guntersblum, Selzen, Dolgesheim, Eimsheim, and Schwabsburg. In order to deprive Bamberger of some of his "best troops," the Hesse-Darmstadt chief minister, Dalwigk, proposed a redistricting of the ninth by adding some hostile territory to the north and detaching the Oppenheim-Guntersblum area to the south. Fortunately the territory north of Mainz was on the right bank of the Rhine and thus in the recently defunct North German Confederation. This meant the Federal Council would have to decide the matter. Bamberger protested to Lasker and to Moritz Busch, one of Bismarck's assistants, and asked for support at the national level. This was forthcoming, and the Prussians rejected any tampering with the ninth electoral district.[82]

With that matter out of the way, there was still an election to win. Bamberger did not expect it to be as close as the previous one, since he hoped to cash in on the enthusiasm caused by Germany's victory over France. Nevertheless, he triumphed by only thirty-eight votes over his combined opponents. Not until the last little town of Wintersheim gave him fifty-six of its fifty-nine votes was his victory certain. The election victory, regardless of how narrow, was very satisfying. "For none of the hundreds of expelled Germans [from France] is there as much compensation," he wrote to his wife.[83]

His two elections in Mainz were the most difficult until the breakup of the National Liberal party in 1879–80. Bamberger had never been happy with the Mainz district, since the composition of its electorate made a close election a certainty. There was also a growing socialist movement which threatened to create additional difficulties. If merely a narrow victory could be achieved during the euphoria over unification, the post-unification normality promised difficult days. An evil omen occurred in December 1872, when his party suffered a sharp defeat in Mainz in the state elections, garnering fewer votes than the democrats and Catholics. For this reason, Bamberger eagerly searched for a new district even as the Mainz committee of the party decided on him as their candidate in the next Reichstag election.[84]

During the latter part of 1873 he moved along two paths, one that led to Halle and the other to the adjacent eighth district of Bingen-Alzey. The Halle candidacy, however, remained vague and uncertain. Far more promising was the move next door. Bamberger had preferred the Bingen-Alzey district in 1868, but it had gone to August Metz, a prominent south German member of the National Association from Darmstadt. When he decided for reasons of health not to run again in 1874, Bamberger was able to transfer to this safe district.[85]

The district of Bingen-Alzey, west and southwest of Mainz, was largely rural, with Bingen and Alzey the only significant towns. It was a land of vineyards and small farms, of rolling hills and a politically alive citizenry. Bamberger was well known in the area and had done some of his most successful organizing for the Democratic Association in 1848 and 1849 there. In the 1870s it was overwhelmingly liberal in outlook, with weak opposition from the Catholic party, since Catholics made up only one-third of the population. There was scarcely a need to campaign. It was the ideal district for Bamberger, who always had his ideas riveted on national affairs. He could now complete his move to Berlin. In the three elections in 1874, 1877, and

1878, he received more than 70 percent of the vote, while in Mainz the liberals were being defeated by the Center party and the democrats.[86]

With the capturing of the election district of Bingen-Alzey, Bamberger could now concentrate his energies on the major focus of his aspirations since 1848, constructing a united German state.

·4·

Financial Unity

Ludwig Bamberger always denied that he was attracted to the idea of a German national state by the increased technical efficiency offered by such a creation. Rather, it was higher political morals, the elevated level of political life, that made a unified Germany so desirable. Nevertheless, Bamberger's major efforts during the first five years after unification centered on technical matters: the creation of a unified and efficient financial struture for the German Empire. Although there was scarcely an issue before the Reichstag between 1871 and 1893 that he ignored, the area in which he felt most at home and in which he was most successful was finance. His most significant contributions to the new empire were in the field of currency and banking legislation, and of all his legislative work he was proudest of his efforts on behalf of financial unity. His achievements in this area were more durable than the Bismarckian empire itself.[1]

Once while he was in the midst of the currency reform debate, Bamberger protested that he completely lacked an instinct for finance and had gotten into it by accident. If heredity influenced Bamberger it should have turned him in the direction of financial affairs. On both sides of his family the banking tradition was strong, and it was precisely this destiny that he tried to escape in the 1840s but was forced into during the 1850s. He did not ultimately regret immersion into the world of finance, but he always regarded it as the means to a more significant end—initially personal survival, and later independence in order to engage himself politically. Nevertheless, he was enormously successful in his financial undertakings even after he ended active participation in banking affairs. His training, which had taken him to London, Antwerp, Rotterdam, Paris, and finally Berlin, had given him exceptional experience in international finance.[2] And it was in exile that he first came to grips with a problem that would immediately occupy him after unification, the gold standard.

Around the middle of the nineteenth century, most German states as well as most European countries had currencies based upon silver. In the Germanies, less than 10 percent of the money in circulation was gold coins, while silver coins composed over 66 percent. The use of silver reflected, among other things, the scarcity of gold, a situation which changed dramatically in the 1850s as a result of gold discoveries in California and Australia. The suddenly more plentiful supply of gold coincided with an increased demand for silver by India, primarily as a result of the American Civil War which shut off the supply of cotton from the United States. Europe's cotton demand had to be satisfied by Indian exports and paid for in silver. This had the effect of increasing the price of silver and making the now relatively plentiful gold inexpensive. The price of gold fell below its par value, and it became profitable to coin gold and melt down silver for export. The use of gold was further encouraged by the general growth of business operations and the ever greater need for funds which gold could more easily satisfy than the bulkier and heavier silver.[3]

The increasing use of gold, although apparently welcomed by the business community, aroused the apprehension of Michel Chevalier, a leading French economist and an advisor to Napoleon III. Chevalier claimed that the increased supply of gold would cause a sharp drop in its value. He advocated that France, a bimetallist country, return to a simple silver standard in order to maintain international monetary stability. Against this background, Bamberger wrote his first monetary essay, "Die Gold-und Silberfrage" ("The Gold and Silver Question"), in 1861. His residency in France and his involvement in international banking undertakings put him in an excellent position to observe the growing use of gold as a medium of exchange. He also saw the ease with which gold replaced silver, a sign of confidence on the part of the business community in the usefulness of gold for international and local transactions. The core of Bamberger's argument was that the increased use of gold would not lead to its debasement but rather to its becoming the basis for an international monetary system.[4]

With this opening salvo, Bamberger's thirty-eight-year involvement in currency questions began. Events during the 1860s confirmed his predictions about the replacement of silver by gold. Led by France, one European country after another had to accept the *de facto* circulation of gold, although most still retained a double or even a single silver standard like Germany's. In 1865 the Latin Monetary Union of France, Belgium, Switzerland, and Italy was formed, and it provided for mutual acceptance of one another's coins. The members seriously considered adopting a gold standard but did not take this step because France hesitated. Although one of the expressed hopes of the Latin Monetary Union was that it would become the basis of a worldwide currency system, only Greece formally joined. One major reason was that the question of a standard remained unresolved. In an attempt to overcome objections, the French called an international monetary congress in Paris in 1867 where the representatives of twenty governments decided by a nearly unanimous vote (the Netherlands dissented) that only gold was feasible as an international standard. Although France continued to investigate the question of adopting the gold standard, in 1870 control of monetary affairs passed from her hands to the newly emergent German Empire.[5]

Germany's political disunity was mirrored in her monetary diversity. The empire had eight different currencies in operation grouped around the thaler, mark, and gulden systems, not to mention the franc system in Alsace-Lorraine. Only the city state of Bremen was on the gold standard; the rest were tied to silver. The leading advocate of the gold standard in Germany was Adolf Soetbeer, who during the 1860s wrote incessantly on its behalf. His efforts were seconded strongly by the Congress of German Economists (Kongress der deutscher Volkswirte). Bamberger and Soetbeer were in constant communication from the late 1860s until the latter's death in 1892, and both participated in the meetings of the Congress of German Economists.[6]

From at least 1861 on, Bamberger was convinced that gold represented the only rational currency base for the future. In 1867 he broached the subject with Otto Michaelis, councilor for financial affairs in the Federal Chancellor's Office of the North German Confederation, and Rudolf von Delbrück, its president. The latter was sympathetic but the former, cool. Ludolf Camphausen, the Prussian finance secretary, was also opposed to the idea of a gold standard, and matters thus moved slowly. In June 1868, the Reichstag of the North German Confederation requested a currency system which would as far as possible pave the way toward a universal monetary system. The following year the Customs Parliament passed a similar resolution. In 1869 and 1870, Bamberger emphasized the need for a gold standard for reasons of monetary rationality as well as national unity. He also wanted currency reform regarded as an affair of the Customs Parliament.[7]

Ultimately the Franco-German War of 1870–71 provided the means whereby the new German Empire could institute monetary reform. Besides completing the political unification of Germany, the consequences of the Treaty of Frankfurt gave the new nation an indemnity of five billion francs. Since a large part of this indemnity was paid in gold or in notes easily convertible to gold, it became possible to withdraw silver from circulation and substitute gold. The first step was taken on July 3, 1871, when the government ended its purchases and suspended the coinage of silver. On November 11, 1871, the decisive move was made with the submission to the

Reichstag of a bill regarding the minting of gold coins.[8] The proposal introduced gold coins in denominations of ten, twenty, and thirty marks. However, it did not allow the free coining of gold, and it gave the states the right to mint the coins. Although it seemed to foreshadow a gold standard, the bill neither restricted a state's right to mint silver coins nor provided for the withdrawal of the states' silver coins.[9]

According to Bamberger, rational currency reform should have been based on the following principles: gold standard, simplicity, centralization, and internationalism. Scored against this standard the government's bill deserved a passing grade, but it was far from perfect. Actually he had hoped to see bank reform come first so that a central bank through a correct discount policy could regulate the currency transformation. Since this step was precluded by disagreements within the Prussian government, one had to proceed directly toward the gold standard. All the events since 1860 had convinced Bamberger that gold was the currency of the future. As it steadily replaced silver in international transactions, except with India, Chevalier's fears of inflation caused by oversupply of gold were not realized. The price of gold declined only 1.5 to 2 percent. This was impressive evidence of the convenience of gold as a medium of exchange and as the basis of an international currency. Only gold, Bamberger claimed, was international in the sense that it had "a value in itself" which was "not determined inside the borders of the country but only on the world market." "A state, which wants to make future transactions," he argued, "must obligate itself to pay in gold." Moreover, a world monetary union would be superfluous if all countries based their currencies on gold.[10]

Bamberger was the first speaker in the general debate after Rudolf von Delbrück introduced the bill. It was Bamberger's first great speech in the Reichstag, and appropriately it concerned monetary reform. He announced that in general he accepted the proposal. However, he chided the government for introducing a temporary double standard instead of taking the definitive step toward a gold-based currency. In reality, he argued, it was impossible to maintain a double standard; rather one created an alternating currency, and the most convenient medium would always be circulated. With a single currency standard based on gold, the country could avoid fluctuations. In order to make clear the government's intentions to adopt a gold standard, no more silver should be minted and it should be recalled as quickly as possible. In addition Bamberger announced that he wanted to see inserted into the law the right of the individual to have gold minted. This would facilitate trade both internally and externally and provide greater flexibility. At the same time he wanted to eliminate particularistic measures in the bill by making the minting of gold and the withdrawal of silver an affair of the empire. He was highly pleased with his first great effort. "I spoke for a full hour and one-half," he wrote to his wife, "and had the utmost attentiveness [of the Reichstag] —an unheard-of occurrence. Everyone compliments me."[11]

The speakers in the general debate added relatively little to Bamberger's presentation. The strongest opposition came from some Progressives and from Moritz Mohl, who wished to retain silver and thus create a double standard. Both hoped that an international currency system patterned after that of the French-led Latin Monetary Union would take shape. The ultimate outcome of the debate was foreshadowed when Bamberger's suggestion that the bill be considered in plenum for the second reading without first being sent to a commission won easy approval.[12]

Karl Helfferich, in his excellent study of the German monetary reform, claimed that the bill regulating the minting of gold coins as well as those establishing a new German currency system and the Reichsbank were examples of the Reichstag's playing a constructive role. Using its expertise and capitalizing on the lack of unanimity within the government, the German legislative body significantly changed and improved the government's proposals. In these three cases, Bamberger was at the center of the legislative improvement. He devoted all his energies to financial reform, withdrawing from the Deutsche Bank and all private business in order to have his hands clean. Although there was no formal parliamentary commission, a "free commission" composed mainly of National Liberals was organized. It was here that Bamberger worked effectively and that most of the amendments for the second reading were decided upon. "The currency affair," he explained to his wife, "is completely under my direction. I have now worked myself so into the stuff that I have the complicated material completely in my head."[13]

During the second reading, when the most significant changes were made, Bamberger's amendments and speeches enjoyed almost unbroken success. He first helped beat back an attempt by Moritz Mohl to introduce the twenty-five-franc gold coin used by the countries of the Latin Monetary Union. Bamberger denied that international commerce required an international coin. Rather it was necessary that all currencies be based on the same metal. Regarding the division of the mark, he successfully proposed that it contain only one hundred pfennigs rather than both groschen and pfennigs. He also fought successfully to amend article 3 to eliminate the thirty-mark gold piece, leaving only the ten- and twenty-mark pieces. He believed that the latter two coins were sufficient for financial transactions, and he also feared that the thirty-mark piece, very similar to the Prussian thaler, would permit the old Prussian system to be smuggled in. To complete the preliminary skirmishing he successfully advocated changing the inscription on the new coins from "German Imperial Coin" to a more dignified "German Empire."[14]

The heart of the bill as Bamberger saw it was not contained in the first five but rather in the next six articles. Article 6 deferred calling in the silver coins and also left in doubt whether the minting of the gold coins would be up to the empire rather than the states. Here was an issue which not only went to the core of financial logic but also was a touchstone of German unification. According to Bamberger, German monetary questions were by definition a matter for the central government to regulate. To eliminate any ambiguity he proposed that the minting of gold coins be an affair of the empire, paid for by the federal government, taking place at all "suitable" mints within federal territory instead of at state mints. He would have gone further, he advised the Reichstag, but out of deference to his colleagues and the state governments he did not request the withdrawal of silver coins. Bamberger's amendment to article 6 met the firm opposition of the Prussian finance minister, Camphausen, who stressed that article 6 was the result of a difficult compromise among the state governments. He particularly called attention to the clause in Bamberger's amendments which would have replaced the phrase concerning the minting of gold at all state mints which declared themselves ready with a more flexible statement about "suitable mints of the empire." This appeared to reduce the role of the states in carrying out the currency reform. Camphausen's reference to previous compromises within the Federal Council served to sway enough representatives to defeat Bamberger's motion.[15]

Defeated on an issue that he considered crucial and for what he regarded as insufficient reasons, Bamberger announced the most dramatic and perhaps most effective step in his entire parliamentary career. Hoping to use his prestige and influence with his colleagues as a lever on the government, he stated that he would support no bill that made the minting and maintenance of imperial coins an affair of the states and which did not make it possible for individuals to have gold minted for their private accounts. This latter measure Bamberger regarded as indispensable for a flexible currency system which would unofficially regulate the amount of gold in circulation. He had introduced a measure to request the chancellor to lay before the Reichstag in the next session a bill which provided that state mints not used by the empire must be available for minting for private accounts. Disheartened by Camphausen's apparent hostility to the idea, Bamberger announced that he was withdrawing all of his pending amendments.[16]

Bamberger's colleagues, especially Eduard Lasker and F. W. August Grumbrecht, took up his amendments. Article 9 was altered so that remelting of worn-out coins was financed by the empire, not the states. Article 10 was changed to prohibit the minting of gold and silver coins unless sanctioned by the bill. Article 11 was amended to emphasize the role of the federal government by making it responsible for financing the calling in of the states' gold coins. It also empowered the chancellor to call in silver coins and to give an account to the Reichstag at the beginning of each session. And finally the Reichstag adopted Bamberger's motion to provide for minting for private accounts.[17] With justification could Bamberger write: "Now finally the main work is done. . . . Yesterday I had a very successful day. . . . Today it was somewhat confusing and I saved the largest part of my amendments finally only through a *fausse sortie* which Lasker seconded in the ablest way."[18]

Although he thought the main work was done, the government was dissatisfied with the changes made on November 18, and Bismarck tried to convince Bamberger to renounce them. As he explained to his wife:

> Bismarck again has his peculiarities and wanted me to throw overboard something which I had pushed through on the second reading. . . . The day before yesterday the finance minister had me called to his office during the Reichstag sitting and made clear that if I did not give up my resistance the bill could be wrecked. I laughed at him politely and offered him a wager that his prophecy would not be fulfilled. The result was that Bismarck, before yesterday's decisive session, withdrew his chicanery. Minister Delbrück . . . had me informed at my arrival in the House that they had given up their opposition and that all of my proposals will be upheld in the third reading. . . . Even if I always thought that I would have a share in these matters in the Reichstag I never would have expected, so to speak, to monopolize them. One must always seek to create specialties for oneself in order to be effective.[19]

It was advice that Bamberger did not always follow.

On November 23, at the third reading of "my currency law," Bamberger heard Delbrück announce that the state governments had accepted the changes introduced by the Reichstag regarding articles 2, 9, 10, and 11, which increased the role of the central government. Article 6 remained unaltered, but the changes in the other articles pointed clearly in the direction of a nationally controlled financial system based on gold.[20]

The law of December 4, 1971, concerning the minting of gold pieces may have signified the ultimate victory of the gold standard. Nevertheless, it was merely the first of three steps that would drastically reshape Germany's financial system. The law had created a *de facto* double standard with gold now added to silver. The gold standard had not yet been reached. And the key support for the entire financial edifice, an imperial bank, had not yet been introduced. Bamberger saw clearly what the order of priorities should be and also understood why this was unrealizable. During the debate on the law regarding the minting of gold coins, Bamberger, as well as others, had called for the introduction of bills regulating the entire currency system and establishing a national bank. The following year he proposed to bring both bills in simultaneously. He recognized that the bank question was by far the more complicated of the two but argued that bank reform should be settled before currency reform. The bank could then preside over and regulate the introduction of the new currency and the withdrawal of the old. Unfortunately disagreements among the German governments and within the Prussian ministry continued to delay action on the bank question.[21]

Thus in February 1873 the Reichstag was presented only with a bill to establish a new currency system. The bill contained few surprises, since it mainly carried through the law of December 1871. Article 2 established the imperial gold currency based on the mark to replace the states' currencies. It was to go into effect no sooner than six months from the emperor's decree. Article 6 provided that the new coins of small denomination (silver, nickel, and copper) would be minted at the cost of the empire.[22]

Once again the first parliamentary speaker, Bamberger welcomed the measure but noted serious shortcomings and omissions. He desired a more explicit statement regarding a "pure" gold standard, believing that a hidden silver currency could still be smuggled into the bill. In particular he wanted the Austrian gulden, a silver-based coin, excluded from Germany. He also stressed the need for a coin between the five- and one-mark silver pieces. And most important of all, he wanted to see inserted in the bill the right to mint gold for private accounts.[23] Bamberger was strongly opposed once again by Moritz Mohl, who argued that the bill as it stood went too far. He wanted a double currency standard which expressly permitted the Austrian gulden to circulate as legal tender in Germany. Mohl's position had relatively little support, while Bamberger's position was generally seconded by speakers from the Progressives and Conservatives as well as National Liberals.[24] Bamberger's motion to discuss the bill in plenum without sending it to a commission was approved, auguring well for his position on the entire measure. The "free commission," in which Bamberger played a major role, once again oversaw the preparation of amendments for the second reading which commenced on April 22. Bamberger's name was attached to sixteen major amendments, twelve of which were accepted by the Reichstag.

Two of Bamberger's major objectives had been to get the change from silver to gold carried through as quickly as possible and to strengthen the federal government's role. Thus he regarded the minimum period of six months for the introduction of the new currency as too long and proposed that it be reduced to three. This was adopted with virtually no opposition. The careful financier also detected an impreciseness throughout the bill about when the goal of the currency reform would be reached. The opening article spoke of an imperial gold currency replacing the state currencies. However, the bill did not provide for a pure gold standard since it allowed continued circulation of silver currency. *When* the remaining silver currency would be called in, and silver coins of only small denominations used, was unclear. Thus, when the currency bill went into effect it would only introduce an indeterminate transition stage. Throughout the bill no distinction seemed to be made between the transition stage and the ultimate goal of the reform, which was a pure gold standard. Bamberger feared that this ambiguity would encourage Prussia to retain the silver thaler in circulation. For these reasons he wanted to draw a sharp distinction between the transition stage and the final goal. He proposed using the term "imperial gold currency" whenever the transition stage was clearly meant and "gold standard" when the ultimate aim was mentioned. No objection was raised.[25]

Bamberger was unsuccessful in his attempt to upgrade the chancellor's role and increase centralization by giving him the power to designate which mints would coin the new currency. The government regarded this as too extreme, and the motion was defeated. However, another of Bamberger's amendments gave the Federal Council greater authority to regulate the circulation of foreign coins in Germany.[26]

The core of the bill for Bamberger was article 11 (12 by the final reading) and a new article (18 by the final reading) dealing with paper money. The first dealt with the minting of gold by private individuals. The government's bill provided for the private minting of gold, but only conditionally, and left the amount of the fee for this service open. The chancellor was empowered to permit individual mints to coin gold for private accounts. The bill, however, contained no general right for private persons to mint gold and left the whole process in the hands of the executive branch, which was not known for its sympathy to the idea. Bamberger saw the government's version as an example of unnecessary control. It was part of a bureaucratic notion that the state must closely regulate the supply of gold. The classical liberal was on the side of those who did not want the government "to order our soul completely into the hands of the state and ask it to nourish, care for, and clothe us." This idea would be restated ever more frequently by the 1880s. His amendment stated that private individuals had the right to mint twenty-mark coins on their own account at mints which coined gold for the empire, so long as the latter were not busy with the government's requests. This general right was necessary to make certain that the German gold supply was in rapport with the needs of business. The situation was always so fluid, Bamberger argued, that the government, even with the best intentions, could not itself regulate the quantity and value of gold necessary for German financial transactions. In the world of international commerce only those directly concerned could do this. Furthermore, the fee for this service must not be set so high as to undercut it. Bamberger's amendment set the maximum rate at seven marks for a pound of fine gold. He was actually in favor of an unlimited right to mint coins for private accounts at no fee, but the government was adamantly opposed and his amendment represented a compromise. He thought that eventually the government would see the benefit of a lower rate. It did, and in 1875 the rate was set at three marks. The government, uneasy about the relative lack of controls and the possible cost to it for private minting, nevertheless accepted Bamberger's proposal when it was clear that it had the overwhelming approval of the Reichstag.[27]

It was only after the government's version of the bill as amended passed the second reading that the entire measure threatened to collapse. Bamberger had been unhappy that the government was so dilatory in preparing a bank bill. He was convinced that one could not establish a new currency system and leave untouched the question of bank notes and paper money issued by the German states. The lack of gold coins in Germany had encouraged the issuance of bank notes of small denomination, which Bamberger as well as others regarded as dangerous since newly minted gold coins would enter the market without steps being taken to reduce or eliminate the circulation of paper money. This would stimulate the export of gold, especially of the new gold coins, which would at the very least mean a setback to the idea of a gold standard. The government, because of internal differences, was slow to move. Camphausen was opposed to the idea of a central bank. Also several states which had issued large amounts of paper money saw the reform of the paper money system taking place at their expense.[28]

These facts were open secrets, and the Reichstag used what pressure it could on the individual states. A resolution in 1871 asking the government to do something about reform of paper currency was passed but had no success. Eighteen months later the Reichstag tried to attach a reform of the paper money system to the reform of the currency system, hoping that the Federal Council would not be willing to see the entire bill fall through. A number of divergent amendments dealing with the paper money question were proposed.[29] All were designed to force the government to begin paper currency reform. Delbrück warned the Reichstag not to go too far in attacking the paper money question. As the debate wore on an attempt to send all of the amendments to a commission was defeated, with the help of Bamberger's eloquence. Warnings that acceptance of an article 18, which the amendments would have created, would mean rejection by the Federal Council of the entire currency bill, were brushed aside. Several amendments were withdrawn, leaving as the major one that worked out by Bamberger and his National Liberal colleague from Bavaria, Marquard Barth. It stated that no later than January 1, 1875, all bank notes not based on the new imperial currency were to be called in. From that date on, only bank notes of not less than one hundred marks, and based on the new currency, might be issued and remain in circulation. The same stipulations applied to paper money issued by the states and by corporations. With one stroke Bamberger and Barth hoped to reduce the amount of paper money in circulation and force the government to act on the bank question, since this would be necessary to carry out the terms of the amendment. According to the stenographic reports of the Reichstag debates, a "large majority of the house" voted in favor of the amendment, and Bamberger was well satisfied with the results of the second reading.[30]

However, the German government was not, and the passage of the bill with the new article seemed to endanger the entire measure. The government, or rather the states as represented in the Federal Council, had several objections to the new article 18. For one thing, the date by which all old bank notes had to be withdrawn and new notes of one hundred marks or more issued (January 1, 1875) was regarded as too soon to accomplish the objectives of the article. Delbrück argued that a sufficient supply of bank notes could not be ready and that the government could not produce a bank bill by then. He asked for a year's extension to January 1, 1876. More serious from the government's point of view was the prohibition of bank notes of less than one hundred marks. The smaller notes circulated best, and to call them in would be equivalent to cancelling them. Nevertheless, the Federal Council, as Bamberger had calculated, was not ready to see the entire bill collapse because of article 18. It had to produce a response to the Reichstag action. Prussia and most of the other German states were willing to see the old paper currency virtually eliminated if it were replaced in part by an issuance of imperial paper money. However, Bavaria in particular proved unwilling to go this route. Most of her paper money was in large denominations which would be little affected by the prohibition of the smaller amounts, while the idea of imperial bank notes was strongly opposed in particularist Bavaria. Thus the Federal Council reached no decision, and Camphausen maintained the government's negative position before the Reichstag while attempting to pacify it with the statement that the Federal Council was trying to resolve the paper money question.[31]

When Delbrück and Camphausen made the Federal Council's position clear and hinted at a rejection of the currency bill if article 18 were upheld, Bamberger reacted vigorously. From the Reichstag's side, he warned, a rejection or strong modification of the article might make the bill worthless. He then proposed to remove the proceedings on article 18 from the agenda until the government produced its proposals on state paper money. Bamberger's pointed motion was replaced by a somewhat softened one which simply removed article 18 and several resolutions from the day's agenda. Nevertheless, the thrust of the motion was clear: until the government took action on article 18, the currency bill would remain in limbo. Very pleased, Bamberger wrote to his wife, "The day before yesterday as a result of a very successful tactic I forced the government to introduce a law on bank notes."[32]

The government's new proposals, however, were not quickly forthcoming. On May 29, June 10, and June 16, questions were asked in the Reichstag about the supposedly impending proposal. The problem within the government centered around the Prussian finance minister, Ludolf Camphausen, who had his own plan for ending the impasse. All state paper money would be called in and replaced with federal paper money to be issued on the basis of one thaler per capita and distributed to the states on the basis of population. This was enormously generous to Prussia, which had been very modest in issuing paper money and counted only 5/6 thaler of paper money per capita. Other German states were not so favorably placed. Saxony had issued 4 1/2–5 thaler of paper money per capita and Bavaria, 3. If all paper money were called in, these states would suffer financial losses. Foreseeing the opposition, Camphausen revealed his plans in part to the Reichstag, hoping to enlist its support. Additional pressure on the states would be exercised by threatening to hold up other lucrative appropriations arising out of the Franco-German war which were to accrue to the states.[33]

Rather than accepting Camphausen's plan, the Federal Council requested the chancellor's office, under Delbrück, to work out a proposal regulating not only paper money but also the bank question. Since this latter provision was anathema to Camphausen, Delbrück, who presided over the Federal Council, used as the basis of discussion a proposal from Saxony which only provided for additional money to be issued to the states in the form of imperial treasury notes. After apparent agreement to this formula had been reached, Bavaria, joined by the Grand Duchy of Hesse, announced that they could not agree to treating the paper money and bank questions separately. By then, June 18, the end of the Reichstag session was only a week away, and the whole matter threatened to be lost. Bismarck, who had remained in the background throughout this question since the technicalities were beyond his comprehension, nevertheless quickly perceived the political ramifications. One could not ignore the objections of the second most important state (Bavaria), especially with national elections approaching. Such an action would only increase the strength of the Catholic Center party. A way out of the deadlock had to be found, and Bismarck sought it through direct negotiations with Bamberger.[34]

The political leader of Germany and the financial leader of the Reichstag met on June 21. Bismarck tried to convince Bamberger that the best solution was no solution and to close the Reichstag without any further action on the currency bill. The idea, said Bamberger, was so "unsuitable and simply impossible that at first I did not even want to believe that I had understood him correctly." Bamberger convinced him that it could not be done[35] and it was he who found a solution in a rewording of that part of article 18 that dealt with state paper money. All of it would be called in by Janaury 1, 1876, a delay of one year, and imperial paper money would be issued. The amendment also mentioned other unspecified relief measures which would be granted the states via future legislation. Although he opposed in principle the issuance of paper money, he regarded one federal currency as preferable to various state currencies. Also article 18 saved the currency bill and compelled the government to resolve finally the bank and paper money questions, crucial items in Bamberger's calculations.[36] The currency bill which was passed on June 23, 1873, and became law on July 9, 1873, was carved into shape by Bamberger, and if anyone should be called the father of the German currency system, it is he.

The currency law also opened the door to new legislation dealing with the paper money and bank questions. It was the former that had to be treated first, as it was more urgent. Within two and one-half years, all state paper money had to be called in, new imperial paper currency issued, and most important of all, agreement reached on distribution of the new money and relief measures to be granted to the states.[37]

The Federal Council united on the issuance of 120 million marks in imperial treasury notes to be distributed on the basis of population at the rate of three marks per capita. This compared with a total of 184 million marks of paper money in circulation. Those states which had issued paper money above the ratio of three marks per capita would receive as a loan two-thirds of the excess amount of paper money, to be repaid in fifteen years without interest.[38] The total amount of treasury notes to be issued totaled 174 million marks, to be reduced to 120 million by 1891.

For the Reichstag and for Bamberger the main question was not how the treasury notes were to be divided among the states but rather how the treasury notes would relate to the general problem of money in circulation. There had been general agreement that as the new mark currency was being issued the old, primarily silver-based, state currencies had to be called in. This was doubly urgent because the French war indemnity of 5 billion marks was repaid by September 1873, two years earlier than originally foreseen. Bamberger warned the German government of the dangers to the new currency system that might be caused by this rapid repayment and the ensuing excess of currency in circulation. All this made it vital that silver be called in quickly. To encourage this, Bamberger had proposed the issuance of currency notes which would be given in return for the cashed-in silver. These notes would then be exchanged for gold coins as the supply became sufficient. Little was done in spite of Bamberger's warnings. The government moved very slowly to call in silver and to issue the new gold currency. By 1874 only 34 million marks in silver had been withdrawn.[39] For these reasons, Bamberger was initially suspicious of imperial paper money, seeing it as a way to be generous to the states, but not as a means to reduce the money in circulation. He accepted the idea in order to save the currency bill, and at least a single paper currency was preferable to numerous state currencies.

The treasury note bill came before the Reichstag on March 26, 1874. Delbrück very modestly spoke of the proposal as a compromise, admitted there would be significant objections from the Reichstag, but hoped for its good will. He did not get it from the first speaker, Alexander Georg Mosle, a National Liberal deputy from Bremen, who damned all paper money as the ruin of a country. He cited Bamberger, "the soul of this paper money decision," as evidence that it was not necessary for financial reasons. Mosle rejected the notion that the compromise on article 18 of the currency bill was necessary, and he called on his colleagues to place principle ahead of expediency. He also proposed that nothing be done regarding paper money until the government introduced a bank bill.[40]

Bamberger proved more sympathetic to Delbrück's request for good will. He regretted that no bank proposal was yet introduced but was willing to wait until the next session. He defended the introduction of new paper money on the grounds of compensation to the states and customary usage by the German people. However, the deputy from Bingen-Alzey still had several reservations about the bill. He opposed the right to exchange notes at the main treasury for specie. He also argued that there was no need to issue more than 120 million marks, since this would undermine the principle of reducing the amount of money in circulation. The bill provided for an initial issue of 174 million marks, compared to 184 already in circulation, and this had to be seen in conjunction with the slow calling in of silver.[41] As had become customary with currency legislation, the bill was not sent to a committee but would be discussed in plenum. The prospects for piloting the bill through without changes which would make it unacceptable to the Federal Council were not especially good. Strong opposition came from those who were in principle against paper money, especially in this case since there were no pressing financial reasons for it, and from those who wanted a bank bill introduced simultaneously with a paper money bill. But the greatest danger lurked in the provisions regarding the allocation of the treasury notes and the extra payments.[42]

The second reading opened with an amendment to article 1 which threatened to upset the compromise in the Federal Council. Instead of distributing the 120 million marks on the basis of population, Bamberger proposed that the amount of treasury notes issued be limited to 120 million marks and that it be used to withdraw the states' paper money. No state, such as Prussia, would get a gift of paper money because of the ratio of population to paper money already in circulation. There would be an extra payment to those states with relatively large amounts of paper money, but it would be a credit out of the "reserves of the empire," that is, in specie rather than paper. This approach would eliminate a significant portion of the paper money in circulation even if the government lost interest by granting the advance payment. The heart of Bamberger's argument was that only 120 million marks were required if the government adopted a rational monetary policy. The matter could not be seen in isolation but must be viewed against the background of hesitation in eliminating silver currency and the rapid repayment of the French indemnity. The government's policies taken together would unleash inflationary pressures.[43]

The debate over article 1 lasted two days. The government, represented by Delbrück and Camphausen, continually referred to the difficult compromise which was worked out by the government and hinted that upsetting this compromise threatened the entire bill. They also pointed to the inescapable fact that their version of the bill also foresaw an ultimate issue of only 120 million marks in treasury notes, after fifteen years. The majority of the Reichstag proved unwilling to throw the gauntlet down to the government, and article 1 passed with only one minor change, an amendment by Bamberger substituting twenty-mark for twenty-five-mark treasury notes.[44]

Defeated on a key issue Bamberger gave his support to an amendment to provide funds to cover one-half instead of two-thirds of the excess amount of paper money and to have it repaid within ten instead of fifteen years. As Bamberger complained, "We no longer stand on the level of accommodation with the governments. We have made loyal offers, but . . . they have not been accepted." It did not help. The amendment was rejected, and article 3 was accepted with the meaningless proviso that the government, to the extent possible, was to pay the excess amount in specie.[45]

Bamberger made one more attempt to alter the bill to his liking. Article 5 stated that the treasury notes were to be accepted at face value by every national and state treasury office and that the main treasury office must at any time give specie for the notes. The government believed that only this kind of explicit support would enable the treasury notes to be accepted by the public. Bamberger moved to eliminate the part of the article dealing with the cashing in of the notes at the main treasury office. Simply writing on the treasury note, Bamberger argued, that it may be cashed in at any time would not assure its convertibility. This was especially true since there was no special fund set aside for this conversion, and in time of crisis the government would have to withdraw this right. In normal times the government would not be overburdened and could handle any ordinary demands. He hoped that when a bank bill was worked out, the treasury notes would be converted into bank notes and only then be redeemable in cash. Once again the government's negative reaction spelled defeat for his proposal.[46] The bill as passed on the second reading was accepted unchanged during the third reading.

Although the law did not meet Bamberger's expectations, it did clear the way for the long desired bank reform bill. The area in which he felt most at home and in which he was most successful was banking. It was here that his personal experiences were strongest and most useful. He brought to the question of bank reform over twenty years of experience in international finance. Before 1871 he had been involved in the establishment of banks in France, the Netherlands, and Germany. The Banque des Pays-Bas was a Parisian bank which officially had its seat in Amsterdam under Bamberger's brother Heinrich. In 1872, after Bamberger had left France, it merged with the Banque de Paris and became one of the most important French banks in the latter part of the nineteenth and early twentieth centuries.[47]

His first major contribution to the German banking system was his role in the founding of the Deutsche Bank. Bamberger's involvement with the planning for the Deutsche Bank began in June 1869, and in January 1870 he was invited to Berlin to discuss the "founding of a large North German bank which is to be a kind of national institute for German maritime commerce." The aim was to extend German foreign banking transactions directly to transatlantic areas. Previously London had served as a middleman, and all German business went via the English capital. Bamberger had had experience in this area during his Parisian years, particularly with South American countries. He was invited to participate in the founding of the Deutsche Bank by Adalbert Delbrück, head of the banking firm of Delbrück, Leo & Co., and a cousin of Rudolf von Delbrück. Bamberger agreed to become a member of the board of directors, and he was also instrumental in finding the bank's first director, Hermann Wallich, who remained in that position for twenty-three years.[48] Bamberger remained a member of the board only until 1872 when, because of his involvement in financial legislation, he thought it better to divest himself of all private business connections. Nevertheless, he gained valuable experience in the intricacies of German banking and made contacts with the leaders of the German banking world which would serve him well in working on the Imperial Bank.

The division of Germany was also apparent in its banking network, particularly as it concerned banks with the power to issue notes. By 1870 there were thirty-three in eighteen states. This abundance of banks of issue was reflected in the amount of bank notes in circulation, which reached 300 million thaler in 1870, climbed to 370 million in 1871, and rose to 450 million in 1872. First steps toward alleviating this situation had been taken in March 1870 with a law making the creation of future banks of issue dependent on federal legislation and through article 18 of the currency law which eliminated effective January 1, 1876, bank notes below one hundred marks.[49]

A final settlement of this question was needed, and the means, Bamberger and others believed, was a central bank for Germany to regulate the issuance of bank notes, the discount rate, and the rate of interest. It should play the same role in Germany that the central banks of England and France played in their respective countries. It was on the question of bank reform that some of Bamberger's most effective writing was done. The banking issue was dry and obscure even for most of the members of the Reichstag, and it was difficult to engage the public. Bamberger believed, however, that pressure would be needed to produce the kind of bank law he thought necessary for the financial health of Germany. He first had to enlighten the public about the need for a central bank to control the issuance of bank notes. Only a central institution could regulate bank notes, since, according to this extreme individualist, "shared responsibility is no responsibility." He also strongly argued that the new central bank of issue need not have complete metallic backing for its notes. Only one-third cash reserves were necessary, since part of a currency is always in circulation. The notes, however, would always be redeemable in cash. What was required was elasticity with security. Some risk would always be present, but that would be true even if the notes were fully covered. The central bank would follow a very conservative policy. It would grant only short-term credit, give no interest, and in general not chase business. His essay "Die Zettelbank vor dem Reichstag" ("Bank of Issue Before the Reichstag"), written in the fall of 1874 just as the government's long awaited bill appeared, has been praised as a model for presenting a complex problem in layman's language and also as very modern in its approach to the question of backing for bank notes.[50]

The bank reform question was not only hard for the public to understand; it was also difficult for the German government to work out. The relatively long delay was caused by Camphausen's opposition and the lack of unity among the German states. The Prussian finance minister was extremely solicitous of the profitability of the Prussian bank, which made substantial sums from minting money and through loans and discount policy. Transforming it into an imperial bank would channel the profits not into the Prussian but rather into the national treasury. Moreover, an imperial bank would be under the direction of the Reichstag.[51]

Additional pressure to produce a bank bill developed by 1874 as a result of the financial crash of 1873 and the ensuing depression. It was argued that one cause of the feverish speculation which led to the collapse was an excess of money in circulation. This seemed to be confirmed by reports of gold being exported from Germany. Rather than see these developments as a result of the currency reform, Bamberger attributed them to the insufficiency of reform, the lack of a central bank to regulate bank notes, and the slowness in calling in silver. To Bamberger, the crash only signified that financial reform had to be speeded up.[52]

A proposal for a central bank had been worked out by the chancellor's office as early as 1872. However, it remained stuck in the Prussian finance ministry, whose approval was required before Bismarck would accept it. So tenacious was Camphausen's opposition that when a bill was finally produced in 1874 it contained no mention of a Reichsbank. This signified the triumph of Camphausen over Delbrück. As the rumor spread in the summer of 1874 that the government's bill would not contain an imperial bank but would reaffirm the leading position of the Prussian Bank, Bamberger met with his supporters and determined to fight.[53] After receiving a copy of the bank proposal from Delbrück, he wrote Oppenheim: "The more I go through the bank paragraphs the more impossible it appears to me to put the affair in order." For him only one thing was important: "As the first act, the Reichsbank, and only later, measures for the small banks." By October 23 his strategy was set. The government's bill should go to a commission, not to amend individual paragraphs, but to work out an authoritative program for a new government proposal which provided for transformation of the Prussian Bank into a national bank.[54] Although his wife was seriously ill in Wiesbaden and in fact died during the deliberations over the bank reform bill, he felt he had to go to Berlin.

The prospects for a major struggle were good when the government's bill came before the Reichstag on November 16, 1874. Even with the best intentions on all sides, a bank bill that would satisfy these diverse forces would have been difficult to write. Since no one took seriously the possibility of simply eliminating the thirty-three existing banks of issue, it became a question of adapting a new law to an already existing and highly complex situation. The bill gave to the empire the right to regulate the issuance of bank notes (article 1) in denominations of not less than one hundred marks, and each bank was obligated to cash in its notes at face value. The proposal set 300 million marks as the value of bank notes in circulation, to be distributed among the banks on the basis of their average monthly balance from 1867–69. If any bank exceeded this limit it would be subject to a tax of 5 percent of the excess. The proposal also placed various restrictions on banks which wanted to operate outside their state's boundaries, as most did, by limiting the financial activities of those banks whose notes exceeded the basic capital. The aim was not only to limit uncovered notes but also to limit the development of banks of issue and to encourage them to concern themselves more with checking and deposit transactions.[55]

Delbrück opened the debate on November 16, stressing the difficulties in establishing a Reichsbank alongside or in place of the Prussian Bank. He did emphasize that the law contained no obstacles to a future national bank. The basic purpose of the bill, he went on, was to reduce the number of bank notes in circulation, and on this basis he defended the special 5 percent tax on excessive uncovered bank notes.[56]

As the second speaker, Bamberger delivered a strong plea for a central bank. He called attention to the success France had in repaying its indemnity to Germany and at the same time remaining not only solvent but financially strong. This would not have been possible, he maintained, without the Bank of France. He also referred to the export of gold that was apparently taking place and that Delbrück had tried to play down. Bamberger admitted that there was no cause for concern but added that a central bank could if necessary take countermeasures. A national bank was also needed to call in small bank notes. Without it, the government's bill would come through as a measure weighted down by the dead hand of a bureaucracy. It was a negative bill which hoped to guard against natural developments by various regulations. It lacked flexibility and did not take into account the unexpected or unusual. It could not limit banks to their home states. That would mean re-creating the pre-1871 particularism. It would also be child's play for banks to circumvent the various other restrictions contained in the bill. To the government's claim that it was impossible to get agreement on the details of a Reichsbank, Bamberger replied: "I accept no law without a Reichsbank, and I accept any law with a Reichsbank." A central bank could exist alongside the older banks, and it would not be especially difficult to transform the Prussian Bank into a national bank. Although the law did hold out the possibility of a Reichsbank after ten years, the financial realist argued that after ten years new special interests would have emerged and taken root making it even more difficult to introduce an imperial bank. He ended his speech with a plea to Bismarck, who was in attendance, not to let the spirit of particularism thrive within the bank reform bill.[57]

Bamberger's long speech triggered an equally long reply from Camphausen, who believed himself to be the target of the liberal's criticism. Although denying any antipathy to a Reichsbank and claiming that Prussia would adapt itself to the wishes of a majority of the Federal Council and Reichstag, he said that Prussia would not take a stand on a Reichsbank until the details were known. He accused Bamberger of being an enthusiast for a "monopoly bank" which sooner or later would toll the death knell of the other banks in Germany.[58] The desire to erect a national bank had the support of the National Liberals and Free Conservatives, with opposition from elements of the Progressive and Center parties. The ultimate outcome of the question of whether to create a central bank was foreshadowed by the vote, 158–127, to send the bill to a commission of twenty-one.[59]

The commission met on November 21 and selected Unruh as chairman and Bamberger as reporter. Before it proceeded to the general discussion it decided by a vote of 13–4 not to discuss the bank bill before a decision was made about the establishment of an imperial bank. No meetings were held until December 17, when Delbrück communicated the Federal Council's cooperation in the creation of a national bank. Then during twenty-one sittings the committee worked out a new bill which contained an imperial bank. The commission's proposals were accepted by the Reichstag in the second and the third readings with only minor changes.[60]

Only a few of the over sixty articles of the bill generated extended debate. The first major exchange came on article 9 of the revised bill, which dealt with uncovered bank notes and prescribed a tax of 1 to 5 percent, even for the Reichsbank, for uncovered notes above a specific amount. On this point Bamberger was outvoted in the committee and took his struggle to the floor of the Reichstag. He was an unqualified foe of a tax on uncovered bank notes, preferring to leave the question of regulation in the hands of the central bank. Realizing that there was no chance to eliminate the quota system, and the suspicion of banks that it signified, Bamberger hoped to increase the size of the quota of uncovered bank notes for the Reichsbank from 250 million to 350 million marks. Even this approach failed as the Reichstag rejected a number of amendments which sought to revise article 9. Ultimately the commission's proposal was accepted.[61]

Beaten on the question of increased quotas for uncovered bank notes, Bamberger registered a success with article 14, which had been inserted into the commission's proposal at his urging. It provided that the Riechsbank was obligated to exchange unminted gold at the firm rate of 1,392 marks for a pound against its notes. The principle contained in this measure went back to the currency bill and the minting of gold for private accounts. At that time, against much opposition, Bamberger had succeeded in getting the principle of "free minting" accepted even though the rate was rather high (7 marks per pound). He hoped that time would bring a reduction of the rate, and article 14 was designed to do that. Henceforth, anyone could present a pound of fine gold at the mint and receive 1,392 marks. This was only 3 marks less than could be coined from a pound, thus making the effective rate only 3 marks instead of 7. Helfferich calls this the "keystone" of the constitution of the German gold standard. For the first time a fixed relationship between raw gold and German currency was created.[62] It was also essential for the relationship between German and foreign currencies. Since the Reichsbank had the obligation to buy gold, all gold that came into the country would flow to the new bank. The bank thus became an intermediary between the German and foreign currency systems. The bank would be a source of gold for export when required by German commerce and could also oversee the rate of exchange. In short, concluded Helfferich, "Only through article 14 was the Reichsbank placed completely in the service of the German gold standard."[63]

The only significant exchange concerning the private banks of issue occurred over article 44. The notes of private banks of issue could not be accepted for payment outside the boundaries of the state unless they met several conditions by January 1, 1876. They had to agree to engage in the same activities as the Reichsbank, that is, buying and selling gold and silver in bar or coins, handling bills of exchange which fell due within three months, granting loans of not more than three months, and buying and selling bonds and debentures. The banks also had to take as payment the bank notes of all other banks whose notes could circulate in the empire. The purpose of the regulations was to make certain that the banks were "solid" and "solvent" and ultimately to restrict the number of banks with the power to issue bank notes. A hole in the web of restrictions was cut by an amendment to article 44 by Georg Siemens which permitted banks that limited their notes to the basic capital to engage in other bank activities than those prescribed for the Reichsbank, namely the granting of credit to industry.

This proposal had been in the government's original bill but had been stricken in the commission at the insistence of Bamberger. Siemens now tried to revive it after industry had complained that one of their most comfortable sources of credit would be eliminated. The debate was extended but not bitter, even though Bamberger's deep resentment against corporations came through. He saw them rather than individual entrepreneurs as the real beneficiaries of the amendment. Still angry over recent financial scandals which he traced to too easy credit and overcapitalization, he saw the amendment as encouraging more of this. Nevertheless, it was accepted by one vote after the Progressive Hermann Schultze-Delitzsch went through the "Yes door" by mistake. He protested but it was too late.[64] A decision on such an important matter could not be decided by accident, and the uproar in the assembly was long and noisy. At the third reading a compromise was worked out which eliminated the heart of Siemens' amendments but permitted the Federal Council on an individual basis to allow a bank to engage in certain credit practices. In fact it was an empty provision, for the Federal Council never made use of the authority.[65]

The compromise over article 44 was the only change resulting from the third reading, and the bill was passed on January 30, 1875, and proclaimed on March 14, 1875. It met Bamberger's basic objectives. It created a central bank which would clearly be superior to the private banks of issue; its quota of bank notes was greater than those of all the private banks of issue combined (250 million marks vs. 135 million), and it would be responsible for supervising currency circulation within the German Empire. The bank was technically a private bank, with only private capital, but under the close supervision of the chancellor and a bank directorate appointed by the Federal Council and emperor. It was thus a semiofficial financial institution. The bank law also made a reality of the right to mint gold for private accounts. Moreover, it encouraged the private banks of issue to give up the right to issue notes in order to avoid the various restrictions imposed by article 44. One-half of the private banks did within a few years.

As the recognized financial authority of the Reichstag, Ludwig Bamberger was well placed to play a key role on behalf of the financial unity and solvency of the empire. He not only demonstrated his knowledge of French financial practices but easily reached to the United States, England, Belgium, and the Netherlands for supporting evidence. As an orator and writer he was unsurpassed. He was also a leading member of the largest party in the Reichstag, for the National Liberals had approximately 40 percent of the seats after the election of 1874. Furthermore, he was on good terms with Delbrück and Bismarck even if cool toward Camphausen. He could be well pleased with his efforts and was. "With the bank law," he wrote in early 1875, "the triple circle in which the currency system rests and is to develop is closed." He was especially satisfied with his efforts because he thought he perceived a larger development at work—parliament's growth in power. The Reichstag had played a significant role in hammering out the financial legislation. It had demonstrated itself to be the equal of the executive branch, a happy sign for the growing importance of the legislature and for the role of liberalism. "Parliamentarianism is ultimately not that fifth wheel on a wagon," Bamberger claimed, "and the liberalism of the national parties, besides the task of being the encouraging support of the imperial government in its enlightened tendencies, has to direct the government back to the right path, where it departs from it."[66] The Free Conservative, Robert Lucius von Ballhausen, agreed with Bamberger that it was the Reichstag that made "usable laws" out of the goverment's bank and currency bills.[67]

Bamberger's expectations about the future of parliament were not fulfilled, and he was one of the first to realize it. Nevertheless, posterity has praised his financial accomplishments. At the beginning of the struggles in 1871, Adolf Soetbeer, the leading scholarly proponent of the gold standard, wrote Bamberger: "My entire hope rests on your effectiveness in the Reichstag."[68] He was not disappointed. Bamberger's protégé, Karl Helfferich, assigned the National Liberal the leading parliamentary role in the legislative struggles. Walther Lotz had only praise for the bank reform act and maintained that the currency reform was successful to the extent that it followed Bamberger's advice and suffered by not accepting some of his proposals. More recently Erich Achterberg has praised his ideas on the need for elasticity regarding the exchange and issuance of bank notes and called them very modern. Bamberger had written in 1876 that the sensitivity of a currency system is an excellent early warning system about a country's economic health. Manfred Seeger agreed with Bamberger on the need to mint a ten-mark coin and with his ideas on paper money. Helfferich summed it up: "His legislative and literary services on behalf of the German currency and bank structure, both for its establishment and defense, represent a major life's work."[69]

Although Bamberger saw the bank law as a great step forward in the collective life of the German nation, he did not ignore the fact that the German currency reform was incomplete until a decisive break with silver was made. He believed that gold was the money of the future, that silver was destined to disappear, and that those countries that accomplished this transformation most quickly would profit most. The dark cloud on the golden horizon was the relative slowness with which the German government withdrew silver currency and melted it down for sale. Bamberger recognized that the longer the process of withdrawal took, the more expensive it would become as the price of silver fell. In "Die Entthronung eines Weltherrschers" ("The Dethronement of a World Ruler"), "Reichsgold" ("Imperial Gold"), and "Das Gold der Zukunft" ("The Gold of the Future"), Bamberger predicted the decline and fall of silver and its replacement by gold. He hoped that the government would draw the proper conclusion.[70] It did not. Bamberger had also noted that even when the gods have deserted a system it could continue for some time, and so it was with silver. But in 1875–76 this was a small stain on the new financial cloth. The future still looked clear, and he could surrender himself to self-congratulation. As he confessed to Karl Hillebrand, "I think with superstition how for fifteen years all programs have turned out to be true."[71]

• 5 •
The 1870s:
Victories Without Triumph

If Bamberger believed that the value of the Reichstag was demonstrated in the legislative battles over the financial legislation, he knew that the parliament's position was far from secure. As a politician and liberal member of parliament, he was concerned about the place of the Reichstag in Germany's political system. He had given up his youthful dreams about a German democratic republic and reconciled himself to the monarchical system. Nevertheless, parliament's position within the system was in many respects unenviable. It existed alongside a powerful emperor, an imposing Federal Council, and an important Prussian legislature, and it had to contend with a chancellor like Bismarck. It was one element—and by no means the most important—within the German governmental structure.

A number of historians have pointed out that German constitutional life developed differently than did western Europe's. Ernst Fraenkel and Reinhard Lamer have emphasized that German constitutional theorists misunderstood the British parliamentary system, viewing it too formalistically and doctrinairely and using "monarchical constitutional" government as a comparative term. They regarded the king as the moving force of the English system and saw aristocratic self-government as part of the magic formula. However, the German parliamentary system did not grow out of the estates, as the English system had, but in opposition to them, and Germany missed the period of "patronage parliament" where parliamentary style and an esprit de corps were formed. German constitutionalists also had to fight against the authority of an entrenched bureaucracy. Moreover, the Germans were suspicious of the pluralistic state and saw it as a sign not of political maturity and self-confidence, but rather of dissolution. Lothar Gall has also stressed in connection with Baden that since the constitution was a gift, the liberals did not see it as part of the basic political order but as an instrument with which to transform the state internally. The constitution did not signify the abdication of the patrimonial state but was merely the means to carry on the struggle. Thus, and not only in Baden, a feudal government faced a constitutional parliament, and the two were to a certain extent in permanent opposition.[1]

In one of his first essays after his return to literary activity during the Franco-Austrian War, Bamberger plunged into the polemics over the validity and usefulness of parliamentary government. The exchange of letters between Thomas Contra and Michael Pro was Bamberger's attempt to come to grips with a host of current questions, including parliamentary government. It is an exchange between a democrat and a liberal, between an idealist and a realist, between an opponent of Prussia and a supporter. Although Bamberger had probably made his decision by then, Thomas Contra was outfitted with strong arguments. For the more progressive Thomas, parliament must not be a sham parliament, but so long as it only proposed rather than acted it was a mere fiction. In America and England, Thomas continued, parliaments were conceivable; "in present-day continental Europe they will always be dependent on the tolerance of the army." For this reason one could not expect too much of it. Its role was to preserve and develop what had been achieved, "not to form what never was there." It was a "bulwark but not a battering ram." Thus whoever establishes a parliament before freedom is a reality "opens the way not to progress but betrayal."[2]

Michael Pro did not reply directly to the charge that a parliament established prematurely would be a fig leaf for absolutism. However, building an effective legislative system, he noted, was a long process that could not be carried out with one bold stroke. One must not set one's sights on a mature parliament and reject everything else. The same message was repeated in 1868 in order not to encourage his followers to expect too much from the Customs Parliament.[3] But Bamberger had to admit that a parliament would create nothing "that has not been accepted by the people. It can only give expression, form, rule, and consecration to that which already lives in the spirit of the age and of the nation." He did not, of course, accept Thomas's conclusion.[4] Parliament, Bamberger claimed, should be constructive and deal with concrete matters. He warned against opposition for its own sake and against speakers who appealed to the gallery or the future. "The more parliament becomes a practical engine of government," he wrote in 1869, "the more one will learn to respect those who calculate their efforts in terms of actual effectiveness.... Parliament is a workshop, not a theater of opinions."[5] "We are not here," he told his colleagues in 1873, "to be edified by theoretical observations" but in order to make "practical decisions for the life of the state" and for "our financial system.... Analyses of concepts belong in the school and not in parliament."[6] These maxims seemed to be in accord with parliamentary developments of the early 1870s, when a great number of major pieces of legislation for the new empire had to be passed. In particular it expressed the role Bamberger had played in the financial legislation. He was an ally of the government but also a constructive critic of its proposals. However, it was difficult to conclude that the Reichstag was becoming more important. For example, after passing thirteen bills, with Bamberger's support, to provide payment for parliamentary deputies, the Reichstag had to sit helplessly by while the government ignored these measures until 1906. The title *Herr Abgeordneter* ("Congressman"), even Bamberger conceded, was rarely used in speaking and then mainly by very "humble petitioners." Moreover, a member of parliament was placed behind a major in court etiquette. Bamberger's proposal for a parliamentary journal containing the day's speeches, which he hoped would educate the populace and provide a substitute for sketchy newspaper excerpts, was rejected. The building of a new parliament building dragged out interminably until Bamberger regarded it as a sign of the low value of the Reichstag.[7] Bamberger also realized that ministerial repsonsibility could not be realized in imperial Germany. At best he hoped first for imperial ministries and second for a sufficient identification in the public eye between a man and his ministry that there would exist a moral obligation to resign if problems developed.[8] In 1866 Bamberger had written that a parliament would get all the respect it deserved as soon as it became the determining organ of the state. Indeed, that remained the problem until 1918.[9]

Two years before unification, Bamberger tried to define the constitutional system. "One party supplants the other," he wrote, " 'go away so that I may sit in your place.' That is constitutionalism as it is positively established and how it would exist in Germany if constitutionalism could be carried through. Party life, party spirit, whether to support or fight the government, is the primeval element of the life of a state."[10] As far as Bamberger was concerned, the party that was best suited to govern Germany in the 1870s was the National Liberal party. It was a direct product of the success of Bismarck's policy. In a physical sense the civil war caused the Progressive party to split, with the secessionists uniting with liberal groups from the newly annexed areas to form the National Liberal party. It was joined by other elements from the south German States in 1871. More than the physical sponsor of the party, Bismarck also shaped its ideological outlook. It was committed to cooperation with the Bismarckian regime to complete German political, economic, and administrative unity. Substantive political goals toward parliamentary government were played down, and the Reichstag was acknowledged to be subordinate to both the executive branch and the Federal Council. The shift in emphasis from liberal constitutional to national goals was symbolized by the slogan "Through unity to freedom."

By the early 1870s the party had divided into two wings. Those on the

right were led by Wilhelm Wehrenpfenning, Johannes Miquel, Eduard Stephani, and Friedrich von Schauss; those on the left, by Bamberger, Eduard
Lasker, Franz Schenk von Stauffenberg, Max von Forckenbeck, and Hans
Viktor von Unruh. What separated these two groups fundamentally was
where to draw the line in cooperating with Bismarck. Both wanted to be on
good terms with Bismarck but not at the same price. What concessions, or
more harshly, what surrenders of liberal principles should be made to obtain
or maintain Bismarck's friendship? The head of the party was the Hanoverian
Rudolf von Bennigsen, who tried to mediate between its two wings.[11] In
social composition there was little to differentiate the two wings, and the
party was preeminently the representative of the middle classes, dominated
by businessmen, lawyers, judicial and administrative officials, and academics,
but also containing an agricultural element. It was a "national" party, not
only because of its goals for German unity, but also because of its geographic
spread and its support in the 1870s by aristocrats, middle-class urban elements, small farmers, and craftsmen. It was strongest in the Protestant areas
and in the smaller cities. In the election of 1871 it received 30 percent of the
vote and 125 seats. In 1874 its share of the vote fell slightly, but a more
favorable distribution and greater success in the run-offs saw it emerge with
155 seats, making it by far the strongest party in the Reichstag. It never was a
tightly organized group. The local party committees selected candidates and
campaigned with little interference from Berlin. The dominant element was
the Reichstag group itself, but even within it many members scarcely knew
each other, very few devoted themselves to party business, and many came to
Berlin only for the most important votes. A relatively small group including
Bamberger, Lasker, Forckenbeck, Miquel, Wehrenpfennig, Stephani, and Bennigsen, the chairman of the parliamentary group, controlled the party. Although it attracted more votes than any other party in the 1870s, it was in no
sense a mass party. Rather, it was a political organization dominated by an
economic and cultural elite.[12]

Bamberger was from the outset an important figure in the National Liberal
party and the Reichstag. In 1870 he was elected to the board of directors of
the party. He lived in Berlin during the sessions of parliament, establishing a
permanent residence in 1874 at 18 Margaretenstrasse. He consulted with and
was regularly consulted by Bismarck, who valued his opinions. He also played
a key role not only in the battles over financial legislation but also in the
struggles over the military bills and the *Kulturkampf*.[13]

Bamberger rarely broached the subject of parties or party unity in the
abstract, and his few statements on the matter were obviously colored by
political events. His close friend and political ally, Theodor Barth, wrote of
him rather naively that he had "no fanaticism about parties" since he left the

National Liberals, the Liberal Union, and the Radical party.[14] He had joined the National Liberal party because it offered the best vehicle for realizing his goals, but without great enthusiasm. In 1866, in the wake of the Progressive party's split but before he believed it was final, Bamberger wrote that it was not necessarily a bad sign if a split occurred in the "bosom of an enlightened party." Forcible cooperation under pressure was not good for a party. However, this seemed to be precisely the history of the National Liberal party in the 1870s, until it became too much even for him.[15] In 1884, under the changed circumstances of the just completed merger of the Liberal Union and the Progressive party into the Radical (Freisinnige) party, Bamberger announced that the "task of a party in a higher sense is to overcome to a certain degree and under certain circumstances differences of opinion and to demonstrate its higher unity." Six years later, after the election debacle of the National Liberals, he chastised them for having compromised themselves to death with Bismarck and having made "the principle of no principles into an official state religion." "Parties," he wrote, "live on the basis of principles or at least basic views."[16] In Bamberger one faces a practical politician whose statements must always be measured against the political, social, and economic background. Revealing for this problem are his views on nationalizing the German railways, an issue much discussed in the 1870s. Publicly he was opposed to the plan, but as he explained to Hillebrand: "When my friends Unruh and [Viktor] Böhmert rack their brains about whether a state or private railroad is better, I tell *you* . . . confidentially: I do not care about the railroads." As long as Bismarck used the issue "to thrash soundly" the middle-sized states, Bamberger was with him "heart and soul."[17] There is constantly the problem of discovering Bamberger's real or fundamental views on a subject. Too often they seemed to adapt themselves to the political situation.

Upon joining the National Liberal party, Bamberger was aware of the tension that existed within it, and the history of the party is the story of the attempt to keep its two segments in harmony. After thirteen years of repeated crises the almost inevitable split occurred, and one is tempted to ask why it did not happen sooner. Even in the years before unification there was talk of a breakup. The series of important legislative measures introduced into the North German parliament between 1867 and 1870 provided ample stimulus for the hostility between the two wings of the party to surface. In 1868 Max von Forckenbeck, as a former Progressive, felt himself increasingly isolated within the parliamentary group. And Wehrenpfennig at the same time was writing to Heinrich von Treitschke of the need to reconstruct the party and to get rid of the Progressive elements. He described heated exchanges with Lasker and expressed the opinion that a split would take place after the elections in 1870.[18] On the other side of the political fence similar sounds could be heard. Although Bamberger considered a split in the National Liberal party "fatal," such people as Wehrenpfenning and Johann Kaspar Bluntschli, law professor in Heidelberg, "force me from time to time to reflection about the N.L. party and our absorption in it. It must be said for it that either *our* spirit, that is Lasker's, [Karl] Twesten's, [Julius von] Hennig's . . . predominates or we really run into the Gothaer corner. They [the other side] are always just looking for a 'good excuse' to anchor in or near power. The next Reichstag or Customs Parliament can lead to a break which, however, should best be completed in a way that the W's and B's are driven to the Free Conservatives."[19]

The difficulties within the National Liberal party were not lessened by unification. If anything, the early 1870s witnessed the growing strength within the party of the right-wing elements. Most of the party's Reichstag deputies from south Germany, with a few exceptions like Bamberger and Stauffenberg, aligned themselves with the right wing. The more progressive elements came from Prussia, and their relative strength within the party dropped by 20 percent so that they were a minority by 1877.[20] And recently the English historian J. C. G. Röhl has suggested that the business slump of 1873 strengthened the right wing at the expense of the left as only very large and presumably more conservative firms were able to survive.[21]

During the early 1870s the tension within the National Liberal party was most pronounced over military issues and to a lesser extent over the clerical question. Disputes over the military budget and the Reichstag's role in military matters had been at the heart of the Prussian constitutional conflict in the 1860s, and the Prussian government made clear its hostility to any compromise on this issue. According to Huber, the issue was whether the strength of the army would be determined by an "act of command" or by a "law." The former view won, and the army remained essentially outside the constitution. In the proposed constitution for the North German Confederation, the government wanted to set the size of the army at 1 percent of the population and have 255 thalers appropriated per man on a permanent basis. This iron budget was fought by the majority of the Reichstag, and a bitter struggle was avoided only by Forckenbeck's compromise regulating the strength of the army for four years.[22] Four years later the government, under the pressure of the recently ended war, was not able to draw up a military budget in detail and finally propose a continuation of the existing arrangement for three years. This merely reopened old wounds.

Bamberger's views on the military dated from the revolution of 1848. Then the European military system was "the lion of the desert with the brain of modern man," and he, like most democrats, supported a popular militia. In the aftermath of the failure of the 1849 uprising, he had recognized the importance of sound military training, and although still suspicious of the army, by the late 1860s he tried to be realistic about military requirements. An army was a necessary evil, required for protection. Germany stood among several well-armed neighbors, he told his south German audience, and could not afford "the dilettantism" of the militia system. That would only mean relying on others, namely Prussia, to defend south Germany.[23]

Although he did not wish to deny the army what it required, Bamberger was not willing to see parliament stripped of its already limited authority. The government's military bill of November 1871 would deprive the Reichstag of any control over the military budget for three years. Since the military budget accounted for most of the federal budget, parliament's budgetary powers would be sharply curtailed. The proposal set off a heated debate within the National Liberal party with Bamberger, Lasker, Unruh, and Stauffenberg on one side and Bennigsen, Miquel, Treitschke, Stephani, and Forckenbeck for the government's bill.[24] Besides objecting on principle, many of the opponents of the bill feared that since the end of the three-year period would not fall before the end of the legislative period, the military question would be a major issue in the next election. On November 30, 1871, the decisive vote in the party showed a small majority (44–40) in favor of the three-year bill. As a compromise the party agreed to introduce a motion to provide a two-year military bill.[25]

Bamberger was the main speaker for the compromise proposal. He had been one of the leaders of the group against the government's proposal and was well aware that the party might fall to pieces over the issue. Even though his friend Oppenheim preached a break, he hoped to avoid one. Bamberger's speech was noticeably flat—as if he were going through the motions—and it indicates that the idea of a two-year bill was nothing more than a face-saving device for him and for the party to avoid a break. Two years may have been better than three for Bamberger, but for the Progressives it was not nearly as good as one and for the Conservatives not as attractive as three. The bill went down to defeat with only some National Liberals in favor. Then the government's version was accepted 152–128 with about forty National Liberals voting against it.[26]

Bamberger seemed almost pleased by the whole affair. As he described it to his wife: "Next to Lasker I had taken over the leadership of the campaign of the left wing of our party, which certainly ended with a predetermined defeat. However, our minority was almost equally strong as the majority—more than we might have hoped. . . . With this affair a deep fissure has developed among the National Liberals. *I* alone am responsible that they did not blow apart. I do not want it because the Lasker half would have too unworldly a leader."[27]

The question of who would lead a new left-of-center liberal party would later plague the left liberals. It should have been Lasker, whose parliamentary activity placed him in the forefront of the Reichstag. However, Bamberger always harbored a reluctance to see Lasker as a leader, which indeed became impossible by the late 1870s because of his declining health as well as his Judaism. But even earlier in the 1870s Bamberger was of two minds about him. They had been close friends and political allies since the late 1860s and were eventually interred under a common headstone. Nevertheless, as early as 1869 he detected qualities in Lasker which tell us not only about his friend but about himself as well. He wrote to Oppenheim of Lasker's "extreme moral sense" which had a "tendency to tyranny." This came to the surface especially in early 1873 when Lasker uncovered a scandal in the Prussian railroad and forced the resignation of the commerce minister. It was Lasker's greatest day, and for a time he became extremely popular in Germany. For Bamberger it was a sign that Lasker might become too much of a zealous moral improver. "He convinces himself that he can introduce a new religion of business morality into the world. There is something of a Christ in him." Bamberger was to a certain extent in the middle, since his contacts with the world of finance and the stock exchange tried to get him to pacify his friend, while the latter brought him the new evidence which he had uncovered. Bamberger tried to moderate Lasker and keep him from implicating Bismarck "whom Lasker would not be unhappy to involve in the defeat of the government." The difference between the two liberals came down to Lasker's "moral cant and my latitudinarianism."[28] Bamberger's lack of rigor in business questions often comes through as a mild cynicism about the world in general, but it does betray a realism toward political questions that made him hesitate for a long time before taking the decisive step of secession from the National Liberal party.

Throughout 1873, Bamberger still saw little hope for a new party, but the military bill once again threatened the equilibrium of the old.[29] The German government was determined to obtain what the emperor and the army had always regarded as the proper degree of freedom from parliamentary interference with the military. Article 1 of the 1874 bill set the size of the army exclusive of officers at 401,659 men unless changed by future legislation. Subsequent articles prescribed the organization of the infantry, cavalry, and artillery. Nothing was said about the budgetary allocation, and technically the Reichstag had the power to deny the appropriation. But having already accepted the size of the army, it would be under a moral obligation to provide the funds.[30]

The bill was sent to a commission of twenty-eight where a number of revisions were made, the most significant being the elimination of article 1. Hoping to reach a compromise with the government, the commission did not substitute its own formulation. Almost two months elapsed between the first and second readings, in part because of Easter, in part because of Bismarck's supposed illness. The chancellor made excellent use of the intervening period to stir up a press campaign against the opponents of the bill, charging them with leaving Germany defenseless and inviting the French to come across the border. He hinted at dissolving the Reichstag and resigning. The prospect of fighting an election on the question of military security was not pleasant for the National Liberals.[31]

The fate of the bill rested in the hands of the National Liberals since they had 40 percent of the seats. The Center party and most of the Progressives were opposed to anything more than an annual military bill, which the government would never accept. Thus a relatively small group of National Liberals could bring the bill down, and in 1871 almost half of the party had voted against the three-year bill. Now there was no chance that the government would accept even a three-year measure. Once again Lasker led a group of liberals against the bill. Starting with a desire for an annual military bill, Lasker was willing by April 3 to accept a four-year military bill in order to avoid a split of the party over this issue. He would go this far but "no further."[32] However, as the government's press campaign mounted, he realized that his troops were deserting him. The more concession-oriented National Liberals around Bennigsen and Miquel were determined to avoid a break with Bismarck on the issue of military preparedness. Finally as a compromise the National Liberal leaders agreed to a proposal setting the peacetime strength of the army for seven years, which Bismarck accepted on April 9. For some twenty hours the National Liberal party waited to hear whether the emperor, whose opinion was final on military matters, would accept the new offer. Stephani's account is still the most vivid depiction of how the National Liberals made weakness and surrender a source of joy. On the afternoon of April 10, Bismarck sent Lothar Bucher to inform the National Liberals that the emperor would accept the seven-year limit if the exemption of officers from communal taxes were restored. "Unparalleled jubilation," wrote Stephani, "running around, I ran to Miquel; we were so happy."[33] What followed in the Reichstag was anticlimactic. Bennigsen made the "great" speech for his party introducing the crucial amendment to article 1. He referred to the popular pressure for the government's bill and to

Bismarck's threat of resignation and dissolution of the Reichstag. He also stressed the need for national defense not only against external foes but also against internal enemies, meaning the Center party. Even Lasker felt called upon to defend the seven-year arrangement, which he viewed not in a narrow military sense, but rather against the backdrop of "the general political situation." The Reichstag was not being forced to surrender one of its rights, and the military received what it thought necessary. "There is now no victory and no defeat," he claimed.[34] The vote on Bennigsen's amendment to article 1 was 224 in favor, 146 opposed. Virtually every single National Liberal and even a handful of Progressives voted for the bill.

Three years before, Lasker and Bamberger had voted against setting the strength of the army for three years. Now they agreed to a seven-year bill which would mean that two legislative periods could pass without a debate on a military bill. They were unquestionably frightened by the popular movement and believed they would be defeated if forced to go to the people on this issue. Even Lasker hinted at this in the above-mentioned Reichstag speech. Bamberger, who did not participate in the debate, did not even seem to regard the outcome of the struggle as a defeat. The day after the arrangement between the government and the National Liberals was worked out he wrote: "Our trial with the emperor is won. *Lasker* has triumphed; instead of eternity the emperor gets only seven years. Compared with eternity that is very little. Furthermore William has behaved very reasonably." Six days later he was still pleased by the course of the Reichstag, primarily because of the favorable turn on the military bill.[35]

The military bill was not the only compromise that the National Liberals had to make during the session. Five days after approving the military bill they had to approve a press law which increased the authority of judges to order the confiscation of printed matter and eliminated a provision which had forbidden the obligatory giving of testimony. These new concessions to the government, which were considered necessary to save the bill, represented a retreat on the third reading from positions taken on the second and again called in question the solidity of the National Liberal party.[36] For someone like Stauffenberg, the desire to secede from the party was strong. After thinking it over he acknowledged that the left-wing group could accomplish more inside than outside the party.[37]

In spite of his brave words to his wife, Bamberger was seriously concerned about the relationship of the National Liberal party to the government, particularly when the government was not following a liberal course. In a revealing essay in 1874 he admitted that because of its military, dynastic, and bureaucratic nature, the government would be conservatively oriented for an "incalculably long time." Thus "a complete identification of governmental thinking with that of the liberal party could not take place without pulling the latter significantly to the right and as a result splitting [the party]." If a cabinet with National Liberal members should be formed, "precisely because of [the party's] unavoidable turning to the conservative direction of any German government, the opponents would then form a new liberal opposition with their neighbors further to the left." The conclusion that Bamberger drew from this prophetic analysis was that the correct policy of the government was to base itself on the liberal parties. A "dual system" of pulling and pushing, of mutual observation and friction, would be more bearable in the long run, more bearable to the liberals than the "complete amalgamation with the organs of a specific government. The time for party government has not yet arrived in Germany, and it remains to be seen whether it is to be desired."[38] So things appeared in 1874, and they offer an insight into the negotiations with Bismarck in 1877 and 1878.

If the military bills of the early 1870s nearly drove the National Liberal party to the breaking point and forced many of its members including Bamberger to compromise long-held principles, a somewhat different picture emerges with the *Kulturkampf.* The struggle between the Catholic church and the German federal and state governments was clearly regarded as a victory for the National Liberal party and as a product of its close cooperation with Bismarck. Although the campaign was over in fact by 1880, at its peak in the early 1870s it offers the viewer a look into the substance of German liberalism and Ludwig Bamberger.

Bamberger's views on the church were not substantially different from those held by many of his liberal colleagues. The church was tied to the forces of the old order, opposed German unification, and fought against modern political and social beliefs. Personally he had no patience or use for religion and dismissed the debate over papal infallibility with the comment, "It stinks to the heavens."[39] He probably would have agreed with the Progressive Rudolf Virchow that the struggle between church and state was indeed a *Kulturkampf.* As early as November 1871 he referred to the fight against the Catholic church as the "signature of the empire. I myself am busy with the affair in the most intimate circles; it will not end for a long time."[40] As the *Kulturkampf* heated up in Prussia, and the law against misuse of the pulpit was followed by the appointment of Adalbert Falk as minister of religion and the enactment of the school supervision laws, Bamberger's enthusiasm for the struggle grew. "The Bismarckian way exceeds the boldest expectations, and I am truly intoxicated to observe how this development so correctly takes the course which my best expectations had demanded of it. . . . The conflict of the state with the church must come, and precisely the way it starts in Germany is a moment of incalculable world historical significance." It was new evidence of the correctness of his decision of 1866.[41] A week later his mood was still exuberant. "One cannot say that Bismarck is incalculable in the great historical tasks. In the great turning points he has always ultimately followed the correct path—1866, 1870, and now, always keeping to the high road of his great mission. One must be a simpleton in order not to do justice to him." Bamberger was pleased that the chancellor was devoting himself to domestic affairs.[42]

Bamberger departed from his National Liberal colleagues on only one issue connected to the *Kulturkampf*, the regulation of the Society of Jesus. For many Germans, the Jesuits not only symbolized the intrusion of religious societies into the secular world but also represented the antinational side of Roman Catholicism. In the province of Posen they were regarded as supporters of the Polish cause, and indeed many of the Jesuits were not ethnic Germans. Public opinion focused on the Jesuits, and protest rallies demanded their expulsion. The government responded with a bill that gave it authority to deny residence to Jesuits even of German nationality and to remove them to another district. This measure, however, did not go far enough for the Reichstag majority, and it was sharpened to provide for the prohibition of the society and the expulsion of foreign members, while German Jesuits could be denied residence in certain places and removed to other areas. The bill, although passionately debated, was passed by a two-to-one majority.[43]

Only a handful of deputies outside the Center party voted against the measure, and among the National Liberals only Bamberger and Lasker voted against the bill. Moritz Busch, Bismarck's confidant, made the point that outside the Center party only Jewish deputies voted against the bill because they had a dark premonition that at some time in the future people would be aroused enough against them to demand a special law.[44] Since it is difficult for the historian to document dark premonitions, we must look elsewhere for an explanation. During the third reading, Lasker sought to justify his negative vote by emphasizing that the purpose of this struggle should be to reconcile spirits, not forcefully suppress opposing views. He critized the lack of legal rights for the accused, who would be subjected to administrative rather than juridical justice. For most of Lasker's colleagues, the war against the papacy overshadowed everything else.[45]

Bamberger voted against the Jesuit bill even though it threatened to cost him support in Mainz. He agreed with Lasker that the right of residence was one of the basic rights of Germans and should not be abridged, especially in such a vague and unregulated way. Also he believed that the law would be ineffective, since one was fighting an idea which was embedded in the entire church. The law in fact would benefit the Jesuits by creating martyrs, enabling them to thrive under persecution. He expressed a similar attitude—

although not a similar vote—in 1878 in regard to the Antisocialist Law. He remained very pessimistic about the possibility of fighting intellectual movements with physical means.[46]

His stance on the Jesuit bill represented his only departure from the liberal norm during the *Kulturkampf* of the 1870s. Otherwise he supported the government because political imperatives demanded it. The Prussian May Laws of 1873, which regulated the training and disciplining of clerics and made it easier to secede from the church, he greeted as a step forward in the "preparation of the great struggle of the Catholic world against the Protestant." He referred to the Center party as "hostile to the state" and "antinational." Its coming to power would mean the end of the empire, and its very strength posed a mortal challenge to Germany. While the conflict went on, he continued, all other quarrels had to recede so that there would only be two parties. Bamberger believed that posing the question in such a way would mean that the German government would be forced along a liberal path. "For the time being we are in the midst of a struggle for survival, and since the great majority of those parties who are fighting for the survival of the empire are of a liberal inclination, it is self-evident to any imperial government to be friendly to those with this view." This policy had already succeeded and would "become even firmer," he maintained.[47]

It may have looked that way in July 1874. Bamberger was registering success in financial matters, the military bill had been passed to his apparent satisfaction, as had the Imperial Press Law and most of the anti-Catholic legislation, and Bismarck was alienated not only from the Center but from many of his former conservative friends. It seemed perfectly correct to conclude that the chancellor would be forced to rely on the liberals and that the German Empire would be pushed in a liberal direction.

However, by 1875 the first signs of the end of the "liberal spring" were apparent, and they involved the Center party. Karl Aegidi, then in the Foreign Office, wrote to Bamberger of a conversation he had with Ludwig Windthorst, the Center party leader. According to Aegidi, Windthorst said that Bismarck could have peace if he wished, but the chancellor deigned not to hear.[48] Bamberger did hear, and by the end of the year he was confiding to his diary that the Center was out to make peace. He was also told by Max von Forckenbeck that two years earlier Bismarck had remarked that he could make peace with the Center any time.[49] The internal situation began to seem more "complicated" during 1876. Bamberger detected an uncomfortable mood in the air as no one knew what Bismarck's aims were. Differences with the chancellor developed over the judicial reform bill, which resulted in another compromise after Bismarck threatened to let the entire measure fall. Once again the National Liberals were forced to make major concessions on the third reading. Bamberger did not play a prominent role in the battles over the judicial legislation; however, he counseled moderation and warned against a confrontation with Bismarck, which Lasker seemed to desire, since the elections were approaching.[50]

The event that made the strongest impression on Bamberger in 1876 was the resignation of Rudolf von Delbrück, the president of the Imperial Chancellor's Office, on April 14. Delbrück had worked in the Prussian and German administration since he was twenty-five. In the 1850s and 1860s he played a key role in the long negotiations with Austria over her attempted entry into the Customs Union. From 1866 on he worked to create a strong central authority for Germany. In his economic and financial views Delbrück was liberal, pushing free trade and supporting Bamberger's financial activities in the Reichstag. He was highly regarded by the National Liberals, who viewed him as a liberal influence on the chancellor. By the mid 1870s, however, Bismarck grew increasingly disenchanted with his chief aide, particularly over what he regarded as Delbrück's desire to control and to centralize everything in his office, which was regarded by his opponents as more Prussian than German. Moreover, Delbrück had become very independent, and his office obstructed Bismarck's plans for tax reform and separate imperial ministries.[51] Bamberger had been aware of Bismarck's increasing distaste for Delbrück for at least five months before the latter's departure and immediately ascribed the event to a conflict with Bismarck.[52] "I take the whole turn [of affairs] tragically," he lamented to Oppenheim, "and see in it the continuation of the retrogressive symptoms which began a year ago with the 'War in Sight' article."[53] "As soon as I heard about his resignation I wrote Delbrück a very agitated letter which came from my heart."[54]

The departure of Delbrück also touched Bismarck's heart—with joy, because he had stood in the way of Bismarck's plans for the reorganization and restructuring of the German Empire. The first clear sign of a change in Bismarck's thinking came in his Reichstag speech of November 22, 1875, on the bill to raise the brewing tax. He used the opportunity to outline his ideas on tax reform. He wished to eliminate the matricular contributions from the states, which formed a mainstay of the federal government's income, and wanted to use indirect rather than direct taxes to provide the necessary financial support for the empire. And in passing he mentioned a desire to return to a tariff system for income.[55] The brewing tax bill was rejected, as Bismarck had expected, but the chancellor had made it clear that this was merely the opening salvo in a long struggle to reform Germany's finances. A similar fate awaited the government's bills for a stamp tax in November 1875 and for retaliatory tariffs against countries (mainly France) which provided export premiums in December 1876. Early in 1877, in a memorandum to

Camphausen, Bismarck once again spelled out his financial program, this time placing greater stress on tariffs.

The elections of January 1877 gave the chancellor some encouragement. They resulted in a moderate defeat for the National Liberals and Progressives, who lost about 20 percent of their seats. The National Liberals, who lost twenty-eight seats, were still the indispensable support for his reform plans. However, Bismarck held little hope of winning the entire party to his program of financial reform, since the left wing of the party was extremely hostile to tariffs and indirect taxes. Nevertheless, he hoped at least to split the party and gain the right wing's solid support for his new program. One of the best ways to do this was to take into the cabinet a prominent National Liberal who could be security for the bulk of his party. Most suitable for this position was Rudolf von Bennigsen.[56]

As Bismarck's new program evolved, Bamberger found himself moving from puzzlement to opposition during 1876–78. His first strong reservation about the direction of German policy coincided with Delbrück's departure and focused on Bismarck's attempt to nationalize the German railway system, which the chancellor believed would provide an additional source of income for the central government. The program was announced in December 1875, but opposition developed from several German states and from within the National Liberal party. As was his wont, Bismarck pushed ahead by having the Prussian legislature accept a measure which provided for the sale of the Prussian railway system to the empire. Unfortunately for Bismarck, the Federal Council and the Reichstag had to give their approval to purchase the lines. The hostility to the measure within the Federal Council was too strong, and Bismarck had to be satisfied with the sale of the railways to Prussia.[57]

Bamberger's attitude toward the railway nationalization question shifted as Bismarck's intentions became clear. Initially he saw the issue as leading to a confrontation with the medium-sized states of Bavaria, Saxony, and Württemberg, whose "great power itch" was once again making itself felt. In Bamberger's eyes, this was now "dangerous" and "once and for all must be driven out." He was not concerned so much about the issue of a state railway versus a private railway, which was more a question of "form" than "substance." He hoped that Bismarck would combine railway nationalization with the idea that "the three kingdoms must really be thrashed soundly," and if so, "I am with him body and soul. . . . All the more as it cannot happen without giving the empire itself a completed constitution. All that *must* happen while *he* lives, otherwise it may not happen at all."[58] This view was in keeping with Bamberger's inclination to support the chancellor when he was carrying out a "progressive" action. Greater centralization and a weaker Federal Council were worth far more than hand-wringing over the constitution of the German railway system. The comment is also indicative of how dependent Bamberger and other liberals were on Bismarck to accomplish their aims.

However, when it became clear that Bismarck was not willing to squash the "great power" pretensions of Bavaria, Saxony, and Württemberg, Bamberger and Hans Viktor von Unruh led the campaign against the nationalization of the Prussian railway system. When the "substance" had been removed, the form became significant. The opponents disliked the idea of providing the government with a permanent source of funds beyond the reach of parliament or the states. Also their opposition grew out of their hostility to public ownership of business. Both Bamberger and Unruh, it should be noted, were deeply involved in railroads, Bamberger as an investor and Unruh as a railroad director.[59]

Several months later Bamberger was once again among the opposition when the government introduced a bill to raise tariffs against countries which provided export premiums. Bamberger was the major speaker against the bill, which ultimately died in committee. In addition to providing technical criticism, the free trader stressed that the measure went far beyond a few tariffs or the height of those levies. The bill signified a change in the government's policy toward protection. He referred in particular to a newspaper story during the summer about a Prussian official in Wiesbaden who called upon the inhabitants to petition against the projected end of the tariffs on iron. The fact that a Prussian official felt free to issue such a summons signified to Bamberger that a "decisive turn in the direction of the Prussian government" was taking place, and the present proposal provided further evidence.[60] At the end of his brief response Camphausen, although denying that any fundamental change had occurred in the German government's tariff policy, announced that "in the future the national side of our position will be more strongly stressed than before."[61]

The government repeated its attempt to push through a retaliatory tariff in April 1877, but with Bamberger in the forefront the Reichstag once again rejected the proposal. He taunted the government by referring openly to the fact that Camphausen, who was given the responsibility of defending the measure, was not enthusiastic about the proposals. In fact, during 1877 Bismarck became increasingly displeased with his finance minister over his dilatory handling of the chancellor's financial program. Bamberger, in a theme he would develop later, regarded the government's measure as a first step in injecting economic considerations into a political body, which would divide the Reichstag into two economic camps.[62] He found further evidence of a change in policy in the apparent failure of the tariff negotiations with Austria in the fall of 1877.[63]

Throughout 1877, Bamberger grew increasingly concerned and disillusioned with Bismarck's policies, especially since the chancellor was away from Berlin most of the year. Rather than decisive action there seemed to be drift. He claimed that in three years Bismarck had had no domestic successes and ascribed this to his relations with the National Liberals: "If parliamentary politics has contributed to his discomfort, the key to it is that he does not want to hold on to the liberal party, and it is indispensable. Officially he is friendly to it, secretly he seeks to subvert it in order to form a party of [unreadable] ."[64] Bamberger described the National Liberal leader, Bennigsen, as "tired and out of sorts": "He says he is through with Bismarck, he who most of all held to him and had the most intimate relations with him. . . . Bennigsen also opposes the view that the Liberal party should let itself be pulled into the government now . . . [and] step into the inheritance of the confused economy and economic disorder of the last years."[65]

In this unclear situation, Bamberger and Forckenbeck agreed on the need to proceed cautiously. Forckenbeck proposed a defensive posture to defend what had been achieved and perhaps to draw the chancellor out on his plans. He arranged a political rally in Breslau for November 22 at which Bamberger was to speak. Appearing before—as Forckenbeck described it—"cultured scholarly elements" from the "upper, middle, and lower-middle classes," in which the National Liberal party had its "firm roots," Bamberger attacked the too powerful personality of Bismarck, warned about a coming reaction, and called upon the middle class to be prepared for a long struggle to defend what had been achieved.[66] Bamberger's Breslau speech, with its (albeit subdued) attack on Bismarck and the fact that the meeting was open to the left (that is, the Progressives), is difficult to evaluate, especially since the rally was held during the negotiations over the Bennigsen candidacy. Although it may have been an attempt to torpedo the negotiations, the Breslau affair was probably designed to demonstrate to both Bismarck and the right wing of the National Liberal party that National Liberal support could not be purchased cheaply. The so-called Bennigsen candidacy for a Prussian cabinet post as interior or finance minister, if it ever was a serious consideration on Bismarck's part,[67] spun itself out over the summer, fall, and winter of 1877–78. Bennigsen and Bismarck first conferred in July 1877, and the details of their meeting are still little known. A second, even less publicized meeting took place in September or October, when Bennigsen was offered the ministry of the interior.[68]

From Bamberger's pen we have several references to National Liberal meetings from November 1877 to January 1878. Feder uses November 13 as the date of one which according to Bamberger's letter to Forckenbeck seems to have taken place on November 23. According to Bamberger, he, Bennigsen, Miquel, Stauffenberg, and Heinrich Rickert met at Lasker's house. Bennigsen gave a report about his discussions with Bismarck, and it became a question of "whether and how. A single entry into the cabinet discussed, the diverse points of program were touched upon. Nothing was yet firmed up." Bamberger did not regard the affair as urgent since Bennigsen claimed there could be no talk of a new discussion with Bismarck until the latter came to Berlin around Christmas time, "for it will depend on his situation vis-à-vis the emperor, whether and how he wants to and can carry out the expressed intentions. Therefore, I do not see the matter as so pressing, since even on our side so much unclarity rules."[69]

The National Liberals who were involved in the discussion, perhaps seven or eight, apparently made Bennigsen's entry into the cabinet conditional on the simultaneous entry of Forckenbeck and Stauffenberg. Eduard Stephani has reported that at a meeting of the National Liberal executive board in February 1880, Forckenbeck all but admitted that his and Stauffenberg's names had been placed in order to torpedo the negotiations.[70] There is of course no admission of this in Bamberger's writings, but in August 1878 he claimed that the purpose of Bismarck's gambit, to have Bennigsen alone enter the cabinet, was to undermine the party or drag it along.[71] If this was Bamberger's view all along—and it is similar to the comments cited above which he made during the spring of 1877—it is logical to expect him and his supporters to force Bismarck to pay a high price for their support and also to guard against the above-mentioned danger. Whether they would have compromised, by dropping Stauffenberg, cannot be ascertained. Bamberger did not return to the theme of the Bismarck-Bennigsen negotiations until shortly before his death, when Bismarck's and Moritz Busch's memoirs appeared. He wrote Stauffenberg that Busch's description of the negotiations, which the latter claimed collapsed not because of Stauffenberg and Forckenbeck but because the emperor himself had not wanted Bennigsen was "probably all Bismarck's lies." He admitted he had little material from the period. [72] Stauffenberg eventually responded to Bamberger's letter and summed up the affair: "Now it is quite clear that Bismarck had no other intention than to get rid of Camphausen, which he even succeeded in doing. We were merely the naively duped ones." In reviewing Bismarck's memoirs, Bamberger dismissed Bismarck's depiction of the Bennigsen candidacy as a fable.[73] If Camphausen was the target, as an obstacle to Bismarck's reform plans, the chancellor finally relieved himself of the finance minister by the spring of 1878.

The negotiations went on until February 1878. Bennigsen's December trip to Varzin produced nothing conclusive. The sketchy evidence available indicates that Bismarck offered Bennigsen the ministry of the interior and that Bennigsen countered with a request for the finance ministry and the simultaneous entry of Forckenbeck and Stauffenberg into the cabinet. Bismarck made no commitment and went on to discuss financial reform. Although there were differences over such questions as direct or indirect taxes, the role of the state's matricular contributions, and the constitutional guarantees for the Reichstag's budgetary powers, they were not unbridgeable. At this moment, at the end of December, the emperor made known his distaste for the Bennigsen proceedings and vetoed even Bennigsen's entry into the cabinet. Whether this really signified the factual end of the negotiations (as Hermann Oncken believes and Dietrich Sandberger disputes) can never be resolved.[74]

Two developments in February 1878, however, definitely signified the end of the negotiations. On February 7, the irreconcilable Pope Pius IX died and was replaced by the more conciliatory Leo XIII. There suddenly appeared the possibility of peace with the Center party, and one could even consider the party a potential government ally.[75] Two weeks later, Camphausen was given the task of introducing into the Reichstag Bismarck's bundle of tax proposals, which faced opposition from the National Liberals because of the lack of sufficient constitutional guarantees. The Reichstag's financial control would be reduced, since the taxes were permanent indirect levies, and there was as yet no imperial finance minister to hold responsible for the reform. Stauffenberg announced the National Liberals' opposition to the plan and asked whether the government intended to supplant the tobacco tax by a more lucrative tobacco monopoly, which the National Liberals also opposed. When Camphausen temporized, Bismarck intervened to say that the tobacco tax was merely the transition stage to a tobacco monopoly. Although Camphausen defended himself on the following day by claiming he had always favored a tobacco monopoly, he effectively destroyed his position not only with Bismarck but also with the National Liberals. His resignation was anticlimactic.[76] Bennigsen, feeling deceived by Bismarck and Camphausen over the question of a tobacco monopoly, went to Bismarck immediately after the session of February 23 to inform him that he would not enter the government. Bamberger reported that the Hanoverian liberal was "shocked" over the "falseness which lay in the scene."[77]

It is difficult, in spite of Sandberger's claims, to see the failure of the negotiations as of "catastrophic significance" to the National Liberals, unless success is measured by a willingness to cooperate with Bismarck. The negotiations remained shrouded in mystery from beginning to end, and Bismarck's ultimate aims are unverifiable. Among the National Liberals of the left there was fear of being duped and taken for a ride toward unacceptable financial reforms. Alone in the cabinet, Bennigsen would not be able to withstand this. Thus the price for cooperation was relatively high—two or three National Liberals in the government and an independent national finance ministry.[78] How difficult even this latter provision would be to obtain was evident during the debate over the bill to provide a deputy for the chancellor, whose long respites at his country estates were becoming more frequent. Besides creating a deputy or vice-chancellor, the bill provided for the creation of several central offices, including an imperial treasury office, but made them subordinate to the chancellor in their specific areas.[79]

Bismarck's efforts to win over or split the National Liberals and to push through his financial reorganization plans thus at best moved slowly in the spring of 1878. He was, however, a patient man. His program of eliminating the matricular contributions and going over to indirect taxes and tariffs was not a "firm program" for which he expected immediate success. He wrote:

> Politics is long lived and requires plans for a generation. So long as I am capable of taking part in the affairs of state as a minister or in parliament, I will not cease in every session, and as often as I find an opportunity for it, to propose and advocate political and economic measures which I consider correct, and thereby believe in the final victory of healthy reason over party tactics and rhetoric. The scholars without a business or property . . . who live off stipends, honoraria, and coupons, will have to subordinate themselves in the course of the years to the economic demands of the people who produce or vacate their parliamentary seats. This struggle can last longer than we live, but I at least am decided even then not to give it up, even if a momentary lack of success can clearly be foreseen.[80]

• 6 •

Antisocialism

Sooner than Bismarck realized, the opportunity would present itself to achieve parts of his plan and to force out some of those who lived off honoraria and coupons. Bamberger had noted that Bismarck was "very impressed by the rise of the Social Democrats and states one must get at them with legislation. How? He himself does not yet say."[1] On May 11, 1878, Max Hödel shot at the emperor and missed. Three weeks later Karl Nobiling shot at and seriously wounded William. Bismarck reacted to the assassination attempts by bringing into sharp focus the struggle against the Social Democrats, which he also hoped would seriously weaken the National Liberal party.

The Social Democratic party grew rapidly in the 1870s, receiving 3.3 percent of the popular vote in 1871, 6.8 percent in 1874, and 9.2 percent in 1877. Bismarck had tried various ways of striking at them. The press bill of 1873 provided punishment for those who subversively attacked family, property, or military duty, but that paragraph was stricken by the Reichstag. The criminal code bill of 1875–76 contained article 30, which forbade attacking the institutions of marriage, family, or property, and inciting one class against another. This provision also failed to win the approval of the Reichstag. The attempted assassinations would provide the occasions for third and fourth attempts to destroy the Social Democratic party legislatively. The two "anti-socialist" bills would also cause a severe moral and political crisis for the National Liberal party and particularly for Bamberger.

As much as any liberal, Bamberger had been concerned since his return from exile about the emergence of an organized workers' movement and the spread of socialism in Germany. During this period he came to grips with the issue in various ways. He had gone into exile as a member of the democratic left with much sympathy for social reform and had returned to Germany as a convinced proponent of laissez faire and extremely hostile to plans for social improvement, which he all too readily labeled socialism. His move toward the political center cannot be traced, but by 1860 he was condemning "suddenly discovered recipes for social salvation" as "pure deception" or "wildly visionary" since "there is no simple way to make something out of nothing."[2] A few clues to his transformation can be found in the exile writings of his close associate H. B. Oppenheim. Oppenheim in 1850 was still emphasizing the compatibility of democracy and socialism. He defined socialism as the liberation of producers and peasants through a "political and pedogogical revolution," through equitable administration and fair taxes, and by increasing and multiplying the productive forces. In this sense socialism belonged to the democratic political movement and provided material for awakening and enlightening the masses. Both Bamberger and Oppenheim stressed the role of the masses who, according to the former, had to be given "their proper weight." Oppenheim regarded the "proletariat as the most powerful lever of the democracy because it was most interested in a radical change of existing conditions." Nevertheless, even then he stressed the difficulty of talking to the masses so that one could be understood and also be truthful.[3]

Nine years later Oppenheim's view of socialism had changed, and he claimed that it could only be realized by a dictatorship. The only lasting solution to the social question was one which was reconcilable "with general and individual freedom, economic as well as political and intellectual."[4] If the ideals of socialism as defined by Oppenheim were realizable only as part of the general movement toward the realm of freedom then there was no need to organize a special workers' party apart from the progressive middle class. Oppenheim thus immediately condemned Ferdinand Lassalle's organization of a workers' party.[5]

Of course Oppenheim's admonitions against a separate workers' party were not heeded. By 1868, when Bamberger entered the election arena, besides the Lassallean party, a second workers' political party was being born. The problem represented by the new political groups—What should be done to improve the condition of the lower classes?—was on the political agenda. In an essay written in 1867, Bamberger referred to the social question as no longer a question but a task. But it was a task that must be tackled within the framework of freedom and democracy. Freedom was the precondition and means for solving the social question. And with an obvious slap at the Lasalleans he went on: "Whoever involves himself with the solution of the social question without subscribing to the basic principle of political freedom, his work is deceptive, his aim is generally to rule through division of those who in truth are bound to common interest with one another."[6] These and other pious generalities were repeated in the election campaign for the Customs Parliament. At one of his speeches, the Lasalleans appeared in force and made counterspeeches, and a speech in the Mainz suburb of Gonsenheim announced as dealing with the problems of the worker was disrupted, apparently by workers.[7] His opponents charged that since becoming a rich man, he had developed a fear of socialism and was seized by the same anxiety that he had found so unacceptable in his moderate opponents in 1848. "Generally Bamberger seems to shirk the social question," it concluded. More correctly it might be said he did not take it seriously.[8]

Although at times Bamberger expressed sympathy for social problems, he had nothing but contempt and hatred for organized socialist movements. He complained about the "growing flood of socialist agitation" and feared that the "vermin" might realize how stupid it was to war among themselves. However, he believed that the "labor pains of the rabble" would always produce successors for the "Hydra head" of socialism. Shortly before the outbreak of the Franco-German War, the socialist supporters of Wilhelm Liebknecht and August Bebel held a rally in the Electoral Palace in Mainz. Bamberger could scarcely contain his anger as he wrote to Oppenheim: "The Mainz City Council was so dumb to concede the Academy Hall to the Marxists for their meeting. The German Michel believes in the honor and party rights of Marx, [Johann von] Schweitzer, and Liebknecht. That will cost us dearly one day."[9]

His hostility toward socialism and socialists was reinforced by the Paris Commune. Like many others, Bamberger saw the commune through the eyes of a worried bourgeois. He feared that the revolt would lead to an "extralegal rule of the Reds with all the insanities of their program" and considered the insurgents capable of "every barbarism." He called it a product of the socialist preaching of class hate and the practical carrying through of socialist ideas.[10] His views seemed to moderate during the 1870s when he described the Commune as the result of an exaggerated desire for federalism at best or mere plundering at worst, and claimed that one should not dignify it as communism or socialism.[11] However, he was quite willing to do so, and under the impact of the Antisocialist Law he once more saw the Commune in ideological terms. "The Commune," he concluded, "was the living embodiment of socialistic thought."[12]

Although his hostility to socialism continued after unification, the 1870s presented Bamberger with a number of problems concerning workers which only remotely could be connected to socialism. Nevertheless, he was quick to see evidence of socialism everywhere.[13] In the first session of the German Reichstag, the government reacted to the increasing number of industrial accidents by introducing a bill which regulated liability for accidents caused by trains and in factories and mines. For the former, liability was assumed by the train companies, but for the latter types of accident the burden of proof was put on the injured. After much debate the bill was passed on May 13,

1871, with no substantial changes. Looking back on the debates, Bamberger attributed the "difficult birth" of the liability law to its adjacency to the area of the "social question." Although he generally supported the government's bill, he characterized all attempts to extend its scope as complete socialism, and the deputies who voted against the bill (mainly Progressives and socialists) as "more or less socialistically inclined" and espousing "class hate." The readiness on Bamberger's part to smear his opponents as socialists would not disappear but grow in later years.

The tendency was more evident in 1872 as the Reichstag grappled with the problem of providing legal recognition for associations, particularly labor unions. This question gave Bamberger his education in workers' problems. As he told his wife: "I am now involved in difficult but interesting work. The commission of the Reichstag on worker and religious associations, strikes, and the like has named me its reporter, and I have to eat my way into material which up till now I knew only superficially."[14]

The author of the 1872 bill as well as two previous ones was Hermann Schultze-Delitzsch, the father of the German cooperative movement. The first bill in 1869 won the approval of the Reichstag of the North German Confederation but not of the Federal Council, and the next two attempts died in committee. Franz Duncker, a supporter of the measures, charged that Bamberger used his position in the commission to delay the deliberations on the 1872 bill as long as possible. The history of the Schultzian proposals is a sad chapter in the liberal's attempt to establish a favorable profile for the newly emerging forces on the left. In this process Ludwig Bamberger helped to destroy any potential for cooperation that may have existed as he fought against a possible link between the liberals and the working class. The issue of the legal position of associations was lost in a dispute over whether the bill would favor the Progressive party and its supporters.

The purpose of Schultze-Delitzsch's bill was to set out conditions which had to be met if an association was to be legally recognized. In most German states, including Prussia, legal recognition was granted at the discretion of the administrative authorities. Getting legal recognition meant receiving the rights of a corporation, that is, to acquire property, sue and be sued in court, conclude contracts, and have members subject to limited liability.

The bill was in no way revolutionary, since Bavaria and Saxony had similar ones, but it foundered because of two fears—that the collection of dues would mask a strike fund, and that the major beneficiaries would be recently formed Trade Unions (Hirsch-Duncker unions) that were closely aligned with the Progressive party. For Bamberger these considerations provided reasons for working against the bill. In fact, he wrote his longest book to warn the German people about the dangers of the Trade Unions.[15] The book, a three-hundred-page attack, dredged up every possible danger connected with them. He attacked the British unions which served as a model for the Trade Unions, warned against strikes, and approved of lockouts; but his major criticism was that the Hirsch-Duncker unions were under the patronage of a political group, the Progressive party. Franz Duncker and the executive director of the Trade Unions, Max Hirsch, were both members of the Progressive party and, according to Bamberger, they had gotten their colleague, Schultze-Delitzsch, to introduce his bills regulating associations. Thus the measure was a move designed ultimately to favor a political group.

Besides being allied with a political opponent, the Trade Unions, according to Bamberger, were nothing more than strike associations. The "natural impulse" of these organizations was toward strikes, and they had their "life's principle in the strike." All statements to the contrary were just so much window-dressing. In fact, he saw no significant difference between the Social Democrats and the Trade Unions. The latter were mere advocates of "peaceful socialism," but even these moderates believed a "drastic means" must remain and that was the strike. It did not matter whether one was dealing with the Trade Unions, the Catholic Journeymen's Association, or the Social Democratic unions: "All this water flows into the same current."

Not content with trying to bury the unions under a cloud of suspicion as radical socialists, Bamberger also worked to undermine their advocacy of devices to ward off labor disputes, such as conciliation and arbitration boards. Although hard pressed to combat proposals whose goal was to avoid strikes, Bamberger warned that they would change nothing, that one should not expect the "better elements" to escape from the hands of those who were "prone to war." Industrial courts, he maintained, were based on the idea of the equality of the opinion of employer and employee. "With that the world is accordingly divided into two halves; from the outset the principle of class antagonism on which the socialistic agitation rests is acknowledged." In Bamberger's view, such a step would be taken as a sign that the state was supporting every workers' organization.

Closely connected with the issue of the legal position of the unions and the boards of conciliation and arbitration was the question of insurance funds for the support of sick or disabled workers and for the payment of widows' pensions. The Hirsch-Duncker unions tried to establish so-called free funds, without government supervision or employer participation. Once again the unions wanted normative standards to be applied to the assistance funds rather than having to accept the discretionary will of the authorities. For Bamberger the assistance funds were secret strike funds. They were a means of "enticing the worker into a sphere of activities run by others . . . and then chaining him to be used for other purposes." Bamberger's notion of individualism was also offended since "self-reliant" workers as members of the unions would be forced to join the funds. Moreover, he regarded the Trade Unions' disinclination to have employers involved in the funds as a sign that the unions were under the influence of socialist ideology. "The more the unions acknowledge that the spirit of their policy is the spirit of separateness, that they are striving for the monopoly of the care and leadership of a separately organized workers' state within the state, the less they have claim to [the Reichstag's] legislative sympathy." When finally in February 1876 a very restrictive bill regulating assistance funds was passed, Bamberger had every reason to be satisfied.

Bamberger's response to the above measures indicated a blind hostility to all measures that might favor workers' organizations. He was also in a key position to sabotage the legislative attempts to deal with the question. In the early and mid-1870s he was at the height of his influence in the National Liberal party and was a major speaker during several of the debates. He was the reporter for the Reichstag commission on associations and chairman of the one dealing with industrial courts, and none of the pro-union bills that went to these committees made it to a second reading. In his book on workers' organizations as well as in newspaper articles in the influential *Augsburger Allgemeine Zeitung,* he continued the attack on the legislative attempts to come to grips with workers' problems.[16]

Concurrently with the battle against the unions, Bamberger waged a vicious struggle against university professors of economics organized into the Association for Social Policy (Verein für Sozialpolitik) but dubbed by Oppenheim "Socialists of the Chair" ("Kathedersozialisten"). It involved a war of words over the role of the state in social problems, and over the presence and cure of current social evils. In the 1850s and 1860s it appeared that a laissez-faire economic policy represented the wave of the future. The proponents of this view had organized the Congress of German Economists, and their basic hostility to the intervention of government in the economic life of the country became the acknowledged position of the bulk of the National Liberal party.[17] However, in the late 1860s serious challenges to this laissez-faire doctrine began to emerge from within the university walls. Professors such as Gustav Schmoller, Erwin Nasse, Gustav Schönberg, and Hans von Scheel called attention to the ill effects of capitalism, which for Schmoller meant the destruction of the old ethical relationship between employer and employee and "the descent into materialism and egosim." He was convinced that in economic activity a variety of ethical considerations often opposed the egoistic impulses of individuals. To uncover these other factors was the task of the economist. Schönberg claimed that laissez faire had fulfilled its mission by releasing the productive forces. Now it was a question of distribution, and only with the help of the state could the greatest abuses be eliminated.[18]

Initially these criticisms of the accepted teaching of laissez faire met little response from the other camp. The professors of economics seemed to be writing for each other. Only toward the end of 1871 did the new trend reach out to the general public and ignite a journalistic quarrel that was to last several years. On October 12, in a speech about the social question before a church group, Professor Adolf Wagner delivered a sharp criticism of laissez-faire social and economic policy.[19] The main response to Wagner came on December 17 from H. B. Oppenheim. The exchange soon involved Lujo Brentano, Wolfgang Eras, and Adolf Held and continued unabated over the summer months.[20] Bamberger, who had remained a spectator of the unfolding verbal struggle, wrote to his wife that "O[ppenheim]'s quarrel with the German professors of political economy has become a public issue."[21]

While the journalistic battle raged, the Socialists of the Chair decided to act. As Schmoller described it: "A number of anti-Manchester political economists . . . have the intention . . . of having a discussion about the social question, especially the trade unions, strikes, factory legislation, and the housing question. There will be public discussions by prominent industrialists, politicians, and editors."[22] The sponsors did try to draw leading figures from the political, labor union, and business worlds. Among those invited from the National Liberal party and the Congress of German Economists were Eduard Lasker, Rudolf Gneist, Johannes Miquel, and even Ludwig Bamberger. Some Socialists of the Chair thought they saw a glimmer of sympathy for social ills in Bamberger's 1867 essay for Berthold Auerbach's *Volkskalender.*[23]

While it is difficult to know Bamberger's thoughts as he read the invitation from Schmoller, his response was clear enough. He feared that between him and Schmoller there was no congruity of views. "I believe namely that one can devote active attention to the recently posed social problem and nevertheless remain on the foundations of the economic teachings established and developed by Adam Smith. . . . I consider it neither acceptable nor salutary . . . to sanctify the opposition between capital and labor by the terminology of scholarship." He rejected the idea that the state should assist the Trade Unions by compulsory measures and charged that the unions served party purposes. Such state action would only encourage strikes, which in his eyes were at least 75 percent due to communist or ultramontane machinations. He also feared that state intervention would threaten much of the recently passed liberal legislation such as freedom of movement, freedom to carry on business operations, free trade, and the ending of restrictions on marriage. A meeting of this kind thus would only deliver "war material" to the extreme right and left.[24]

Not only did Bamberger reject the invitation, but he and Oppenheim worked to convince Lasker not to attend. The appearance of a man whose incorruptibility and fairness were conceded even by his enemies would redound to the credit of the congress. Bamberger's letter betrayed the scorn of the businessman for the desk-bound and unworldly scholar:

> Since I studied [Lujo] Brentano's two volumes [*Arbeitergilden der Gegenwart*] with care I really despise the type. It is pure propaganda for class hate, seemingly armed with great knowledge of the facts but actually insipidly immature. When I wrote to Oppenheim that I did not consider you completely armed against the enticement of this congress, my fear was the *residuum* of various, in part "older" expressions which left me with the impression that you viewed the totality of great industry and finance generally with a certain mistrust and . . . as more or less illegitimate.

Lasker finally excused himself with a cold.[25]

The congress to discuss the social question was convened at Eisenach on October 6, 1872, and Rudolf Gneist, a member of the Congress of German Economists, was made chairman. Although little of a concrete nature was established, the meeting aroused much attention and was commented on in many newspapers.[26] While the congress met, Bamberger prepared a number of articles to expose the errors and shallowness of the Socialists of the Chair.[27] Besides trying to characterize them as a special species of socialist, Bamberger tried to dismiss the economists by challenging their ability to make pronouncements on "real" problems without ever having left the study hall. His sharpest attack was directed at Lujo Brentano, who in his book on labor organizations had portrayed the English trade unions as the ideal labor unions for the nineteenth century. He was a staunch supporter of the Hirsch-Duncker unions.[28] Referring to Brentano, Bamberger charged: "He may have gone through the factories of half the world, he may have studied the documents of all the English strikes; still he gains only a poetical view of practical business life, if he does not know firsthand the actual problems of business leadership." He claimed the economist's work was permeated by an anticapitalist bias akin to that of the socialists. In fact, wrote Bamberger, "a common band ties all shades from the wild Russian Bakunin to the tamest German instructor."[29]

In many respects Brentano was an unfortunate target for Bamberger. He was among the most liberal of the Socialists of the Chair and claimed that if he were a member of the National Liberal party he would belong to its left wing.[30] The instructor was also every bit as tenacious a fighter as Bamberger and believed that right was on his side. As he remarked of Oppenheim, "He feels like a bourgeois; we have bigger hearts." Or later, "Why do I have scorn if not to express it?" Even Schmoller cautioned him to tone down his remarks to avoid making the dispute worse than it was.[31] Brentano was suitably angered by Bamberger's "libel" and was determined to "scatter" his attacks like "chaff," because "with the prominence which Bamberger enjoyed in the political world and his brilliant style of writing, his attacks found echo everywhere in the press."[32] Brentano's main counterattack came in a series of articles published under the title *Die wissenschaftliche Leistung des Herrn Ludwig Bamberger (The Scholarly Effort of Mr. Ludwig Bamberger),* in which he "publicly exposed Bamberger's gross ignorance, his distortions and denunciations with the same malice with which he attacked me." Even fifty years later Brentano still could not conceal his anger over the events of the 1870s.[33]

Although the verbal struggle between the two economic groups continued at a subdued level after the first congress at Eisenach, several attempts were made to bring the warring parties together.[34] However, the path to cooperation was rocky, and Bismarck added a new dimension to the quarrel by dispatching Rudolf Meyer and Hermann Wagener to the 1874 meeting of the association. Meyer was the editor of the archconservative *Berliner Revue,* and Wagener, likewise an extreme conservative, had been Bismarck's adviser but had been forced to resign in 1873 because of Lasker's disclosures of misdealings in railroad contracts.[35] Although neither one participated in the debates, the affair brought to the surface in Bamberger and others the fear that Bismarck might desire to turn from a liberal policy and be interested in an alliance between left and right behind a program of state-supported social policies which would threaten the liberal measures of the early 1870s. These gains had scarcely been achieved, and they would once again be placed in jeopardy. It is perhaps this desperate fear that made many of the liberals react so strongly to suggestions of tampering with the recently introduced laissez-faire economy. Also, the fact that the Socialists of the Chair were coming to dominate university teaching made it appear inevitable that future generations of German leaders would be infused with ideas which to Bamberger at least were subversive.[36]

Bamberger in particular was attuned to the larger political ramifications of Wagener and Meyer's visit to Eisenach in 1874 and refused to be swept along by the reconciliatory currents at work between the two economic camps. For him the Wagener-Meyer episode was symptomatic of the dangers inherent in the academic socialist movement. To call on the secular arm of the state for help meant to run the risk of reopening the doors to the conservatives. If once a regime wanted to use such appeals for help for illiberal measures, then the rhetoric of the professors would provide a welcome cover. He reminded his readers that Wagener had close relations with the Lassalleans and that Lassalle himself had called on Bismarck for help.[37]

The negotiations toward reconciliation between the two groups nevertheless continued until Bamberger almost torpedoed them on January 27, 1876. During the debate on proposed revisions of the penal code, Bamberger intervened with a stinging attack on the academic socialists. He charged the professors with making attacks on industry unsurpassed even by socialists. He also made references to abuses of freedom of teaching which could have been regarded as an attack on the principle itself, although he denied any such aim.[38] Brentano's reaction seems fair. He complained to Lasker: "Is it acceptable to assail men with calumny without cause, in a place where defense is denied them? . . . What is one to make of this honesty which in one and the same breath demands freedom for scholarship and denounces this freedom as dangerous to the state?"[39] For the negotiations to continue, Bamberger was forced to write a letter of apology, although he did so with the greatest reluctance. Finally in 1876 and continuing until 1879, joint meetings of the Congress of German Economists and the Association for Social Policy were held, although little more than some good will resulted.[40]

Bamberger had from the outset seen the Socialists of the Chair as providing socialism with intellectual respectability and the government with an excuse to turn away from liberal policies. He recognized them as the enemy, and with a persistence that is remarkable hounded them as long as he could. He was, it seems in retrospect, unfair to Brentano since they had more in common than was initially apparent.[41] What also remains from this stormy dispute is a residue of genuine hatred by Bamberger for any measure of state intervention. One is almost ready to conclude that he regarded liberalism as a seamless cloth whose one tear would destroy its value. What must be remember, however, is Bamberger's uncertainty about Bismarck and the former's basic distrust of the still conservative Prusso-German state. Until such a state was genuinely infused with a liberal spirit, it would be suicidal for liberals to grant it increased authority over individuals. What might be granted to a liberal state could not be permitted a conservative one.

In spite of all the rhetoric the renegade academicians were, after all, merely a manifestation of a much greater problem, the rapid growth of the Social Democratic party. Bamberger attributed the rapid rise of the Social Democrats to a number of factors such as universal manhood suffrage (which he regarded as an unnecessary gift from above); the intellectual and social support that socialism got from willing allies among professors, Catholic leaders, and Conservatives, whose hostility to liberalism only helped the socialist cause; generally improving economic conditions which led to a revolution of rising expectations; and finally a weakness in the German character, which had a great affinity for "eccentric and disturbing thoughts." With these factors as his basic assumptions, he never regarded the social question as a real problem. Rather it had been artificially stimulated from outside. Once this outside nourishment was cut off, the epidemic would be under control.[42]

Since these factors were beyond his power to change, what could be done to halt the socialist menace? In light of later developments it is worth mentioning what he refused to countenance as a means of dealing with the problem. The use of force to upset the existing order should of course be met in kind, but beyond this he was reluctant to go, at least in the early 1870s. "May our talents," he wrote in 1872, "guard us against experiencing socialist-baiting. To whom the frivolity of such police measures has not become clear from history, he may in his anxiety seize on such hopeless means." He was equally dubious about the effect of restrictive legislation. "Against the spread of mere theories one does not make any laws. What does it help to forbid erroneous teaching?"[43] His opposition to the Jesuit Law was based on the same arguments: "Nothing has proved itself less powerful for half of a century than the attempt to fight currents of the public spirit, be they good, be they bad, with police repression . . . the cure is worse than the illness."[44]

Bismarck too had been concerned about the spread of socialism in Germany, particularly after the two factions united at Gotha in May 1875. He responded with his most serious attempt to curb the Social Democrats, via a thorough revision of the penal code. The bill would have changed more than fifty articles in the code. Articles 85 and 11 were to be changed so that the definition of high treason would include those who approved of attempts to "incite" to riot or disobedience to the law, while article 128 placed new and vague restrictions on associations whose "effectiveness" rested on secrecy. The key provision, however, was article 130, which stated that anyone who publicly incited various classes of the population against each other in a way that endangered the peace or who in the same manner publicly "attacked" the institutions of marriage, family, or property was to be punished with imprisonment.[45]

The bill was justified in the most urgent terms by Minister of State Gerhard Leonhardt, causing Eduard Lasker to remark that if the situation was so serious the government should not bother to revise the code but should introduce exceptional laws. Since Lasker was not convinced of the imminent danger, he regarded the paragraphs regulating assembly, association, press, and public discussions as a direct threat to the rights of every German. Very aptly he called the articles rubber ones that could be bent or twisted at will.[46]

Six weeks later the debate on article 130 took place. This antisocialist paragraph was recognized as the most important and dangerous article in the bill and was the subject of the longest discussion. The government's spokesman, Count Botho zu Eulenburg, recited a long string of supposedly incriminating quotations from socialist sources, causing the Social Democratic deputy Wilhelm Hasselmann to applaud the minister's speech because of the "enlightment it contributed to the final goals" of the worker's movement, but also to warm him that his speech would fall under the scope of article 130 for inciting one class against another.[47] When Lasker characterized the article as an attack on freedom of the press and discussion, whose continued existence he saw as the best corrective to erroneous views, Eulenberg attacked this "too idealistic" viewpoint. He argued that only the educated, who read several newspapers, could weigh opposing viewpoints, while those who read socialist newspapers read only one and swore by it.[48]

At this point Bamberger intervened to announce that Lasker's position was not that of the National Liberal party and that he, Bamberger, was not blind to the "quite serious dangers" to Germany connected with the "socialistic-communistic" movement. Proudly the liberal recounted that he had read the socialistic stories thirty years before and had even translated Proudhon. He admitted that he did not, like Lasker, believe in the idealistic aspects of the socialistic movement. While his colleague might have read the theory of socialism, "I have read the biography of Lasalle; I have become acquainted more or less with the whole personal history of this agitator; I have read the last exchange of letters . . . and know that the founder of this party spent the last days of his life in a most immature amorous escapade" and that "he was driven to socialism by satiety and ennui for the normal course of things." After presenting his credentials as an expert on socialism, Bamberger went on to say that although there were honorable men among the socialists he did not believe that they represented the general element in the movement and still less did he believe their protestations of legality. "I believe that if the gentlemen . . . could murder us and through it introduce their regime they would do it. I am not so idealistic that I believe, like Lasker, that if an unfortunate constellation would come in Berlin as in Paris [in 1871] the hands of the peaceful citizens would suffice to protect us." He also did not share Lasker's certainty that with free discussion the truth would triumph: "Oh, the empire of lies is so great." The danger of socialism was greater in Germany than in any other country "because its whole complexion" afforded more advantage to this view. Here he referred to various groups, among others the Socialists of the Chair, who for one reason or another furthered the socialist cause, and he even raised questions about freedom of teaching. Nevertheless, he was equally certain, at the conclusion of his scattershot speech, that article 130 was not the answer. "These old wives' remedies with press paragraphs cannot help us in such questions. . . . To lay a hand on these institutions is to destroy the principles on which the German Empire was formed." The article was overwhelmingly defeated in the second reading. [49]

A brief footnote to the discussion on article 130 was written on February 9 during the third reading of the bill. Bismarck appeared and spoke for the article in what was obviously a hopeless cause. His words were not reassuring to the liberals. He chided the deputies for not answering directly the charges of the socialists and made known his desire for greater discussion of the theoretical aspects of socialism. In portentous words the chancellor remarked: "A great deal new has been brought forth in socialism and many of us have never, at least never attentively, read or studied a socialist paper but judge it only by hearsay. . . . I must confess that I am not so well instructed as . . . Bamberger; more enlightenment can still be brought to me about it, and I am ready to hear more." [50]

In spite of his hostility to the socialists, Bamberger, at this stage, could not bring himself to support a bill designed more to limit freedom than to eliminate socialism. As he explained in a speech in Dresden later in the year, he did not think the socialist danger was becoming significantly greater, and he hoped the slowdown in economic growth would make the workers less demanding and more humble. There was therefore no need to take additional precautions. He also warned his listeners that they should not let fear of socialism be a cover for reaction. In this sense socialism presented a threat to the free development of the nation, as reactionaries could argue that there was a choice only between them and the socialists. He even hinted that certain conservative groups secretly hoped to encourage the socialists to an uprising with the intention of wiping out liberalism in the process of restoring order. [51] The point he stressed was that the socialists had taken no violent action to realize their goals, and "only where the realm of action begins and the empire of thought ceases, does the legislator have the right to enter with the sword." [52]

It may be an exaggeration to say that socialism was an obsession with Bamberger, but he rarely missed an opportunity to enlighten the public about it. Even his rural constituency of Bingen-Alzey, where the socialists had yet to receive a recorded vote, was given a crude exposé of socialist aims. [53] His most serious attempt to come to grips with the problem of socialism appeared in the form of an essay entitled "Deutschland und der Sozialismus" ("Germany and Socialism") in the *Deutsche Rundschau* in February-March, 1878. He had written it because "certain ideas about the necessity of remodeling human society on new, untenable, never tested foundations have overpowered minds in Germany in a striking and serious way." [54]

Much of the essay contained arguments made on previous occasions. The personal motives of the leaders were the driving force behind the socialist dynamic. The Socialists of the Chair, most newspapers, Catholics, and conservatives all received their reprimands for futhering socialism. Universal suffrage and relatively frequent elections also stimulated the growth of socialism. Strikes which involved violence indicated the tendency toward violence inherent in workers' movements. Hints were dropped that voting restrictions and lengthened legislative periods might help, and the solution to the social question was still to be found in "an increase in free movement, in diligence, and in goods." What is more interesting are his comments about various aspects of German society and politics. German society, he claimed, had not been reformed, and too much of the old survived. There was no triumph of the middle class. It had not absorbed the old class system, which still existed. Thus there was no feeling "for the great common interest," and each group thought of its own interests. He pointed out that the popular vote for the so-called antinational groups within Germany such as the Poles, Welfs, "Swabian Democrats," Alsatians, and Ultramontanes almost equaled that of the "national" parties—2,395,000 of 5,535,000. What Bamberger was really admitting by his emphasis on the splintered nature of German society and the lack of integration was that German unity, which he supported and fought for so long, was perhaps a mistake at worst or premature at best.[55]

If German society was compartmentalized, Bamberger nevertheless detected an exaggerated veneration of the state. The Germans, he noted, used the word "state" where the French said government. The word "state" signified an abstraction, something almost godly, to which one could concede unlimited confidence. "The idea that the state is outside the individual system with superhuman intelligence and morality has already overpowered the minds and completely pushed into the background the idea that the state too is composed of individuals sometimes acting alone, sometimes acting together. The more one . . . claims greatness and power for the state externally and internally, the more cautiously must the limits of its power vis-à-vis the freedom of movement of individuals be delineated."[56]

This statism applied to the middle class, which was his audience and Germany's future. The German bourgeoisie refused to live up to the role history had assigned to it. "For a long time it has not felt itself responsible for its preservation. It lives in the tradition that the higher authority . . . cares for peace and security. For that reason it does not defend itself against the attacks which are directed against its own camp."[57] He warned his middle-class audience not to look to Bismarck for aid. It was Bismarck's method, said Bamberger, proving himself more of a prophet than he perhaps realized, to make use of every lever of pressure which was available to him. Thus "the middle class is . . . not absolutely sure of the domestic policy of the great statesman." It would never be, he continued, as long as it "proves itself too weak to push him to the conviction that it offers the true, healthy support."[58] This was the program of the 1860s based on the hope that Bismarck would realize what was "life-giving" to a nation. If Germany was ever to grow out of the appearance into the reality of a parliamentary state, the bourgeoisie would have to gather itself into a "solid, compact body with consciousness and recognition of its duty to self-preservation, strong enough to defy the oppositional elements above and the advancing elements below."[59]

Even if the bourgeoisie would not heed his advice, they still bought his essay. Bamberger was pleased by the public response and wrote to his mother that his tract had made quite an impression and "procured many compliments for me." Even Bismarck was favorably impressed and called Bamberger to his office for a personal conversation after the first half of the essay appeared. It was perhaps the last private meeting between the two men. The chancellor complimented him on his article but was eager to find out what remedies he would propose in the second part of the essay. The liberal replied that he had no patent cure for the socialistic disease, whereupon Bismarck remarked: "If you do not want chicks you have to crack the eggs." Sixteen years later Bamberger called Bismarck's comment the "quintessence of the [Anti] socialist Law." At the time, however, he saw no danger in it, telling his mother: "Even Bismarck, who otherwise does not read much, has regaled me with compliments."[60] In the preface to the reprint of his *Deutsche Rundschau* essays, Bamberger admitted that Bismarck was not the only person who had expected him to provide a solution to the social problem and hence felt slightly deceived when none appeared. Bamberger could only reply that this had not been his intention.[61]

Scarcely two months after the appearance of Bamberger's essays came the first attempt to assassinate the emperor, followed three weeks later by a second and nearly successful effort. Bismarck now had an opportunity to push through his restructuring of the empire.[62] Although the immediate reaction was the introduction of a harsh bill against Social Democrats which had been part of Bismarck's long-range plans to control them, he also suspected that the severity of the bill would provoke a rejection by the National Liberals, giving him a new election slogan against them. And the liberals themselves were well aware of this possibility.[63]

Bismarck once remarked to Lucius von Ballhausen that in the administration of justice, speed was more important than fairness. "A policeman with his noncommissioned officer's reasoning . . . is just as good as a learned judge."[64] Within nine days of the first assassination attempt and over the objections of some of the ministers, Bismarck won the Federal Council's approval of a bill for the "defense against Social Democratic excesses."[65] The bill was clearly an exceptional law directed against the Social Democrats but vague enough to frighten others. Article 1 gave the Federal Council the authority to forbid printed matter and associations which "follow the goals of Social Democracy." Articles 2 and 3 gave the police the right temporarily to ban the distribution of materials and to dissolve meetings which served the goals stated in article 1. Violations of the law were to be punished by imprisonment, and the law was to be in effect for three years.[66]

Except for the German Conservatives, the response to the bill was negative. The National Liberals critized the Social Democrats strongly but seemed to reject the idea of a special law and warned against hasty action. When the government's bill became known they objected to its vagueness. So little chance did such a bill have that some speculated that Bismarck was counting on a rejection, which he could then use against the National Liberals in the next election. Contrary to more customary procedure on important matters, there had been no prior consultation with the party about the bill.[67]

In spite of the preponderantly negative attitude of the party, some twenty to thirty deputies around Treitschke and Gneist were ready to deal with the chancellor, arguing that the party's parliamentary position as a support for Bismarck was crucial to its success. These differences were revealed at the meeting of the National Liberal executive committee at Lasker's house on May 21 and at the full meeting of the parliamentary group a day later. The executive committee agreed that the bill as it stood should be rejected, but there was no agreement about whether the National Liberals should offer anything to Bismarck. Thus Bennigsen was left without precise instructions since, as Bamberger said, the National Liberal leader "will know how to pull the diagonal out of the parallelogram of forces." Bennigsen was to stress the party's awareness of the danger and its willingness to sharpen the penal code or to discuss a law on associations.[68]

The debate on the first antisocialist bill ran its course on May 23–24 with few surprises. Bennigsen hinted at Bismarck's ulterior motives for bringing in such a bill, but he devoted most of his speech to attacking the Prussian government for having a permanent ministerial crisis. Almost as an afterthought, he did say that the National Liberal party would be ready to cooperate with the government in working out a general law regulating associations or to enact legislation based on respect for the civil liberties of all groups. He left little doubt that he did not expect this until the fall session. Only most Conservatives and a few National Liberals ultimately voted for the government's bill, which was defeated 251–57.[69]

The expected dissolution of parliament did not take place immediately after the rejection of the government's bill. Before Bismarck decided on his next step, a second and more serious assassination attempt took place on June 2. Capitalizing on his good fortune, the chancellor had the Reichstag dissolved on June 11 and new elections scheduled for July 30, 1878. The campaign was the most bitter and vicious of the eight-year-old German Empire. Bismarck initiated a press campaign that indeed focused on the Social Democratic menace but also intimated that if the National Liberals had passed the government's May bill there would have been no second assassination attempt. The chancellor's press allies also stressed that there was an opportunity for the healthy core of the party to separate itself from the doctrinaire left wing around Bamberger and Lasker.[70] The government even distributed copies of Bamberger's "Deutschland und der Sozialismus" to use against the liberals. Besides being on the chancellor's elimination list, Bamberger was also under attack by economic groups for his free-trade views.[71]

The National Liberals, if not Bamberger, were vulnerable to a campaign based on hysteria. Immediately after the second assassination attempt the views of the National Liberals did not seem to change. While joining in the feeling of revulsion over the deed, they still cautioned against an overhasty and overzealous entry into the field of special laws and advocated instead that the penal code be sharpened. This initial reaction quickly changed when they realized that they had not gauged the popular reaction properly. Under mounting pressure from their constituents, they became ready to countenance more energetic action against the socialists. However, it was too late to prevent a dissolution of the Reichstag—and also a severe election defeat which placed the National Liberals once again in a crisis situation.[72]

While the election campaign took on the appearance of a crusade against the socialists and indirectly against the liberals, Bamberger returned to his relatively peaceful constituency of vineyards and small towns where the socialists had not yet even placed a candidate. He escaped the pressures to which other National Liberals were subjected, and thus his statements perhaps reflected his actual beliefs. He had not participated in the debate over the May bill, but his views were made known in a letter to the editor of the *National Zeitung* which was occasioned by references in Bennigsen's and Lasker's speeches to the supposed noble goals of socialism. He denied as he had earlier that the "goals of humanity" had anything in common with the aims of the socialists to transform society. What disturbed him even more, he went on, was the inappropriateness of the government's bill to deal with all manifestations of socialism. The measure, he claimed, would still grant a patent for every socialistic attack on society, provided it did not come from the Social Democrats. These other sources of socialistic teachings were the truly dangerous ones, and by ignoring them the country would be "deceived about the true nature of its illness."[73] It was not a new theme with Bamberger, but it would smooth the way to acceptance of the Antisocialist Law and the use of physical means to counter intellectual currents.

The second assassination attempt did not cause a shift in Bamberger's thinking. For his immediate reaction we have the testimony of the diplomat Joseph von Radowitz, who met the liberal on the day of the assassination attempt. Radowitz reported that he expressed his "scalding hot" indignation to Bamberger about the harmful tolerance by liberals of his stripe toward instigators of such heinous acts as Nobiling's and asked him whether he still thought the goverment had exaggerated the danger. Even at this moment of Bamberger's most emotional reaction, according to Radowitz, the deputy did not seem to change his opinion in the least and still denied the need for exceptional laws to deal with such situations.[74]

With such an attitude, but concerned about the prospects of the National Liberals, Bamberger returned to his secure constituency of Bingen-Alzey. He had been elected and reelected in 1874 and 1877 with over 70 percent of the vote, and it required little effort on his part to keep his district loyal. His main opponent was from the Center party, and usually it was difficult even to find someone to run against him.[75] The Hessian Progressive party, as the local National Liberal branch was called, indicated via its election manifesto that it was standing apart from the more heated campaigns in other parts of Germany. The party cautioned the government to remain within the limits of the German legal code. It demanded the suppression of any threat to the social order, but it rejected any attempt to acknowledge legally the opposition of the classes by singling out the Social Democrats for exceptional treatment. The party subscribed to Bamberger's belief that intellectual movements must be fought with intellectual weapons and that repressive measures would only drive the movement into secrecy.[76]

A few days late in Mainz, Bamberger set the tone for his party's campaign in Hesse by delivering the keynote speech at a meeting of the state's provincial election committee. It was a very cautious effort in which he assumed a negative attitude toward an exceptional law against the Social Democrats. He conceded that the socialist movement had brought Germany fact to face with a new condition which was similar to a foreign threat aimed at the country's very existence. But even so, it could not be met by temporary measures like an exceptional law limited to several years. He traced the socialists' success to the unwillingness of other groups to isolate them. For this reason legal regulations alone were insufficient to cure the disease. "Only through a change in the spirit of the nation itself, which has played much too frivolously with the fire of the socialist idea," would the danger be eliminated. He did not think, however, that such a cleansing action was occurring, especially since the government's press campaign seemed to be directed more against the liberals, the most consistent opponents of socialism, than against the socialists. He warned his listeners that the election campaign seemed to be a Napoleonic plebiscite on the issue of an exceptional law, and by accepting such a measure they would be encouraging Bismarck in his "dangerous tendencies" toward more state power.[77]

But if there was to be no exceptional law against the Social Democrats, what should be done? "I must admit," he told an Alzey audience toward the end of July, "for my taste I would prefer a general diluting of the common law so that the German people will remember day in and day out that it must cut out of its national body the harms of Social Democracy in order to regain full freedom." A special law would make "us more easily forget that we still nurture an evil in our midst which can constantly threaten us anew."[78] The recipe, then, was no special law but perhaps a more general measure that would strike at or frighten his major targets, the so-called allies of the socialists.

Bamberger's concern about the question of freedom, and in particular free speech, appears to have been genuine. During the campaign he wrote Oppenheim that a law against the Social Democrats will make it "ever more difficult to speak and write in a popular way. I am anxious, only for this reason, about my next speeches in Alzey and Bingen, and I would like to recapture something of the freshness and directness with which I spoke years ago at such occasions."[79]

The election was never in doubt. Bamberger remarked that with his voters he belonged to the right wing. "That is a pleasant feeling. In prior years I always had a certain ill feeling about this left-wing consciousness."[80] His general concern about freedom struck a responsive chord among his voters, and he won by a larger percentage than in 1877, polling 75 percent of the vote. In contrast to the rest of Germany, voter participation in his district had dropped 16 percent since the 1877 election. The inability of the socialist danger to penetrate the comfortable vineyards of Rhenish Hesse was demonstrated.[81]

If Bamberger's constituents showed themselves singularly uninterested in the socialist menace, the voters in many National Liberal strongholds made known their desire for a tough approach to the Social Democrats and forced many liberals, against their better judgment, to declare themselves in favor of a special law.[82] In spite of their more accommodating approach to the idea of an antisocialist measure, the National Liberals were the major losers in the campaign, dropping from 127 to 99 seats while the two conservative parties increased their representation from 78 to 116. Although Bamberger had expected a defeat, he was nonetheless bitter about it. There was much to say about the election, he wrote Oppenheim, but "this says it all: This people is made for politics as the donkey is for lute-playing. Never will anything come of it." To Stauffenberg he remarked that Germany, as in 1848, was headed toward a "miscarriage."[83]

The miscarriage at first threatened to affect the National Liberal party, which was heading toward its final crisis. The government as expected produced a new bill against "the efforts of Social Democracy which are dangerous to the public." Instead of the curt six articles of the May proposal, the new bill was a more thorough product of twenty-two paragraphs. Article 1 forbade associations which served "Social Democratic, socialistic, or communistic" purposes aimed at "undermining the existing state or social order." Public meetings and printed matter which served such purposes were also forbidden. Punishment of offenders was set at either a fine or imprisonment. Protests against decisions of the state police could be appealed only to the Federal Council. In districts where "public security was threatened," the state authorities with the approval of the Federal Council could for one year require prior police approval for meetings, ban distribution of printed matter, and deny residence in certain areas. The law was given no time limit. [84] Except for its more generalized version of article 1, the bill did not present any concessions to its opponents. Nevertheless, this was September not May, and the National Liberals' will to resist was no longer so strong. The questions were: on what terms could one make a deal with Bismarck, and could the entire party unite behind a compromise with the chancellor. Bismarck, by his silence as to his ultimate aims, only increased the discomfort of the National Liberals.[85]

In view of the uncertainty regarding Bismarck's intentions, the first reading of the bill took on the appearance of an "oratory tournament." If so, August Bebel rather than Bamberger captured the prize. The socialist leader laid bare the government's inability to prove any connection between the would-be assassins and the Social Democrats. He also ridiculed the government's contention that the socialists needed to be treated as outcasts by revealing Bismarck's earlier relations with Ferdinand Lassalle. He warned the deputies that by placing the socialists outside the law, the bill would have the very consequences the government wanted to prevent: the socialists would be driven into the arms of anarchism. Arguing that the Social Democrats were not committed to violent upheaval but to a peaceful transformation of society, Bebel claimed that the bill was a true spur to radicalism. His two-hour speech, and especially his revelations about Bismarck's contacts with Lassalle, made a deep impression inside and outside the Reichstag.[86]

In spite of Bebel's fine speech, the Social Democrats with their nine seats would have little effect on the outcome of the deliberations. The Progressive,

Socialist, and Center parties would vote against the bill, and the two conservative parties would vote for it, leaving the decision once again in the hands of the weakened but still significant National Liberal party. Bamberger gave the party's position on the proposal. His opening remark that the bill shoud be referred to a committee of twenty-one was taken as an indication that the National Liberals were willing to cooperate in working out an acceptable law. The remainder of his speech was replete with qualifications and equivocations, as he was in the uncomfortable position of seeming to advocate something that he fundamentally disliked. He gave the impression at one moment that he would never accept the bill and at another that he had convinced himself of the bill's political necessity.

The deputy from Bingen-Alzey admitted that there had been no massive eruption in Germany as in France in 1848 and 1871 and that the government was unable to prove a direct connection between the two would-be assassins and the Social Democrats. However, there still existed a danger in Germany, and the government was determined to do before the catastrophe what other governments had been forced to do after one.[87]

The National Liberal leader still had to admit that the government was trying to regulate an intellectual movement, and it faced a difficult problem in determing when words become a threat to the state. He refused to accept the charge, however, that the bill represented an exceptional law directed against the Social Democrats, even if the government's statements might have contributed to this erroneous conclusion. The words "Social Democracy" did appear in the bill, but this in no way meant that a definite group of people would be subject to its provisions. To Bamberger it was obvious that instead of a special law against certain people one had an "impartial exceptional law" which would limit the freedom of all persons. For this reason, he went on, one had to make sure that the law did not cut too deeply into everyone's civil liberties. In other words, what did the government really mean by the movements designated in article 1? And here Bamberger got to the major point of his speech. He was happy to see the word "socialistic" mentioned in article 1 and regarded it as indispensable. He did not view it as merely another term for Social Democracy but as the real source of the present danger. Anyone who believed that questions of production, distribution, and consumption of goods could be determined by legislation was on the inclined plane from socialism to Social Democracy. As long as one thought that social problems could be solved by the state, one fed the socialistic stream.[88] Realizing that he was casting his net wide, Bamberger noted the difficulty of suppressing these other manifestations of socialism, but it was precisely these respectable socialists whose writings stirred one part of the population against the other. The law must work as a warning to those who had wittingly or unwittingly contributed to the spread of socialistic teachings in Germany. A definition must be found which forbade this most characteristic trait of inciting one class of the population against the other because of property relations, "and then just those writings of the kind which I have described to you [Catholic and conservative] will also fall under the law." Bamberger also wanted certain "guarantees," such as a time limit, written into the bill and wanted the right of appeal made more effective.[89]

Bamberger's speech signaled the intention of the National Liberals to work with the government to bring forth a law but left some doubt about the details of the compromise. Albert Hänel, the Progressive party's spokesman, confessed that in the final analysis he simply could not tell what Bamberger "really wanted." He considered extremely dangerous the National Liberal's desire to include "socialistic" activities within the scope of the bill, pointing to the dangers this might contain for scholarly research.[90] Bamberger acted surprised that Hänel had misconstrued the "most important point" of his speech and claimed that his goal was just the opposite of that outlined by Hänel. Since one could draw no line between the Social Democratic and the merely socialistic, the latter term must appear in the bill, but "since I do not want to oppose scholarly and serious intellectual efforts I must search for other criteria in which one can discover liability for punishment." These other criteria remained unstated.[91]

The bill was sent to a commission of twenty-one which contained seven National Liberals and was chaired by Bennigsen. The lack of unity within the party was evident. With Lasker leading the attack in the commission, an effort was made to modify the bill according to the points raised in Bamberger's speech, and initially things went well. In the article forbidding associations, meetings, and printed matter which served to "undermine" the existing state and social order, the term "overthrow" was substituted for "undermine." Lasker also succeeded in limiting the bill's duration to thirty months and in modifying the Federal Council's role as the only court of appeal. The council would now contribute only four of nine members to an independent commission, the others being judges. The provision requiring prior approval of the police for meetings in case public order was declared to be threatened was removed for Reichstag or state election meetings. Under similar conditions threatening public order, no one could now be expelled from his place of residence. A report regarding the execution of either of these two measures had to be presented to the Reichstag.[92]

As Lasker was able to register a number of successes, Bismarck began to believe that the deputy wished to make the entire bill unworkable. Once again he mounted a press campaign against Lasker and the National Liberals, threatening a dissolution and new elections. The message reached Bennigsen and caused him to "mediate" with Bismarck, which meant that the majority of the National Liberal members of the commission deserted Lasker and that several changes made in commission would be eliminated in the second reading.[93]

The second reading was bitter and long, but it was marked by Bismarck's apparent pleasure at the new tractability of the National Liberals. His call to them to unite with the conservative parties behind the Bismarckian banner found a sympathetic echo in Bennigsen's speech.[94] On this basis the bill was to move forward toward adoption. Lasker and his supporters were left with little but recriminations.[95]

Bamberger participated only once in the debates of the second and third readings, in the debate concerning article 6, which he seemed to regard as the heart of the bill. It aimed to forbid printed matter in which Social Democratic, socialistic, or communistic efforts directed at the overthrow of the existing state or social order were represented in a way that endangered public peace. The Center party leader and future German chancellor, Baron Georg von Hertling, had attacked the article as an attempt to censor printed matter. In particular he stressed the implications of Bamberger's speech on September 16, in which the latter cited as socialistic the belief in the use of legislation to effect a transformation in the "organic development of social and . . . economic life." The Catholic deputy claimed that this would lead to "the absolute rule of the Manchester theory."[96]

That this was Bamberger's purpose was soon apparent as he made an eloquent plea for censorship of the press and attempted to justify his acceptance of the law. He conceded that the regulation of the press was "uncivilized," but "the press is so prominent, one could almost say . . . so exclusively the lever by which any confusion is brought into and spread in the world that not to work out a regulation . . . of the press is the same as renouncing from the start any effectiveness for the law. We are making a law which limits and endangers the general freedom of the press, of association, and of assembly," he admitted. "In it lies the justification for the great reproach which we make to the Social Democrats: that they drive us toward reaction, that they ruin our legislation." Rather than supporting a reactionary measure, Bamberger went on, he and his colleagues were upholding a measure designed to forestall a major reaction in the future.

The acceptance of the law signifies: We find that a danger for the empire is present in the excesses and transgressions of Social Democracy. The rejection of this bill would mean the denial of this danger and . . . I do not know how I, without nullifying all of my thoughts and actions, could reject this law and with it permit the conclusion: No, it is not true that Social Democracy is a danger for the empire.[97]

However, as Bamberger continued, it became evident that for him there was no dividing between Social Democracy and socialism and that the law was a weapon to be used against all those who in one way or another abetted the socialistic heresy. Whoever presents socialistic teachings as something permissible "lapses into the Social Democratic tendency of necessity."[98] He asserted that he was not advocating censorship of teaching. "I repeat: no limitation on freedom of teaching, complete respect for free movement of German scholarship, but . . . the government has let these things go in such a way for a number of years that if it had not been so tolerant or indifferent, things would not have come to such a pass." The close connection between government and university would have sufficed to stifle any socialistic propaganda.[99] Bamberger convinced himself of the necessity of the law in the hope of seeing the "allies" of the Social Democrats struck into silence and in the belief that the law would be used against "right-wing socialists."

The final vote on the bill took place on Saturday, October 19, at about quarter past two. The outcome was not in doubt, and no National Liberals defected. Bamberger, Lasker (almost against his better judgment), and Stauffenberg all voted for it, contributing to the 221 favorable votes versus 149 opposed.[100] The law that Johannes Miquel supposedly called "the most infamous law, a law which has set us back thirty years," the measure which Johannes Ziekursch said signified the end of the liberal era in Germany, was set on its twelve-year course.[101]

Although he had made two long speeches during the debates, Bamberger accepted an invitation to speak before a charitable organization in Leipzig because, as he stated, there were still some things that had not been said during the long deliberations.[102] Whether things worked out as he hoped would depend on the interpretation given the law. Would it be used as a club against the Social Democrats or as a sign that the nation had awakened to the falseness of "socialistic project-making." Only the latter gave it lasting worth. He even acknowledged that he was indirectly striking against freedom of teaching but defended himself by claiming: "I do not say that the state should urge teachers to think otherwise but . . . they must become clear about their relationship to the state, on whose side they stand, because the state has declared war on Social Democracy. . . . If the Socialistic [scholars] are right, the Social Democrats cannot be completely wrong. . . . If one agrees with the law, he must free himself from socialistic ideas."[103]

If Bamberger's main reason for accepting the Antisocialist Law was the belief that it would serve, not as a stick to beat the Social Democrats into submission, but as a warning to the nation to turn away from error, he must have been sadly disappointed. It soon became apparent that the minister of the interior intended to interpret the law so harshly that scarcely any part of the Social Democratic apparatus would escape persecution. The legal niceties that the National Liberals inserted into the law had no apparent effect in preventing the government from striking swiftly and devastatingly against the Social Democratic organization. Of their political newspapers, only two escaped suppression by changing their names and declaring themselves politically neutral. Other scholarly and popular periodicals were suppressed, as were the unions' welfare funds. In the first month 153 associations, 40 periodicals, and 135 nonperiodical publications were silenced. By June 1879 the numbers increased to 217, 127, and 278, respectively; and by October 1879, to 244, 184, and 307. Immediately upon publication of the law the Prussian government declared a state of seige in Berlin and expelled sixty-seven Social Democrats. Bismarck even had Social Democratic Reichstag deputies arrested. Bamberger, who assiduously read the daily press, must have realized that the law would not be anything but a means to eliminate Social Democracy in Germany.[104]

However, when Bismarck introduced a bill in March 1880 to renew the law for five years, only Lasker, who had just left the National Liberal party, recognized publicly the failure of his expectations and drew the necessary conclusions. In a speech depicting the misuses to which the law had been put, he announced his opposition to an extension. But he was virtually alone as the National Liberals, including Bamberger, voted to extend the measure for three and one-half years.[105] The reason is perhaps to be found in the growing crisis within the National Liberal party.

·7·
𝔓rotectibe 𝔗ariffß and 𝔖eceßßion

The National Liberal party had thus far survived the crisis situations that had become almost the norm within its ranks. But beginning in 1878 with the Antisocialist Law, and continuing with the struggle over Bismarck's new financial plans and the dismantling of the *Kulturkampf*, the party stumbled toward dissolution. During the election campaign of 1878, Bamberger wrote an essay on the current political scene which he decided not to have published. He came across it five years later, decided that it might still be relevant, and had it printed unchanged in the *Deutsche Rundschau*.[1] Bamberger tried to explain recent developments and suggest their significance for the future. What was most important to him was the growing discord between Bismarck and the National Liberals, which was inevitable once the National Liberals were considered to be something other than the "engine of the master." He traced the change, beginning with Delbrück's dismissal, through the Bennigsen negotiations, Camphausen's resignation, and the Deputation Law, that made certain Bismarck would have no equals but only underlings in the government. The business slump, induced partly by international difficulties, also gave Bismarck an excellent opportunity to cut his ties to the liberals. By 1877–78 it was time for Bismarck's new program to begin to emerge. The plans, Bamberger wrote, were known only in outline, but "they are enormous." However, there was still liberal opposition in parliament, making it necessary to find a new means to force the liberals to the wall. This was provided by the assassination attempts. The Social Democratic excesses, he feared, would be a welcome excuse to overcome liberal parliamentarianism. "One must inject the dangerous material of freedom in the concentrated form of Social Democracy into the body politic in order to get rid of the sickness of middle-class liberalism." Bamberger did not foresee a change in the democratic base of the empire, that is, universal manhood suffrage, but the executive would be strengthened and parliament weakened. Without the liberals parliament "must lead a very feeble existence," even if parliamen-

130

tarianism in Germany had never led anything "but a mock existence." What would the liberals do? "When the liberals see this coming they will accommodate themselves to it." They could not maintain completely their present position, but by concessions they could carry forward a part of their program. Even Bismarck realized he could not have it all his own way. The chancellor, according to Bamberger, was a practical statesman who wanted to bind part of the middle class to his new program. The future looked like this: a concentrated state power borne by popular institutions to the favor of the lower class, with lucrative indirect taxes which indeed "hit the lower classes but are not felt by them," a well-apportioned protective tariff, and everything secured through a "firmly disciplined military force." "To western industry as to the eastern latifundia the dark proposals which the prince carries in his head must appear as the sure promise of redeeming acts."[2]

Indeed they did. Bismarck took major steps in carrying through his new economic program on November 12 and December 15, 1878. On November 12 he instructed the Federal Council to establish a commission to draw up a new tariff schedule, and on December 15, in a letter to the council, he laid down the guiding principles for the revision of the tariff. It was clear that 1879 would be the year of the tariff.

It should not be surprising that commercial policy provided the occasion for a titanic political struggle that sharply altered the German political scene. Since at least the 1850s, if not earlier, commercial questions had been regarded as preeminently political matters that had ramifications far beyond whether a particular duty should be fifty pfennigs or one mark. Besides affecting the economic interests of important social and political groups, commercial questions were also at the center of negotiations between Austria and Prussia during the 1850s and 1860s. It has been argued that Prussia's dominant position in Germany was due to her success in fending off Austria's attempts to join the Customs Union. The device which Prussia used during these two decades was to move in the direction of free trade.[3] Free trade became the dominant element in Prussian and later German commercial policy between 1850 and 1875. It was in accord with the political aims of the Prussian government as well as the economic goals of Prussian agriculture and large elements of the German middle class. It formed the basis for a community of interest between otherwise disparate groups which continued even during the Prussian constitutional conflict of the early 1860s. As Werner Schunke points out, to be a free trader was to be considered an agent of Prussia.[4]

Free-trade interests in Germany were organized most effectively in the Congress of German Economists, which was established in September 1858 through the efforts of Viktor Böhmert and Otto Michaelis. Although not originally designed to be a free-trade organization, it was gradually taken over by elements who favored free trade. Its aim was the "dispersion of correct economic principles and views and their introduction into daily practical life on the basis of full economic liberty of the individual as well as the nations." Its membership in the 1860s was composed of lawyers, publicists, merchants, government officials, chambers of commerce, banking houses, insurance firms, and a small number of manufacturers interested in export. The relatively small number of the latter has been cited as a weakness. The free-trade movement used the same arguments as its counterparts in England, but it could not appeal to the same export-oriented industrial groups. Instead it was more of an intellectual or journalistic movement.[5]

The Congress of German Economists was at the height of its at best modest influence from 1867–76. Besides its propagandistic activities, one of its members, Michaelis, was appointed to the federal chancellor's office, where he worked closely with the already convinced free-trade advocate Rudolf von Delbrück. Moreover, several members of parliament, including Ludwig Bamberger, were members of the organization.[6] Bamberger joined the Congress of German Economists in 1869 and was quickly coopted to its standing committee. What attracted him to the organization was not only its advocacy of free trade but also its support for a laissez-faire economic policy and a rejection of state interference in economic matters. Bamberger was a convinced proponent of Adam Smith, and the word "individualism" sums up his political, social, and economic outlook. It is a thread running through his entire life and all his activities. His views on noninterference and individualism, although first formed while he was a student at Heidelberg, received their strongest imprint from the French writer Frédéric Bastiat in his *Sophismes économiques*. Even in old age, and aware that Bastiat's reputation had sharply declined under the impact of scholarly research, Bamberger could not hide his fondness for the Frenchman's works.[7] Bamberger's triumph over adversity in exile (although considerably aided by a sympathetic and well-to-do family) and his years in a privately owned bank where personal decisions affected the investment of large sums of money could not but strengthen his individualism. His one experience working for the government, when he edited a government newspaper in Alsace, was enough to convince him of the evils of bureaucracy. Bureaucrats, he complained, did not know how to differentiate between a subordinate clerk and an independent man who offered his services.[8]

Because the movement of individual life was so "manifold and tortured," it was impossible to determine whether one was hurt or harmed by a measure. Thus the role of legislation was to lay down only the broadest guidelines. "Within these guidelines, the individual determines himself. A state cannot go from interest group to interest group."[9] His emphasis on individual activity made him hostile to corporations. Here, as he put it, he was a "monarchist." He wanted a business where a "man stands on his own" and cannot hide behind a collective entity like a board of directors.[10] The idolization of individualism also meant that he valued very highly the "importance of the geniuslike personality." "No sentence is falser than that there are no irreplaceable persons," he wrote.[11] Whether this attitude smoothed the way for his acceptance of Bismarck is difficult to say, but it did lead him to bemoan the fact that Karl Twesten had died prematurely. He wondered what would have happened if Twesten had lived and taken Lasker's place as the counterpoise to Bennigsen.[12] With such a pronounced view of the primary role of unrestricted individual activity and a deep hostility to government intervention, Bamberger very quickly and easily found himself in the free-trade camp on his return to the German political arena.

His activity in the Customs Parliament immediately placed him in the midst of commercial questions, as a major struggle developed over a new tariff program which was a moderate step in the direction of free trade. To make up for a loss in revenue the government proposed new taxes on petroleum, mineral oil, and tobacco. This initiated a quarrel extending over the life of the Customs Parliament. Not until the third try in 1870, and only after the government dropped its request for a petroleum tax, did the Customs Parliament approve the tariff bill.[13] Bamberger opposed the petroleum tax on the grounds that it was illogical to eliminate one tax only to replace it with another. But more important was his belief that the petroleum levy was too heavy a burden on a necessity of life for the lower classes. His basic dislike for all indirect taxes, whether on imported or domestic goods, came to the surface with this issue. He believed that they all penalized the lower classes even if the pain was not as intense as with direct taxes which had to be paid all at once. This issue brought forth one of Bamberger's few concrete proposals to help the lower class and might have been the reason he was invited to the Eisenach conference on the social question. He told his colleagues that he favored replacing the funds lost in the reduction of the iron and rice tariffs by levying an estate tax on the well-to-do. "I believe that the system of direct taxes on the estates of the well-to-do is not yet sufficiently utilized. . . . The well-to-do classes are not . . . taxed enough by us, [especially since] they have recieved so many advantages from the progress of the economy brought about by new developments in Germany."[14] Besides the social ramifications of a petroleum tax, there were also political consequences, and for the National Liberals these were most important. They were reluctant to grant the government a permanently lucrative source of income which could make it more independent of the legislature.[15]

The major loss of income due to its tariff reform program came from a reduction of the tax on iron products and pig iron. From 1868 until 1877, iron duties were more controversial than any other. The government did not intend to introduce free trade in iron products, but it was forced to go further than originally desired in order to placate parliament. In 1870 the duty on pig iron was reduced by two-thirds, with corresponding reductions for iron products. Bamberger had advocated the immediate elimination of all iron duties to ease the burden on consumers. Delay would also introduce an element of uncertainty among the iron manufacturers. Humanity, according to Bamberger, demanded the immediate abolition of the iron duties for the same reason that a criminal sentenced to death should be immediately executed.[16] He nevertheless applauded the tariff law of 1870.

The success of the free traders only spurred them on to demand further reduction of the iron tariffs. They were aided by the indemnity from the Franco-German war, which reduced the effectiveness of the government's claim that the iron tariffs were needed for revenue. Strong support for a reduction of the iron duties came from agricultural groups in northeastern Germany who wished to purchase farm machinery at the cheapest price to replace a declining labor force.[17]

The government responded to the pressure from liberal and conservative groups by introducing a tariff reform bill on June 20, 1873, which was highlighted by the elimination of the duty on pig iron and most iron products, particularly farm machinery. So strong was free-trade sentiment within the Reichstag that the iron interests could only delay the inevitable for a few years. Johannes Miquel and Friedrich Hammacher, both allied with the iron industry, proposed a compromise which contained the immediate elimination of the duties on pig iron but put off until January 1, 1877, the abolition of duties on other iron products. Even the staunchest supporters of the iron industry, Karl Ferdinand von Stumm and Wilhelm von Kardorff, accepted it, although with heavy hearts.[18]

The opposition to the compromise came from the extreme free traders, among whom was Bamberger, who would accept nothing less than the immediate abolition of all iron duties. He pointed to the current prosperity of the iron industry and suggested that its previous complaints that tariff reductions would ruin it had not been borne out. Thus one should not give credence to its present prophecies. Delaying the end of iron duties would only give the iron producers an opportunity to organize a protectionist movement.[19]

Bamberger's prediction was not far wrong, but before the iron producers and other economic interest groups could organize a protectionist movement to counter various free-trade organizations, they were aided by the crash of

1873 and the ensuing economic depression. The so-called great depression lasted until the mid-1890s, and it tended to discredit the basic economic, social, and even political tenets of nineteenth-century liberalism. As the previous two decades of prosperity were regarded as a confirmation of the correctness of free competition and nonintervention, the subsequent recession years were taken as a sign that liberalism had outlived its usefulness. The effect of the depression was compounded further by the relative weakness of liberal forces in central Europe compared to their counterparts in western Europe. The depression thus provided the backdrop for a turning away from a policy of laissez faire to one of increasing state involvement in economic and social questions. This was a development that German liberals, particularly those around Bamberger, found difficult to accept. Liberal policies were still viewed as the wave of the future, and to see them called into question before they had triumphed gave a tone of impatience and rigidity to liberal arguments. Believing that the enemies of liberalism were using an international and "normal" economic downturn to reorient Germany's economic and social policies, the left liberals were inclined to see every legislative battle as Armageddon. The depression was not uniquely German but extended to most western and central European countries, as well as the United States. However, it hit Germany with dramatic suddenness toward the end of 1873 with a stock market collapse, and by early 1874 its effect on industry was felt. Over sixty banks and one hundred industrial firms had to be liquidated. According to Ivo Lambi, "the economic crisis which broke out in 1873 was the basic cause for the reversal of German tariff policy."[20]

One of the industries that claimed to be most affected by the economic downturn was iron. The industry had been blessed by a series of good years as it cashed in on the booming German economy. Demand and prices were high, and spurred by the conversion to the Bessemer process, production rose 93 percent from 1865 to 1874.[21] Beginning in 1874 the situation changed for the worse, although not as severely as the iron interests claimed. Iron production still increased about 15 percent from 1872 to 1878, and iron products began to find foreign markets. Germany for the first time began to enjoy a favorable balance of trade in primary and semimanufactured iron and steel products as imports generally decreased. The difficulty was that the rise in exports could not make up for the dampened internal demand. Consumption of iron fell by 30 percent between 1873 and 1879, and the price dropped 50 to 60 percent in that period. This classic case of overextension and overproduction put many iron and steel companies in the red and led to the discharge of workers and reduction of wages.[22]

Although the depression of the mid-1870s extended far beyond the iron industry, it was the iron industry that took the lead in organizing a protectionist movement. It was helped by a variety of factors. In its broadest sense the economic crisis could be seen as a crisis of liberal economic beliefs since at least in Germany, it had followed in the wake of a number of liberal reforms. Various writers representing different social and economic beliefs led an onslaught against the idea of laissez faire in general and free trade in particular. Conservatives who were upset by the liberalization of Germany, Catholics who were concerned by the social question, Socialists of the Chair who believed that laissez-faire ideas were not suited to problems of the modern world, and anti-Semites who denounced the "judaization" of Germany called for an end to the liberal era or an increased role for the state in economic and social affairs. Other writers began to develop an alternative philosophy to free trade, fastening on the writings of Henry C. Carey, who argued that protection of industry was in the interests of both industry and agriculture and advocated a moderate policy of autarky by curtailing imports and exports. His ideas were popularized by the Free Conservative leader and iron producer, Wilhelm von Kardorff, in *Gegen den Strom (Against the Current)*, which even Bamberger found impressive if not convincing.[23]

But in spite of a possible change in the public mind, more credit for the success of the industrial protectionists is due to their organizational and propagandistic work, led by the iron interests. They at first demanded a postponement of the removal of the iron duties beyond January 1, 1877, and when opposition from free-trade groups made this seem unachievable, the iron interests began to seek allies in other industries. They were also able to foster a belief in the crisis condition of their branch of industry and to convince key individuals that the health of the iron industry was the key to the health of the German economy. The major pressure group was the Central Association of German Industrialists, which was organized on January 19, 1876, and headed by Wilhelm von Kardorff. The key figure, however, was Henry A. Bueck, who was also associated with the Union of German Iron and Steel Manufacturers and the Union for the Promotion of the Common Economic Interests of Rhineland-Westphalia (or Longname Association). The Central Association comprised, besides iron groups, cotton spinners, soda manufacturers, sugar interests, and hat and leather producers. It carried on an extensive program of public enlightenment including press releases, lectures, and petitions. It established its own newspaper, the *Deutsche Börsen- und Handelszeitung*, and made several attempts to penetrate traditionally free trade–oriented organizations like the Congress of German Economists and the German Chamber of Commerce. Starting with a demand to maintain the status quo of 1873, the association developed more far-reaching aims which called for the introduction of new tariffs and the raising of old ones.[24]

In spite of their intensive agitation, the gains of the protectionists up to

1878 were meager. In December 1875, on the occasion of a debate over petitions from the Union of German Iron and Steel Manufacturers to retain the duties on iron, the oratory grew more intense as the proponents of protection made dire predictions about the future, and the opponents replied in an uncompromising way. Bamberger's attitude in 1875 set the tone for the free traders and was an omen for the future. He admitted that the German economy was in a recession but that still the great outcry was only partly justified. The prosperity of 1871–72 had been artificial, and one could not expect those golden years to continue. Once conditions had changed and the feverish demand diminished, protective tariffs were sought to keep prices high. "Gentlemen, that is also socialism," he tried to convince his listeners, and he warned them that tariffs on iron products and textiles threatened the agricultural population whose interests he represented.[25] In the Reichstag his language was harsher. He claimed that his warning of 1873 was coming true and attacked the iron industry for bringing its private interests into the highest tribunal of the land. His heart only hardened when he heard their laments, for he mistrusted people who publicly exposed their wounds while begging for alms. Tariffs were merely a state subvention which if granted should be given to the workers rather than the employers. The old Listian argument that tariffs help infant industries, he went on, did not apply to the iron industry, which was in fact too big and overextended. Too much of the French indemnity had found its way to that industry. Furthermore, it was not the only industry in difficult circumstances and should not be singled out for preferential treatment. But the major danger he saw in the protectionist agitation went far beyond the question of tariffs. After the great exertion in forming the German Empire, a slight relapse occurred, and people were beginning to think about their individual interests rather than the common good. First one asked whether "one could not alter something of the freedom of movement, another tries it with freedom of business operations, the third with freedom of trade, another tries it with other freedoms."[26] Protectionist agitation in Bamberger's eyes was part of a broader onslaught against the liberal foundations of the German state, and for this reason one had to attack protectionism in so uncompromising a fashion. As early as 1870 he had advocated free trade because it "leads to progress, to peace, and to freedom." Where protection led was self-evident.[27]

The debate proved inconclusive, but it was an indication of the strenuous efforts being made on behalf of protection. The initiative in this question was passing out of the hands of the free traders, who were now merely trying to defend the status quo, while the protectionists had the momentum of change on their side.

The apparent success of the free traders in 1875 did not prove decisive, and Bamberger was not fooled into thinking that it was the last battle. As he predicted to Oppenheim: "In any case with the protectionists we are going to have a major go-around this time, and I am not as calm about the outcome as the last time. Hoffman [Delbrücks's successor] will probably prefer to adopt the new course, but it depends on which strings Bismarck thinks it proper to pull."[28] Which strings Bismarck was going to grasp would not become clear for some two years. However, by the end of 1876 protectionist pressure was growing. The Russian government had recently required gold as the means of paying its tariffs, which had the effect of raising them. At the same time, the Center party introduced a motion to extend the iron duties for two years, until January 1, 1879. Moreover, the government was proving itself partially receptive to demands for help from the iron interests, who focused their attacks on the export premiums *(titres d' acquit à caution)* that France granted to various industries, but particularly iron and sugar.[29] A bill prescribing retaliatory tariffs on a country's products aided by export premiums found its way to the Reichstag in December 1876, releasing anew the free trade–protectionist furor. Once again Bamberger made the major speech for the free traders. He showed that they had been stung by the protectionists' attempt to brand them as unrealistic and mere theorists much he had tried to label Lujo Brentano. He denied that all that stood in the way of the reintroduction of iron and steel duties was a group of theoreticians in the Reichstag who rode their hobbyhorse of free trade. He refused to admit that the iron industry was facing a crisis and traced the "momentary" dislocations to the threat of war in southeastern Europe. Although the matter was relatively insignificant, since France sent less than 1 percent of its iron production to Germany, Bamberger still regarded it as a major turning point in government policy. This was merely the opening wedge to strike at the real competitor, England, and for a full-fledged onslaught on free trade. The iron industry's arguments that free trade caused their difficulties and that tariffs would cure them, if accepted by the Reichstag, would be used by every other branch of industry. Furthermore, the government's bill asked for power for the Federal Council to decide when to impose the retaliatory tariffs. This Bamberger found entirely unacceptable.[30]

The free-trade majority once again had its way. It buried the government's bill in committee and rejected the Center party's, 201–116.[31] Nevertheless, the protectionist drive was incessant. On the occasion of the budget debate concerning tariffs and consumer taxes, Wilhelm von Kardorff once again used the opportunity to plead the case for iron. In a similar fashion, Bamberger was into the breach to defend the tenets of free trade, pointing out that depressed conditions existed everywhere, even in countries with relatively high tariffs, and calling on the protectionists to end their agitation.[32]

They did not, and a month later a new proposal was before the Reichstag, inspired by Kardorff and others, but supplemented and eventually replaced by a government proposal. In March, Kardorff proposed that the tariffs on iron products, which were eliminated on January 1, 1877, be restored. The government approved of Kardorff's bill but for the sake of appearances decided to introduce a virtually identical one of its own which provided for a tariff of fifteen marks per ton on those iron products deprived of their tariffs on January 1, 1877.[33] According to the government, the main purpose of the bill was to compensate German producers for unfair practices by other countries. While quick to deny that it was inaugurating a protectionist measure, the government maintained that it could not follow the "radical free traders" and remain indifferent to the actions of other countries.[34]

As one of the major speakers in both the first and second readings, Bamberger demonstrated little inclination to compromise on what he regarded as a matter of principle. He rejected the importance of the French export premiums. They were an integral element of the French tax system rather than something invented to harm the German iron industry. He also tried to show the inconsistency of the government's proposal by pointing out that certain iron products, such as machines which were specially favored by French export premiums, had been left out to placate Prussian agricultural interests. He denied that the "problem" of the iron industry was caused by legislation. Rather, he said, it was due to poor business practices or to worldwide factors that had little to do with tariffs. The problem, in Bamberger's picturesque language, was overeating which gave the iron industry indigestion. "Do you propose to stuff it in an artificial way? The sick stomach must be put on a diet." Ever willing to grasp the most convenient argument, he now tried to placate the conservatives, whom he thought might be enticed by tariffs if they could be seen as part of a political retrogression, by denying that the government's proposal involved political reaction. Rather it was a question of favoring certain segments of society, big industry, and capital, which would lead to the division of parliament according not to political views but to economic considerations. "Where an evil spirit could lead the German Empire, not to mention the German Reichstag, with the development of such a thought, I . . . will not enlarge upon today."[35]

There was no need to. The free traders still had the votes and were able to defeat the government's bill 211–111. The Centrist Burghard von Schorlemer-Alst talked of Pyrrhic victory by the free traders, and indeed it was their last major triumph.[36] Perhaps, as Lambi claims, the main difficulty of the free traders was their inability to adjust to a new situation. Their aggressive tactics were formed at a time when free-trade beliefs were in the ascendancy, and they were unable to develop a new approach. They refused to compromise and thus gained a reputation for being unrealistic and dogmatic. It is possible that had the free traders been willing to reach some accommodation with the iron interests they would have forestalled the later alliance between industry and agriculture. However, Bamberger and others believed that one concession to industry would merely encourage other demands. "Do not be led astray by the thought that the reintroduced iron duties would have saved us from the economic reaction," he wrote to Stauffenberg, "*L'appétit vient en mangeant.*"[37] Moreover, even as late as May 1878, Bamberger could not believe that tariffs on grain were possible. "I am convinced that no German Reichstag and no German government which thinks seriously about it will turn out to decide on grain tariffs." Nevertheless, he acknowledged that a tariff on grain could be the purchase price for industrial tariffs. This extra inducement was necessary since the first "offer" of the free importation of agricultural machinery was insufficient. In spite of his certainty he tried to convince the agricultural forces thay they were being offered a mere decoy that would only ensnare them to accept industrial tariffs. A bad grain harvest would result in the removal of any grain tariffs, leaving only the industrial duties. Thus agricultural tariffs were a mistake.[38]

Bamberger had glimpsed the future but refused to believe his eyes. Alone, the iron or even the industrial interest would not have been strong enough to win over the Reichstag to industrial duties. Two additional factors were required: a threat to German agriculture which led to its turning away from free trade, and Bismarck's conversion to protection. There was always something politically anomalous in the alliance of liberal commercial groups with conservative agricultural elements around a policy of free trade, and neither side was entirely comfortable about it. The conservatives had been shunted to the sidelines during the early 1870s. Only after they were convinced that there was no future in incurring Bismarck's enmity did the German Conservative party revive at the polls, doubling its votes between 1874 and 1878 and garnering fifty-nine seats in the latter year. The Conservatives had been avid free traders because their main supporters were in northeast Germany, and the leadership of the party came from the strongholds of large-scale agriculture. They produced for the national German market and were also able to export grain to England and Scandinavia. They did not fear competition for their German markets and were happy to be able to buy their farm machinery in the cheapest market. However, the situation for the large landowners became distinctly less favorable by the late 1870s. English and Scandinavian markets were increasingly lost to United States agricultural products. At the same time, the German market was under pressure from Russian and Austrian farm products. Thus the price of grain fell between 1876 and 1879, and the farmers did not believe they were compensated by the elimination of the iron duties. Against this background, proposals for cooperation with industry and opposition to the general aims of liberalism were to take on a new significance.[39]

But first it was necessary to organize. In 1876 the agrarian conservatives organized the Union of Tax and Economic Reformers, recognizing that "we live in an age of material interests." Initially the organization was not in favor of protection but demanded an end to direct taxes, wanted a tax on the stock exchange, and in general wished to strike at the "middlemen" whom it held responsible for its growing difficulties. By 1877 the group made a noticeable shift toward protection as its economic interests were directed to domestic rather than export needs. It demanded a tariff of 5 percent on grain products, which it called only a financial duty. Also in 1877 the agrarians began to cooperate with the industrial groups organized in the Central Association of German Industry. In the Reichstag, the friends of a change in the government's commercial policy organized the Free Economic Association, which was able to enroll 140 members from the two conservative parties, the Center, and even some from the National Liberal party. They proposed establishing a commission to investigate the state of German industry and agriculture. The bill was defeated, but the cooperation between the two economic groups continued, and a joint committee was established to forge a common economic policy.[40]

All that remained, as Bamberger remarked earlier, was for Bismarck to pull the strings. The chancellor was perhaps being modest when he said of the free traders: "It is remarkable how ... Richter and Bamberger always concern themselves in their speeches about me and not about the issue. The person is immaterial. 'How did I think previously? How did I come to it? I have permitted what I previously fought ... I am a geniuslike dilettante full of contradictions, always inclined to experiment haphazardly.' What is most important to the subject they speak of in passing."[41] The truth probably lies somewhere in between. Bismarck's views on commercial policy, as on most issues, were pragmatic and susceptible to various pressures. His aims were much broader than merely helping a few industries in distress. He recognized, as Helmut Böhme maintains, that a new "supporting pillar" for the Prusso-German state had been created by the emergence of big industry and high finance, and it was equally important as the agrarian one. With increasing industrialization this new force was bound to grow in significance. A conflict between these basic elements would usher in a crisis in the unreformed German state, unless it was avoided by the solidarity of agrarian and industrial interests. Thus it was not agricultural or industrial tariffs alone that moved Bismarck toward protection but rather the sociopolitical aim of uniting key productive forces behind the existing Prusso-German monarchy.[42]

A corollary of this view was the downgrading of the political function of the Reichstag. Rather than see political viewpoints represented in it, the chancellor wanted it transformed into an economic body openly representing various interest groups. His most biting scorn was reserved for those "scholars" without a business, who lived on "honoraria and coupons." Or as he wrote later: "If our parliamentary activity is to run parallel to the practical problems of our life, the consideration of material interests must be put more fully into the foreground than now." The "scholars without a business" were of course the free-trading and left wing of the National Liberal party around Bamberger and Lasker, which he hoped to detach from the healthy mass of the National Liberal party and transfer to the Progressive party.[43]

Besides diminishing the role of parliament and making the National Liberal party an ally on his own terms, Bismarck hoped that the move toward protection would help solve the financial problems of the empire by providing the central government with a secure source of revenue that once granted could almost never be rescinded. This would make the federal government independent both of the matricular contributions of the states and also of the Reichstag, whose already limited budgetary powers would be further reduced.

The move toward protection was slow, as Bismarck had foreseen. The outcome could not be predicted, and chance would play a role, giving him an opportunity to be quickly grasped. In 1876 he gave his assent to the proposal for retaliatory tariffs against France and in 1877 accepted the bill for the reintroduction of the iron tariffs. Negotiations for a commercial treaty with Austria-Hungary were spun out until they nearly broke down. Finally the old treaty was extended, but by an exchange of notes, by-passing the Reichstag. By the early part of 1878, Bismarck was ready to move more directly. Camphausen was forced out by February to be replaced by Arthur Hobrecht, who promised to make no difficulties for the chancellor's financial plans. Shortly thereafter, Heinrich von Achenbach, the Prussian commerce minister, was replaced by Albert von Maybach. In the Prussian cabinet on April 5, 1878, Bismarck raised the question of the restoration of the iron tariffs, and he included agricultural tariffs in his plan.[44]

The decisive event in the process was the near assassination of William I and the resulting election of 1878, which returned a protectionist majority to the Reichstag. Whereas in 1877 the Free Economic Association had only 140 members, the following year it had 204, a majority of the Reichstag. The core of the group came from the Center, 87 percent of whose members joined, while 69 percent of the Free Conservatives and 60 percent of the German

Conservatives were also members. The fourth largest element came from the National Liberal party, 30 percent of whose members subscribed to the petition. The statement of principle carefully avoided the term "protection" but mentioned the need to "harmonize the real and supposed controversies between interest groups" which "cannot be solved through the slogan of free trade and protection." On October 19 its chairman, Baron K. F. von Varnbüler, asked Bismarck to act on the tariff question. Bismarck needed little encouragement and requested the Federal Council to set up a commission to draw up the new tariff. On December 15 he outlined the reasons for revising the tariff schedule: Tariffs were designed to provide the federal government with a sufficient source of income. They would make possible a reduction of the direct tax burden. They would end the conflicts over tariffs between the various branches of production since all products entering the country would be equally affected; and all individuals, since they are both consumers and producers, would find the advantages and disadvantages evenly distributed. The new tariff policy would also improve economic conditions, increase wages and salaries, and, it was hoped, discourage the spread of Social Democracy.[45]

The ground was being laid for a major legislative battle affecting both Bamberger and the National Liberal party. Bismarck was indeed correct when he complained that Bamberger and his supporters tended to personalize issues around the chancellor and see him as the beginning and end of the question. Apparently not writing in jest, Bamberger complained that Bismarck was led to the idea of nationalizing the railroad system because a train he waited for was late. Similarly, Bismarck was said to oppose the demonetization of the thaler and its replacement by the five-mark piece because one could tip a thaler; now he would have to use the more valuable five-mark piece. Even the chancellor's social insurance program, which hurt the private insurance business, Bamberger traced to Bismarck's belief that private insurers were charging him excessive rates. And finally, in Bamberger's eyes Bismarck was led to protection because of the agrarian problem and in particular because Bismarck owned forests which were to be protected.[46] Personal or not, this was the issue that dissolved a ten-year relationship and made the two men increasingly bitter antagonists.[47]

It also led to a renewed crisis within the National Liberal party. Only with extreme difficulty had the party united behind the Antisocialist Law, and the left wing had been upset by what it considered Bennigsen's too accommodating attitude toward Bismarck. At the same time, party opposition to Bamberger and Lasker became obvious in February 1879, when they were reelected by unimpressive majorities to the executive committee.[48] The National Liberals were divided on the issue of tariffs, and nearly 30 percent of the party associated themselves with the Free Economic Association. The party's election manifesto in June 1878 pointedly stated that tariff questions had never formed a part of the party's program, and it admitted that there were differences of opinion.[49] On New Year's Eve, 1878, several National Liberal leaders—Robert von Benda, Rickert, Bamberger, Lasker, and Forcken-beck—met to plot strategy. They agreed on a minimum program of opposition to Bismarck's "reckless" domestic policy, no new financial burdens but at most a substitute for the matricular contributions, and no tariffs on the necessities of life.[50] Nevertheless, it was difficult to find broad support for this proposal, and it became impossible to keep the tariff question from becoming a divisive issue within the party.[51]

The protectionist element was centered around Schauss, Völk, and Miquel, all of whom favored industrial tariffs. Miquel, the mayor of Osnabrück, advised Bennigsen to accept the industrial tariffs but to try to isolate the agrarians. To carry out this compromise policy, he went on, it would be necessary to restrain the uncompromising free traders.[52] Unfortunately the free-trade proponents were in no mood to be accommodating. "Won't pure opposition become an obligation?" Forckenbeck asked. He suggested collecting signatures against the intended tariff program and announced that although he wanted to march with Miquel and Bennigsen, he would also go without them. He would not swim with the reactionary current.[53]

Neither would Bamberger. As early as October he wrote his mother: "The end of the antisocialistic and the beginning of the antiprotectionist campaigns join hands, and I am right in the middle."[54] By November, as the government's intentions became known, Bamberger's reaction was predictable and firm. "The violence of the quarrel over commercial policy . . . will erupt in full force in the next Reichstag. . . . The business is all the more thankless as growing stupidity and corruption make a victory very improbable. However, now I am right in it and can no longer climb out. And if I am convinced of the importance and goodness . . . of any cause, it is this one. It is a true question of civilization."[55] In spite of his determination he was highly pessimistic. "I am still not made to be a loyal subject," he wrote three weeks later. "When I wade through the present-day flow of saliva of loyalty, I think with longing of those countries which are delivered from such kind. . . . Germany is now strongly in a political and spiritual retrogression, and it is not joyful to behold. But I say to myself: if one has enjoyed the good times, one must also live through the bad ones. . . . I have also limited my field of battle to commercial policy, and it is some consolation that in other countries, including France, it is much worse than with us."[56] To Karl Hillebrand, he wrote the same story: "We now get the dregs of B[ismarck]'s personality which marries itself to the slime of the population. . . . The barbarian genius becomes ever more visible. My suppressed manuscript[57] predicted all of this. What you fight in the school is already enthroned by the state: ignorance, bungling, quackery."[58] And to Oppenheim he could scarcely restrain himself: "Bismarck will get everything. biennium [biennial budgets], railroad [nationalization], [anti]Socialist Law and state disability funds. . . . If the Margaretenstrasse [Bamberger's residence] which I view as my intimate fatherland, is run through to the Potsdam railway station I do not yet know if I will not move to Vaduz."[59]

Besides expressing these private sentiments, Bamberger led the publicistic attack on the chancellor's program. On January 11 he delivered a major speech to the Economic Society of Berlin and shortly thereafter he published many of the same ideas in a statement to his constituents.[60] He called Bismarck's protectionist proposal an anachronism which ignored the growing economic interdependency of the last two decades. He refused to admit that there was any general economic misery,[61] but according to the unreconstructed individualist, the people who were crying the loudest were "those who have managed worst. The more one understands how to run a business, the more he knows that he is on his own; the less one is up to the problems of a business, the more he demands that others help him." He ridiculed the idea that by some magical means foreign countries would be forced to pay the bill for the tariffs. This mistook the "natural elements of price formation," just like unions who demanded that employers should pay as much in bad times as good. Such a "genuinely socialistic" proposal would never work. One should not be fooled by the claim that the system favored domestic production. "Who is production?" he asked. "It is not a person. Production is an abstract conception which neither eats, nor drinks, nor pays taxes, nor serves in the army. Her name sounds rather like a pagan deity, and everyone has to lay a penny at her altar. The priests who take the offerings are firstly the sellers. Behind production stand the property owners." A few sellers were favored at the expense of the mass of buyers. "In other words, the many are working for the few when they pay more than they have to." And the priests who garnered the tribute were the great bankers, large stock companies, the iron lords and textile bosses, and the owners of large estates. It was easy to demonstrate that his constituents, mostly small farmers who had at best a local market, would profit little from a tariff that would be more than offset by more expensive bread, wood, and leather and industrial goods. But most of all, "the protective tariff would drain the marrow of the nation and undermine the morale of the country."[62]

The tariff question was a crucial struggle for Bamberger since it seemed to determine the course of the German Empire, and he poured into it all his energies. As he wrote to his mother: "For many years I have not been so overloaded with work." It was strange, he continued, how the public came to identify him with the question of free trade, as they had to a lesser extent with the socialist question. For a politician, this would be good if it were not for the "sterility" of German politics, "which strongly reduces the joy of participation. It is a hard, barren soil on which 90 percent of the seeds are ruined. Now the turn of fate wills it that I come to hefty blows with Bismarck."[63]

The confrontation with Bismarck was not long in coming. Even before the tariff bill was presented to the Reichstag, the preliminary skirmishing began. The speech from the throne spoke disparagingly of Germany's tariff policy since 1865, and the free traders replied in the debate over the commercial treaty with Austria-Hungary. It had been negotiated over a two-year period and when finally initialed would last only one year, presumably to avoid binding the government's hands as it worked out a new tariff schedule. The debate was begun mildly enough by Rudolf von Delbrück, now a deputy, but was heated up by Eugen Richter, who used the occasion to launch a general attack on Bismarck's new tariff departure. Bismarck replied that there would be a far-reaching struggle of economic interests, pitting the free traders and the coastal cities against industry and agriculture. "That is completely unavoidable. . . . The battle will occupy us for years."[64]

Bamberger roamed beyond the Austro-Hungarian treaty in his speech. As an opponent of government intervention, he criticized the reference in William I's speech about aiding employment. "The purpose of the protective tariff is not to bring forth certain products but to cause specific work. It does not ask what or how much or how usefully something is produced but how many arms are set in motion. . . . That is the quintessence of the protective tariff." But the bulk of his speech was directed at Bismarck, who was in attendance. He stressed his past loyalty and that of his party, expressed astonishment at the chancellor's statement that he had been unhappy about Germany's tariff policy for some time, quoted from Bismarck's speeches to demonstrate that he had apparently changed his mind suddenly, and still made clear his deep respect for the chancellor. But he warned his listeners that Germany could not be saved in economic matters by his "genius." Even a genius could not feed, clothe, and house the inhabitants of a large city. "Economic conditions lie in the freedom of people themselves, in their own activity; they cannot be determined by political combinations, and just that has made us so alarmed by the policy which the chancellor has inaugurated."[65]

This first relatively mild salvo was repeated during the debate on the budget. Each of its three readings took on the appearance of a tariff debate, and each time Bamberger was in the forefront. His speeches centered on an attack on the investigating commissions set up in July 1878 to gather material for a possible revision of the tariff system. Bamberger as well as others attempted to discredit the commissions as partisan bodies. It was not too difficult to do. The commissions to a large degree were stacked with friends of protection, and from the start it was difficult for the free traders to be heard either as members of the commission or as witnesses before it. Industrialists from the north and east who were free trade-oriented were ignored, as were the smaller iron producers. He charged that most of the "expert" witnesses called before the commission on the iron industry had been proposed by the strongly protectionist Central Association of German Industrialists and the Union of German Iron and Steel Industrialists. But most suspicious of all, Bamberger claimed, was the fact that the material assembled by the investigating committees was still kept secret. He feared that it would be released after the government's tariff proposals were laid before the Reichstag, making it difficult for the opponents to evaluate the documentary collection. And finally he appealed to the Federal Council to weigh very carefully the tariff proposals presented to it. So intent was Bamberger on destroying the commissions' stature as impartial bodies that he even attacked his National Liberal colleague Hermann Meier, who was a member of the committee on iron. Meier was a free trader but, according to Bamberger, was too old and phlegmatic to escape being dominated by the more aggressive Free Conservative iron producer, Karl Stumm. This breach of etiquette created an uproar in parliament and could not have won sympathy for Bamberger's otherwise dispassionate speech and telling criticism.[66] He had written to his mother that he intended to focus on a few things and would keep silent on everything that did not belong in his department. This still left quite a few topics.[67]

If Bamberger was expecting help from the Federal Council, he was sadly mistaken. The council accepted the protectionist proposals of the commissions as the basis for its discussions and formed subcommittees to deal specifically with a new tariff proposal. Six of fifteen members of the various committees would be slected by Bismarck. The chairman of the tariff project was K. F. Varnbüler, of Württemberg, an old opponent of Bismarck's German policy, who made his peace with the chancellor on the tariff question. As his deputy, Bismarck named the head of the Imperial Chancellery, Christoph von Tiedemann, the "general staff chief" of the protectionists, who also headed the subcommittee on agricultural products. The strongest free traders, from the coastal states, were assigned to deal with gunpowder, playing cards, calendars, literary and art objects, and pottery. It was certain that the commission would approve a protectionist program. The deliberations lasted until the end of March and, although events did not run as smoothly as

Bismarck hoped, the tariff group still produced a proposal that was largely in accord with his desires. Only the level of the agricultural tariff displeased him, and he called for an upward revision by the Reichstag. The committee's proposals came before a plenary session of the Federal Council in early April. With Bismarck having already prepared the state governments by playing on the fear of Social Democracy and calling for speedy approval, the council gave its consent on April 4, 1879. The same day, the bill went to the Reichstag.[68]

The new tariff proposal provided duties for virtually all industrial and agricultural products imported into Germany. It exempted raw materials required by German industry, such as coal, cotton, rubber, and iron ore. For industrial products the duties amounted to 10–15 percent, for agricultural products 3–5 percent, graded according to the value and amount of labor expended on the manufacture of the product. Article 5 gave the Federal Council the right to double tariffs against countries who discriminated against German products. The most important tariffs were those on textiles, iron, and agricultural products. Cotton goods were taxed at a level often exceeding the tariff of 1865. Iron products had rates higher than the law of 1873 but as a rule less than that of 1865. Agricultural products, which had been the cause of a major crisis in the tariff committee, were given rates in many cases higher than those of the 1860 law.[69] It was a table from which everyone could select what he desired, said Bismarck.[70] Bamberger was determined to limit the menu.

The debates over the tariff bill were the longest in the up to then longest parliamentary session. The summary of the discussions required nearly sixty pages. Although those committed to tariff reform apparently had a majority, there was agreement only on generalities, with the real test coming as specific duties were worked out. Also the tariff bill, although rather generous, did not satisfy various groups; iron and textile interests demanded increased duties. Bismarck himself was displeased by the agricultural tariffs. The tariff bill was a package, and final approval would mean satisfying a number of groups. Finally, the tariff proposal was supposed to be part of the government's tax reform program, but no provision had been made for controlling the new tariff revenue, particularly from the agricultural duties. This was an issue that threatened to detach protectionist supporters from the Center and National Liberal parties, especially since the National Liberals were already hopelessly split over the bill. Thus it was not all smooth sailing, and the tariff bill required two and one-half months of intensive parliamentary work before it was passed.

The debate opened on May 2. Reading the speeches, particularly those of the opening debate, gives one the feeling of having heard it all before. The question of tariff reform had been so much debated since the mid-1870s that there was scarcely anything new to be said. Yet the first reading lasted six days. Bismarck introduced the government's proposal, laying greatest emphasis on the need for financial reform, in particular the need to relieve agriculture of direct taxes. He tried to portray Germany as already having moderate protection and claimed that the government was asking only additional protection. The proposed duties, he stressed, were lower than those in force only fifteen years before. Germany was also facing increasingly high tariff walls in France, America, Austria, and Russia, and thus was becoming a dumping ground for foreign countries.[71] The strangest speech of the first reading was probably that of Rudolf von Delbrück, who spoke for the National Liberals. Rather than speaking in generalities or giving a theoretical defense of free trade, Delbrück delivered a long and detailed critique of the bill's supposed contradictions and errors. Whether this was part of a plan to sow dissension among protectionist ranks, as Lambi claims, or a poor move by the National Liberals in selecting someone devoid of theoretical argument, or a sign that the National Liberals were so split that the first speaker had to limit himself to a technical critique, is difficult to say. In any event, the Reichstag was treated in mechanical fashion to a long speech about cotton, glass, wool, machines, rubber, copper, linen, packing cloth, paper, silk, eggs, and wood. Nothing was said about iron and grain because, according to Delbrück, they were too well known.[72] The following day, August Reichensperger announced the Center party's support for Bismarck's protectionist policy. This representative of a party once designated as an "enemy of the state" referred to the free traders as cosmopolitans, unable to see the problem from the viewpoint of Germans. To follow an open-door policy was to leave oneself open to exploitation. However, the party's approval of the tariffs was conditioned on how the matter of taxes and tax revenues was settled. He stressed that the Center was not ready to give up the matricular contributions, although they would accept their reduction.[73]

The proceedings were considerably enlivened when Bamberger spoke. He admitted that the protectionists had the votes. Still certain things had to be said, even though he had said many of them before. There was the old argument of playing into the hands of the socialists, since the notion that the state can be the benefactor of the people was precisely what socialists claimed. He once again blamed the chancellor for the new program. Only he could have altered the opinion of the country and adopted a policy which would inflict deep economic and moral wounds on the nation. He stressed the inequity in indirect taxes for the average man. The tariff policy was nothing but a plan to help the very wealthy. The march toward protection would trigger a chain reaction which would isolate Germany and compartmentalize

Europe. He accused the tariff commission of ignoring and distorting perti-
nent material gathered by the investigating committees. He pointed out that
iron ore, which was indispensable to the iron industry for armaments, came
from Spain, duty free of course. Germany would thus never be independent
of other countries for its weaponry. At the end of his two-and-one-half hour
speech, Bamberger again demonstrated his pessimism about the results of the
debate. Germany, he said, would "survive" Bismarck's policy, but "we wash
our hands in innocence, and time will show who truly cared for the well-being
of the German nation."[74]

Bamberger was happy about his speech. "For me the main pleasure is
that . . . this work is done and gone off without harm; in so aroused a house
and in so difficult a matter, every major speech is like a sea voyage."[75]

The difficulties that the bill presented to the National Liberals became
clear three days later. Bennigsen spoke for those who were neither "free
traders" nor "protectionists," but his speech made clear that he leaned
toward protection. He criticized a number of points in Bamberger's speech
and called the agricultural and industrial tariffs reasonable. "I consider it not
excluded," he concluded in his usually cautious way, "that on the basis of the
new tariff rates . . . and of the tax relations in the individual states a foundation is created for our economic activity still more favorable than that which
now exists." His speech was followed by that of Lasker, who dissociated
himself and his friends from the accommodating policy of Bennigsen and
attacked the chancellor's tariff and financial program.[76] Lasker's speech
occasioned an extremely bitter reply from Bismarck, who returned to the
Reichstag to answer him personally. The National Liberal was denounced as
one who represented the policy of the propertyless and of whom the
Scriptures wrote: "They do not sow, they do not reap, they do not toil, they
do not spin, and yet they are clothed." It was Bismarck's settling of accounts
with the professional politician whom "our sun does not warm, our rain does
not make wet, . . . who engages neither in industry nor agriculture nor any
occupation" except representing the German people all year. Lasker's problem, according to Bismarck, was that because he lacked "interests" the
deputy lacked the sympathy for financial and economic problems that
property ownership gave a minister like himself.[77]

To deal quickly with crucial items like iron and grain, which were the
hinges for the entire tariff package, the Reichstag discussed them in plenum
rather than committee. Bismarck and many agrarians still hoped for higher
agricultural levies; otherwise the threat of agrarian opposition to the iron
duties was present. The iron rates came up first, on May 15, and Bamberger
delivered the major speech for the opponents. He attributed the success of
the iron interest to their financial power and effective propaganda. He

pointed out that in iron production Germany was virtually tied for second place with America. This was not an "economically" weak industry. German production of raw iron had almost reached the figure of the boom year of 1873; imports of foreign iron had dropped by 70 percent while Germany was finding new export markets for its iron. If some businesses were suffering, it was due to poor management and alliances with the banks and the stock exchange, which resulted in overcapitalization and inability to pay dividends. Most of it had been said before in previous two-hour speeches, and Stumm's effective reply gave the opponents a powerful argument.[78] This in many ways was the crucial test for the protectionist alliance. Friedrich von Wedell-Malchow, a German Conservative, believing that neither the iron nor the grain tariffs would benefit German agriculture, proposed a lowering of the iron duties by 50 percent to fifty pfennigs per hundred kilograms. This would test the agrarian-industrial united front. It held as the amendment was defeated 192–125. The proposed duties on raw iron were then accepted 218–88. Symbolizing the lack of unity of the National Liberal party, Bennigsen voted to reduce the duties but then accepted the original proposal.[79]

A similar scene developed over the agricultural tariffs. The actual debate centered not on whether there would be grain tariffs but on their level. Encouraged by Bismarck, Baron Julius von Mirbach proposed doubling the duty on rye. Bismarck spoke eloquently and in great detail of the plight and importance of agriculture. It did not help, and Mirbach's amendment was defeated 173–161. The grain duties originally proposed were accepted 226–109. Again Bennigsen and a number of National Liberals voted against the increase but then accepted the government's proposal.[80] To Bamberger nothing indicated more clearly how large the protectionist majority was than the vote on the higher grain duties: "Everyone who is not completely corroded voted for us, and we still had only a twelve-vote majority."[81]

The National Liberal party had left open the tariff question because of their inability to agree on a common approach and in order to avoid a party crisis.[82] However, the left wing around Bamberger, Forckenbeck, and Lasker was determined to push matters to a crisis. Most of its members would have agreed with Swiss professor Karl Hilty, who wrote: "On the whole nothing is harmed if with the National Liberal party the truly liberal side separates from the other. One cannot make it just with nationality alone; it also required character and a liberal idea."[83]

By the end of May, Bamberger was also ready to leave the party. The crisis for him seemed to come on May 21, the day of Bismarck's major speech defending agricultural protection. The chancellor had stressed the need to preserve the conservative agricultural population, which gave the state security, and asked that agriculture be treated just like industry. Although through the mist of nearly a century the speech has lost some of its vitality, its effect on Bamberger was cataclysmic. "How could everything that rolls down like an avalanche be compressed into one letter!" he wrote Stauffenberg:

> Bismarck's speech today completes the program: The war of the agrarians against modern civilization with the Social Democratic eruption at the finish. . . . In my opinion on the basis of this speech the split of the party should be carried out, simply around the slogan "For or against Bismarck." If you were here and healthy it would happen this evening. . . . And now do not torture your head and heart with thoughts of the future! We must try to salvage from the shipwreck of the major thing, as far as possible, the individual joys of life.[84]

Bamberger's thoughts about an impending split in the party were echoed and reechoed during May and June, 1879.[85] However, the widely predicted split of the left wing of the National Liberal party did not take place for a year, primarily because of the outcome of the struggle over the tariffs. The relative success that the protectionists had on the second reading only seemed to whet their appetites for more. Bamberger's prediction that their appetite would grow as they ate was proving true. The producers of cast iron demanded higher duties for their products, but the strongest claim for more favored treatment came from the agrarians, who still demanded a 100 percent increase in the rye duties. In June, Bamberger had remarked that the "alliance of rye and iron" was "not yet ready."[86] A month later it was, and a bargain was struck on July 11, when the higher rye duties were accepted 186–160.

The tariff negotiations witnessed a growing intimacy between Conservatives and Catholics which threatened to make the disintegrating National Liberal party expendable. Bennigsen tried to be useful to Bismarck, and although he opposed the increased grain duties, he was prepared to accept the tariff package. What he would make a matter of principle was the disposition and control of the tariff revenues. He had been willing to support a tariff increase because of his desire for thorough financial reform, particularly the elimination of the matricular contributions of the states. He also wished to make certain that the Reichstag would have a voice in the disposition of the funds, since the taxes, once granted, did not require annual approval. Bismarck agreed with Bennigsen on the need to free the federal government from the states' purse strings, but he also realized that he needed the votes of the Center party for his tariff program. The Center party, however, wished to preserve the federal structure of the empire and was opposed to unitarian or centralizing tendencies. It finally united behind the "Franckenstein clause," which proposed to give the federal government only 130 million marks annually from the tariff revenues and to return the rest to the states. Thus the government would still require financial support from the states. It was the matricular contributions slightly refurbished. The National Liberals proposed the annual approval of some of the tariffs as a means of control. The decisive vote was in the hands of the two conservative parties, who looked upon annual approval of even a part of the tariff schedule as anathema. Bismarck decided he needed the votes of the Center more than those of the National Liberal party. Thus the vote of July 9 showed 211 for the Franckenstein clause and 127 against. On this one issue, the National Liberal party appeared united.[87]

Three weeks earlier Bamberger had written that if the left wing of the party held together everything might turn out well regarding the left wing's position within the National Liberal party. In the debate on the Franckenstein clause, Bennigsen had announced that he and the great majority of the party would vote against not only the matricular contributions but also the entire tariff bill if the Center's proposal was accepted. This infuriated a small group of National Liberals around Völk, Schauss, Julius von Hölder, and Benda, and the first very sharply attacked Bennigsen's stance.[88] His attack aroused not only the left wing but enough other National Liberals to demand satisfaction. More than thirty members announced they would secede if Völk was not censured for his breach of party etiquette. By a vote of 45–35 the National Liberals voted for censure, forcing Völk out of the party. Fifteen other members left with him. Thus the left wing had unexpectedly won the internal battle, but the war was to continue.[89]

Bamberger was under no illusions about it. Speaking a day before the tariff package was passed, he tried to sum up the significance of the previous seven months, which he found in the vote on the Franckenstein clause. "I have always told my political allies who do not share my economic views," he explained, that the "questions of economics and politics are inseparably bound. The economic reaction pushed to a certain point leads to political reaction. The solemn vote on article 7 [Franckenstein clause] has demonstrated that the house divided right and left, and it will be so in the future."[90] Bamberger could only have felt strengthened in his belief in a political reaction when during June and July Bismarck purged his Prussian cabinet of the remaining liberal elements—Hobrecht, Falk, and Rudolf Friedenthal—and replaced them with conservatives like Karl Bitter, Robert von Puttkamer, and Robert Lucius von Ballhausen. The cleansing operation was carried down to the lower echelons of the administration.[91]

The tariff struggle marked the great turning point in Bamberger's relations with the German government and Bismarck. It is true that he had opposed Bismarck's proposals in the past, particularly the military bills, but he always had tried to work with the government, always believing in the government's good will and claiming that it represented a progressive force. When Bamberger convinced himself that Bismarck was turning his back on the forces of the modern world and the political party that embodied them, the liberal had to take on a new role.[92] The remaining fourteen years of his parliamentary life would see Bamberger almost always on the defensive and in almost continual opposition. From 1879–93 virtually no government initiative won his approval. In everything the government did, he saw retrogression and reaction. From a camp follower of Bismarck he became the most persistent and perceptive critic of the chancellor's policies. He discovered how difficult it was to find the middle road between the acceptance of the accomplished fact and the fruitless negation of it. And if during the 1870s he tended to adhere to the former, the 1880s found him on the other side. As he told the Reichstag in April 1880, during the debate over the military bill:

> I also believe that politics is a practical art, which . . . must work with the instrument of compromise. I have made many a compromise of this kind and have not yet regretted it for a moment. . . . But it is no compromise when the government demands all that is humanly possible and I grant all that is humanly possible. . . . Representative Rickert . . . has referred to the better time when we laid the most essential foundation of German legislation by compromising with the government. . . . Today it is thoroughly different. That government with which . . . Rickert and I together have concluded compromises no longer exists for me. For me there exists today only a government who makes a compromise with me in order immediately to work against me, and with such a government, I say openly, I know no compromises.[93]

The thirteen months from July 1879 to August 1880 were dominated by the so-called great secession from the National Liberal party, which had already been weakened by the departure of Völk and his supporters. After the close of the parliamentary session, Bamberger hurried to his summer home in Interlaken to recuperate and to take stock of the political situation. His assessments were consistently gloomy. "Party conference is a matter of indifference to me," he wrote Lasker. "Separation from Bennigsen is the main thing." "Without strenuous opposition," he told Oppenheim, "a return to better conditions is . . . no longer thinkable. If only one were fresh enough to carry on."[94] Where was one to find allies? "All attempts to deal with the Progressives were futile. . . . With how few persons can one completely go together!" he lamented. In this tragedy, " 'most horrible, most horrible' [in English] is fitting."[95] It was time "for us to go to sleep . . . when I see what triumphs . . . it appears they are right and 'I am out of time' [in English] ."[96]

Pessimism was all he seemed to have left as he contemplated Bismarck's coming program. "Reichstag and state parliaments alternating every two years, no more consent to taxes, the whole parliamentary and political process relegated to the background, workers' assistance and other socialistic paternalism. All of that will now be made with the Center and gobbled up with zest by the philistines. . . . The nationalization of the railroad lays the iron ring around the whole thing."[97] The gloomy comments and expectations were confirmed by the Prussian state elections in October, which resulted in another major defeat for the National Liberal party and the failure of even Lasker to be reelected. Bamberger had refused to sign the party manifesto for the Prussian election because he considered it indecisive and demoralizing.[98] He regarded the results of the election as not "surprising" and believed they reflected most on the German people. "As I see the people, I find it ever more excusable to have tried it with Bismarck than with the people, and I can still rather think of trying it one more time with him than against him, but I also prefer not to do that."[99]

The winter of 1879–80 was a period of jockeying for position within the National Liberal party. The right wing around Miquel hoped to come to an arrangement with "the better elements of the Free Conservatives" and with the government.[100] Among the left wing there was talk of a "liberal middle party," but it remained vague. Feelers were put out to the Progressive party but nothing came of them. At the end of February, according to Stephani, new bitterness within the National Liberal party was created by recriminations over the Bennigsen candidacy.[101]

For Bamberger the period between the tariff bill and the secession in August 1880 indicated that he was increasingly out of step with both the legislative program of the chancellor and other developments in German society. Bismarck, in keeping with his desire to restructure the tax system of Germany so that it relied more on indirect taxes, introduced and saw passed in 1879 a stamp tax on bills of exchange and a tax on tobacco. An attempt to increase the stamp tax the following year and to increase the beer tax in 1879 and 1880 failed. In April 1880 an attempt was made to provide financial support to a trading company in the South Seas, an effort that was rejected by the Reichstag, primarily due to Bamberger's efforts.[102]

Bamberger also strongly opposed the government's action in May 1879 to halt the sale of silver. After the German monetary reform was completed, there still remained the problem of disposing of the now excess silver which the government was calling in. Bamberger had originally pressed for its immediate sale, foreseeing a steady drop in its price. The government hesitated, and the price continued to fall. The drop in the price of silver was traced by many to the German government's sales. Bamberger on the contrary believed it was simply the inevitable consequence of the world's move toward the gold standard. Halting the sale of silver would have no effect on its price, but—and this was Bamberger's major worry—it might encourage those who wished to see Germany depart from the gold standard. Lord Odo Russell, the British ambassador to Germany, publicly intimated that the German government was considering a change in its currency policy. Bamberger and his allies discussed whether to interpellate on the issue. Bamberger was initially opposed, not wishing to get into Bismarck's bailiwick of foreign affairs. He would have been satisfied with a public denial of Russell's statement, but this was refused by the government. He then accepted the idea of an interpellation. [103]

Bamberger was concerned because Bismarck's private banker, Gerson Bleichröder, was a known opponent of the gold standard and was thought to be involved in the decision to halt the silver sales. Bamberger also believed that Russell got his information from Bleichröder, who was an English general consul and a member of the governing committee of the Reichsbank. Bismarck responded to the interpellation by insinuating that Bamberger's involvement with the Deutsche Bank, which had profited from the silver sales, was the main reason for the interpellation. The discussion ended without Bismarck's revealing his deeper motives for halting the silver sales, although it seemed to have been done because of his personal intervention. [104] Bamberger was pleased by the debate and told Oppenheim that in the currency question "our attack" acted as a "deterrent." Nevertheless, he saw Bismarck behind the agitation against the gold standard and claimed that the chancellor would "let loose his hounds until the public is sufficiently prejudiced toward his coup." [105]

The "coup" Bismarck was carrying out reached beyond silver to the army. The Reichstag session of 1880 brought forth a new "septennat," calling for establishing the peacetime strength of the army for seven years. Here was an old issue that not only found Bamberger against the government but also caused a deep division within the National Liberal camp. It was also a poor issue on which to secede, as Bamberger recognized. He feared that the military question might be made binding on party members so as to force them out. If it came to a separation, Bamberger went on, it should be not on account of the military question but because of a "general *incompatibilité d'humeur* as with a divorce." With a separation based on a special question one always came out on "the short end." [106] Regardless of how the secession was motivated, the fact that it coincided with the left liberals' opposition to the military bill would cast an unpatriotic light on their action. "The truth is," Bamberger explained to his mother, "that we three [Forckenbeck and Stauffenberg], as well as Lasker, have a great desire to leave the [National Liberal party], which has become too philistine for us," but "now one bothers us to try it for a little longer. Thus we in fact lie in a watery waste." [107] In addition to the unsuitability of the moment and hesitations on the part of potential supporters to make the final break, Forckenbeck's involvement in Berlin affairs as the lord mayor and Stauffenberg's illness in March delayed the ultimate step. [108]

Thus the military bill came and was passed essentially according to the government's desires. The major thrust of the left National Liberal attack on the bill concentrated on article 1 and sought to limit the effectiveness of the bill to three years instead of seven. How embarrassing this issue was for the left National Liberals was obvious when Rickert opposed the three-year motion and spoke in favor of seven. The motion to substitute three years for seven was defeated 180–104 in the second reading. Bamberger's speech in the third reading, therefore, was in the nature of a general reckoning with his opponents. The real significance of the bill was its impact on political life inside Germany. He disputed Rickert, who had advocated acceptance of the law because he feared an emotional election campaign over this issue. "We do not have too much of the exuberant political life in Germany," he admonished, "but an excess of still life. The nation should finally learn to come out of the political dead-end into which she has been led through the material struggle of interests, and again address itself to general questions. If one wants political representation, if one wants elections, if one wants parliamentary representation, then as a consequence one must wish that the people bother themselves about political affairs, for one without the other is a contradiction in itself." The only thing the German parliament had in common with most of the other representative bodies of central Europe was a name. If the German Empire was created by the efforts of the army, then as a result of the military "the German Reichstag sinks down gradually to a shadowy appearance." Bamberger's speech, although containing much that was true, passed over in silence his previous comments about too frequent elections, his satisfaction with the compromise of 1874, as Rickert quickly reminded him, and ignored his own claim that the military issue was a bad one on which to secede. Few other National Liberals joined him in rejecting the entire bill. [109]

The Reichstag session ended May 10, and Bamberger, in spite of the defeat on the military bill and the permanent crisis within the National Liberal party appeared satisfied with his efforts. [110] Unfortunately he had to stand on the sidelines during the final presecession legislative struggle of the National Liberal party in the Prussian legislature. In May, Bismarck laid before the Prussian parliament a bill to ease some of the restrictions placed on clerics by the May laws of 1873. This so-called discretionary powers bill once again found the National Liberals deeply divided and the Prussian assembly evenly split on the issue. Bennigsen, in order to prevent a Conservative-Center alliance, won over enough National Liberals and Conservatives to push through, by a few votes, a watered-down version of the bill. [111]

This customary tactic of Bennigsen's proved to be the final blow to the already fragile unity of the National Liberal party. [112] The extent of Bennigsen's active role in the passage of the church law shocked even his old opponents. To Forckenbeck it was a "ruinous compromise," and he demanded a public separation from the leader of the National Liberal party. Stauffenberg wrote that "something must happen," not just a separation but a new party. There must be no "procrastination." [113] Bamberger could only write to Lasker that the latter was fortunate to be out of the party "before the shame became so great. Not even for the next session of the Reichstag was it possible to remain together with Bennigsen." "Bennigsen was definitely the corrupting element," he added later, "who did not make the weakness of the party alone, but who enlarged it beyond measure, and cherished and legitimated it." The formation of a new liberal party was to follow the separation from the Hanoverian. [114]

Serious planning for the secession began at the end of July, when Forckenbeck visited Bamberger and Stauffenberg. [115] Providing additional impetus to the separation was the fear that the left-wing National Liberal constituency would drift to the left into the Progressive camp. As Rickert expressed it, "The cities almost collectively, immediately or later, would have almost marched off to the left. The Progressive party and the even further leftist elements would have taken over their leadership." [116] While it may be an exaggeration to say, as Martin Philippson does, that the secession sprang entirely from the ranks of the voters who demanded it, this factor should not be overlooked. Bamberger spoke of the "serviceable public" turning to the future secessionists and away from Bismarck. Nothing must be done openly to encourage it, but quietly "we cannot do enough to stimulate and strengthen it where the tendency to the left and to a break with Bennigsen shows itself." [117]

In spite of the agreement on principles, the formal separation was difficult to consummate. At least five individuals—Bamberger, Forckenbeck, Lasker, Rickert, and Stauffenberg—had to be coordinated and agreement reached on not only a separation but also a new party. For Rickert it was essential that the break lead to a great liberal party or else the whole affair was pointless. [118] Even as late as August 13, Bamberger believed that because of Rickert's hesitation everything was undecided and uncertain, and he feared that they would make themselves laughable with all their "pedantry and preparing." [119]

The declaration of the secession was finally published on August 29 and was scarcely a printed page in length. It was a very moderate document designed to unite various liberal groups. It spoke of the desire for a "truly constitutional system," firm opposition to the retrogressive movement in Germany, and maintenance of "our not easily achieved political freedoms." It tied political to economic freedom, rejected indirect taxes and tariffs, and stressed the importance of religious freedom, which meant that schools must not be subjected to church authority. It closed by announcing the readiness of the twenty-six signers to work for a union on these bases. [120]

For Bamberger the significant fact was "that the main thing happened," and he was pleased that the "great surgical operation" was over. He hoped that no attempts would be made to plaster over the split. [121] However, future difficulties could not be ignored, and his comments to Karl Hillebrand seem more candid: "I place no hope at all in the secession. I joined because the profoundly indifferent Bennigsen and his following . . . no longer had anything at all in common with me. Furthermore, my new party appears somewhat 'Old Catholic.' Officers without soldiers who hold fast to the pure Christianity of the old National Liberalism, several doubtful bishops like Rickert and Lasker." [122] It was the lament of the 1880s and beyond.

Always the politician and publicist, Bamberger immediately plunged into writing a justification of the secession which appeared anonymously at the end of 1880. *Die Sezession (The Secession)* was an instant success, going through four editions within two months. It angered Bismarck considerably, and he covered the pamphlet with marginalia. [123] The essay contained little that Bamberger had not said or written before, but several things are worth stressing. He defended the old compromise policy of the National Liberal party on the grounds that it had offered the most effective means to modernize Germany. The compromises, he reminded his critics on the left, were agreements on how progressive a piece of legislation was to be. Thus for Bamberger they were positive steps, which although not achieving the liberal ideal, at least brought Germany closer to it. Moreover, one had to strike these compromises while there was an opportunity. The choice was not between a compromise now and total victory later, but between compromise and stagnation. It was better to take what was available if it represented progress. By 1880 there was no reason for compromise, since any agreement would be retrogressive rather than progressive. One could not surrender that which made one's existence worthwhile. [124]

The new direction of the imperial government was not merely backward in a general sense; for Bamberger it signified a return to the police state and patriarchal world of the eighteenth and early nineteenth centuries. The greatest part of his essay was devoted to economic matters which he saw as the heart of the issue, and he considered these sections the best part of his work. Economic difficulties were the root cause of the change in the German government's policy, he claimed. Limitations on economic freedom vis-à-vis foreign countries would gradually lead to limitations on economic freedom internally and finally to limitations on political freedom, so interconnected were these social factors, at least in Bamberger's mind. Furthermore the government, in spite of the rhetoric about national solidarity, was appealing to the selfish interests of various groups. It was the antithesis of a healthy national policy and would only unchain material interests and appeal to what was worst rather than best in people. [125]

His fear of a limitation on political freedom, which he first expressed during the debate over the Antisocialist Law, reemerged during the writing of *Die Sezession*. He described to Hillebrand the great strain put on him as he worked on the essay resulting from the fear of criminal prosecution for slandering ministers. With some exaggeration he wrote, "I have never felt more vividly than with this last work how deep we have sunk.... I tried to judge completely without prejudice ... and ... I still had to examine every letter so that the state's attorney would not surprise me with a chicanery." Advised to leave Germany, he refused. "Are the Germans less brutal and base if I am not present? And does it concern me less if I am not present?" [126] The year from the end of 1879 to the end of 1880 was painful for Bamberger, not only because of the falling-out with Bismarck and the secession from the National Liberal party, but because of the emergence in a significant way of political anti-Semitism in Germany. [127] From this phenomenon there was also no "running away," even if "the shadows which are cast into the soul of the nation, into one's own soul, by this appearance darken backward and forward one's whole life."[128]

·8·

In Opposition:
The Early 1880s

The appearance of an anti-Semitic movement was one further manifestation of a new era emerging in Germany in 1879–80. From 1881 on, Bamberger's response to it took three directions: to try to organize a great liberal party, a task in which he never seemed to have much faith; to defend the achievements of the 1870s against state intervention and regulation; and to act as a critic of German society. The last eighteen years of his life were a bitter period for Bamberger, who found himself increasingly out of step with German history.

He had been a widower since December 1874, but even before his wife's death, his growing involvement in German politics had caused them to be separated for long periods. He lived alone during his frequent stays in Berlin in the 1870s. His wife was content to remain in Paris, and she apparently gave him no encouragement in his new pursuits. Nevertheless, the tie between the two was exceptionally strong, and her premature death affected him deeply.[1]

From 1875 on, he led a settled existence. He bought a house near the Tiergarten at Margaretenstrasse 18 and in 1876 a villa in Interlaken where, without fail, he spent the summer months. Although a widower and determined not to remarry, his wide circle of family and friends provided the basis for a very active social life.[2] His letters are replete with reference to illnesses of various kinds, but his health seems to have been good enough to enable him to attend virtually every Reichstag session and not to slow down his writing.

His political activity in the early 1880s revolved around the new Liberal Union (Liberale Vereinigung), as Bamberger's group called itself, and the Reichstag. The Liberal Union was faced with a serious contradiction. It was regarded by its members as only preparatory to the formation of a new liberal party, as merely "the core of a party."[3] The reluctance to become just another liberal group, plus the fact that the Secessionists were notables who had little zest for the detailed and dogged work of political organizing,

161

impeded the establishment of a well-grounded party network in the country-side. Forckenbeck was content to have an organization embracing the parliamentary delegates and a few other prominent individuals. Only Rickert, who had been a key figure in the National Liberal party organization, was an exception. It was in part because of him that the Secessionists did relatively well in the elections of 1881. As Stephani put it: "Who has our [National Liberal] records, Rickert perchance?" No more than fifty local associations were formed.[4] It was difficult to engage the Reichstag deputies—let alone those outside parliament—for party work. The problem of absenteeism remained even after the fusion with the Progressive party in 1884.[5] By then there existed the rudiments of a party structure, a party newspaper, and annual party congresses, although the latter was more like a "discussion among friends" than an institution. The only significant decision reached at these meetings was that of 1881 against a general election alliance with the Progressives.[6]

The question of the place of the Liberal Union in the liberal spectrum preoccupied the group. It was hoped that the party would serve as a rallying point for sympathizers in the Progressive and National Liberal parties and that the new party would be ready when the aged William I was replaced by his supposedly liberal son, Frederick William. Eduard Lasker undertook to work toward rapprochement with the National Liberals via Bennigsen, both before and after the Secessionist victory in the 1881 election. Bennigsen, who was getting contrary advice indirectly from Miquel, remained cool to Lasker's overtures.[7] Although Bamberger hoped for National Liberal defections to the Secessionists, he was more disenchanted with Bennigsen than was Lasker, who seemed to harbor a belief that he could lead the National Liberal party leader to the right path. On the eve of the 1884 election Bamberger wrote to Stauffenberg: "The miserableness of the National Liberals has exceeded our worst idea. This sort was always the misfortune of German politics." To Theodor Barth he wrote, "In what a dumb situation we are. We defended a third estate which looks for protection behind the coat of our and its enemies. I am thoroughly tired of it."[8]

The lack of success on the right was duplicated initially on the left. The major stumbling blocks were Eugen Richter on the one side and Bamberger and Forckenbeck on the other. Richter talked of fusion with the Secessionists in terms of capitulation. He feared that they still looked more to the right than the left for their future activity. Only when they took a "progressive" position on key questions could there be talk of a fusion. Richter thus replied very cautiously to Lasker's suggestions about cooperation between the two liberal groups, claiming that the Progressives must know the Secessionists' entire program before cooperation could become a reality.[9] Richter's coolness was matched by Bamberger's. Even before the secession had become official, Bamberger was preaching that all attempts to make a deal with the Progressives were "futile" and that Richter was not "the man to think of a union with us." Bamberger hoped to exploit the tension between Richter and his chief lieutenant, Albert Hänel, by encouraging Hänel to break with his chief, "and then perhaps our plan is effected by a connection with the moderate Progressives, which a similar one with the left National Liberals could follow."[10] The latent opposition to a close identification of the Secessionists with the Progressives was apparent at the Liberal Union party congress at Halle on January 29, 1881. A motion for a general election alliance with the Progressives failed to win acceptance. Secessionists like Bamberger and Forckenbeck believed that only by preserving their identity could they attract dissatisfied elements on the left and right.[11]

Whether they would unite with the Progressives or serve as a rallying point for other liberals, the Secessionists believed that they needed a forum for their views, and Bamberger was interested in founding a daily newspaper. From early 1880 his attention focused on the *Tribüne* which was sympathetic to the left National Liberals. By the end of the year he had collected enough money to purchase and reshape the paper so that it appeared twice a day starting February 21, 1881.[12] The venture was in difficulty almost immediately. By April, one-fourth of the subscribers had been lost after it became obvious that the paper was a Secessionist organ.[13] The end came in February 1883, barely two years after Bamberger had become directly involved in it, and it cost him a sizable but unknown sum of money, about which he complained bitterly. He tried to arrange the announcement of the newspaper's collapse so that it would attract as little attention as possible, and Richard Wagner, so he wrote to Stauffenberg, "did me a favor for the first time in his life by dying at the same time and absorbing the attention of the public."[14]

The experience with the *Tribüne* did not make Bamberger receptive to the idea of a political weekly. *Die Nation* was actually the brain child of Theodor Barth, a legal representative of the Bremen Chamber of Commerce and from 1881 on a member of the Reichstag and a Secessionist. As a convinced free trader and Smithian, he had opposed the tariff bill, the tobacco monopoly, and the absorption of Bremen into the German customs area. His activities incurred the ire of Bismarck, who pressured the Bremen government to have Barth forced out of his semiofficial position.[15] He decided to take up the battle anew and asked for Bamberger's opinion about founding a political-economic weekly which was to be the organ of "individualism." He hoped for at least one article per month from Bamberger.[16]

In spite of Bamberger's unencouraging reply, Barth went ahead. The following month he was in Magdeburg and Gotha on a fund-raising trip and reported encouraging responses from various insurance company representatives who were threatened by Bismarck's social insurance program. The thrust of the proposed journal was to be against the chancellor's program of "state socialism." By September Barth reported further progress with the insurance interests and had a mailing list of twenty thousand which, during the weekly's best days, yielded three thousand subscribers. Bamberger contributed regularly to the journal and helped out financially.[17] *Die Nation* had considerably more success than the *Tribüne.* Its first issue in October 1883 was the start of a twenty-four-year life. It outgrew its origins as a voice opposing state socialism and became an elegant weekly devoted to social affairs in its broadest sense, due in no small part to Bamberger's contributions.

The Liberal Union, besides trying to find allies on the left and right and establish journalistic organs, had to carve a place for itself in the German legislative picture. This would be the measure of its political success. Its first battles were fought in the Reichstag session of February 15–June 15, 1881. Shortly before the opening of the Reichstag, Bamberger wrote that he saw his task as telling people "what I consider useful, even if unpleasant, truths."[18] Bismarck's legislative program gave Bamberger ample opportunity to state unpleasant truths. The Secessionists continued to be concerned about the government's intentions regarding the gold standard. The early 1880s had seen a reduction in Germany's gold reserves caused by a worldwide reduction in gold production, an unfavorable balance of trade with the United States, and the export of gold to Italy. This, plus the decline in the value of silver, led to calls for a double standard or even a return to a silver standard and the convening of an international conference in Paris to discuss currency problems. Bamberger was easily alarmed on the issue of currency changes and used the occasion of a discussion of petitions for a double standard to defend the German currency system and call for a recommencing of the sale of silver. It was impossible, he claimed, to establish a firm relationship between gold and silver, as the advocates of bimetallism demanded. Gold was always preferred to silver in international commerce. Moreover, Germany's gold supply was second only to England's, and the world's gold supply was by no means exhausted, he contended, pointing to recent Australian discoveries. The debate elicited from the government the statement that it did not intend to tamper with the currency system but would try to enhance the value of silver. This proved satisfactory to Bamberger, and the Paris currency conference broke up without accomplishing anything.[19]

Equally satisfying but still unsettling were the rejection of both an increase in the beer tax and the institution of a two-year budgetary period; the latter Bamberger regarded as an attempt to diminish the importance of the Reichstag. Similarly defeated was the attempt to establish an imperial economic council as a kind of "counterparliament." On the question of a tariff, he had to be partially satisfied. The one chink in Bamberger's free-trade armor was opened by wine and its necessities. A government bill to tax grape imports won Bamberger's support because he regarded it as merely a further interpretation of the already existing tariff on wine. His opponents saw the interest of his constituents behind this interpretation. The grape tariff passed, along with increased flour and textile tariffs which Bamberger opposed bitterly.[20]

The two issues that agitated Bamberger most during the session were accident insurance and anti Semitism. Both were main themes in his speeches, essays, and correspondence during the 1880s and 1890s, and he regarded them as fundamental ills of German society.

On no single issue was Bamberger's hostility to Bismarck's policies so categorical as that of social welfare legislation.[21] We can best ease ourselves into the problem of Bismarck's social welfare program and Bamberger's reaction to it if we start a few years before the accident insurance bill was introduced. In March 1878, the government sponsored a bill to change the regulations regarding Sunday work. Employers henceforth could not obligate their employees to work on Sundays or holidays. But businesses whose nature could not tolerate delay or interruption were excluded. This rather weak rewording of article 105 of the industrial code was sharpened and made more detailed in committee. It specifically forbade Sunday work in factories and at construction sites and set hours of free time for those businesses which engaged in night work. In concerns whose work could not be interrupted, a worker had to receive every second Sunday free. With only minor changes the commission's proposal passed the second reading by a vote of 123–117.[22]

The government, supported by the National Liberal chairman of the committee, Heinrich Rickert, strove to get the original, weaker version of article 105 accepted, and Bamberger spoke for this attempt. The government's proposal, he claimed, represented the dividing line between what was permissible and what was not, that is, between promoting general welfare and forbidding "the adult worker to strike the choice between the advantages which beckon to him in the free enjoyment of a weekly rest or in the additional gain of money." In the latter alternative, Bamberger saw a direct procession to the "socialist state" or even a "police state," because the police and courts had to decide exceptional cases. Ignoring the Progressives, who supported the bill, he saw it as an attempt to enforce religious worship, and he conjured up visions of a maximum workday and maximum prices as corollaries to limiting the working week. How far he would go in intervening in the conditions of work was indicated by a reference to Belgian legislation which permitted children from the age of ten to work in coal mines. This was a "monstrosity" that went too far even for him, but he quickly tried to excuse Belgium's regulations. Her senators were motivated by the lurking dangers of socialism and the belief that the problem had to be handled by the mine owner rather than by legislation. It was not indifference or raw egotism that motivated the Belgian legislator, but a recognition that the spread of socialistic ideas necessitated very careful action in the social field.[23]

In this speech, Bamberger set the stage for his reaction to almost every government proposal in the field of social welfare for the next twelve years. The main theme of virtually all of his speeches would be that the government was taking the high road to the socialist state. Dealing in generalities, Bamberger was often the opening speaker in the debate. Rather than try to deemphasize the ideological aspects of the bills, he posed the issue each time as that between good and evil. Even his colleagues' advice to soften the ideological emphasis was to no avail, and his cry of socialism at every turn was to wear thin and lead to ridicule by his opponents.

In the debate on Sunday work, Bamberger was on the government's and the winning side as the Reichstag voted 133–132 to accept the government's original proposal.[24]

If Bismarck indicated little enthusiasm for measures to protect the health and morals of workers, he was far more open to regulations which would provide sickness, accident, and old age security. As early as 1871 he had written that the only way to stop the threat of the socialist movement was for the state to accept "what appears justified in the socialist demands and in conformity with the state and social order."[25] In spite of his occasional attention to social policy, Bismarck's preoccupation with other matters, the basic liberal orientation of most of his ministers, and their relative independence from the chancellor's supervision made it unlikely that anything would be attempted in social insurance.[26] Toward the end of the 1870s, however, Bismarck's growing estrangement from the liberals plus his ever closer ties with the Conservatives and the Center party opened the pathway to social legislation. The most direct impulse for the social insurance program came from the Antisocialist Law. Even Bismarck recognized its "regressive" content and proposed to fight the resulting dangers with "positive measures directed toward the improvement of the lot of the working classes.[27]

The apparent inadequacy of the Employers' Liability Act of 1871 also encouraged new social legislation. This law placed the burden of proof of responsibility for factory and mine accidents on the worker, and in only 40 percent of the cases had workers been able to establish such evidence of responsibility by their superiors or the owners. Workers also complained of the actions of private insurance companies who, having insured the employer, were loath to see him convicted and often intervened on his side. The threat of a long lawsuit made the needy worker settle for less, and it was generally too expensive for a worker to insure himself privately against accidents.[28]

Such deficiencies in the law led to calls in parliament in 1878–79 for new social insurance legislation. Although the government had been noncommittal during the debates, the Prussian ministry had been studying the whole area of social insurance. In fact, by 1880 Bismarck had embraced the project of a mining and steel industrialist, Louis Baare, who had suggested a plan for accident insurance. By November 30, 1880, a bill was ready.[29] The chancellor saw the issue of social policy through the prism of his own experiences and the needs of imperial policy. As the owner of two paper mills and a sawmill, Bismarck was sensitive to governmental interference in his factories and thus unreceptive to the idea of factory legislation. Even his hostility to insurance companies may be traced to a painful personal experience. Although he held himself open to various groups and persons, from socialists of the street to Socialists of the Chair, from industrialists to his estate neighbors, he did hold firmly to several fundamental points. He opposed a revision of the liability law, for it involved exhausting legal battles. The new program must be compulsory, to keep rates low. He rejected participation of the private insurance companies in the new system, for he saw industrial accidents as a moral problem which could not be the object of speculation and dividends. The exclusion of the insurance companies was the one issue on which he would not compromise. Besides moral considerations, the accident insurance program had to provide a role for the state in the form of an imperial or state insurance office which would contribute to the fund. This would document the state's role and lessen the cost to worker and industry. The insurance program had to provide a role for the state in the form of an imperial cause them to realize they were dependent on the state for their well-being. According to Hans Rothfels, Bismarck aimed at the "fulfillment of authoritarian duties," and he saw the state as the institution "which, through all external changes, safeguards individual existence."[30] He was intoxicated by the "state-forming" purposes of social policy, and his intentions in the field of social policy went far beyond providing security to the worker. He wanted to create a new social and political structure, and the insurance program was to serve as a basis for a new ordering of society. Accident insurance was secondary, he admitted in 1883; the main aim was to establish occupational organizations for all branches of industry and so lay the foundation for a future legislative body alongside or instead of the Reichstag.[31]

If Bismarck sketched his social insurance program in such elemental strokes, Ludwig Bamberger was no less alarmed by the emerging picture. "To carry on social policy," he wrote, meant "to want to lead the state from its up to now essentially political problems to the program of socialistic postulates whose realization . . . would transform the state from the ground up." Bismarck might have agreed. The insurance schemes were merely the opening salvos in an attack designed to destroy individualism and to force Germany into a collectivist strait jacket. Pious phrases concerning human charity, compassion, or Christianity were merely slogans to clothe dangerous plans in innocent garments. Social policy could not be regarded as poor relief or as a product of Christian compassion; rather it reflected the government's fear of the worker. It was, Bamberger repeated ten years later, the entry of the masses into political participation that led toward socialistic experiments. [32] Bamberger saw the program creating a great clientele at the cost of individual independence. Each dissatisfied group would call on the state for aid, and it would soon turn into a general competition which would lead to a demoralization and degeneration of public life.[33] Bamberger did not believe that in the long run the individual could be helped from above. Any momentary gains he achieved would be at the cost of his freedom.

On March 8, 1881, the government's bill on accident insurance for workers was sent to the Reichstag. All those who worked in mines, salt mines, refineries, factories, foundries, and at construction sites, and whose annual wage was not over 2,000 marks, would be insured against accidents through a national institution in Berlin. Accidents causing incapacitations of more than four weeks were covered, and payments were up to a maximum of 66 2/3 percent of the normal wage. Premiums would vary according to the job risk and would be paid as follows: Those who earned less than 750 marks would have their premiums paid by the employer (two-thirds) and the state (one-third); between 750 and 1,000 marks, the ratios were two-thirds from the employer and one-third from the employee; over 1,000 marks, it was half from the employer and half from the insured.[34]

The initial reaction was mixed. Catholic-oriented newspapers generally favored the proposal while stressing the need for revisions; the Conservative press also was friendly to the bill; while the National Liberals, although hostile, refused to reject the plan on principle as Progressive and Secessionist circles did.[35]

Bamberger opened the parliamentary debate and admitted to the Reichstag that he had been urged by his friends and colleagues to limit his discussion to a criticism of the concrete proposal and to touch as little as possible on the question of principle. Such a request he could not honor, for the principle of the law was of such significance that he had to come to grips with it. But first he discussed the specific shortcomings of the measure. He defended the old liability law against its critics and praised the activities of the private insurance companies. He pointed out that nine or ten new companies had been formed since 1871, and that 860,000 workers were insured and had received 17 million marks in awards. Moreover, some 20,000 individual entrepreneurs had insured their workers against accidents. Ten years ago, he lectured his colleagues, Germany's legislation had called the private insurance companies into existence, and now the government intended to destroy them. He took up the insurance companies' claim that the number of cases involving court suits was not exceptionally high, only 2 percent, and denied that excessive friction between employer and employee resulted from them. It was not the business of the insurance companies to desire lawsuits, he emphasized, since this only damaged their reputation and might hurt their business. He was not at all convinced that the state would be more humane and generous than the insurance societies were.[36]

Although Bamberger apparently had no direct ties to the insurance companies they did support the Secessionists and in particular Barth's establishment of *Die Nation*.[37] The old law had stimulated the growth of insurance companies, and the majority of them had prospered during the 1870s. Of course they bitterly opposed the government's bill and claimed that state insurance would not be cheaper than theirs. They denied being responsible for the long trials and pointed to deficiencies in the law. It was not the occurrence of accidents but rather their absence that yielded dividends; hence, they too would be interested in accident prevention measures.[38]

After upholding the efficacy of the existing liability law and the accident insurance companies, Bamberger attacked the proposed imperial insurance institute. Too few people were insured to justify such a structure. He also criticized the lack of payments for the first four weeks of incapacitation and was not pacified by the promise of a future sickness law to cover this period. But the major deficiencies of the bill were that the level of the premiums, the classification of the risk, and the actual arrangement between the employee and the insurance institute were to be worked out later by the Federal Council. Enormous power to influence all the businesses covered by the law was to be given to a body beyond the control of the public.[39] The remainder of Bamberger's speech contained a charge of socialistic experimentation against the government and a defense of the "night watchman's" state which he admitted was his ideal.

No clearer example of the divisions among the liberal parties in the Reichstag was given than in this debate. In the second of what was to be five major speeches from the liberal side, Wilhelm Oechelhäuser, a National Liberal, made a spirited defense of the insurance companies and liability law and repeated many of Bamberger's arguments. For the Progressive leader, Eugen Richter, the imperial insurance office and subsidy were not really socialistic but communistic devices which would lead to class conflict.[40] Baron Adolf von Marschall-Bieberstein, speaking for the Conservatives, supported the government's exclusion of the private insurance companies but opposed the allocation of premiums. He wanted even the lowest-paid worker to contribute to his insurance in order to preserve the self-help aspect of the bill and probably to lower employer contributions. The Center party, through Hertling, supported the bill in principle but voiced objections to the large role granted the federal government through the imperial contribution and insurance office.[41]

Faced with opposition from the liberal parties and only qualified support from the other major parties, Bismarck entered to defend his bill. Something had to be done, he claimed, to remove the legitimate complaints of the people, and under a monarchical and patriarchal system only the state could undertake the task. He made clear to the delegates that his interest in the bill would disappear as soon as the state subsidy was dropped. He was indifferent to the charges of socialism or communism, replying that his program represented "practical Christianity."[42]

With widespread opposition, it was inevitable that the bill would be heavily amended in committee, and a coalition of Centrists and Conservatives worked to reshape the measure. State insurance offices were substituted for the imperial insurance office; the role of the Federal Council in establishing premiums and risk factors was eliminated; the waiting period was reduced to two weeks; and most important, the imperial subsidy was dropped and a two-to-one ratio of employer to employee contributions was inserted.[43]

It was doubtful that the government would accept these changes, and the second and third readings were stormy.[44] Bamberger's only participation in the debate came with the discussion of article 13, which dealt with the allocation of premiums. It had been revised in committee to eliminate the government's contribution, placing the fate of the bill in doubt. In order to salvage something, the German Conservative Hans von Kleist-Retzow introduced an amendment which proposed that the federal states pay one-third of the premium for those whose annual wage was under one thousand marks. He portrayed his proposal as a way to reduce the financial burden on the little man. The government announced that it would accept Kleist-Retzow's proposal for a five-year trial period.[45]

Bamberger characterized Kleist-Retzow's proposal as trying "out socialism for five years" and claimed there were no arguments against such idiocy, only "quiet smiles." Nevertheless he spoke for an hour, and his speech took him through the length and breadth of the bill as well as the Antisocialist Law, which he now said he regretted voting for, and the tariff issue. After several further asides on colonial questions and tobacco monopolies, an attack on Kleist-Retzow, and a defense of Manchesterism, he could only conclude that it was easy to find shortcomings in society but more difficult to discover the means of repair.[46]

As the debates foreshadowed, Kleist-Retzow's amendment was overwhelmingly rejected and the commission's proposal accepted. A similar fate befell the government's plan for an imperial insurance office, which was dropped in favor of state offices. Bamberger had voted in favor of a National Liberal amendment to revive the imperial insurance office, regarding it as the lesser of two evils. On the final vote, Bamberger voted no as the bill was accepted 145–108.[47] True to his threats not to accept a law which eliminated the federal subsidy, Bismarck had the Federal Council reject the Reichstag-approved bill and immediately had work on a new accident insurance bill started. The debates revealed Bamberger's basic approach to the question of social insurance. Less interested in the specifics than opposed to the general principle, he ultimately turned his speeches into tirades against the government's new political, social, and economic program. His fears, it should be stressed, were not wildly implausible.

The following year the government introduced accident and sickness insurance bills thus meeting some of the objections of the previous year. The major innovation was a large measure of decentralization, as the program would be administered by the locality or even factory or trade associations. The government subsidy for premiums was eliminated although, for accidents, the government would pay 25 percent of the damages while the employers would pay the remainder.[48] The bills languished in committee for over a year, with the accident bill dying there because of continued opposition to imperial financial involvement. The sickness bill emerged and passed the Reichstag on May 31, 1883, over Bamberger's negative vote.

Although he did not participate in the debate on the two bills, Bamberger used the budget debate of May 5, 1883, to emphasize his deep-seated hostility to them. He focused his attack on the occupational associations contained in the accident bill. He saw them as a threat to parliament, particularly since they followed closely the government's attempt to set up an economic council alongside the Reichstag. The progress of the century, Bamberger claimed, had been to organize around the principle of civil equality into a common body, the Reichstag. The ultimate aim of the government, he saw accurately, was to dissolve the Reichstag into a medieval assembly of estates. The bill was another link in a chain to restrict the effectiveness of parliament, and this in part accounts for his unwillingness to discuss the factual contents of the bill.[49] One could not be a party to political retrogression.

When Bismarck made his third try for accident insurance in 1884, Bamberger once again cried socialism and warned about the role of the trade associations, which he saw as an attempt to "reconstruct old forms which have been exploded by modern developments." It did not help this time, for enough National Liberals supported the bill to insure passage on June 27, 1884.[50]

If 1881 started Germany down the road to socialistic experimentation with social insurance, the year also ushered the anti-Semitic movement into parliament and into Bamberger's electioneering.[51] Although there are scattered references to Jews and Judaism in his writings during the 1860s and 1870s, and some of them very uncomplimentary, there are virtually no references to the problem of anti-Semitism. In 1870 he did complain of the difficulties in getting nominated for an election district outside one's local area due to the "complications with Judaism." And two years later, in one of his rare involvements with Jewish matters, he requested the chancellor, at the time of anti-Jewish outbursts in Rumania, to do his utmost to see that such excesses did not occur in the future. The Reichstag accepted a motion to this effect.[52] These two manifestations, however, were regarded as mere echoes from the past destined to disappear in a more enlightened age.

Anti-Jewishness, or anti-Semitism as it was called by the late 1870s took on a new configuration at the end of 1879, when it was given respectability by the renowned historian Heinrich von Treitschke. The tone of Treitschke's anti-Jewish comments, which appeared in the *Preussische Jahrbücher*, was mild by the standards of anti-Semitic writers of the 1870s, but the fact that they were written by a well-known historian and political figure was alarming. They led to a great debate about Jews in Germany over the winter of 1879–80, in which Bamberger participated. His essay "Deutschtum und Judentum" ("Germandom and Jewry") appeared in the "very kosher Christian" review, *Unsere Zeit*, whose editor and publisher were "pure Germans."[53] Always politically sensitive, Bamberger was convinced that Treitschke's essay was part of Bismarck's plan to crush the more progressive variety of liberalism, represented by Bamberger and Lasker, by identifying it with Jewry. To his mother he wrote that the affair emanated from the political reaction, since "we are the pioneers of progress." Treitschke was merely the "happy trooper" earning praise from above, this time from Bismarck. "This [Treitschke's] manly pride," he wrote to Oppenheim, "on its face" before royal power, "is a special plant of the German professorial species."[54]

Besides the political ramifications of the new anti-Semitic assault, Treitschke's essay was significant for what it indicated about German nationalism. "The cult of nationality," Bamberger warned, "could easily be transformed so that hatred for other nations becomes a sign of genuine German feeling."

And "from hatred against what is foreign across the border to hatred against what is foreign inside is only a short step. The more hate the more virtue. When national hate directed against foreigners reaches a limit, then the campaign is opened internally."[55] The dangers Bamberger saw in this development were heightened by Bismarckian methods and German character traits.

> [Bismarck] who now dominates us, gives over to the rule of the worst rabble everything that he cannot control with his own hand. That is the only collaboration which he suffers. Perhaps it has always been so. However, it is doubly bad when the theory of brutality is commended to a people with barbarous tendencies, as a species of idealism, power, masculinity, and morality. ... Out of it grows the infamous spirit which now takes over at the universities.[56]

In the wake of the Treitschke affair, a petition was circulated which received 225,000 signatures, calling for the limitation of Jewish immigration, the elimination of Jews from leading positions in state and society, and the reinstitution of a special Jewish census. The petition first led to an inconclusive interpellation in the Prussian House of Delegates in November 1880. It then became a major political issue in April 1881, when the organizers of the petition sent birthday greetings to the chancellor, who acknowledged them. For this he was called to account by Eugen Richter. Bismarck, who replied during the discussion of the accident law, remarked that if it gave anyone pleasure to represent him as a supporter of anti-Semitic movements he would not begrudge him it. He went on to say that if someone like Lasker could characterize the government's policy as an "aristocratic policy," then it was at least understandable that another group could find a similarly pungent phrase "which I will not state" for the opponents' program. He also singled out Bamberger's paper, the *Tribüne,* for publicizing Lasker's phrase.[57] Bamberger was convinced that with this speech Bismarck had "unveiled himself as the anti-Semite that I have not doubted him to be for two years; not from conviction but from method. It is part of his general barbarism. Thiers put it well: *'C'est un barbare du génie'.*"[58] Eighteen years later Bamberger still saw Bismarck's anti-Semitism as governed by a need for political success.[59]

Not only in parliament but also in Bingen-Alzey, anti-Semitism was beginning to be a factor. Although Bamberger had been elected by substantial majorities in 1874, 1877, and 1878, his secession from the National Liberal party had alienated many supporters. If protectionism and anti-Semitism made headway, his constituency was no longer secure. As early as 1879, Bamberger was concerned about protectionist agitation in the area as several localities drafted petitions favoring higher tariffs.[60] By May 1881 he was worried about the "Jew stories" and believed that the chancellor was behind them. "Bismarck is using every means to agitate against me," he complained, "because I more than all others—and that indicates how human affairs change—am hated by him. For the same reason I will not let myself be so easily suppressed. It is a small duel in the shade."[61] After a number of speeches in Ober Ingelheim, Wörrstadt, and Sprendlingen, he was convinced that the reports of serious opposition were unfounded. "That is especially joyful to confirm in the case of anti-Semitism. Not the softest suggestion dares come forth. . . . With true joy I experienced . . . with what abhorrence they [the electorate] spoke of the Jew stories. Bigoted elements of the Protestant clergy, without a doubt directed from Berlin, are at the head of the movement against me, but they have nobody . . . behind them and other clergymen support me enthusiastically. . . . In these troubled times this has its worth."[62]

Nevertheless the election campaign would not be the easy triumph of previous years. He would have to explain the secession and his opposition to Bismarck. He soft-pedaled the first, tracing the split to a disagreement over the seriousness of the reaction. His group merely wanted to form the core of a new liberal party, and he announced to his constituents that the liberal groups in the Reichstag had been united in opposition to the accident insurance, economic council, and stamp tax bills. Even Bennigsen was praised. He told his listeners to ignore party labels and vote for a liberal man.[63] Toward Bismarck he was cautious but firm, putting the responsibility for the evil state of affairs not so much on Bismarck as on the German people. "I have always said," he told his constituents, "first the German Empire must be created, must have a unified constitution. If the German people are in the majority a liberal people, they will take care, even with this constitution, that their freedom is maintained, with Prince Bismarck, without Prince Bismarck, and if need be even against Prince Bismarck. . . . If we lose our freedom it is not the chancellor's guilt but our own. . . . If the German people want to surrender everything to Bismarck, then he will have no respect for them."[64]

Bamberger left Bingen-Alzey in June feeling fairly optimistic about victory. Even though he had alienated some of his former supporters, they were unable, as late as October, to agree on an opponent. Thus he seemed to be facing only a Center candidate and was confident of victory.[65] By the middle of October the non-Catholic opposition united behind the Free Conservative Karl M. Heyl, and even Bamberger admitted that he had won a number of mayors and clergymen and "a lot of people" with the slogan "grain tariff and no Jews." He no longer expected a first-round victory and hoped that the run-off election would be between him and the Center candidate, Philipp

Wasserburg. Otherwise, he believed, all that would decide the race for the Center voters would be "merely the question, Christian or Jew." What might save him would be an awareness that Heyl had been an extremely energetic *Kulturkampfer,* and that Bamberger had at least voted against the Jesuit law. The worst happened. Bamberger, although the leading candidate with 6,461 votes, was forced into a run-off with Heyl, who received 4,787 votes, while Wasserburg was third with an important 3,298. He believed his chances exceedingly poor since he expected most of Wasserburg's votes to go to Heyl.[66] Bamberger won the run-off election by a scant 436 votes. "It is a *wonder,*" he wrote, and he triumphed in spite of the fact that 80 percent of Wasserburg's votes went to Heyl. Bamberger's victory was due to his ability to pick up the 200 or so Social Democratic votes that Bebel had received in the first round, a few hundred Center votes, but most of all his and his party's ability to bring out 1,200 additional voters for the run-off.[67]

"All in all, the reunion will be even better than we had dared to hope," Bamberger wrote to Lasker on the morrow of the 1881 election. The Secessionists were no longer merely the "core of a party" but had won forty-six seats. The election of 1881 was a defeat for Bismarck and a victory for the left liberals as the Progressives won fifty-nine seats. The National Liberals and the two conservative parties together lost ninety seats. Equally unsettling to Bismarck was the fact that the Social Democrats won nine districts, as many as they had had in 1877. As Bamberger wrote Lasker, "Here [Mainz] and in Frankfurt everyone is flabbergasted by the triumph of the Social Democrats."[68]

The overall significance of the election is difficult to grasp. More than 60 percent of the seats won by the Secessionists were taken from National Liberal constituencies, in part because of the party's disarray after the secession.[69] There was also general dissatisfaction with Bismarck's new economic policy, which appeared to mean more taxes and higher prices. Brentano referred to the "shamelessness of the Mammonistic interests, which now under the mastery of the protectionists has actually become even greater. The yearning for leaders without special interests, like Lasker and even Bamberger, was surely not alone decisive for the election result of 1881, but the vote against Bismarck's policy of the protection of national labor was evident."[70] This notion of a defeat, however, should be balanced against a 4 percent rise in the popular vote for the German Conservatives, a nearly 2 percent decline for the Social Democrats, and a decline in votes for Secessionists and National Liberals as opposed to National Liberals alone in 1878. Bismarck also pointed this out.[71]

Although the left liberals celebrated the election of 1881 as a victory, Bismarck was not deflected from his goals. True to his statements to try again if unsuccessful at first, and convinced that the struggle against liberalism would be long, he pushed forward with his plans for a social insurance program, an economic council, a tobacco monopoly, and the economic annexation of Hamburg. For Bamberger, now on the defensive, victory meant defeating a government bill, even if such a negative stance left him open to charges of rigidity, sterility, or at worst being an enemy of the empire. "It may indeed from outside appear dumb," he wrote, "that one struggles so with the mob, but if one still has even one iota of combativeness in his body, it is most pleasant and refreshing to give tit for tat unremittingly."[72]

What Bamberger fought most in the early 1880s was the denigration of parliament. Rudolf Morsey contends that the Reichstag was continually shunted to the second rank legislatively, first by the chancellor's office, then by the Federal Council. Initially the liberal groups were pleased by the active role of the former, which was regarded as a weapon against particularism. But by the late 1870s the Federal Council achieved a greater degree of legislative initiative than the Reichstag.[73] Permanent indirect taxes, a two-year budgetary period, a longer legislative period, the absence of per diem for representatives, the establishment of trade associations for the social insurance program, all were regarded by Bamberger as attempts to undermine the already weak position of parliament, the only voice of the unified German nation. The most blatant step in this direction was Bismarck's attempt to create a German economic council. In Böhme's words, it was to be the final stone in Bismarck's new edifice, and it was designed to push parliament to the side or to get around it. The first move was made at the end of the 1870s with the creation of the Prussian Economic Council. Composed of representatives of industry, commerce, agriculture, and the working class, it was supposed to help economic legislation by giving expert advice. In fact, the Prussian council proved to be dominated by the supporters of Bismarck's new protectionist program. In 1881, the chancellor moved to change the Prussian body into a German Economic Council by adding some fifty non-Prussian members, and he requested the Reichstag to grant 84,000 marks as per diem and travel costs for its members. The government's proposal was defeated 153–102 by a coalition of liberals and Centrists.[74]

Never one to be deterred by a defeat, Bismarck reintroduced the measure at the next session, in the face of the liberal gains in the recent election. In defending his measure, the chancellor denied any intention to weaken parliament and claimed that often bills originated with a ministerial councillor who had no practical experience. The council was necessary to help the government rather than weaken parliament. At the same time he claimed that major economic questions could be better answered by experienced industrialists, agriculturalists, and merchants than by the academically educated and in the main oratorical members of the Reichstag. And he warned the deputies that this would not be the last time the request would be made.[75]

Although Bamberger had not participated in the previous debate on the council, he rarely missed an opportunity to answer the chancellor, especially when it was a question of defending the Reichstag. In Bamberger's eyes, the fact that Bismarck would return to the Reichstag with the proposal so soon after its rejection, in the face of the election results, and promise to do so again and again regardless of the outcome, reflected his low opinion of the representation of the people. The liberal deputy denied that the method of selecting members for the council would provide an impartial body, since the government could choose directly or indirectly more than half the representatives. It would either have whatever opinion the government wished or represent very narrow interests. The members of the Reichstag, he claimed, could easily gain the necessary expertise to handle supposedly technical questions. As expected, the budgetary request for the German Economic Council was rejected by a two-to-one majority.[76]

Bamberger's views on the role of business interests in the legislature were not clear-cut. He removed himself from the Deutsche Bank and the Stolberg Mining Company to keep his hands clean for the major financial questions of the day. However, in his memoirs he regretted having to do this, since such occupations would be very instructive in preparing legislation.[77] In the 1870s, Bamberger in fact bemoaned the dearth of industrial and commercial interests in the Reichstag. "The business world," he wrote, "must . . . not let itself be forced away from high politics and the national legislature by legal scholars, professional politicians, estate owners, and bureaucrats." Practical men of affairs were needed in the working out of legislation.[78] This, of course, should be done within the confines of the Reichstag, not in an economic counterparliament. However, by 1881 he was complaining that the Reichstag was becoming a battleground for various interests.[79]

Bamberger viewed the issue of the economic council as part of a broad attack on politics and politicians, on those who neither reaped or sowed, a theme he developed in an essay entitled "Verdirbt die Politik den Charakter?" ("Does Politics Ruin Character?"). He viewed the antiparliamentary statements and the social welfare program as examples of Caesarian demagogy, which aimed to drive a wedge between the middle and the lower classes and overawe the former. Napoleonic France provided the most recent model. He admitted that politics often was not pretty. Unfortunately there was "no flight from life's problems without putting one's life in jeopardy. . . . One must get at what is demoralizing in these concerns another way than by flight. Those who place some worth on the goodness of their character, those who still have something of it to lose, must do exactly the opposite of what they are advised. They must, by their intervention, strive to ennoble that part of life which one would like to spoil for them."[80]

His article on politics and character led to a public and private exchange with his friend Karl Hillebrand, who had favored an aristocracy of wealth to take care of political problems, which he believed could not be entrusted to the common man.[81] Bamberger's more pessimistic remarks appeared in a bitter letter to Hillebrand written in the midst of an election swing through the Mainz area. He denied that one could escape the increasingly democratized world by fleeing to a romanticized past where high-principled aristocrats ruled. "If you could only see Mevissen, Stumm, and the other rich speculators bowing and scraping before Bismarck." But nothing would help, Bamberger sighed. "We must live and die with the democratized world, willing or unwilling," and he preferred the lower-middle class and peasantry to the "avaricious Junker" who "from narrow-mindedness as from instinct is striving to confiscate the entire economic life."[82]

The gloomy mood persisted through the early 1880s. Whether the government was a little more liberal or conservative made no difference. "I envy the colleagues who still believe enough in themselves to take it [German politics] so very seriously," he confessed. "What makes the present reaction so painful for one of us . . . is that it represents the spirit of hate, of loathsomeness, of unfriendliness which lives in the clergy and Junkers of the land, . . . not the political but the human intolerables sour one's existence." "I won't be surprised," he wrote later, "if a motion is brought in to reintroduce torture. If Bismarck did it, Treitschke would speak in favor of it, and it might find a majority."[83] It stood "written in the stars that Bismarck outlives and overcomes us all; I am convinced of the evil consequences."[84]

The most revealing letter during this period of depression was written shortly before Christmas, 1882. He announced to Hillebrand that he did not intend to go before the voters for reelection, in part because of the spreading anti-Semitic "loathsomeness." He cited a letter from a Frankfurt friend which referred to the "fanatic hatred of Jews" among that city's teaching body. "They may have discovered ethnological and ethical explanations for it," Bamberger continued:

What does that change? It has become an obsession which does not let one loose and inhibits everything! Do you think it is easy for me to make the confession to myself of a completely unsuccessful and bankrupt life? Only with difficulty, confidentially with the understanding of a true friend, do I speak of it. However, I cannot close my eyes to what is. I do not take it more tragically than necessary, and I am completely clear about it. I definitely could not have entered upon any other path through life after 1866 than I did. My faith was my . . . good fortune and at the same time my punishment. I atone for the fact that perhaps ambition affected my belief, although by the coldest self-criticism I believe myself able to say that my desire for a political life and my joy in political development were honorable. What does it matter whether one way or another one's life's dream has dissolved? . . . My soul is out, and if the devil fetches it he will no longer bring it back.[85]

◆ 9 ◆

Colonialism

In spite of the pessimism and forebodings, Bamberger was too much of a professional politician and fighter to succumb to resignation. Whenever there was the smallest chance—and even when there was no chance—to defeat the government, he was at his post in the forefront of the attackers. His long and often hopeless speeches were products of his belief that the Reichstag was the only stage from which one might reach the German people. To educate the public rather than to convince his colleagues was his purpose.

Two of his more successful forays during the fifth legislative period were against the government's attempts to create a tobacco monopoly and to initiate a colonial policy. The tobacco monopoly proposal was in part a product of the financial difficulties of the federal government. The tobacco tax had always been a major source of income for the central government, and it was also attractive to Bismarck because it was an indirect tax. But better even than an increased tobacco tax (which was approved in 1879) would be a tobacco monopoly. State control of the production of raw tobacco and the production and marketing of tobacco manufactures promised to be a lucrative source of funds. During the election of 1881, Bismarck put forth the idea of making the income provided by the tobacco monopoly the "patrimony of the disinherited" and using it to finance his social insurance program. In spite of the unfavorable outcome of the elections and in spite of the fact that the Reichstag the previous year had unmistakably made known its opposition to the tobacco monopoly, Bismarck proceeded with his plans. In May 1882, the Reichstag was presented with a bill which provided that the state would buy raw tobacco and take over the production and marketing of tobacco products. The importation of raw tobacco and tobacco products would also be controlled by the monopoly administration.[1]

The fruitlessness of Bismarck's effort was a foregone conclusion. Only the Conservatives, and not all of them, favored the proposal. Nevertheless the first reading stretched over three days as each party spun out in great detail

180

the basis for its opposition. The bill was sent to a commission which, as expected, recommended 21–3 the rejection of the bill and further announced its opposition to any additional increases in the tobacco tax.[2]

Despite the certain defeat of the bill, Bismarck at the second reading delivered a long and caustic defense of his proposal. It contained a tirade against parliament and the parties, all but accusing them of a lack of patriotism and praising the dynasties as the upholders of the national idea. Even when referring to the struggles of Emperor Henry IV against the "particularists," Bismarck inadvertently blurted out the word "Secessionists," causing a great uproar in the Reichstag. The conclusion of his speech was the occasion for a raucous outburst by his supporters and opponents, which was ended only with difficulty.[3]

Bamberger was the first to reply. He had already expressed his attitude toward the tobacco proposal in March, when he wrote that the "battle for the [tobacco] monopoly is the battle for Bismarck's dictatorship."[4] And his speech made this perfectly clear. He was not, he admitted, a fanatical opponent of the tobacco monopoly, and it was not the details of the bill that offended him most. Given the choice between the monopoly and the rest of Bismarck's socioeconomic program, he would choose the former as the lesser evil.[5] However, he was an opponent under present circumstances. The tobacco bill was not just a tax measure; it symbolized a clash of systems. It was symptomatic of the chancellor's policy of indirect taxes, which Bamberger characterized as a "psychological policy" of taking money from nobody in order to give something to everyone. It also epitomized Bismarck's method of singling out pariahs or scapegoats, like merchants, insurance companies, or tobacco manufacturers, to pay the bills.[6]

But Bamberger was not interested in discussing a universally rejected bill; he wished instead to follow Bismarck along the path of high politics. He accused the chancellor of having a very narrow view of what was national. "Everything that he [Bismarck] wants is national; what others want is particularist." Only groups that did his bidding were considered upright. At the same time, Bamberger reminded Bismarck of the latter's surrender of the national idea when he accepted the Franckenstein clause and when he agreed to an insurance scheme operated by the state governments. The hallmark of the government's program was rather the sowing of discord among various elements of the population. One had "sunk as low as a dog" to stir up disharmony. Not even the dismantling of the *Kulturkampf* could right the wrongs of the past decade, since Bismarck's policy had given its "special imprint to the struggle." About the liberal imprint Bamberger was silent.[7]

When Bismarck replied two days later, the bulk of his speech was designed to rebut the detailed attack on the bill delivered by Richter. For Bamberger he had only a few remarks. He referred to Bamberger's long residence in France and wondered whether his mode of thinking was still not attuned more to Paris than to Berlin. "Bamberger would, if that were permissible in France, . . . be a *sujet mixte.*"[8]

Stung by the remark, Bamberger retorted by defending his efforts on behalf of Prussian-led German unity and continued, "Where does he [Bismarck] get the right to interpret in this way the opinion of another who has an unblemished life behind him? . . . I have no so great and deed-filled and fame-crowned life behind me but, praise God, I also have a blameless and well-known life behind me, and may he yet see where he finds cause to call me a *sujet mixte,* . . . a contemptible expression, an expression which if it had been German must have been censured by the president [of the Reichstag]."[9] His parliamentary comments notwithstanding, Bamberger wrote his mother that he did not for a moment take it "tragically. This arch comedian told pure untruths, and when I showed him in a very clear way that I saw through him, it made him furious. I took it quite easy."[10]

The first article of the bill was defeated 277–43, but the government refused to withdraw the proposal, thus forcing the Reichstag to reject all seventy-two articles.[11] As Bamberger expressed it: "The affair was so unpopular that it perished of its own accord."[12]

If Bamberger was only one of several participants in hindering the establishment of Bismarck's tobacco "dictatorship," his role was decisive in delaying Germany's colonial program. As a belatedly unified nation, without a significant overseas tradtion, Germany until the 1880s possessed no colonial empire. The motives for Bismarck's colonial policy, or rather his turn from an anticolonial stance to a procolonial position, have been variously listed as a desire to achieve a rapprochement with France, to embroil Germany with England in order to damage the pro-English stance of the crown prince, to strike at his left liberal opponents who in the main were anticolonial, to get Germany out of the depression, and to win an election, to mention only the most prominent. A recent and detailed study by Hans-Ulrich Wehler seeks to place the problem of German colonialism within the framework of late nineteenth-century economic development. Using the work of Ronald Robinson and John Gallagher as a base, he applies the concept of free-trade imperialism to Germany and claims that there was a broad ideological consensus in the Reichstag from left to right over the need for overseas expansion. The divergence was over the kind of expansion—the traditional method of the informal empire versus the need for secure colonial possessions. Bismarck in the 1860s and 1870s was an adherent of an informal empire. The change to a more comprehensive system derived from the economic problems of the 1870s and early 1880s. It sprang from a belief that the future strength of a state would depend on the share of the world that it controlled and a fear that Germany would be shut out of Africa. Imperialism would also be of psychological value in demonstrating to business groups that the state was ready to intervene in their favor. In this sense, says Wehler, the expansionist policy was to contribute to overcoming the depression and enlivening the capitalist dynamic. Moreover, Bismarck exploited the colonial movement for political purposes even though he recognized it as a "swindle." It would attract attention away from domestic problems, conceal social tensions, provide a new integrating element, and win elections.[13]

Bamberger might have agreed with Wehler's analysis. As a banker he had had experience in investment in Latin America and North Africa, and the Deutsche Bank was founded to facilitate overseas trade. His later opposition to colonial expansion contradicted the policy of Siemens and the Deutsche Bank, who actively supported the program.[14] This early experience seemed to leave no positive colonial impressions on Bamberger. In his memoirs, in fact, he traced his opposition to a colonial policy in part to his experience with chimerical mining ventures. This essentially negative stance was reflected in his attitude toward government support of companies overseas. "I am a decisive opponent of all those theories which desire that states intervene internationally for their citizens when the latter . . . get into an entanglement on account of their financial interests. As much as I . . . agree . . . that where, without cause, a German citizen is injured, the whole power of the German Reich is not enough to intervene for him, as little do I acknowledge the theory that where a citizen tries to earn 10 percent abroad instead of 4–5 percent here, we have to support him."[15] His views on colonial policy were rarely expressed in the 1870s when the issue seemed to belong to the past. They were clearly stated, however, toward the end of 1876 in the debates over retaliatory tariffs. "The entire colonial policy," he explained, "which now has changed, sacrificed peace, repose, and the taxpayers' money in order to chase after chimerical advantages of trade abroad. A sound policy reverts evermore to the conclusion that a people, through peaceful work, through peaceful agreements with its neighbors, best provides for commerce and industry."[16] This confession of "free-trade imperialism" represented the firm conviction of a lifetime.

As with so many other things, by 1879 Bamberger was becoming less certain of the government's attitude toward overseas expansion.[17] His first extended treatment of the subject of colonialism came during the debate over the friendship treaty with Samoa. German firms had been active in Samoa and the neighboring islands since the 1830s, and beginning in the 1870s Germany sought to regulate its relations with the isles by friendship treaties, which granted freedom of trade, most-favored-nation status, and coaling stations. The treaty with Samoa was concluded in January 1879 and presented to the Reichstag for its approval in June. It was apparently a small matter, a friendship treaty with a tiny island thousands of miles from Germany. State Secretary Bernhard Ernst von Bülow reassured the Reichstag that Germany intended no colony and no monopoly. It only wished to secure rights for German shipping and trade as the Americans had recently done. A slightly different twist was given to the debate by the National Liberal deputy from Bremen, Alexander Mosle, who announced his support for colonies, praised recent colonial writers like Friedrich Fabri and Wilhelm Hubbe-Schleiden, and hoped that the friendship treaty was only the first step toward an ambitious colonial program.[18]

Whether this speech spurred Bamberger to take the floor is not known, but he admitted he was worried by Mosle's view and wondered whether his or Bülow's statement was accepted by the chancellor. However, he supported the government's efforts to widen commercial opportunities for German merchants and warned against permitting any nation to win a trading monopoly in Samoa. Thus he voted for the treaty.[19] But ownership of colonies was another matter. When he came across a newspaper report in August 1879 that Germany intended to buy a pair of Pacific isles, he wrote: "We are spared no piece of folly."[20] Germany was spared that particular piece of folly as the newspaper report proved unfounded, but within eight months Bamberger found his worst suspicions confirmed by a new and larger piece of folly.

In the spring of 1880, the government introduced a bill which provided a guarantee of 4.5 percent interest on its capital to the South Sea Trading Company for a period of twenty years. The guarantee was actually for the trading house of Johann Cesar Godeffroy, which had been engaged in the South Sea trade since the 1830s. Godeffroy had speculated in mining ventures, was on the verge of bankruptcy, and had to mortgage part of his holdings to the English banking firm of Baring. However, he was not only a relative of Bülow's, but also a protectionist and a director of the North German Bank, which controlled the *Norddeutsche Allgemeine Zeitung,* a government newspaper. In the summer of 1879, a request for financial support for Godeffroy went to Bismarck. The chancellor, impressed by the trading possibilities in the Pacific and fearing a loss of the German position in the area, encouraged a bank consortium to organize the South Sea Trading Company to channel financial support to Godeffroy. The imperial guarantee would make the venture palatable to the financiers. At the same time, the press played up the issue as a national question.[21]

The Reichstag debate began on April 22, 1880, with Undersecretary Adolf von Scholz justifying the measure as a way to prevent harm to German trade and the national interest. He was followed by the colonial enthusiast Hermann von Hohenlohe-Langenburg, who advocated a more energetic colonial policy.[22] Bamberger's speech of April 22 and the subsequent ones on colonial matters are among his best. He disciplined his oratory, avoided any hint of standing on principle or being dogmatic, and had his facts well marshaled, gleaning them from directories, medical journals, and even from Samoan newspapers. He denied that there was any inherent connection between free-trade principles and his opposition to the subsidy. He asked the government why, if it was interested in in supporting commerce, it had to turn to bankrupt companies. He saw no "national interest to support those who have failed." Other companies had failed without the federal government's intervening. He then went into the history of the company, its financial difficulties in the 1870s, its indebtedness to Baring, and the connections to the North German Bank and the *Norddeutsche Allgemeine Zeitung.* Part of Godeffroy's troubles, Bamberger stressed, was due to mismanagement in the South Seas. The company had a bad reputation in the area; its officials had abused their position as counsels and had dealt with an American adventurer, Colonel Albert B. Steinberger, to get trade advantages for the company. Its major difficulty was the insolvency of the plantations, which other companies did not possess: only a small portion of the huge holdings was being farmed, and their real worth was only one-fifth of the claimed value. The key problem was the lack of workers to develop cotton and coconuts. The islands offered no export market for Germany since most of their trade was with England. He also denied that they would be attractive to immigrants, who could not be pushed to certain places but would go where the opportunities seemed greatest, North America. After this opening salvo he moved that the bill not be sent to a committee but be discussed directly in plenum.[23]

The government appeared stunned by Bamberger's charges and asked for a day to prepare a reply. When it came, it offered little to rebut his claims other than that his information was taken from hostile sources. Nevertheless, Bamberger was not sure about the attitude of the Reichstag, and another deputy even believed that a small majority was in favor of the bill.[24] For the second reading, Bamberger reached deeper into his well-stocked bag of South Sea information. He denied that Godeffroy dominated the South Sea trade and cited statistics which proved that the company's share had to be far less than half. He then passed in review the economic significance of the Samoa-Hamburg trade: tortoise shells for 1,850 marks, mother-of-pearl for 380 marks, and only six ships per year to Germany. None of these statistics showed a recent steady increase or even any increase at all. He then read his colleagues medical reports describing the dangers of elephantiasis. To claims that Germany's honor and prestige were at stake, he retorted, "What will foreign countries say if we reject this proposal? I will tell you exactly what foreign countries will say: nothing at all! . . . Nobody cares a rap about it." The only people who were watching were Baring and the other bankers, and Bamberger's advice was, "Don't pay them."[25]

The Reichstag did not, defeating the proposal 128–112, as a combination of left National Liberals and the Center outvoted the Conservatives and a minority of the National Liberals. A sizable minority preferred to remain on the sidelines, perhaps dissuaded from supporting the government by Bamberger's revelations.[26] He had no doubt about his own role in the affair. "Had I not destroyed Samoa we would now also have the beginnings of such nonsense" as the French *"folie coloniale."*[27] He noted that

> The Samon affair has caused a great stir. . . . It has made a deep impression on Germany and called forth hate and love in abundance. . . . I had a correct flair [in English in the original] for how the matter could be handled and for what could be made of it. I prepared myself carefully for it well in advance while *no* one else cared about it, and the government as well as the opposition stated that the affair would go through like a letter through the mail. Apart from the satisfaction of preventing a truly shabby trick, it also is worthwhile to take revenge for various things. . . . Completely alone, at my own expense, I have paid him [Bismarck] back with interest.[28]

Bamberger's victory still had little effect on the swelling tide of colonial enthusiasm. Even he admitted that the question engaged the public's interest, and he considered it a new phenomenon that passions could be so aroused by economic and colonial questions. In 1882 the German Colonial Association (Deutsche Kolonialverein) was founded with Johannes Miquel as a leading member. Two years later the Society for German Colonization (Gesellschaft für deutsche Kolonization) was organized. Although the world may not have cared what the Reichstag did about the Samoa proposal, it did seem to care about colonies, and in 1882 England, in spite of Gladstone's protestations, found itself in Egypt. England and France also seemed to be moving toward a partition of West Africa. By 1884, Germany stood on the verge of colonial gains on the east and west coasts of Africa through the efforts of Karl Peters, Gustav Nachtigall, and Alfred Lüderitz. On April 24, Bismarck placed Lüderitz's West African possessions under the protection of the empire. But the area which once more brought Bamberger into the colonial storm was the South Seas.[29]

In June 1884, the government presented a bill to organize and support regular mail service to East Asia and Southeast Asia, which would be in the hands of private companies and receive an annual subsidy of 4 million marks for fifteen years. Bismarck saw this as another means to help German shipping and the export industry, a move which would help restore business confidence and enliven the economy. The move had been discussed by the government since 1881, but only toward the end of 1883 did enough potential support manifest itself to move to the bill-producing stage.[30]

The proposal was recommended for adoption by Postal Secretary Heinrich Stephan, who called it a "national affair." He portrayed it not as a piece of colonial policy or state socialism, but as a practical measure to satisfy a need and to help German trade. "You build with those postal ships a bridge over the ocean to lands rich in products with a trade-oriented people which is very accessible to the progress of European civilization." Moreover, subsidized lines of this kind were used by England and France, and German trading houses had to use foreign mail ships.[31]

Almost reluctantly, Bamberger attacked the presentation of the very popular postal secretary. Although he recognized that including the measure in the postal budget would make it seem less objectionable, he was convinced that the "project" was "as foolish as possible."[32] He tried to explain his reasons to the Reichstag. His speech was in many respects a copy of his Samoan efforts—very factual, devoid for the most part of his biting humor, without personal attacks or an ideological stance, even "boring" as Richter conceded, but always to the point. He took the government to task for its weak and sketchy motivation of the bill. The Reichstag was provided with almost no information on which to make a decision in either the bill or the introductory speech by Stephan. Nowhere was it stated whether the subsidy was necessary because trade with the area was good or bad, and there were no details about the kind of contract the government would make with the private companies. Thus, Bamberger went on, he had had to gather the statistics for his case himself, and they provided a weak justification for the government's position. The fact that other countries supported steamers was no justification for Germany to follow suit. England, whose subsidy was the same as that suggested by the government, had far more extensive interests in the area. For Germany there was no justification of the subsidy and monthly mail steamers on the basis of freight, people, or mail to be carried. There were already enough steamers operating in the area, including fourteen German ships, and he pointed out the difficulty the German shippers had in getting a full cargo for their ships to Asia. It was "false chauvinism" to want German goods to be carried only in German boats. German trade, on the contrary, profited from using the shipping of other countries and could dispose of its products to a far wider market. He claimed that after studying the consular reports he could find only one complaint about a lack of a direct mail connection between East Asia and Germany. The total mail sent between Germany and East Asia was some three hundred thousand letters annually or a few bags of mail per month, which he calculated would cost one hundred marks per letter to send. There was, furthermore, no large group of passengers waiting to be ferried across. In fact, the entire Asian trade was so insignificant that he could see no reason to build a fleet for it. The government's claim that mail ships somehow would increase trade was like "warming the thermometer with the hand so that the temperature appears to rise." He further emphasized that even without subsidies Germany was able to ship one-third of its exports to overseas markets. And finally, France, with all its subsidies for South Sea commerce, was still behind Germany in trade, and its subsidized companies were not prospering.[33]

Bamberger's speech, ably seconded by Richter, received only weak replies from Bismarck and Stephan. The chancellor's speech was flat and resigned, giving rise to claims that what he really wanted was an election issue rather than a steamship subsidy law. The most important speech of the day, however, was given by a Centrist, August Reichensperger, who admitted that he had been deeply impressed by Bamberger's arguments and could discover no significant answer by the government. With the Center opposed to the proposal, its chances of reemerging from committee were dim.[34]

The referral of the proposal to a commission only two weeks before the end of the session appeared to mean its burial. But to everyone's surprise, Bismarck appeared at the commission meeting for the first time since 1871. He requested a new plenary discussion of the bill, admitted the steamer subsidy proposal was an integral part of a new colonial policy, and made clear what one of the themes of the fall election would be. All he succeeded in doing was to provoke Bamberger to reveal confidential information about which groups would profit most from the bill. Once more given information by a confidant, Bamberger was made aware that an old enemy of his, Adolf von Hansemann, and others were moving to cash in on the government's proposal. They bought up Baring's shares in Godeffroy's company for 20 percent of their face value, and as the subsidy bill became known they could sell plots of land in Samoa at speculative prices. Furthermore, Hansemann had interests in New Guinea which also would be favored by the bill. And lastly, Hansemann was related to the government councillor concerned with colonial matters, Heinrich von Kusserow. That there was collusion could not be proved, but Bamberger's revelations destroyed any chance that the bill would find its way to the Reichstag before the session ended.[35]

The subsidy bill had two repercussions. During the discussions in the commission, Bamberger hinted at the relationship between Hansemann and Kusserow and as a consequence was challenged to a duel by the latter.

Bamberger was forced to deny any suggestion of collusion between the two or any intention of maligning Kusserow. Bamberger continued to shake his head for a month thereafter, trying to understand how he had made such a blunder after waging an impeccable campaign.[36]

The debate over the steamship subsidy bill was not over. It erupted in a particularly bitter form in the discussion about the friendship treaty with Korea. The latter was scarcely mentioned, as most of the speakers seemed to have their eyes on the next election and passed in review the past two decades of Prusso-German history. The core of the debate involved Bismarck and Richter, who spoke five and seven times respectively. It was clear from the chancellor's statements that colonialism would be the key issue. Bamberger figured in the debate primarily because of his statements during the commission meeting of June 23 which Bismarck characterized as a "scornful persiflage of all German colonial efforts." In his reply, Bamberger admitted his general skepticism about all of Germany's colonial efforts, and he bemoaned the fact that such an important matter as colonies, which would involve Germany in serious foreign policy questions, was discussed in a "carnival atmosphere." He stressed that foreign policy complications might develop with England if Germany embarked on an ambitious overseas program and how vulnerable Germany was to English displeasure. He admitted that he saw a "piece of Samoa" behind the latest proposal and called the bill the government's "revenge for Samoa." As his ideal regarding overseas policy he singled out America, which he claimed had rejected a colonial policy. The foundation of American policy abroad, he said, was "We want trade not dominion."[37] After getting the steamship subsidy debate out of its system, the Reichstag passed the Korean friendship treaty bill with no opposition and virtually no debate.

As expected, the colonial issue was a major topic for debate between June and the October election. The government press and colonial organizations played up the issue. Bamberger's former National Liberal colleague, Wehrenpfennig, announced in the *Preussische Jahrbücher* that when Bamberger maintained that trade was more important than dominion, he was upholding the standpoint of a "haggling Jew."[38] Anti-Semitism had become another weapon of the colonial enthusiasts.

Although Bamberger was clear about his own intention regarding Bismarck's colonial program, he viewed the "shallow enthusiasm" and "intoxication with maritime power" as a dangerous political weapon which played to all the "false instincts of the nation.... The contrast between the childish belief in B[ismarck]'s ideal strivings and the true facts" angered him. "Many a time I say to myself, he pushes the colonial system perhaps only in order to lead to an alliance with France against England, which would reconcile the angry neighbor. And such a goal would be comprehensible." Two weeks later, however, he saw the anti-English campaign as a way to strike at liberals close to the crown prince and his English wife and make "parliamentary capital out of it. He [Bismarck] leaves no stupidity unused." He believed that Bismarck's theory of colonization, that is, utilizing charter companies to do the administrative work, "disappears already with the first close look, and we are setting Germany on a maritime course of major dimensions."[39] One almost feels that Bamberger did not know whether to laugh or cry over the "colonial frenzy" which found "gallant Germans . . . swimming in beer declare waterless Angra Pequena one of the inspiring sources of national welfare." As a "cast-off public benefactor" he could look on "how, under the enlightened commercial policy of the Pomeranian Junker and the Holy Inquisition, even in . . . Polynesia or Hottentotland, masters examinations combined with phalansteries, a solution of the social question, reproduction of the corporative structure, continental blocks, compulsory guild membership, and right to work are produced, all in connection with an aristocratic officer corps. That must be marvelous, I would like to be there." He envied Hillebrand his residence in Italy: "That is the great profit of absenteeism; you can keep your cake because you don't eat it."[40]

First he had to return to contest the seat in the Reichstag which he had retained in the last election only by a narrow margin. He faced three candidates, the National Liberal Schauss, the Centrist Wasserburg, and a Social Democrat. The main challenge came from Schauss, who had seceded from the National Liberals in 1879 but was nevertheless running under their banner. Recently relations between the two men had reached a point where Schauss challenged Bamberger to a duel as a result of the latter's comments during the debate on the accident insurance bill of 1884. The matter was settled peaceably, but the enmity remained strong.[41] From afar it looked as if Bamberger would not have an easy time, and Karl Schrader, his party colleague, even asked Stauffenberg to make a speech on Bamberger's behalf in Bingen-Alzey. The government tried to make the campaign a plebiscite on the colonial issue, and its newspapers lashed out at colonial obstructionists like Bamberger and Richter, recently united in the newly formed German Radical (Deutsch-Freisinnige) party. They played up the anti-English campaign and implied that the colonial opponents were doing England's work, charges which could also be used to embarrass the crown prince and his English wife. Schrader bemoaned the German's susceptibility to such arguments and claimed: "Our political education, as with all other nations, must and will be completed only through experiences of an evil kind."[42]

While calling attention to and criticizing the hate campaign, Bamberger did not lessen his opposition to the government's policy. "If I wanted to be in the

Reichstag at any price," he wrote Hillebrand in July, "I would not preach my godless steamer heresy in the villages." His attitude, although confident, was "I don't care a bit." "Actually," he wrote Stauffenberg unconvincingly, "I would prefer to be defeated, for I am tired of the battle with the majority which is enthusiastic for the ideal goals of Bismarck." Nevertheless, he did not think Schauss had much of a chance even though he was trying to exploit the issue of anti-Semitism. Schauss had little support among the Center because he had been too active in the *Kulturkampf.* "The Center people," Bamberger claimed, were "much more ardently for me than I myself. Even my opponent, Wasserburg, has visited me twice without my lifting a finger or conceding a word. Sch[auss] must be furious." He believed, however, that he had to play down the cooperation he was receiving from the Center since it might alienate his own anticlerical supporters. Bamberger was also helped by Max Broemel, who spoke on his behalf in the district and delivered a sheaf of material on Schauss supposedly documenting his ardent anti-Catholic attitude and his otherwise insignificant role in the Reichstag.[43]

Bamberger gauged the election well; in the first round he was only some six hundred votes ahead of Schauss and far from a majority because of the other candidates. In the second round, approximately two-thirds of the Center's votes went to Bamberger, as the candidate who was independent of Bismarck and had voted against the Jesuit Law, giving him a comfortable 56 percent of the votes. About 38 percent of his district was Catholic, making it virtually impossible for the Center to win unless it could get allies for the run-off, which never happened. In 1887 and 1890 the party did not bother to put up a candidate, giving Bamberger easy first-round victories.[44]

For the rest of the Radical party the election results were less pleasant, as the colonial campaign claimed its victims. The party lost the equivalent of 18 percent of its popular vote and 37 percent of its seats, returning with sixty-seven representatives. The German Conservative party was the major victor in terms of Reichstag seats, going from fifty to seventy-eight while the Free Conservatives held their own. The National Liberals made striking gains in the popular vote (33 percent) but were not able to win more than four additional seats. The other victor was the Social Democratic party, which increased its votes by over 70 percent and its seats by 100 percent to twenty-four. Thus it could be said that the election tended to push German society to both the right and the far left.

For Bismarck it was a pleasing victory and a signal to press on energetically with his colonial plans. In September the English had recognized Germany's protectorate in Southwest Africa, and in July 1884 the German flag had been raised in West Africa. In February 1885 protection was accorded to Karl Peters' acquisitions in East Africa, and in May 1885 the possessions of the

New Guinea Company under the leadership of Adolf von Hansemann, head of the Diskonto Gesellschaft, were put under the German umbrella. Finally, from December 1884 to February 1885, Bismarck presided successfully over the Congo Conference in which France and Germany cooperated against England.[45]

One of the first measures Bismarck took in the new session was to reintroduce the postal steamship subsidy bill, now enlarged to include a line to Africa and an increased subsidy.[46] The new proposal pushed the postal interest into the background and stressed instead trade and a general colonial policy. Pleased by the more honest statement of aims and playing, as he said, the role of the devil's advocate, Bamberger again denied that he opposed the venture on principle. Emphasizing the commerical aspects, he claimed that no significant trade was to be gained from these ships. No one would buy German goods simply because they came on German ships. The goods that would be shipped did not require the express boats provided for in the proposal. Germany exported about 50 million marks worth of goods to these countries, and for them the taxpayer was to pay 5.4 million. Again he emphasized that the English and French subsidies were either required by the enormous interests of England or, in the case of France, produced no significant results. Moreover, the world suffered from overproduction, and markets were full of goods. Thus, he concluded, great profits could not be expected. On the whole, the proposal represented an "unproductive business" on which the taxpayers' money should not be squandered, especially when the budgetary situation was so unpromising.[47] The debate proceeded relatively quickly, and the matter was referred to a commission where after several changes the reworked bill was rejected 14–7. Decisive for the vote was the Center, which demanded concessions in other fields as its price for supporting the measure.[48]

As the postal steamship company bill was being debated in committee, Bamberger was able to score minor victories in the colonial skirmishing as the Reichstag cut budgetary requests for consulates in Asia and Korea. As the major speaker against motions to restore the funds, he demonstrated a knowledge of conditions in both areas that government representatives and supporters could not or would not match.[49] The most bitter struggle developed over a relatively minor item of twenty thousand marks to create a new department in the Foreign Office, which was to be responsible for economic, commercial, and consular affairs. The budget commission recommended that the twenty thousand marks for the new director be stricken, touching off a major debate. The opponents of the new allocation saw a colonial office in it even though they stressed purely financial considerations. The government emphasized the vastly increased workload in commercial affairs, often requiring a special expertise. Bismarck, however, posed the question as one of confidence or lack of confidence in him and his "oath of office," since he claimed the addition was necessary to carry on German foreign policy. In spite of this assertion, the Reichstag in the second reading rejected by a vote of 141–119 a proposal to restore the cut funds, with the majority coming from the Center and Radical parties.[50]

The vote, however, caused a major crisis in the Radical party, as the government drummed up public opinion against this supposed parliamentary outrage. Petitions supporting Bismarck poured into the Reichstag, and the party's susceptibility to national or patriotic pressures was evident. A sizable group led by Rickert, Schrader, Broemel, and Forckenbeck decided to support the government on the third reading, while the bulk of the party behind Richter continued its opposition. Bamberger joined the latter group. He rejected a suggestion to abstain on the third reading because he believed it would harm the party more than a little obstinacy. "For my part I am for no in the third reading. But if any of us stays silently in his corner we will be severely ridiculed. . . . I consider that worse." The question of a few thousand marks, he claimed, could not be isolated from the rest of Bismarck's then very active colonial moves. "Even *after* the petitions' comedy and in the face of the great Southwest Africa policy, I regard it morally impossible for us to say *yes* in the third reading because this would be an assent to Bismarck's entire policy, a joining in the insipid submission; and I say to you after quiet reflection that I consider that the worst, even worse than [a divided party]. No one is going to get *me* to say yes."[51]

Bamberger was particularly incensed by the recent reemergence of the Samoan clique of Hansemann and Godeffroy, whom he had viewed as the chief beneficiaries of the steamer subsidy bill in June 1884. The center of operations was now New Guinea, which was regarded as suitable for large plantations. On December 23 the northern half of New Guinea was placed under German protection. This confirmed the fears Bamberger had expressed in the summer. "It proves only that my source was so good that I do not doubt in the least that Hansemann [was] behind it as my informant knew. But are we also silently to accept the South Sea annexation in all its glory?" He would oppose it regardless of the party's desire and if it [the party] does not wish it I will leave. What the devil does one still have to lose?"[52] Thus this was not the time to give an indication of approving Bismarck's colonial program by supporting the establishment of a new Foreign Office department.

Bamberger did attempt to mediate between the two groups, who were essentially split into Secessionist and Progressive wings, but this failed, and the party was forced to declare the budgetary question open. The long debate in the third reading was enlivened only by Rickert's announcement that he and a number of colleagues would vote for the government's original request for a second director of the Foreign Office. A sufficient number of Radicals followed him to enable the government to win 172–153.[53]

But all of the budgetary debates in this colonial Reichstag represented mere shadowboxing for the major battle that took place when the mail steamers subsidy bill emerged from the commission in March 1885. The second reading extended over five days as the Reichstag was faced with a commission proposal that was itself rejected by the commission 14–7. The rejected report had reduced the lines from three to one, leaving only the East Asia line, and lowered proportionally the subsidy figure. It also laid down certain conditions that the contracting companies had to meet regarding regularity of sailing, safety, speed, and place of construction of the boats. Majorities could be obtained in the commission for individual sections of the bill, but each change alienated another group so that it was impossible to obtain a majority for the whole bill. In the long debate, the first indication of the sentiment of the Reichstag occurred on the fourth day as a progovernment majority voted to close off discussion of article 1. Parliament then approved lines to Australia and East Asia but rejected the African connection by majorities of ten to fifteen votes.[54]

Bamberger did not participate in the second reading but delivered a two-hour effort in the third round. By then the outcome was clear, and it was only a question of scoring points. He regretted the more frequent use of military terminology in reference to economic matters, particularly in regard to a trade struggle with England. He also tried to argue the case for only an Asian line where there was at least a chance for significant trade increases. The attempt failed by fourteen votes.[55] The five-year struggle had finally ended in a government victory. Bamberger might, however, have drawn some satisfaction from the future development of the subsidized steamship lines. The Australia-Samoa line proved extremely unprofitable and was given up in 1893. The East Asian line required ten years before it began to show a profit, but from the mid-1890s on it carried an increasing share of East Asia's trade, which increased sharply.[56]

The following years found Bamberger still occupied with colonial questions, and his position did not change. It was still all "hot air" which would only make Germany an object of general hostility. "One day," he wrote, "all of the accumulated hatred of all the nations will break loose against us. To get us into a quarrel with everyone is B[ismarck]'s aspiration."[57]

·10·
New Unity and Continued Opposition: 1884-1890

The colonial debates in the Reichstag illuminated more clearly than any other issue the wide gulf separating the left liberals from the National Liberal party and pointed up one of the failures of the secession, the inability to form a great liberal party. Under Miquel's leadership, the National Liberals had become more governmental than ever. In the colonial debates of 1884 and 1885, as well as with the accident insurance bill, the party had supported the government's proposals without reservation, making a connection between the two liberal groups difficult. Since the National Liberal leadership, in Bamberger's words, was the "misfortune of German politics," the Secessionists would have to turn to the left for support.[1]

The Secessionists had proclaimed at the outset that their group had its *raison d'être* only as a gathering point for liberal forces. By the end of 1883 the sporadic attempts at cooperation with the Progressives and National Liberals had yielded nothing; nevertheless some move seemed urgent. The election victory of 1881 was regarded as ephemeral, being due to a certain organizational advantage coming from Rickert's adherence to the Secessionists and dissatisfaction with the recently passed tariff legislation. But perhaps the most telling argument for the fusion with the Progressives was the desire to provide a strong base of support for the eighty-seven-year-old Emperor William's son, Frederick William, when the expected succession occurred. As early as 1879, Forckenbeck had discussed the question of a great liberal party with the crown prince; and in 1882, 1884, and 1886, Bamberger had conversations with him.[2]

Finally, it has also been suggested that Lasker's death and the ensuing quarrel with Bismarck drove a number of Secessionists to the left.[3] In response to Lasker's death, the United States House of Representatives sent a message of condolence to the Reichstag which Bismarck refused to accept. Ostensibly the chancellor was disturbed by a passage that praised Lasker's useful parliamentary work, regarding this as an implied criticism of the government. But in the course of a speech explaining his actions he made clear that what disturbed him most was the political capital Lasker's friends sought to make from his death and burial. He accused them of exploiting it in a "usurious way" and proceeded to review all the supposed sins of the deceased representative.[4] The high point of this campaign of "exploitation" was Bamberger's memorial speech. The memorial service was kept separate from the burial service to give the former, as Bamberger admitted, a "politically liberal character." Although he hoped that several colleagues would participate in the "political memorial service," Rickert and Forckenbeck declined, leaving him the only speaker. His speech indirectly attacked Bismarck as he praised the deceased as one through whom the German nation spoke for ten years, although now "Lasker's spirit" was considered "dangerous." He also defended his friend against the charge of being impractical, stressing his effective parliamentary work in committee and in the party caucus. The speech was a surprising success, especially with the crown prince and his wife, and was reprinted.[5] Bismarck's wrath was understandable.

If fear of the next election, long-range political ambitions, and momentary anger pushed the Secessionists toward the Progressives, the motives of the latter were less clear. According to Felix Rachfahl, the motive for the fusion was the impending election. The Progressives' election chances, at least to Richter, seemed dim, and he was afraid of taking the blame. Thus, to improve his party's chances and diminish his own responsibility for a possible defeat, Richter went along reluctantly.[6] Gustav Seeber, in his pathbreaking work on left liberalism, argues that Richter and the other leaders of the party feared a burgeoning popular movement on their left. Faced by a choice between "a popular struggle against Bismarck or turning away from the popular movement, the leadership of the Progressive party chose the latter path. . . . Out of fear of the working class, the leadership of the Progressive party turned to the decidedly upper middle class elements and pushed the union with the Secessionists."[7]

Seeber's use of the term "pronounced upper middle class elements," athough possibly correct, seems to rest on insufficient evidence. The interests of the Deutsche Bank may have been well represented by Siemens and Schrader, but this did not stop the Secessionists from opposing Bismarck's colonial policy. There were indeed connections with the insurance companies, but these were sought out by the Secessionists after they had announced their opposition to Bismarck's social insurance program. Of greater concern than the profits of private insurance companies was the maintenance of constitutional rights, and Seeber admits that it was precisely this consideration that was paramount to Lasker, Stauffenberg, and Forckenbeck.[8] Although Seeber does demonstrate the makings of a popular movement against Bismarck, its impact on Richter is not easy to discern, and it was Richter who, on January 25, 1884, asked Albert Hänel, known for his sympathy for a union of liberal forces, to feel out the Secessionists on the subject. The negotiations were led by Hänel for the Progressives and by Bamberger, Forckenbeck, and Rickert for the Secessionists.

Although Bamberger's political roots had been democratic, and thus closer to the Progressives than to the National Liberals, his move toward the right in the 1860s drew a curtain over his past. Even when his opposition to Bismarck in the 1880s seemed to confirm the predictions of his democratic acquaintances, Bamberger refused to concede anything. In 1883 Carl Vogt still represented an "outdated democratic attitude toward German affairs" which did not "even stimulate me to a discussion because he differentiates much too little in evaluating why I belong to the opposition." He had equally uncomplimentary words for his former democratic friends in Mainz, who were the "source of all misery for us."[9]

The Progressive party and Richter might not have been very "radical," but to many of Bamberger's constituents they were dangerous enough. In 1884, shortly after the fusion, Bamberger's supporters in Alzey canceled an election rally because, Bamberger believed, there was a possibility that Richter might show up. Even Stauffenberg admitted that the fear of Richter "in our circles" was "very general and not unfounded."[10] Thus, with deep reservations and little enthusiasm, Bamberger joined in the negotiations with the Progressives.

The discussions proceeded smoothly until Bamberger raised objections to any reference in the common statement to per diem for Reichstag deputies and to ministerial responsibility. Hänel was rightfully surprised by his opposition to per diem since he had voted for it in the 1870s, as did virtually all the Secessionists.[11] Stauffenberg, who because of ill health and involvement in Bavarian politics did not participate directly in the negotiations, still had great influence. For him there was only one path to take, to a fusion. "Now above all, in spite of reservations, the affair must be made; it cannot be rejected. For us things lie so: with a rejection we will surely be ruined, for our entire position can only be tenable in passing." He did add prophetically: "With the acceptance [of the offer for a union] we can also certainly suffer shipwreck." He advised Bamberger to give up his objections to per diem and ministerial responsibility. Only two things were important: that the Secessionists have a dominant position in the new party and that defections from the Liberal Union be kept to a minimum. In spite of his strong hostility to any mention of a responsible imperial ministry, Bamberger dropped his opposition.[12]

The Secessionists, nevertheless, were able to achieve a dominant position, with the Progressives making most of the concessions. Stauffenberg was named chairman of the central committee which, as Bamberger noted, gave "the affair the signature of our firm"[13] In the program or points of agreement that Bamberger drafted, the Secessionist view on the military budget triumphed, and the document called for the military budget to be approved once every legislative period rather than annually. Even the demand for a responsible imperial ministry did not specify responsibility to parliament, as the Progressives' 1878 program had. Also dropped from earlier Progressive platforms were calls for factory legislation, which Bamberger opposed, the widened use of jury trials, and improved public education for the working class.[14] The declaration, with its vague phrasing and omissions, could be positively interpreted by Richter, as if nothing had changed, and at the same time it might attract some National Liberals, which even Hänel hoped for.[15] If anything, it was to provide the basis for future discord.

Stauffenberg's desire to keep the number of Secessionist defectors to a minimum was realized. The negotiations had been kept secret until their successful conclusion was announced to the two parties' Reichstag groups on March 5. Although there was some grumbling from both sides, the fusion was accepted by great majorities. On March 15 and 16, the party congresses gave their assent.[16] When the Reichstag opened on March 6, the new German Radical party was the largest, with ninety-nine deputies. Its effectiveness would depend on its inner cohesion. The major point of friction, from the point of view of the former Secessionists, was Eugen Richter, who was regarded as vindictive and doctrinaire, ready to maintain opposition at any price, and too interested in short-term "election tactics" at the risk of losing more important long-term prizes.[17]

Immediately, however, Bamberger seemed pleased with Richter's behavior, particularly his silence during the Lasker debates and during the opening stages of the debates on extending the Antisocialist Law. "I see right now even more how correct we were with the fusion. R[ichter] is a politician and so few are."[18] Nevertheless it was not long before the party went through its first crisis. During the negotiations over the fusion, Stauffenberg had written Bamberger of the crucial importance of the Antisocialist Law. "On this depends the whole future of the liberal party . . . we cannot accept the old law."[19] On March 8 the government introduced a bill to extend the Antisocialist Law for two years. By proposing a mild extension of only two years, Bismarck wanted to force the Radical party either to betray its principles by helping to pass the law or, as he preferred, have the bill rejected, dissolve parliament, and run an antisocialist campaign against the left liberals.[20] The latter were faced with a dilemma. Although a general election was scheduled for the fall of 1884, they desperately wanted to avoid one so soon after the fusion, particularly one in which they would be branded enemies of the empire. On such an issue, Bamberger admitted, "we will lose heavily in the voting." There was also substantial pressure from the party's strongholds to vote for a renewal of the law.[21]

Bamberger, nevertheless, intended to vote against extending the law. In 1883, in the debate on the accident insurance bill, he had admitted: "I do not know if we acted wrongly in an exceptionally agitated time, but such an exceptional law cannot remain permanently without harming the whole nature of the people's lives and of the state constitution."[22] The following year he justified his change of heart on the basis of the government's actions in the social field since 1878. The government by 1884 stood "up to its shoulders in socialism," and socialistic ideas were being spread by leading elements of German government and society. The Antisocialist Law was suffocating public discussion and blinding people to the truth that underneath the mantle of the law the socialist state was being introduced. To end the law would be to bring people to their senses, to force them to realize that the apparently harmless ideas they permitted among themselves were the same ideas that were discussed by the Social Democrats.[23] Bamberger had now reversed himself. In 1878 the law had been necessary to make the socialists of the salon aware that they were playing with dangerous ideas. In 1884 the law was no longer necessary to show these same people that their ideas were the ideas of Social Democrats. It was not one of his more convincing speeches, especially as he had already been a part of a plot to make certain that the bill passed.

If Bamberger's intentions regarding the Antisocialist Law were clear, this was not the case with a number of his colleagues, who were under strong pressure from their constituents to vote for its extension. He hoped, however, that the Center would provide the votes for a majority but added that it would not at all hurt "if we deliver a dozen apostates." When Stauffenberg apparently wrote him that the party was obligated to vote against the law, Bamberger was quick to deny this. The phrase in the party program, "equality of the parties before the law," he replied, did not mean an unconditional obligation to vote against the law. At the discussion with the Progressives, it was pointed out that a majority of the Secessionists would vote against an extension, but "we did not hide the fact that there would also be dissenters." Thus there should be no talk of making the issue a party question. Realistically, Bamberger continued, even if Richter would threaten the dissenters with the "death sentence," "silently he would also like to deliver a few deserters in order to escape a dissolution which he fears even more than we." The key to the situation, Bamberger went on, was to place Richter "before the accomplished fact. I am also not afraid of [doing] it. In a small group he is quite reasonable. I think it will come as you and I wish: the great majority of the party votes against, among them all the leaders with the exception of Forckenbeck." He expected only eight or ten to vote for the bill.[24]

The silent struggle within the new party went on. When Theodor Mommsen publicly announced his support for an extension of the law and said that he would not vote against the bill even if he were sure of being in the minority, Richter, so Bamberger reported, was held back from an attack on the historian only with the greatest difficulty. At the same time, however, Bamberger was assuring Mommsen that the vote on the bill would not be made a question of party discipline. "In this sense not merely we [Secessionists] are united, but the agreement of the former Progressives is on the whole certain, perhaps even without exception."[25]

Further discord was created by other Radicals who wished to bring in amendments designed to weaken the bill. The expectation was that Bismarck would reject these and in so doing would push wavering Radicals into the opposition. Richter opposed the amendments on the grounds that such temporizing would harm the party's election chances with the left, whose votes he regarded as necessary for the run-offs. Bamberger, however, discounted the idea that there were any votes to be won from the Social Democratic side and argued that what counted was how the party voted on the entire bill. This perhaps fundamental difference of opinion reappeared in subsequent debates over the military bills. An inability to decide where its constituency was to be found seemed only to result in weak compromises and to drive potential voters to the Social Democrats and the National Liberals.[26]

How the bill would fare could not be predicted. The commission meetings were chess matches, as the Radicals wished to put the onus for the passage of the bill on the Center to avoid a dissolution, while Bismarck wanted the bill rejected to smash the new party. Commission members were ordered to absent themselves or change their votes to avoid giving the other side an advantage. Finally the government's proposal failed to win approval of the commission.[27]

Within the Radical party, things rapidly came to a climax when Forckenbeck announced that he would vote for renewal and justify it publicly. On May 5 Bamberger, Richter, Stauffenberg, Rickert, and two others met to plan strategy for the second reading. It is best to let Bamberger describe it: "Quite coolly Richter brings forth a note with probability calculations, how many votes our group would have to deliver so that the law is accepted. He states that twenty-five are needed and explains with the most innocent candor that if some wanted to abstain it would be much better if they voted for [the bill]. In short there was no more eager propagandist for acceptance." And for the sake of security, some who would have voted no were sent home and all those for the measure fetched to Berlin. "Such a naive turnabout from the comedy of indignation to the opposite performance, one has perhaps never experienced." It was a "buffoonery without equal."[28] More than providing comedy, the affair demonstrated to Bamberger how useful for the Secessionists the fusion was. Without it, they, from whose ranks the great majority of the no votes came, would have had to pay the bill and be singled out as great sinners by Richter.[29]

The farce played itself out during the Reichstag debates of May 8–10. Speaking for those Secessionists who had changed their minds since 1878, Stauffenberg made known his disappointment with the interpretation that the administration had given the bill. He and his friends, he complained, had been "deceived" about the character of the law. Although the external effects were favorable, in the sense of the apparent destruction of the Social Democratic organization, the "psychological effects" were extremely harmful. "When a great number of citizens are placed outside the law for an indefinitely long time, it cannot help but force them ever more from the path of legality." All the law would achieve in the future was a radicalization of the Social Democrats and a growth in anarchism.[30] The three-day debate was highlighted by an embittered exchange between Bismarck and Richter that scarcely touched the Antisocialist Law. The chancellor, unaware of the arrangement of May 5, ended his speeches with a plea not to "elect any Progressive deputies" if one wanted to be rid of the socialist danger.[31] The roll-call vote yielded an unwanted government victory, 189–157. Besides the National Liberals, Free Conservatives, and German Conservatives, thirty-nine Center and twenty-six Radical deputies voted for the law. Of the twenty-six, twenty-four were former Secessionists. In addition, thirteen Radical and eighteen Center representatives were absent. Bamberger voted no.[32]

The Secessionists had won the first tug of war within the party and kept the way open for a possible agreement with some of the National Liberals. Bamberger and Hänel held conversations in April with Arthur Hobrecht of the National Liberals, which led nowhere. Still Bamberger sounded pleased as he wrote Stauffenberg. "I spoke with Hobrecht and Blum in order to remind them how little, after this experience, they were right to fear that we had fallen into Richter's hands."[33] In spite of the pleasure over the outcome of the struggle, the much feared election, as already noted, decimated the ranks of the Radicals as Bismarck was able to play the colonial card against them. They were perhaps also hurt by their opposition to the Accident Insurance Law of 1884.[34]

The short life of the Radical party, from 1884 until 1893, was marked by continual tension between its two wings. The two groups were never truly united in a homogeneous party. In the party committees, the always odd numbers of seats were divided so that former Progressives outnumbered former Secessionists by one. Both groups had their own newspapers which periodically engaged in heated exchanges with each other. Finances were in part separate, and even local organizations belonged clearly to one group or the other. Richter and Rickert both served as *de facto* organizational chiefs.[35] If anything, the former Secessionists should have felt at home in the new party, since the internal quarrels could almost be regarded as a continuation of those within the National Liberal party. The union had been carried out almost against the will and better judgment of both groups, and the outcome of the election of 1884 was not designed to convince the leaders that they had made the right move. Particularly antipathetic were Schrader, Barth, and Rickert on the one side and Richter on the other, whom the former accused of trying to make the party his personal instrument. While Bamberger shared many of the attitudes of his Secessionist friends, he tried to play a mediating role, although he seceded once again in 1893.

As early as October 1884, Bamberger was complaining that Richter was making himself unpopular with the crown prince. Frederick William, the Secessionists' main if not only hope for the future, had been pleased by the fusion, and not to alienate him was a cardinal principle of the Secessionists. [36] By 1885 Richter and Rickert were hurling criticisms at each other through their respective newspapers. In the summer of 1885 Richter had founded the *Freisinnige Zeitung,* ostensibly a party newspaper, but in reality his personal instrument. The newspaper war elicited from Bamberger the first admission that the fusion "was a great blunder."[37] As he told Stauffenberg, he tried to do what he could to end the wrangling, but he seemed to have little success. In November he even considered it a gain that the Reichstag party group met together to plan strategy and "at least shared in the work." It "once again gave the Reichstag group a sense of purpose." He also hoped to divert the warring newspapers toward the real enemy, the "arrogance and insolence of the Junkers." That should be made the "war cry in the entire press" rather than the fostering of dissatisfaction within the party. By December he asked Stauffenberg, the titular head of the party, to come to Berlin, since "until now I have taken on myself the function of the buffer between the alignments in the parliamentary group."[38]

Internal relations improved in early 1886, when the party united in an unsuccessful opposition to the third extension of the Antisocialist Law. [39] More successful was their united opposition to the brandy monopoly. Although divided on the proposed Prussian legislation to end the *Kulturkampf* by revising the May Laws, the party agreed to disagree. Bamberger, as a non-Prussian, did not participate directly in the legislative struggle, but the affair was a major concern of the party since the liberals had played a large role in passing the anti-Catholic measures. The party split, with Richter and Bamberger arguing for a yes vote and Schrader and Rickert opposed.[40]

However, the major test for the party during the sixth legislative period was to be the military bill. Although a new bill was not required for a year, Bismarck found 1886 a very suitable time for such a proposal. In the Balkans a crisis had developed as a result of the interests of the great powers in Bulgaria and the Ottoman Empire, while in France the emergence of General Boulanger could be regarded as a direct threat to Germany. At the same time, Bismarck had suffered some defeats in the Reichstag with the brandy monopoly and the brandy tax. Even the Antisocialist Law passed in 1886 would last for only two years rather than the five originally proposed. The Center party, although pleased by the dismantling of the *Kulturkampf,* would not be the reliable instrument that Bismarck desired. And there was still the ever present danger of the throne change, which would bring in the liberal-oriented crown prince. Perhaps it is an exaggeration to claim, as Seeber does, that the Bismarckian dictatorship was facing a crisis,[41] but a military bill could serve a number of purposes. In view of the foreign dangers it could be easily justified; it would meet the stiff opposition of the Radicals and perhaps the Center and thus stood a good chance of being rejected. This would open the door to new elections, or a "terror campaign," as the liberals called it, around the issue of national security. Such emotional single-issue campaigns had worked in 1878 and 1884. A severe weakening of the Radical party and a strengthening of rightist forces would tie Frederick William's hands and destroy the idea of a liberal ministry. There was thus much to gain and little to lose by bringing in a new military bill.

The measure provided for a 10 percent increase in the peacetime strength of the army, raising it to 468,409, and it would be in effect for seven years. The increase would require 24 million additional marks, a 7 percent budget increase. The army budget composed over 70 percent of the federal budget, which had run deficits the two previous years.[42]

The initial reaction of the Radicals to the military bill was to see it as the means to dissolve the Reichstag,[43] and their attitude is in some ways reminiscent of 1884. The party platform, which reflected the Secessionist rather than the Progressive viewpoint, called for parliamentary approval of the military budget once every legislative period. Although most of the Secessionists had voted against the last septenant in 1880, Rickert had voted for the bill and Forckenbeck had left the hall during the voting, indicating that even the Secessionists might not be united behind the party platform. As early as April 1886, Bamberger foresaw difficulties over the military bill. "The last time," he complained to Stauffenberg, "*we* voted against the seven years, and our program ties our hands." This implied willingness to avoid an entirely oppositional stance was made more firmly in October when Bamberger stated that he was working to get Richter to avoid absolute opposition to "any" enlargement of military expenditures. One ought to "hold still" or talk only in "generalities," he advised. There was no reason to "commit ourselves before we have to." By November, Bamberger reported that Richter agreed to tone down, his criticism of increased military expenditures, and he appeared satisfied with the course of negotiations with the former Progressive leader.[44]

The party was concerned about three elements of the military system: the length of service, the size and cost of the army, and the duration of the military bill. Richter, who delivered the opening speech in the Reichstag, stated his party's belief in a two-year term of service and annual approval of the military budget; however, he announced that a triennial military bill provided sufficient constitutional guarantees.[45] The parliamentary commission on the military bill, dominated by a Radical-Center coalition, approved a strongly amended version of the government's proposal in the first reading. It provided for only a fourteen-thousand-man increase for three years with an additional nine thousand for one year. However, when it became clear that the government would have its dissolution at anything but the original price, it became difficult to hold the Radical party to the commission's initial resolutions. The party was determined, or so it thought, to deprive the government of the military bill as a viable election issue. In order to cover up its retreat, the Radicals drew up a plan for a national income tax to finance the increased military expenditures. The progressive income tax rate would range from 1/2 to 3 percent and apply to those whose incomes were over six thousand marks annually. It was supposed to provide 30 million marks per year, more than enough to cover the increased military expenses even for the government's original request. Its purpose, according to Bamberger, was to make the "well-to-do classes alone" bear the burden of the increased military costs.[46]

Although the tax plan attracted attention and seemed to provide a dramatic way to establish a basis for popular support, Bamberger had no illusions about the possibility of its being accepted by the Reichstag, not to mention the state governments. In fact it did not come to a discussion in the Reichstag during that session.[47] The income tax proposal might have been slightly embarrassing to the government, but it did not save the liberal opposition from having to retreat in the face of determined government and popular opposition. Nearly eight hundred petitions with 120,000 signatures poured into the Reichstag supporting the government's bill, while only a handful opposed it. Over the Christmas vacation, and after strenuous discussions, the party agreed to accept the government's requests for men and money but to limit the duration of the bill to three years instead of seven. This, it was hoped, would defuse the military bill as a campaign issue.[48]

It did not. The Reichstag debate lasted three days, and it had the sound of an election campaign. Even when it became obvious that the opposition would accept "every soldier and every penny," as Windthorst said, but only for three years, Bismarck's intention to dissolve parliament remained firm. It was not a "question of time," he claimed, but "a question of principle." The issue was whether the German Empire was to be "protected by an imperial army or a parliamentary army."[49] This set the tone for the discussions, which ranged over the previous twenty-five years of German history. For Bismarck it was an opportunity to heap scorn and abuse on the Reichstag, whose majority he referred to as the "consortium of the majority." He acted amazed that it dared to question the makers of Germany's foreign and military policy and accused the opposition of desiring a war with Russia on account of Bulgaria, whose German-born prince had been overthrown by a supposedly Russian-inspired coup. The prince had close ties to the crown prince's family, and an anonymous article in *Die Nation* seemed to favor such a war. Bamberger was attacked by the *Kölnische Zeitung* because of it, but in fact he had been advising his friends not to do anything that would give the impression that they were pursuing such a goal.[50]

In spite of—or perhaps because of—this attack, one of the mildest speeches of the three-day debate was delivered by Bamberger, the final speaker of the third day. His speech was in essence a defense of the Reichstag rather than of his party's amendment. The government's aim in introducing the military bill, he charged, was to have an excuse to dissolve parliament to obtain a more obedient Reichstag. "He [Bismarck] has longed to achieve this goal for twenty years, with diplomacy, with power, with authority, with everything that is available to him. He has gradually come somewhat closer to the goal, and he has always known to grasp the moment when he believed that the iron was so hot that he could once again bend it to his advantage. Such a moment now appears to have come again. . . . Not to let this majority come into being, which blindly subordinates itself, and . . . abandons the empire and the entire welfare of the nation, that is our task."[51]

The dénouement of the oratorical duel came on January 14. Stauffenberg's proposal to reduce the duration of the military measure from seven to three years was approved 186—154 and the entire article, 183—154. Bismarck then read the notice he had already drawn up dissolving the Reichstag.[52] The Center and Radical parties defeated a Conservative-National Liberal coalition. The election that all the deputies foresaw was to take place February 21, 1887, leaving only five weeks for campaigning. The Conservative and National Liberal parties were better prepared than their opponents and formed an election cartel on January 15, confirming Bamberger's comment that the National Liberals were "spineless Bismarckian troopers."[53] The government, ignoring the fact that the Reichstag had granted its manpower requests, charged in effect that without the seven years the French would be across the border the next day. It stressed its "constitutional authority" for the defense of the nation, which the Reichstag majority was now trying to usurp.[54]

Shortly before the Reichstag's dissolution, Windthorst asked Bamberger, "Are you also sure of your people?"[55] Bamberger seemed to be reasonably confident, although he recognized as the major enemy "the clever philistine" who "says: you should have given him the seven years in order to take away from him the excuse [to dissolve parliament]. Our main effort should be applied against *this argumentation.*"[56] Such a "clever philistine" was Bamberger's good friend, Anna von Helmholtz. Describing a dinner gathering at which Bamberger was present, she wrote, "One walks as if on eggs on account of high policy. I cannot understand friend B[amberger] with his fruitless opposition on principle. We cannot have an army subject to recall and revocation like France." And even if Bamberger was an expert on currency and tariff questions, she went on, he could still entrust foreign affairs to Bismarck and military matters to General Helmuth von Moltke "without harm to [his] soul." Instead of helping keep Bismarck in reasonable bounds, "the so-called liberals do everything to exasperate him . . . and destroy their own work. . . . It is no misfortune for humanity if liberalism and its idealism come into ill repute—because always and everywhere it shows its inability to replace those ruling. Papa's sigh, one cannot rule with the liberals, comes to me so often."[57] Perhaps it was she who Bamberger had in mind when he wrote: "It is unbelievable how many entirely liberal and reasonable people here [Berlin] have voted for the cartel candidate."[58]

In his own district the campaign was the easiest since 1878. After his victory in 1884 he had as usual claimed that it would be his last election campaign, but by 1886 this was forgotten, and he was busy preparing for the next election. In 1887 he received active support from the Center party, an outgrowth of their cooperation on the military bill, and won an easy three-thousand-vote victory over his National Liberal opponent.[59] The same could not be said for the bulk of the Radical party, for whom the election was a disaster. It brought out more voters both absolutely and relatively than any previous election. Nearly two million more people voted in 1887 than in 1884, clearly responding to the government's emotional campaign. And most of the new voters voted for the cartel parties, which increased their votes by 55 percent and their seats by 40 percent, giving them 220, a clear majority. The Center's totals remained unchanged, while the Radicals paid the bill. Their vote total dropped slightly, which, given the large number of new voters as well as the cartel, made for a catastrophic defeat. The party lost over half its seats, emerging with 32.[60]

"What can we say to ourselves?" Bamberger wrote Stauffenberg after the first-round results were known. He once again blamed the defeat not on anything the left liberals did or did not do, but rather on the German "philistines," and he saw the Reichstag as a true reflection of the German public: "Junkerdom and Catholic Church who know very clearly what they want, and a middle class, childishly innocent, politically immature, and requiring neither justice nor freedom." He heaped scorn on the National Liberals whose "spirit, pompous servility," was the "expression of the German middle classes."[61] Besides the "philistines," Bamberger blamed Richter and claimed that the election was evidence that "the fusion was a mistake (joined in by me with open eyes). . . . One should have given more weight to the weakness of the German people which sees in Richter its *bête noire.*" The future looked bleak, and only "new constellations" might make a new start possible.[62]

A first step toward correcting the error of the union with the Progressives involved reducing the power of Eugen Richter, by forcing him to give up his newspaper or the leadership of the executive committee. This was the plan of Bamberger, Barth, Broemel, and Schrader, who believed that Richter was using his journal to attack party colleagues. Moreover, Schrader could not escape from the mirage of the throne change, and with Richter as its leader, the party would be compromised in the eyes of the crown prince. The attempt to reduce Richter's role failed, and Bamberger never did seem to take it seriously, admitting a greater "resignation than before the election" with regard to party problems. "What can make this misery any greater?" he sighed to Stauffenberg, and referred to the latest conflict as a "tempest in a teapot." From Bamberger's viewpoint although the campaign against Richter was unsuccessful the former Secessionists had made him more cautious, and they were able to make one of their own men, Hugo Hinze, the party's business manager. As Schrader admitted to Stauffenberg, as long as the Secessionists were able to win the policy debates, there was no need to push things to a break.[63]

The internal wrangling was over by April, but the party still faced the prospect of three years as a minor parliamentary group faced by a powerful cartel. The government's first action set the tone for the next three years. Before the run-off elections were even settled, parliament was called into session to deal with the new military bill, which was a repetition of the government's first offering. It required only three brief sessions to see the proposal passed.[64]

With the military bill as an indication of future events, Bamberger envied the sick Stauffenberg his absence from the "empty parliamentary stage." Since the opposition was "broken," Windthorst "depressed," and the Radicals "decimated," the struggles appeared as "miserable shadowboxing."[65] The main hope for the Radicals depended on their ability to work with the Center, a party which Bamberger had previously ridiculed but on which he now depended for his reelection. He supported the government's efforts to end the *Kulturkampf* even if this damaged the Radicals' chances. "We must," he wrote, "make it through this probably long transition period in order to get rid of the *Kulturkampf,* and then take up on a new basis the struggle for the liberal cause." It appears that Bamberger believed the ending of the *Kulturkampf* would rob the Center of its *raison d'être* and provide a new field for liberal activity. It was a vain hope. Equally vain was Schrader's plea that the party take up more clearly the cause of the "little people" and become a "more radical party." This should be balanced by Rickert's stricture against the "radicals" who stirred up the masses against the liberals by slandering "proven men of the people." Nor did Bamberger seem to take Schrader's advice seriously. When Alfred Stern suggested an opening to the left embracing even socialists, Bamberger replied that this advice demonstrated how difficult it was to judge German events from afar (Zurich). Even if an occasional by-election such as Greiffenberg-Kammin did demonstrate the possibility of such a connection, it "was not symptomatic."[66]

Bamberger was thus unwilling or unable to look to the left when it suddenly became unrealistic to look above for help. The left liberal dream of a new beginning under the crown prince began to fade by early summer 1887, when the first news of the crown prince's illness leaked out. Bamberger told Stauffenberg that he did not "believe in the recovery of the crown prince." He had experienced the "same deadly course" with a close friend. Quoting an acquaintance, he continued, "even if it were not cancer, he would no longer regain his health. What a misfortune."[67]

The prospects for the seventh legislative period thus were not very promising, but publicly Bamberger tried to find a silver lining. He admitted that the government would have its way on the change of the industrial code to strengthen the guilds and on the upward revision of the agricultural tariffs.

On these issues the government could dispense with the National Liberals and rely on the Center and Conservative parties. Thus the National Liberals would suffer defeats on economic questions because they helped the Conservatives. At the same time, he hoped that the Center and the National Liberals would stand together with the Radicals on the most "decisive questions" of constitutional changes or the introduction of monopolies.[68] The hope proved ephemeral, and the three-year session was undoubtedly the least successful for Bamberger. Although he continued the strategy of defensive victories, a progovernment majority was generally available for most issues. As he had predicted, when there were National Liberal defections the Center party often provided the margin of victory for the conservative parties. Bamberger's speeches took on an increasingly bitter tone particularly with regard to the National Liberals, who became his special target for their supposed betrayal of their last remnants of liberalism. He explained to Alfred Stern that "I contain in the quiet of my bosom so low an opinion of our present parliamentary life that this *nolens volens* becomes visible in my expressions and works provocatively as scorn." "Powerlessness," he wrote of the National Liberals, "united with the appearance of high position," was a "miserable thing."[69]

For a liberal of Bamberger's persuasion there was much to be provoked about. The Conservatives, joined by the Center, continued their assault on occupational freedom and were able in June 1887 to push through a law to increase further the regulatory power of guilds. The effect of the elections was even clearer after the passage of a previously thrice-defeated measure to make it easier for courts to exclude the public from trials or enjoin secrecy on those present. Another bill whose passage the 1887 election made possible was the measure to increase the tax on brandy and revise the regulation of the brandy industry. It signified a further extension of the indirect tax system and provided various benefits to those landowners, generally in the northeast, who also operated distilleries. It was also helped through the Reichstag by the National Liberals led by Miquel, which angered Bamberger greatly.[70]

The apparent benefits that would accrue to the agricultural brandy producers were supplemented by others that would fall to the grain producers as a result of the tariff act of 1887. When the tariff bill of 1879 was passed, Bamberger hoped that the unfavorable public reaction would dampen the enthusiasm of the tariff reformers.[71] It did not, and the next eight years saw major tariff laws which raised the rates on iron, textiles, and agricultural products. Bamberger remained a constant critic of the government's tariff program, and in October 1878 he had founded the Association for the Promotion of Free Trade (Verein zur Förderung des Freihandels). It was the major center for free-trade agitation, organizing meetings and publishing a newspaper and other materials.[72] He continued to raise his voice in parliament in the early 1880s against further tariff increases. The major thrust of his attacks centered on the heavy burden to consumers, evidence of which he saw in the use of cheaper substitute products and calculated as 51 million marks. It was difficult to deny that there had been a business upturn in the wake of the 1879 measure, but Bamberger attributed it to the general worldwide business improvement that affected all countries. The harmful effects, which he had predicted in 1879, would come later, in "decades." "Things do not change so quickly," he now had to concede.[73]

In his speeches in the early 1880s Bamberger still seemed to think it might be possible to reverse or at least halt the protective tariff momentum. He chose to regard the early tariffs as exceptional measures. In 1885, however, the government introduced a measure which provided for wide-ranging tariff increases as broad as the 1879 law. The permanency of the protective tariff system could no longer be denied, and Bamberger was forced to fall back on the old arguments that the government was unchaining an open war of material interests. "If there is a national policy," he told the Reichstag, "it is above all one which wishes to view the German nation as a common unified interest and not a conglomerate, dissolved into atoms in which, in the future, the wild hunt for individual advantages and the war of all against all is unchained."[74] By the middle of the debate on the 1885 bill he publicly announced his disillusionment with the government's program and in effect dropped out of the proceedings, telling the Reichstag: "I am indeed glad that other colleagues and for the most part younger ones, who have fewer painful experiences, still have the bravery to defend what I call the good cause. But I concede openly to you: I lack the desire to speak in this house about tariff matters."[75] The desire did not return two years later, when the government introduced a new tariff bill to raise the duties on agricultural products from 67 to 100 percent above the 1885 rates. Supported by a coalition of Conservatives and Centrists, the government's recommendations were accepted virtually unchanged.[76]

The inability to influence the course of parliamentary events, especially when the Center party was willing to support the government, as it did on the tariff bill of 1887, was never more obvious than in connection with the colonial debates and the bills to lengthen the legislative period and extend the Antisocialist Law. At every opportunity Bamberger made himself heard on colonial matters, usually in connection with budget proposals or bills to introduce German law and administration into the protected areas. His speeches continued to show the same careful preparation based on wide reading of both pro- and anticolonial materials. There was no opportunity to repeat the victories of the early 1880s, but it was still necessary to fight the national enthusiasm which seemed determined to ignore the realities of

Germany's African possessions, this "expensive toy for the national fantasy." He never tired of telling his colleagues that Africa was left alone so long because it was unsuitable for Europeans, at least in those areas where the Germans settled. "Who enters the business with music exits with torn soles," he remarked disdainfully.[77]

The brunt of his criticism was directed against the various companies who administered the colonies on behalf of the government, particularly in Southwest and East Africa. Both companies he portrayed as on the verge of bankruptcy with only a precarious hold on their territories. In Southwest Africa the German Colonial Association, encouraged by the government, had taken over Lüderitz's interests. The company, composed of prominent bankers and industrialists, hoped to discover minerals, but as one of those involved remarked: "We have had to bite into this sour apple because the Foreign Office urgently desired it." Complications developed when the British moved north from their Cape colony into the hinterland of the German area to sign treaties of friendship and protection with the local rulers. Quickly, under the guise of a research expedition, the Germans concluded treaties with the rulers, and their government declared its protection of the area. Naturally the British spoke of a "shadowy protection," and this appeared confirmed when in the fall of 1888 a rebellion forced the company's representatives to seek refuge with the British in Walfish Bay.[78]

The events in Southwest Africa confirmed the devastating criticism of the company and its prospects which Bamberger had made in 1887[79] and set the stage for a renewal of the discussion in January 1889, on the occasion of the budget debate. Once again he reviewed the various problems that afflicted the Southwest Africa company, claiming that it had mismanaged affairs and scarcely existed in reality. Over 50 percent of its capital was gone; attempts to drill water wells failed; there were no prospects for cattle-raising or farming; the company was under British protection in Walfish Bay; and for three years there had been no official reports about the company. He also brought to light the difficulties the company was having with a local ruler who was threatening to declare null and void all its mining concessions and to turn them over to an Englishman. The Germans, he suggested, lacked authority, which in reality was more significant than the pieces of paper called treaties. He asked what the intentions of the government were, especially since it was asking for additional funds for the colony. He again tried to convince his listeners that the German government should not feel bound to come to the rescue of every business which, because of involvement in a dubious venture, faced financial ruin. This was a false conception of German patriotism and national honor.[80]

Bismarck replied that the German government was at present involved in sensitive negotiations with England, and Bamberger's revelations about worthless treaties and nonexistent companies would severely damage the German position. He argued that English interest in the area was proof of its value, ignoring the fact that they might only be interested in creating a buffer between Germany's possessions and the Cape colony. He then suggested that the Foreign Office would never ask the Reichstag for funds for a "sandbox" and implied that Bamberger had demonstrated a lack of patriotism as well as good sense.[81]

Bamberger denied revealing any secrets, claiming that all of his information came from public sources. Calling for more factual information from the government about the colony, Bamberger concluded, "everything that has happened in the last four or five years since we have inaugurated our colonial policy proves me more correct than him [Bismarck]." Rather than more light he received additional heat from Bismarck, who now accused Bamberger of an "unpatriotic" act, even if the liberal was technically correct in his statements. Kardorff added his voice to the attack on Bamberger, all but accusing him of being responsible for the deaths of German marines who were trying to put down a rebellion in Samoa. The uprising, Kardorff charged, was due in part to the way the whole Samoa question had been handled since 1880, meaning Bamberger's obstructions.[82] The tone of the debate was quickly declining into little more than accusations, and almost as an afterthought the budgetary requests were approved.

The debate was resumed in the next session of the Reichstag, and in the intervening period Bamberger could take solace from the fact that events gave added weight to his criticisms. The government was forced to dispatch troops to bring a temporary end to the uprising. It was nevertheless necessary for the liberal once again to defend himself against charges of being antinational. Colonial policy, he argued, should be viewed as an economic task, and seen in this light "the whole colonial policy is a luxury, a luxury of certain educated classes who have read history." One could have doubts about Angra Pequena or Dar-es-Salaam without "being a traitor to the fatherland." What was the difference, he asked sarcastically during the debate on the renewal of the Imperial Bank charter, between a Reichsbank that has existed fifteen years and a still undiscovered mine in Southwest Africa? If someone doubted the worth of the undiscovered mine, he risked being labeled a traitor. But if someone undertook to undermine a healthy banking institution that has worked well for fifteen years, nobody found anything evil in it.[83] Southwest Africa languished for another twenty years until the discovery of diamonds and copper promised to make the colony valuable; however World War I brought these dreams to an end.[84]

The East African affair had many parallels to that of Southwest Africa, including a native uprising and a nearly insolvent company. By November 1888 the German government was faced with the alternative of giving up the East Africa protectorate or using force. The former could have internal repercussions as a blow to the cartel, some of whose supporters were financing the German East Africa Company, and as a victory for the parliamentary opposition.[85] Thus the use of force seemed preferable. The intervention would be carried out under the guise of suppressing the slave trade, a method which won the approval of the cartel parties as well as the Center, which was interested in Catholic missionary work in the area. In fact it was Windthorst who first introduced a motion calling on the government to do what it could to fight the slave trade. A month later the government requested 2 million marks to fight the slave trade in East Africa. It also proposed the appointment of an imperial commissioner to oversee the activities of the East Africa Company.[86]

It was not an easy issue to oppose, but Bamberger did precisely that. Windthorst's resolution, he argued, would legitimate intervention in East Africa and would help bail out the bankrupt company. The motion was accepted but merely served as the prelude to the government's bill.[87] This much longer debate again brought Bamberger into conflict with Bismarck. The liberal's evidence again clearly demonstrated the essential worthlessness of the protected area and that only the company's backers stood to gain from the government's bill. It was a bill not for the protection of German interests in East Africa but for the protection of the East Africa Company. He ridiculed the government's high-sounding motive of fighting the slave trade and claimed that only the elimination of slavery itself, which the government did not propose to undertake, would make it possible to end the slave trade. He painted a picture of a German expeditionary force getting bogged down in an endless war of attrition as the French had in North Africa and Mexico.[88]

In this debate Bismarck was more willing to play the national card. He admitted the East Africa Company had made mistakes but insisted that Germany could not ignore its compatriots in distress. They symbolized a great national movement against which the spending of 2 million marks was insignificant. Bamberger, the chancellor charged, viewed the German Empire too much as a "financial institution but not as a national institution of the German nation."[89] The bill was passed a few days later, and a military expedition was dispatched to crush the uprising. Bismarck, however, held the reins of the colonial enthusiasts (people "with full mouths and empty pockets") under control; he wished to do nothing to damage relations with England. By the end of 1890 the Heligoland Treaty was signed, in which Germany surrendered many of her claims in East Africa. At the same time Germany formally took control of the colony from the company. The total cost was 20 million marks. Again Bismarck's dreams of a series of colonies operated by charter companies at a minimal cost to the empire dissolved.[90]

The East African affair continued to cause problems even after Bismarck was gone. The uprising proved more difficult to bring under control than first realized, and the government had to request additional funds for the military operation. In 1890 the government's budget contained a request for 4.5 million marks to continue the East African operation. The new chancellor, Count Leo Caprivi, admittedly no colonial enthusiast, defended the proposal as necessary to permit Germany to complete successfully the task already begun. Privately Bamberger believed that Caprivi shared his view of colonial undertakings,[91] but nevertheless he announced on May 12, 1890, his and his party's continued opposition to the East African venture. Softening his position, however, he denied that his party was an unconditional opponent of a colonial policy; it was opposed to colonial policy as it developed in Germany. Undeterred by charges of having a shopkeeper's mentality, Bamberger emphasized the economic side of colonialism. One could not ignore the profit motive, and like Bismarck, but publicly, he recognized that patriotic enthusiasm did not bring forth investment. "Colonial policy is economic policy," he claimed, "and economic policy must balance." It did not in East Africa, and the colony as well as German colonial policy in general only bred local uprisings and international disputes. He charged that the action to end the slave trade was in the interests of the plantation owners, and their interests as well as the desire for a large colony were the real motives behind the operation.[92] As under Bismarck, the Radical party's opposition was fruitless, since the Center supported the government.

The East African story had its parallel in New Guinea, where the charter company asked the government to take over the administration of the colony in order to give the company more opportunity to pursue economic ventures. What, asked Bamberger, were the company's economic pursuits? The request was convincing proof that Bismarck's much heralded inexpensive approach to colonial undertaking, utilizing charter companies, was a failure.[93]

Although defeated on these colonial issues, Bamberger and his small band of colleagues at least acted as a loyal opposition, forcing the government to defend and explain its actions and to provide the Reichstag with more information than it originally wished to disclose. Windthorst, who opposed Bamberger on the East African issue, conceded that the liberal was "the most objective opponent" of German colonial policy and one who usually "suggested a series of considerations to which one . . . should have paid attention more often than has happened."[94] There was of course an element of tilting at windmills, but for Bamberger this was the way the loyal opposition played the game, even at the risk of seeming doctrinaire or possessing a bookkeeper's mentality. This attitude was also in evidence in the debates over the bill to lengthen the legislative session to five years.[95]

The issue of the length of the legislative period had been discussed in 1881 as part of the government's request for a two-year budgetary period, but it was overshadowed by the latter. A motion on behalf of a five-year period also failed in 1885, but in 1887 the proposal was jointly sponsored by the cartel parties. It was painful for Bamberger to oppose the government on this issue. During the 1870s, on at least two occasions, he had come out in favor of lengthening the legislative period. In 1874 he had complained of the "completely insufficient three year voting period" and regarded the necessity of closely spaced elections as "inappropriate for the Reichstag, inappropriate for the country, and also inappropriate for the government." It was "wrong" to rouse and agitate the voters every three years, especially since the chancellor had the right of dissolution. With a three-year session, he suggested, this right of dissolution would become a dead letter. The short session and also the lack of per diem contributed to a "restless" parliament. He was particularly disturbed by the fact that so many members of the 1871 parliament chose not to run for reelection. Of the 397 deputies in 1874, 221 were new.[96] He made similar comments in 1878 in his article "Deutschland und der Sozialismus." He singled out the three-year period as a major stimulus to socialism. He not only proposed that it be lengthened, but even went further and wondered aloud whether universal suffrage could not be undercut by introducing more rigorous residence requirements. He seemed almost disappointed that nothing could be done to revoke universal manhood suffrage. In 1878 he was pessimistic about any of his suggestions' being enacted into law. Parliament lacked, he said, a feeling for national rather than particular interests.[97]

All of the above statements were carefully noted by his opponents in 1888, and the debates over the bill to lengthen the session at times seemed to be nothing more than a discussion of Bamberger's previous statements on the issue. It was not easy for Bamberger to explain them away. He tried to portray the question as not involving liberalism and conservatism since many constitutional countries operated under five-year or even longer sessions. Rather it was a "question of opportunity." One had to look at the whole political picture and determine who would be hurt or strengthened by the measure. It was a question of power. The decisive factor was whether parliament would be strengthened or weakened, and under the present circumstances parliament would be weakened by an extension of its term. The government, he charged, would run a scare campaign every five years which would far overshadow the 1887 election. Somehow with a three-year period the opposition would have a greater opportunity. In 1874, with over one hundred and fifty National Liberals, Bamberger could contemplate peacefully a longer legislative period. In 1888, after two dissolutions and two "terror campaigns," with his party reduced to a handful of deputies, a longer period no longer looked inviting.[98]

The bulk of his two major speeches during the debate dealt with the alleged sins of the National Liberals because of their alliance with the conservative parties, rather than the bill itself. With the outcome of the vote not in doubt, Bamberger was apparently appealing to the National Liberal electorate, especially those voters who had deserted the Radicals in 1887. [99] When reminded by Bennigsen that the National Liberals had also worked closely with the right-wing parties from 1867 to 1877, Bamberger answered, as he had eight years before, that the early years had generated progressive, not retrogressive, compromises. Cooperation then advanced the cause of freedom in Germany. It had given the German people a unified political structure, a parliament, and the vote. Cooperation in the 1880s favored the aims of the political and economic reaction.[100]

Although a tiny minority, the Radical party was nothing if not resourceful. It introduced an amendment to the bill which provided that per diem and travel costs would be paid Reichstag deputies. Realizing that the government and the conservative parties had fought this, but that the National Liberals had generally favored it, this was a way if not to defeat the bill at least to embarrass the National Liberals. Bamberger himself had no firm views on the issue. Initially favoring per diem in the early 1870s, he opposed it in his 1878 essay on socialism on the ground that it would help the Social Democrats, and also at the time of the fusion. No matter, the occasion called for the measure.[101] The Radicals' attempt failed as the Reichstag ruled the amendment out of order on the grounds that it had no "essential" relation to the bill, which passed the second reading by a two-to-one majority.[102]

The bill to extend the legislative period brought into sharp relief the fact that Bamberger's attitude toward political rights for the working class was conditioned by considerations of momentary political gain, and the struggle over the Antisocialist Law suggested some parallels. Bamberger had convinced himself to vote for the Antisocialist Law in 1878 out of the need to preserve the unity of the National Liberal party and a hope that the bill would silence those in the middle and upper classes who played with socialistic ideas. By 1884 he recognized the incorrectness of both assumptions and from then on voted against renewal. The most trenchant (even if somewhat exaggerated) statement regarding Bamberger's attitude toward the law was delivered by the *Sozialdemokrat*. The "greatest evil," it remarked, was that Bamberger had approved the law in 1878 when his position was of the "greatest and most harmful significance; presently [his opposition] is as irrelevant as possible."[103]

In 1886, in the aftermath of the third renewal of the Antisocialist Law, the government returned to a harsh interpretation of the measure and of the penal code. A new strike decree of April 11, 1886, sought to brand all labor activity as Social Democratic and all strikes as potentially revolutionary. It made a punishable offense the attempt to convince workers to strike.[104]

The Social Democrats interpellated on May 21, and Wilhelm Hasenclever, their spokesman, taunted the liberals about their lack of response to this threat to the right to organize and strike. "It is the only pretty child you have. Now one would have thought that liberalism, like the lioness, would have defended this child, but liberalism has not been a lioness for a long time. It is extremely tame, otherwise it would step forward in this question much more sharply, more energetically than we. It is your cause that I now represent, that you really should have represented."[105] There was no direct reply, but Bamberger did use the debate to expound his views on strikes and to attack the government. To Hasenclever, he protested that he laid more worth on freedom to organize than the Social Democrats imagined, because it was "the key, the foundation stone of our whole view of civil society."[106] He viewed the strike pattern of 1885-86 as an attempt by the workers to carve themselves a larger share of the economic pie and thus to improve their economic condition. With all of the government's pronouncements about improving the lot of the working man, he continued, who could deny that the only permanent improvement in working-class conditions would come as a result of an increase in the workers' share of the profit? The strike movement was the only effective means of action left to the worker, and to prevent him from striking "would take away from the worker not merely a formal right but a material right."[107] Bamberger had come a long way since the early 1870s, when he viewed strikes with great suspicion and claimed they were an integral part of the Social Democratic revolutionary movement. Or was it a brief detour made necessary by the political landscape?

As the toughened antistrike decree did not have the desired results, Bismarck sought in 1888 to strengthen the Antisocialist Law to permit expulsion of "agitators" not merely from their place of residence but also from the country. This would prevent the spread of socialism into the countryside, where expelled "agitators" had previously been sent. The bill also made it possible to banish and deprive of citizenship those who had taken part in a group which had as its goal weakening the execution of the law. This could have meant almost any Social Democrat. The new law would run for five years. Such was the success of Bismarck's antisocialist crusade after a decade.[108]

Paul Singer, a Social Democrat, opened the debate and began the methodical destruction of the government's case. The brunt of his well-documented two-hour attack fell on the use of police informers and *agents provocateurs* who worked under the direction of Puttkamer and who had only encouraged extremism within the party. Puttkamer, who tried for two hours to explain away or reject Singer's accusations, could not entirely dissolve the residue of truth which lay in the socialist's speech. The prospects for the government's bill diminished greatly when the Center party announced it would reject the bill in its existing version.[109]

The following day, Bamberger gave his last major speech on the Antisocialist Law, and his task was to demonstrate that now was time to reject the law finally. One had to decide, he began, whether the law was a temporary measure to meet an exceptional situation or a permanent act, as the government seemed to believe. If the former, which Bamberger claimed was the original intent of the law, it should be rejected after ten years. He charged that the law was causing "deep harms" to public life, to private morals, to the whole administrative and legal structure extending into international relations. He supported Singer's charges and even adduced evidence of his own which added weight to them.[110]

Bamberger also betrayed the first signs of a new attitude toward the socialists. He looked back to the 1820s, the era of student agitation, and wondered whether in fifty or sixty years people would not view the socialists' strivings as one did those of the post-Napoleonic period, that is, as relatively harmless. Only toward the end of his speech did he turn to the specifics of the bill. In particular, he attacked the banishment provision. To the former exile, such a measure appeared as a sentence of death. The aim of the regulation, Bamberger contended, was to make it impossible for a Social Democrat to sit in the Reichstag. To the old socialist-hater this now seemed horrible. "I am even more convinced that it is a very healthy sign that we have Social Democratic deputies in the Reichstag, and I would regret it if they were no longer here to take part in our debates. I would truly regret it if the last means were taken from them to justify themselves before the nation, to shed light on the injustice which has befallen them, and to discuss their ideas freely. And should you decide that a commission is to be set up for the law, I will ask my party to make a seat available to the Social Democrats at our loss so that they can participate." [111] Bamberger closed his speech with the admission that "if I have to choose between the responsibility of lengthening such an exorbitant law with all the excrescences it has shown, or to take on myself the danger of an upheaval, I prefer the latter."[112]

The outcome of the debate was decided by the National Liberals. Their spokesman, Heinrich von Marquardsen, once more dredged up what was probably the most quoted speech in the Reichstag, Bamberger's of October 12, 1878, in which he justified his support for the first Antisocialist Law, in order to announce the National Liberals' acceptance of a law against the

Social Democrats. But as Bamberger had predicted, the National Liberal stated the party's unwillingness to accept the new version and so made certain the adoption of the old law.[113] Out of the commission came a recommendation that the current law be extended for two years, which was approved 164–80. Bamberger took no public role in the debate of 1889–90.[114]

The balance sheet after twelve years showed that 155 periodicals and 1,200 nonperiodical papers and pamphlets had been prohibited. About nine hundred people were expelled and fifteen hundred convicted of various infractions, while 322 associations were dissolved.[115] Until 1884, Bamberger had contributed to such results. Only once after the expiration of the law did he comment on it. He was rather philosophical and apologetic about it. He regretted that in the early stages he had given his assent, but, he went on, "the experiment was unavoidable. If it were never tried people would have said it would have succeeded. There are things from which one has no rest until they once have been tried." The law, he admitted, did help the Social Democrats, but this too was only a matter of time. "When things are in the air everything helps them, force as well as forbearance."[116]

If anything was in the air for Bamberger during the seventh legislative session, it was defeat. Besides fighting unsuccessfully against the bills to extend the legislative session and to renew the Antisocialist Law, he had to accept the final installment of Bismarck's social welfare program—old age and disability insurance. Sick throughout most of the deliberations, he appeared only toward the end of the debate, once again to warn his listeners of the dangers of playing with socialistic ideas. It is doubtful whether this helped or hurt his cause. He had hoped that the bill could be defeated and conceded that it was better that his advice to level an attack on principle against the bill was not followed. Not only should a factual treatment of the bill be undertaken, but as he confessed to Stauffenberg on May 5: "Rickert maintains correctly that compromising Manchesterians like me would do better to keep quiet and leave it to the more kosher loyalists to brew their soup together so that none of the opponents is frightened off by the bad company. I incline to this view." Nevertheless, Bismarck's speech the same day drew Bamberger into the arena once more. The bill, although in jeopardy throughout the proceedings, was approved by a twenty-vote majority when a handful of Centrists behind Georg von Franckenstein gave their support to it.[117]

Undoubtedly the high point of his parliamentary work during the 1880s was reached on financial questions, and they produced virtually the only government bill that Bamberger supported during the dismal cartel years. He always regarded his role in the passage of the financial legislation of the 1870s as his most important legislative achievement, and during the 1880s defending that work became one of his most important tasks. On this issue he had the unusual satisfaction of being on the government's side. One of the major financial issues of the 1880s concerned the question of the proper basis for the German currency system, gold or gold and silver. Although Bamberger had regarded the issue as settled in the mid-1870s, by the early 1880s the supporters of silver were staging a determined counterattack. The German government, as already noted, had suspended the sale of silver in the spring of 1879, but the price of silver continued to drop sharply because of the conversion to gold, the new silver strikes in the United States, and the decline in India's demand for silver. Along with the collapse of the silver price, the production of gold did not keep pace with the increased demand, and since it was the basis of the German currency system, money was tight and prices fell. The lower prices especially hurt the large, market-oriented grain producers in northern Germany. Also, because of declining prices of goods in terms of gold currencies, the farmers and manufacturers of silver standard countries seemed to enjoy an export advantage in relation to gold-producing countries. Thus the fall in grain prices and increased competition brought the East Elbian estate owners into the currency battle on the side of the bimetallists, believing that bimetallism would bring them higher prices and reduce competition. The major bimetallist spokesman in parliament was the Free Conservative Wilhelm von Kardorff, and the 1880s repeatedly witnessed long exchanges between Bamberger and him over the merits of a gold standard or bimetallism.

Bamberger argued that the fate of silver was sealed, and he pointed to the series of international monetary conferences held in the 1880s and 1890s which at most called for a greater use of silver and less of gold, as at Cologne in 1892, or could reach no decision, as in Paris in 1881 and Brussels in 1892. He also traced the evolution of the Latin Monetary Union, trying to indicate that, in spite of itself, it was moving toward a *de facto* gold standard. The union recognized that in case of dissolution, debts among member states had to be paid in gold, demonstrating, said Bamberger, the falsity of the double standard theory. The union might proclaim the double standard in principle, but it refused to abide by it in case of liquidation.[118]

The appearance of the Junkers in the forefront of the silver advocates by the mid-1880s nevertheless worried Bamberger and made him see the issue as part of the seamless web of political and economic reaction. He viewed their agitation as a drive for cheap or overvalued money so that they could write off their debts. The debtors in Germany, he pointed out, were not the poorest part of the population but among the wealthier elements, another reason to deny them sympathy. Also he recognized that both within and outside the Reichstag there was a suspicion of money and those who lived off its manipulation, which could be exploited by the opponents. People "view everything that does not appear to create matter or form as a parasitic doing. They overlook the fructifying and creative power of money, which is the handiest vehicle for transference of matter."[119]

Thus, in spite of his certainty about the correctness of the gold standard, he recognized that the supporters of bimetallism included influential elements in the Reichstag, and given the general direction of German politics, he did not rule out a retrogressive step in currency matters. As early as 1882 he took very seriously the agitation of the silver advocates, and he played a key role in organizing a counterattack. His desire to uphold the gold standard ironically brought him into close contact with the otherwise hated protectionists and colonialists, Bueck, Stumm, Friedrich Krupp, and Friedrich Hammacher, as he helped found the Association for the Protection of the German Gold Standard (Verein zum Schutz der deutschen Goldwährung) and organized the chambers of commerce against the silver onslaught.[120]

Besides the external agitation, much depended on the Reichstag and the government. In the Reichstag, Kardorff or his allies periodically introduced resolutions requesting a change in or reexamination of the German currency system. In 1882 his proposal was not acted upon because, as Bamberger sarcastically wrote Soetbeer, "something positively dumb finds a majority only when Bismarck is for it." [121] In this case neither Bismarck nor the German government seemed to favor bimetallism. Bismarck's attitude remained obscure, but the heart of the opposition to the double standard was centered in the Finance Ministry in the person of the minister, Adolf von Scholz. [122] In 1886, when Scholz proposed to appoint Otto Michaelis as president of the important Prussian bank, the Seehandlung, Bismarck warned the minister to make sure that Michaelis had dissolved his "free-trade Bambergerian relations." Scholz's ministry, he continued, should not run the risk of "nourishing a Bambergerian snake at the breast."[123] It apparently did.

The monetary picture improved somewhat in the early 1880s because of an increase in the supply of gold caused by the Reichsbank's purchases and a favorable balance of trade. By 1884 Bamberger, despairing of the government's resuming the sale of silver, looked on the status quo as the best that one could hope for. To defend this meant, as with so many of the earlier achievements, to score important victories under the changed conditions of the 1880s.[124]

However, by early 1885 the bimetallists led by the agrarians were once more attacking, spurred into action by sinking grain prices which they blamed on the government's hard money policy. Kardorff took the initiative and proposed that the German government recall the international currency conference, which had been broken off in 1881, to reintroduce the minting of silver coins at their full value. Bamberger was pessimistic about the outcome of the resolution, since Bismarck's attitude was still unclear. He tried to mobilize the chambers of commerce to send in petitions opposing Kardoff's resolution, with limited success. The debate of March 6, however, was a victory for Bamberger as the resolution was rejected. He had stressed in his speeches that not gold, but increased competition, was responsible for reduced grain prices. The margin of victory was provided by a part of the Center party behind Windthorst and a few Conservatives. Bamberger confided to Soetbeer that "a stone" was "lifted from his heart." He believed not very modestly that it was one of the few cases where he was able to change the opinion of some Centrists and Conservatives by argument.[125]

The agitation against the gold standard did not cease but seemed to increase in intensity, and Bamberger, as one of the main targets, became increasingly pessimistic. "If one did not find his reward within himself," he wrote Soetbeer, "public activity in Germany would truly be the dumbest thing that one could carry on." [126] Without success, Soetbeer tried to convince Bamberger to concentrate on the currency question and withdraw from the struggles against colonialism and state socialism. This momentary fit of despair passed, and Bamberger was again at the ramparts a few months later to defend his legislative work. The debate, which extended over January and February, 1886, was far more bitter than the previous one. Kardorff sharply attacked Scholz and claimed that the spirit of Bamberger still reigned in the government even though Delbrück and Camphausen were gone. Scholz in turn delivered what could only be called a very uncommon attack by a government official against a loyal government supporter. In words that Bismarck usually reserved for the Radical or Social Democratic parties, Scholz charged that anyone who loved his fatherland and did not want to betray it would oppose the bimetallists. This unheard of attack convinced Bamberger that Bismarck must have approved it beforehand. The resolution that was finally formulated merely requested the government to reexamine the currency question and to communicate the result of such an investigation to the Reichstag. In such a meaningless form the resolution was accepted, and Bamberger was highly satisfied with the outcome.[127]

After this onslaught, and in view of the government's firm opposition to tampering with Germany's gold-based currency, the bimetallist agitation ebbed for the rest of the Bismarckian years. It did reemerge in the mid-1890s and Bamberger continued to lead the fight against it, first as a Reichstag deputy and after 1893 as a private citizen. By this time he was ably seconded by Karl Helfferich, who proved himself the equal of Bamberger in the journalistic currency wars. The German government, although showing signs of weakness at times, refused to alter Germany's gold standard, even if it did talk about doing something for silver. The dénouement came first in 1896, when the British government declared it would not surrender the gold standard and second as a result of the gold discoveries in Australia and Alaska.[128]

If the struggle to maintain the gold standard was one of his few satisfying efforts in the 1880s and 1890s, Bamberger's one major victory in the cartel Reichstag was the renewal of the Reichsbank. The imperial bank was never subjected to the concerted attack that the gold standard had withstood, but its structure and policies did meet with opposition. The major demand was that it be nationalized instead of remaining a private institution under imperial supervision and acting on behalf of the empire. Issuing from this was the claim that nationalization would provide a profit for the empire which now went into private pockets. The opponents also argued that the bank had become more and more the instrument of the large financial interests and that it ignored the needs of the little people and agriculture. They wanted the bank to become more of a credit institute for agriculture, whose products would provide the security.[129] The opponents' case was weakened, as they had to admit that the Reichsbank had performed its functions well. They, however, wished to give it additional tasks.

Although the supporters of revision continually stressed that their major aim was to increase the income of the empire rather than to cater to the needs of agriculture, the other side viewed the latter motive as decisive. The cry for revision was regarded as a device to grant easy credits to the Junkers or, as Bamberger put it, to grant money to individuals who were not solvent.[130] Bamberger also opposed nationalization of the bank on the grounds that the Reichsbank would become too much of a political arm of the government. There should be, he had warned in 1887, no mixing of bank policy and foreign policy. Instead of "Jupiter" (Bismarck) guarding the bank, one needed a more modest "Mercury." He was also reluctant to tinker with an institution which, even its opponents acknowledged, had done a commendable job. The government's proposal in fact suggested no significant changes in the 1875 act. Moreover, on this issue the financial and economic interests of the Radical, National Liberal, and even a part of the two Conservative parties dovetailed, providing a comfortable majority for the government's bill. Bamberger's two speeches merely showed him in the uncomfortable position of speaking for the government.[131]

If the legislative work contained few rewards for Bamberger, the end of the 1880s saw the evaporation of another dream that he and his colleagues shared, the reign of a liberal emperor.[132] How liberal Frederick William was remains uncertain. Andreas Dorpalen has given a reasonable interpretation when he claims the crown prince was convinced that liberalism was the wave of the future, with which the monarchy would have to come to terms. "But at the same time he sensed uneasily that a liberal victory would mean a diminution of royal power, a prospect thoroughly distasteful to him."[133] Still he represented a vast improvement over his predecessor and at least embodied the possibility of a liberal future.

Yet even before Frederick William's accession to the throne, Bamberger had expected the worst, and when the throne change occurred it was merely a question of how many days or months the new ruler could survive. "For how long?" Bamberger wrote a few days into the new reign. "One can not deceive himself about that." A month later he quoted Mackenzie, Frederick's doctor, as saying: "I am afraid it is cancer."[134] What should one do? By April Bamberger had become an unofficial secret adviser of at least the empress and through her probably the emperor. Referred to as the "neighbor" and working through an intermediary, Baroness Bogumilla von Stockmar, Bamberger participated in the aborted reign of Frederick III. Not much was accomplished, but given the circumstances not much could be expected. The major achievement was the dismissal of the minister of the interior, Puttkamer, who was widely regarded in liberal circles as symbolizing the reactionary government. Puttkamer's dismissal had been discussed since the throne change, but it was Bamberger who recognized the appropriate opportunity to force Puttkamer's resignation. It did not matter who replaced him, he argued, but that the minister left. He was the symbol of all that the Radicals hated, and this action would at least give a liberal aura to Frederick's short reign. That Bismarck, for his own reasons, accepted the dismissal is also clear.[135] Besides his contribution to Puttkamer's removal, there was not much to be done. The empress seemed most concerned about her daughter's marriage to the recently deposed Bulgarian ruler, Alexander, and the emperor was busy bestowing medals on deserving liberals like Forckenbeck and Virchow.

Frederick III's death on June 15, 1888, left Bamberger and the Radical party without the support that had been perhaps their strongest prop in the 1880s. Schrader, as usual, could talk of developing a "long-range strategy," "shaking off what is opposed to liberalism," even if it cost them a district or two, and going back to "pre-1866" attitudes. This would be coupled with a campaign to portray Frederick III as the embodiment of liberal ideals.[136] Theodor Barth, however, wrote of the "old-timers among us" who "now slowly give up hope that they will yet experience a return to reason."[137] Bamberger also described the "passivity" of a part of the leadership:

Stauffenberg, who stands closest to me . . . is so depressed by the antipathy which he draws to himself as a prominent individual that he has withdrawn to his Bavarian sphere where he still possesses influence, effectiveness, and sympathy. So even in the best the reaction appears in the form of a resurgent particularism. Forckenbeck has withdrawn entirely to his city hall, Virchow lives for his scholarly work, Hänel remains in Kiel . . . and . . . Richter is absorbed by his newspaper. So besides Rickert most of the work falls to me, and I no longer believe in it.[138]

To Stauffenberg, who rarely appeared in the Reichstag during this period, Bamberger admitted: "You are missing absolutely nothing here. . . . It is all dull and unprofitable." [139] For the moment or longer there was not much to do. "It will be some time," he wrote his Bavarian friend, "until the cultured middle class, without which nothing is to be done, again becomes politically usable. I will probably not experience it if it really comes again." [140] The cartel had put the seal on a great internal development in Germany. "The true division [in Germany] ," he explained, "was not between north and south but between east and west. . . . The task of us liberals was to overcome the spirit of the east with the spirit of the west," but "today the east has triumphed over the west in the deepest meaning of the word. The spirit of the feudal east has subjugated the middle-class west and made it a worshiper. In the language of the day, one calls that cartel."[141]

Although the National Liberals' turn to the right had helped the "Junkers into the saddle," Bamberger asked rhetorically whether "we" did not further this development "with the fusion." [142] Even if Bamberger had his doubts about the correctness of the fusion, the normal friction between Richter and some of the former Secessionists paled in comparison with the general political situation. [143] One could let party affairs slide, Schrader had written, until it was a question of a "new beginning." When that occurred, he asked, "Can we still use Richter?" [144] Such a new beginning seemed possible by the spring of 1890.

· 11 ·
The 1890s:
A New Beginning?

In early 1889, in a series of articles in *Die Nation* under the title "Die Nachfolge Bismarcks" ("Bismarck's Succession"), Bamberger raised the previously unasked question of who or what would follow Bismarck. Although he claimed that his party had no reason to desire Bismarck's removal since the successor regime was likely to be even more reactionary, Bamberger nevertheless speculated about it. He sought to deflate the possible candidacy of Bismarck's son Herbert, arguing that it was ridiculous to compare Bismarck's offspring with Pitt the Younger, who was a "self-made" man. Herbert, on the contrary, had been advanced through the efforts of his father. Admitting that Bismarck would never bow to the will of a Reichstag majority, Bamberger suggested that the day might nevertheless come when Bismarck lost the confidence of the crown and was left in the lurch by his presently fervent supporters. Only this could force him to yield the stage.[1] The purpose of the essay, he wrote, was to get the question of Bismarck's succession on the "agenda," since "that is not an advantage to him. His opponents will see to it that the theme no longer disappears."[2] What inside information or premonition Bamberger had about coming events is not clear, but his articles appeared at an opportune time.

The dismissal of Bismarck did not issue from Bamberger's efforts. It grew out of irreconcilable personal and political differences between Bismarck and the young emperor, William II, aided by Bismarck's belief that the greater the difficulties, the more indispensable he would seem. By the end of 1889, the cartel was showing deep cracks as a result of differences over relations with Russia and the Antisocialist Law. Bismarck's unwillingness to compromise on this latter issue in order to insure a further extension of the law has led to speculation that he was counting on a growing political crisis to continue him in office, even as he realized that he was losing the support of the emperor. The two men also split on the issue of the government's attitude toward the working class. A day after the rejection of the bill to renew the Antisocialist

226

Law (January 26, 1890), the emperor announced plans for calling an international conference about workers' protection. Given Bismarck's well-known opposition to any workers' protection bill, this was regarded as a direct blow to the chancellor.[3] Even more surprising was the emperor's speech from the throne at the close of the Reichstag session in January 1890. It contained no reference to the Antisocialist Law, and he spoke warmly of the working class and the need for additional legislation to satisfy their justified interests.[4]

Bamberger could only respond: "What a surprise the speech from the throne was. No one had any idea." Everyone was convinced, he went on, that the emperor would deliver a declaration of war. "Ony with great effort did I hold Richter back yesterday from delivering a major speech which *antici-pando* was to be directed against this speech from the throne. How good that I was successful. . . . How this speech from the throne is to agree with the whole direction in the affair of the Antisocialist Law nobody can explain." Also striking was the absence of Bismarck.[5] Another unexpected development occurred ten days later, on February 4, when the emperor's manifestoes calling for an international conference on worker protection specifically mentioned the prospect of regulating the length of the working day. William had also signed the decrees over Bismarck's objections. These announcements, in Bamberger's words, fell like a bolt of lightning into the election campaign and signified the real end of the Antisocialist Law. He joked about Bismarck celebrating his seventy-fifth birthday as a private citizen.[6]

The Radical party's prospects for the February 1890 election appeared good to Bamberger, "even if one of our kind no longer dares to hope for much." Pleased by the "soft speech from the throne," the Radicals did not have to fear a "terror" campaign. In Bingen-Alzey, Bamberger regarded his reelection as certain, since he was assured the support of the Center party and faced only weak National Liberal and Social Democratic opposition.[7] His electoral predictions were borne out as the cartel parties lost almost 40 percent of their seats, while the Radical party more than doubled its share to sixty-six and the Social Democrats tripled their representation to thirty-five. The latter also drew more popular votes than any other party. The election of February 20 was a resounding rejection of the cartel parliament. In Bingen-Alzey, Bamberger polled almost 60 percent of the votes to win an easy first-round victory. Bismarck survived the election by one month. The time for a new beginning was at hand.

Shortly after Bismarck's dismissal, Bamberger wrote Stauffenberg: "We are glad that the evil man is going, and that we were not even in the least responsible for it." The chancellor's departure even improved his health, he claimed.[8] The man who had filled the pages of his life was gone from office but not from Bamberger's mind or pen. He devoted two long essays to

Bismarck in the 1890s, and virtually every other article he wrote during that period contained references to the fallen leader. He confessed to Broemel, "I am of the view that one must in a moderate way always be reminded of his shortcomings."[9] His literary efforts demonstrate this clearly. Although he considered it inappropriate to deny "with dialectical contradictions Bismarck's true merit," he could praise only Bismarck's foreign policy, and that with reservations. He could not help mentioning some "shortcomings." At the time of the growing rapprochement between Russia and France, he felt justified in asking whether Bismarck's policies had not contributed to it, particularly his role as the honest broker in 1878, in founding the Triple Alliance, and in the financial measures against the Russians that drove them into the arms of the French financiers. By the mid-1890s he could even write that Germany's relations with other countries had become better under Bismarck's successor. "The world looks more peaceful today than ever in the three decades during which the greatest diplomat of his time" led the foreign affairs of Prussia and Germany.[10] In 1887 he had privately applauded the action against the Russian bonds and claimed that the cautious French investors would never buy the risky Russian securities.[11]

Leaving the field of foreign affairs, Bamberger was convinced that "the last ten years of the Bismarckian regime have brought incalculable harm to Germany, because they have undermined whole ranks of the nation in their innermost moral and intellectual existence." He called attention to the chancellor's manipulative talent. The German leader was unequaled in managing the government machine and in using popular currents for momentary successes. Although a Junker, he had no aristocratic prejudices but only differentiated between those who "adapted themselves to him or not." He grasped everything that promised to be useful for a particular purpose, and the theme of his tenure could be the "manipulation of public opinion." Bismarck's main sin, according to Bamberger, would be his impact on future generations. He detected the emergence of a Bismarck cult, which would stress all the wrong characteristics. The greatness of his personality did not rest on the "pedestal of psychological esteem but on the accomplished fact," and the authors of books for young children, Bamberger noted, would have trouble finding evidence of nobility or magnanimity. There was in Bismarck an absence of humanity, and the liberal wondered about the effect on the younger generation if the "questionable ideal of martial energy with all of its excesses was developed into the highest expression of the national character." Nevertheless, at the end of his last work devoted to Bismarck, only a few months after the former chancellor's death and shortly before his own, he could not help asking rhetorically what would have been the outcome if

Bismarck had cooperated in building a healthy constitutional life rather than opposing it.[12] All liberal roads still went via the great chancellor.

Soon after Bismarck's dismissal, Bamberger wrote Otto Hartwig that the "not unfounded feeling of its own inadequacy makes the nation on the whole unenthusiastic to get on with the business [of state]."[13] Not Bamberger himself. In spite of his fears for the future, he was always a creature of the present, and that meant facing the problem of his and his party's relationship to the new regime under Bismarck's successor, Caprivi.[14] The party greeted Caprivi as someone with whom cooperation was possible. The general was regarded as unemotional, without the bitterness and hate that seemed so necessary to Bismarck. In particular, the former Secessionists saw considerable possibilities under the new regime since the chancellor seemed to be convinced of the need to get along with the Reichstag. Moreover, he was regarded as sympathetic to the Radical position on colonial and commercial policy and vigorously opposed the growing anti-Semitic movement. Also, as Bamberger wrote, Caprivi's successor would only be worse.[15]

When Caprivi spoke for the first time in the Prussian House of Representatives, both Richter and Rickert replied, the first saying in effect, "I will fight you just as your predecessor," while the latter implied: "If you call me I am ready any time."[16] For the former Secessionists the question immediately arose whether the party could be a suitable instrument for cooperation as long as it was headed by Eugen Richter. The apparent answer was no, ushering in the major party crisis between 1884 and the dissolution of 1893.[17] Only a few days after Bismarck's dismissal, Bamberger, although now claiming that the founder's removal and the election results justified the fusion, gave the first indication that a move was planned against Richter. He wrote of reorganizing the internal structure of the party. Unfortunately at a party meeting Rickert "revealed too much of his heart in which he divulged what we had discussed among ourselves several days ago about preparing for the reorganization" of the party.[18]

Besides differences over the party's attitude toward the Caprivi government, the specific causes of the dispute were the Secessionists' old claim that Richter was misusing his position as editor of the *Freisinnige Zeitung* to attack his colleagues and the fear that he desired the party as his personal instrument. A quarrel also broke out over the party's relations with the National Liberals, whose support Hänel, among others, needed in the February election.[19] The ultimate aim of the oppositional group led by Rickert, Schrader, and Barth was to remove Richter from the chairmanship of the "committee of seven" which was in charge of party affairs. The thirteen-member executive committee (seven former Progressives and six former

Secessionists) was responsible for the election of the members of the committee of seven and its chairman. Bamberger, although clearly sympathetic to the efforts of Rickert and Schrader, nevertheless tried to play a mediating role in the early phase of the conflict, primarily because he more than the others was convinced of the absolute necessity of avoiding a break in the party precisely when so many new possibilities seemed to be opening up. Secondly, it appears that by being or sounding conciliatory he could exercise more influence on the fair-minded Stauffenberg, whose support was considered essential to Richter's opponents.[20]

The problem for the Secessionists, since they were a minority in the party and the executive committee, was to win over or silence a former Progressive. Bamberger worked on Rudolf Virchow, attempting to convince him that Richter's removal from the board of directors would be beneficial. "It is hard to find someone who recognizes Richter's ability and achievement more than I," he told Virchow, "but when the conversation turns to his personal relation to the party I have a great deal of trouble. Do you believe that a *man,* to whom it is a question of the cause and not petty egotistical purpose, searches in every way secretly to incite one part of the party directly against the other? . . . When a prominent leader himself so undermines his party, it *must* be ruined." After unburdening himself and even hinting at what was planned, Bamberger quickly reassured Virchow that he hoped the parliamentary work would push the intrigues into the background. "From the other side, I mean the old Secession, one wishes nothing more than to keep the peace."[21]

It is difficult to take seriously Bamberger's last comment to Virchow. Two weeks later everything was set for a "test of strength," as Bamberger relayed developments to the ill Stauffenberg. The central committee of the party, which included all the members of the Reichstag and the state parliaments, was to be called together to elect a new executive committee of thirteen. The Secessionists hoped to replace Robert Zelle, who was believed ready to resign and was one of Richter's men, with Hugo Hinze, who stood with the Secessionists. This would give the latter a clear majority. Barth, Schrader, and Broemel were even threatening not to accept their own election to the executive committee or the board of directors if Hinze were rejected by the party's central committee. Bamberger looked on with mixed feelings at this power struggle between "hostile brothers." His friends were "right," but he did not expect success, since he believed that Richter had a majority of the central committee behind him. He tried to dissuade his colleagues from pursuing the affair, hoped to postpone the meeting, and tried to enlist Stauffenberg's aid. He admitted his pessimism about the future of the Radical party and seemed to agree with a comment of Forckenbeck's that in the long run it would not be held together. For the moment, however, one needed to win time.[22]

The climax nevertheless came unexpectedly and quickly. Richter convinced Zelle not to resign, and Bamberger convinced Hinze to continue his party work without being a member of the executive committee. Thus the conspirators' plans seemed to be upset, and the old executive committee was reelected on May 19. Then surprisingly Richter insisted on the immediate election of the new committee of seven. Bamberger had expected this at a later date when Stauffenberg could be there. Virchow was also absent. While the bulk of the party retired to an inn, the eleven members met, with Bamberger presiding, to elect the new board of directors. "Now comes the coup! Chairman of the committee of seven: 6 Schrader, 5 Richter. Tableaux! Deputy: 7 Zelle, 2 Rickert, 2 Richter. New Tableaux. You should have seen this," Bamberger continued. "He [Richter] was speechless but submitted silently." "That was always my program," he now revealed. "The election of Hinze [to the executive committee] would have meant nothing to the world," but this outcome signified "that we do not need the head of the *Freisinnige Zeitung* as chief of the party," which was to be the message for the press. Unsaid perhaps was the hope that with a more accommodating leader the party would be more useful to the government.[23] Rickert had been Zelle's predecessor, and since both leaders were removed, one could argue that this was no attempt simply to punish Richter. With both Stauffenberg and Virchow missing, the former Progressive, Albert Hänel, cast the decisive vote for Schrader. He had never been happy with Richter's leadership and had recently quarreled with him during the February election over the question of accepting National Liberal support, which Hänel desperately needed in Kiel.

Richter was not prepared to submit silently to his dethronement and immediately began a counterattack. Two days after the crucial meeting, Virchow formally protested the holding of the vote for the committee of seven in his absence and without his even being invited. Hänel's reply that Richter himself had requested the election did not end the matter.[24] In the ensuing three weeks, a heated newspaper war raged between the two wings, with Richter's supporters charging that he was the victim of a shabby trick and that Schrader, with his financial connections, was unsuited to be the head of a "peoples' party."[25]

The Secessionists were hard pressed to maintain their position. Bamberger defended his group's action to Stauffenberg and saw Virchow being used by Richter to undo the decision of May 19. He claimed unconvincingly that Richter's deposition was greeted with approval except by a few fanatics and argued that if the Bavarian would stand firm, Richter would bow to the inevitable. The sharp attacks against Barth, Schrader, Rickert, and Broemel, he went on, were forcing them to make it a point of honor not to give in. He claimed that his "oral efforts" had succeeded "in keeping their displeasure in check." Bamberger also tried to convince Stauffenberg that the original action against Richter simply happened and had not been prepared before-hand. It was merely a sudden decision forced upon them when Richter was able to forestall the election of Zelle. The thought of acquiescing for five years in Richter's leadership was too much. "Without even having a moment to discuss it, everyone said to himself: things *cannot* proceed this way. Had I voted for Richter, our friends would have exploded.... You know how impartially I think in the matter, but *this* line I aso had to follow, and I count on your support. We are now in possession and let the others come."[26] They did, and two days later even Schrader was no longer sure about the course of the "campaign," since his group was being depicted as "secret intriguers" by several newspapers. He was searching for a graceful way to retreat.[27] In spite of Schrader's letter, Bamberger still encouraged Stauffen-berg to stand firm and claimed that Richter would "cringe." "We all do not doubt that. No, it is a question of making a decision at all costs, and this *vabanque* must finally be played. The fellow is too wretched. I could not expect our friends to endure for another five years this insolent, mendacious system of intrigue."[28]

In the midst of the newspaper war, Richter's journals began to suggest that the Secessionists wanted him out of the way because they intended to be conciliatory on the military question. Seeber argues in effect that this lay behind the entire affair. In 1890 the government requested an increase in the army of some eighteen thousand men, once again raising a painful issue for the Radical party. Opposition in 1887 had cost them dearly, and in 1890 at least one wing of the party believed there was much to be gained from cooperation with Caprivi. In April, Bamberger, although assuring Stauffen-berg that he stood on his side, presumably against the bill, wrote of a "disposition to yield" if the government's request was not too extravagant. By May he believed that the military bill would run smoothly with the great majority of the party voting in favor of it, "probably even I in order not to carry on a cheap policy of being outvoted" (that is, to vote no when you are aware that a majority will vote for a bill).[29] The party crisis, however, coincided with an intensification of the struggle over the military bill when the war minister, Julius von Verdy, said on May 21 that the bill was only the first of much greater demands. This gave Richter a new weapon to use against his opponents and also made it difficult for them to cooperate on the military question. The following day Bamberger wrote that he would vote no. If Stauffenberg would do the same, the "external demarcation line [between the two factions of the party] is also wiped away." The military bill, he predicted, would "cause us even more headaches than the party agony. Such is life."[30] He hoped to get even Barth and Rickert, who were perhaps the most yielding on military matters, to vote against the bill. "Then perhaps the whole party will vote no and through it avoid a greater evil than the open break with Richter." In spite of warnings from Caprivi that a rejection would mean a dissolution and possibly a revision of the constitution with Bismarck's return, the Radical party voted against the military bill. Bamberger even proposed the introduction of two-year service for the infantry, which of course was rejected.[31] The bill passed because of the support of the Center party.

Hoping to defuse the military issue as an inner party weapon, Bamberger still believed that his faction could have its way as long as they stood firm and emphasized the "true reason" for the dispute, "Richter's relationship with the *Freisinnige Zeitung* and its attacks." He continued to pressure Stauffenberg to support his friends. His defection, Bamberger threatened, would cause his friends to refuse to accept a party office, "and you remain alone with Richter. We goad you on in this embarrassing situation in order to ease your conscience."[32] Stauffenberg remained unconvinced by Bamberger's efforts, and by June 1 both sides seemed ready for a compromise. Bamberger even changed his tone and spoke of a party recovery rather than a break coming out of the crisis.[33] The compromise of June 9 drawn up by Bamberger provided for an alternating chairmanship of the committee of seven between Richter and Schrader. Although Richter was in effect first chairman, he and Schrader would each have the power to call meetings.[34]

The crisis was overcome, but the basic incompatibility remained. Richter regained his position but nominally had to share his authority. Nevertheless, he still seemed to be in control of the party to the extent that any person was able to control it.[35] Bamberger, although apparently equivocal at first, gradually assumed the role of a hard liner, and this probably represented his position all along. His apparent initial neutrality was more pose than belief, adopted because of the need to lead Stauffenberg on. For the professional politician, the change of government created a unique opportunity to play a role in this new regime, but with Richter at the helm the chances for cooperation would be very uncertain. Thus the party needed a new profile. Although the attempt was at best partially successful, the government could not fail to note that some elements in the party were ready to support it.

In spite of the Secessionists' pleasure over Caprivi's chancellorship and their willingness to be cooperative, they demonstrated their readiness to oppose the government on a number of key issues. The Radical party without exception voted against the army bill of 1890 and against the government's major federal tax measure, the sugar tax bill. It also helped kill a bill to reduce the immunity of Reichstag deputies.[36] With Bamberger in the vanguard, the party continued to fight the government's colonial program from 1890 to 1893. Every possible occasion—budgetary requests, the government's assumption of administrative responsibility for a territory, the dispatch of troops to quell a rebellion, or the sending of a scientific expedition—was used as a springboard for a general colonial debate. Even though Bamberger was again accused of a lack of patriotism, the debates were not as heated as in the Bismarck years. Since Caprivi was obviously unenthusiastic about the colonial ventures, the Radicals were not inclined to overemphasize their differences with the government, and as Bamberger admitted, both sides had reached a "state of immovability." The discussions added little to the arguments of previous years. Bamberger was convinced that events such as rebellions in East and Southwest Africa, the failure of the steamship connection to Samoa, and the untenability of Bismarck's charter company approach vindicated his decade of tenacious opposition. He did not exaggerate greatly when he said all that remained of the colonial intoxication was the "hangover and the expenses." Neither the witty phrases, nor the factual arguments he continued to present, nor even the government's admission that his charges were correct could change the outcome. Pleading for more time for the colonies to demonstrate their value and stressing the issue of honor and patriotism, the government won every vote. The margin of victory was provided by the Center party, which accepted the colonial requests as part of a scheme to eliminate the slave trade and spread Christianity.[37]

Opposition to Caprivi's policies was accompanied by an air of regret rather than the rancor that had been a part of the debates of the Bismarck era. By March 1891, through an old schoolmate of Caprivi's, the Secessionist wing of the Radical party came into direct and regular contact with the chancellor, with Schrader as the intermediary. Whether this was ever known to Richter's wing of the party is doubtful. The issue that formed the basis of this cooperation was commercial policy.[38]

Since 1879 German commercial policy had moved increasingly in the direction of higher tariffs, particularly on agricultural products. The grain rates formed the center of the protectionist movement of the 1880s and 1890s, and the tariff laws of 1885 and 1887 raised these duties from one to five marks per hundred kilograms. The major beneficiaries of the grain duties were the estate owners of the northeast, who saw their economic interests threatened by the importation of cheaper grain from North America and Russia. Operating relatively efficiently but cursed by poor soil, burdened by heavy mortgages and high valuation, and believing themselves hurt by the gold standard, the Junkers saw their salvation in higher tariffs.

By 1890, however, the old arguments for agricultural protection seemed less compelling, and Caprivi was impressed by other considerations. Germany's tariff increases had closed off German markets to agricultural exports from central and eastern European lands. German industry, which viewed these areas as prime fields for export, was sensitive to complaints about high agricultural tariffs and threats of retaliation. A major goal of Caprivi's commercial policy was to consolidate central Europe into a market for German industrial goods. Moreover, there were important political reasons for being conciliatory on this question. He could strengthen the Triple Alliance by removing sources of friction between Germany and Austria-Hungary and Italy. In the early 1890s Germany also suffered a severe economic depression, which coincided with bad harvests and rising grain prices. The price of bread rose 50 percent in Berlin between 1890 and 1891. To make matters worse, Russia also faced famine and forbade the export of rye and wheat. To the public, the most obvious remedy was to lower the grain tariffs, and bills to this effect were introduced into the Reichstag. The government moved to permit the importation of American and Scandinavian pork and undertook to negotiate a series of commercial agreements.[39]

The Radical party was kept informed of the negotiations over the commercial accords, and Bamberger recorded Caprivi's statements in favor of tariff reductions on grain products and about the "harmfulness of a policy based on [special] economic interests." The liberal was apprised of the wide range of the chancellor's plans and his intention to conclude commercial agreements not only with the Triple Alliance partners but also with Russia. He also tried to drum up urban support for the treaties, particularly in Mainz.[40]

The first round of treaties—with Italy, Austria-Hungary, and Belgium—was signed by December 1891 and immediately introduced into the Reichstag. A fourth treaty, with Switzerland, went to the Reichstag in January 1892. They provided for the reduction of the duties on wheat and rye to 3.5 marks per 100 kilograms, as well as reductions for certain types of wine and grapes, the latter reduction of special concern to Italy. Coming at a time of food shortages and high grain prices, the treaties met little opposition. The first three passed 243–48 on December 18 and the Swiss treaty, on January 23. Only from the German Conservative party did a majority vote against the treaties, while all the Radicals, the Centrists, and the Social Democrats voted for them. Bamberger spoke relatively little during the debates, but he did intervene on behalf of the articles dealing with wine and grapes, stressing that he supported them even though he came from a wine-producing area.[41]

The treaties represented the zenith of Caprivi's chancellorship, and he was made a count for his efforts. Three months later, as a result of the failure of his school bill and his increasing dislike for the Prussian minister of finance, Miquel, Caprivi resigned all his offices but was finally persuaded to remain as chancellor. Moreover, during the summer of 1892 the government was embarrassed by its apparent vindictiveness against Bismarck in connection with his visit to Vienna. Public opinion seemed to rally around the aggrieved ex-chancellor, and the government appeared petty and mean in comparison.[42]

As Caprivi received these blows, Bamberger recognized that it was the Radicals' task to help keep the chancellor in office. He told Broemel and Stauffenberg that the Radicals had to get along with Caprivi "in spite of everything," since "nothing better would come after him." He believed that Caprivi's salvation lay in a commercial treaty with Russia, which the two countries were then attempting to negotiate. The affair was more significant politically than economically, he wrote. A successful conclusion to the talks would be a "slap in the face" to Bismarck, who had been trumpeting that the wire to St. Petersburg was broken, and a "great triumph" for Caprivi. The one development that might come between Caprivi and the Radicals, Bamberger remarked, was a new military bill. "If one could only convince him to delay it for a year so that no apple of discord comes between us," Bamberger wrote hopefully. Unfortunately the trade negotiations with Russia dragged on through 1892, even degenerating into a tariff war by the summer of 1893, and by the end of 1892 the "apple of discord" was sent to the Reichstag. [43]

The second or "big" army bill of Caprivi's tenure was introduced on November 23, 1892. Concerned by recent French military reforms, which produced more recruits annually than Germany in spite of the latter's larger population, the government determined to make the idea of universal military service more nearly a reality. This meant an increase of 84,000 enlisted men at a cost of 60 million marks. The human increase was as much as all the previous military bills since 1871, while the financial cost added to an already overstrained budget and would necessitate tax increases. Such major increases, Caprivi was convinced, could be wrung from the Reichstag by offering concessions such as a reduction in the duration of the law and the term of military service. The seven-year life span was reduced to five, corresponding to a Reichstag legislative period. Also, after much squirming and hedging, the emperor accepted a *de facto* reduction of service to two years for the infantry.[44]

The prospects for the bill were not good. The Center, since Windthorst's death in 1891, missed its brilliant leader's sure hand and was divided on the measure, with the larger so-called democratic wing of the party behind Ernst Lieber opposed to it. The two Conservative parties had come to regard Caprivi as an enemy by 1892 as a result of his commercial policy and the beginnings of a decline in grain prices. They were ready to support the growing anti-Semitic movement and the soon-to-be-organized Farmers' League (Bund der Landwirte) as a means of destroying Caprivi and his policies. They were not averse to seeing him humiliated because of the military bill. The Social Democratic party, which by 1892 counted thirty-five deputies, would also oppose the bill.[45]

The Radical party was once again placed before the issue that was the bane of liberal existence in Germany. In October, Barth announced the Radicals' position that Germany's financial condition did not permit such an increase even if concessions were made on the term of service and duration of the bill. Even before the measure was formally introduced, Barth and Schrader saw Caprivi, who according to Bamberger was very "upright" but "completely unbending. All or nothing. Flag on the mast. If rejected then *finis Germania*. Thus probably dissolution." In the opening debates Richter, as expected, delivered a harsh critique of the justification for the bill. However, the latent tension within the party surfaced as Rickert pointedly stressed that the Secessionist wing of the party had supported military bills in the past. Several weeks before, Bamberger had predicted that Rickert would be receptive to concessions from the government, but he (Bamberger) did not expect them to be forthcoming. The Radicals as a whole would have been willing to grant the additional funds needed to convert to two-year service but none to increase numerical strength.[46]

The bill was referred to a committee, which met twenty-eight times from January until March to find a solution to the military problem and avert a dissolution. The issue seemed most painful for the Radicals. Bamberger reported the spreading feeling among his colleagues that a dissolution or Caprivi's resignation would be of doubtful worth and saw evidence of a willingness to compromise. "Rickert is already very soft, and the others of our color would prefer anything than to see Caprivi go or a dissolution with new elections . . . even Richter. . . . But the devil will have to find something that does not compromise us and appears acceptable to the government."[47]

The military committee could not. After its extended discussion it rejected the government's bill but was unable to agree on a substitute behind which a majority of the committee could unite. Even after the end of the committee meetings, the second reading of the bill was delayed a month to permit further efforts to compromise. During this period Bamberger was in contact with the army about a compromise solution. In April he had his "last conference" with Caprivi. The chancellor presented the government's final offer, a reduction of 14,000 troops from the government's original request, plus "nonessentials." Bamberger told him "categorically" that only ten or twelve deputies from his party would support it, "among them *not* I. . . . I implored him to make more concessions in any form." When they parted after a very "quiet and friendly conversation," it was with the expectation of a rejection and a dissolution. "My formula is," Bamberger informed the ever ailing Stauffenberg, "I will not nail anyone to the cross who wants to help if he is *sure* of helping to produce a majority, but [I will nail] everyone who offers unsuccessful concessions. If without harm to the party the dissolution can be avoided, I consider that a relative benefit. For one thing is certain: Caprivi and the Junkers are divided by a steadily growing mutual hate, and we will never again get a chancellor who possesses this good quality."[48]

The final act played itself out from May 3 to May 6, during the second reading. The key vote would come on the motion of a Center deputy, Carl von Huene, who proposed a 14,000-man reduction and a firm commitment to a two-year service period. Even as late as the last day Bamberger was uncertain about the outcome, and he still hoped a few defectors might provide the necessary majority. He reported a last-minute plan by Hänel to offer the government support in return for a permanent establishment of the two-year service. Caprivi, according to Bamberger, wavered but appeared at the final Reichstag sitting with the dissolution statement already prepared. A final attempt to play for time by adjourning instead of closing off debate and forcing a vote failed. Huene's proposal was rejected 210–162, and the Reichstag was dissolved. The Social Democrats, most of the Center, and most Radicals provided the majority against the amendment.[49]

The postscript for the Radicals was written quickly. Six members of the Radical party had voted for Huene's motion. At first Bamberger was pleased that the number of defectors was so low, since it would have required twenty more, an impossible number Bamberger claimed, to have provided a majority for the bill. The Radicals would have merely looked foolish if more had voted for the bill and it had still failed. Although he maintained that Richter would have preferred to see Huene's amendment pass, he hoped the former Progressive would not make too great a "scene" about the six. Bamberger even admitted that up to May 6, Richter had "behaved quite correctly, and one cannot reproach him for absolutely anything." The fact that Schrader and even Rickert and Barth (the latter two with extreme difficulty) voted against the amendment, Bamberger regarded as a hopeful sign. He believed that a split could be avoided.[50]

Bamberger was wrong, and Barth, who had predicted that dissolution would mean the complete destruction of the party, was proved correct. "*Consummatum est,*" Bamberger wrote Stauffenberg after the Radical party meeting on the evening of May 6. By a vote of 27–22 the party voted to expel the six "apostates." As a consequence, twenty-two members, mostly former Secessionists plus a few old Progressives around Hänel, left the party to escape "Richter's dictatorship." The new secessionists organized themselves as the Radical Union (Freisinnige Vereinigung), and the group around Richter changed its name to the Radical People's Party (Freisinnige Volkspartei).[51]

The split that all the participants seemed to recognize as inherent in the fusion finally occurred over the issue that had been the Achilles' heel of German liberalism since the 1860s. The question will never be settled whether the fundamental issue was clashing political conceptions, issuing from different socioeconomic bases, or the unwillingness of the Secessionists to submit to Richter's authoritarian leadership. I incline to the latter view. Richter may have been forced by his public's opinion to be unbending toward the military bill, but this public support failed to materialize in the election. The most that can be said is that Richter's party lost fewer seats than Barth's group, winning twenty-three to the latter's thirteen, making for a loss of over 40 percent of the Radical party seats. It was 1887 but on a smaller scale, probably because Caprivi refused to organize a "terror" campaign as Bismarck had done. The party's so-called readiness to compromise scarcely could have had worse results in 1887 and 1893 than its final decision to vote against the military bills. For the Secessionists at least, even after they voted no, the major concern was to reassure their voters that they were more ready to compromise than they actually were. Reasonableness rather than stiff opposition seemed to be their key to success. One should not blame them for not being Social Democrats. Admittedly there was a reservoir of opposition to government policies, as the election results showed, but could it have been exploited by any other party than the Social Democrats? Moreover, it cannot be demonstrated that the military or antisocialist position of the party was responsible for its disastrous showing in the election. As Ziekursch points out, the propaganda of the recently organized Farmers' League plus the anti-Semitic agitation probably took its toll of liberal constituencies. The Anti-Semitic party increased its vote from 47,500 to 263,900 and its seats from five to sixteen.[52] Bamberger did not seem to understand the election either. "What," he moaned, "had influenced the minds of the electorate? Certainly not the debates in the Reichstag. . . . On the minds of the wisest and most foolish the question must force itself, what then actually sways the opinion of the masses? In any case, anything but logic. . . . The German character is the least political in Europe," and the Radicals had failed because they were the only "purely political party left in Germany."[53]

His views on the 1884 fusion continued to fluctuate. He admitted that "there were so many mistakes it would be difficult to know where the first ones were and on which side." He believed that Richter's strategy all along had been a party purge and personal control, but "from his standpoint" Bamberger could not blame him. The most "inexcusable of all mistakes," however, was the "egoism" of the six dissidents who instead of abstaining gave Richter his opportunity.[54] But a month later his and his friends' "greatest error," he claimed, "was the fusion" since it "canceled our best move, the secession. . . . Without the fusion, parliamentary developments in Germany might well have taken a better course, even if the main thing, the unpolitical nature of the German people, would not have been overcome as the basic evil."[55] Five years later, at the appearance of Philippson's biography of Max von Forckenbeck, Bamberger complained that neither in the book nor in the reviews had he found the "true truth" about the secession and the fusion. Bamberger himself seemed not to know it.[56]

The most immediate consequence for Bamberger of the party split was the end of his parliamentary career. On the day of the separation he telegraphed his district that he would not be a candidate for reelection. He had often talked of not runing for a seat but always found a reason to offer himself once more. As late as April, he indicated that if the Reichstag were dissolved he would be a candidate; his constituents, he said, would *"nolens volens"* make him their candidate and not even expect him to campaign actively.[57] However, the "last horrible proceeding in the party was the limit." That plus the increased anti-Semitic agitation drove him away. "Had it been a joy to be there," he wrote Hartwig, "I could still have held my own quite well. But I would seem like a fool if I expected to continue the unthankful work, more Sisyphean, less friendly, and inwardly more upsetting than before."[58] He remained unmoved by the entreaties of his friends and even by a gracious letter of support from Richter.[59]

Leaving the Reichstag did not signify getting out of politics. During the last six years of his life he was still involved politically, doing what he could for a "healthy" national policy and acting as a critic of German society. The rest of 1893 saw Bamberger's friends, particularly Barth, Schrader, Broemel, and Rickert, trying to put together a new liberal group. The hastily organized Radical Union had won fourteen seats in the Reichstag election, which Bamberger regarded as the best that could be expected. He had strong doubts, however, about the direction the new party was taking. He feared that in its eagerness to support Caprivi, the party would move too far to the right and still not be able to prevent Caprivi's fall or "subjection to the Junkers." He seemed to regret its unanimous support for the military bill, which was accepted 201–185 in July.[60]

As Bamberger surveyed the liberal scene in 1893, it looked like a "picture of misery" with "no way upward," and he was convinced of the "hopelessness" of Barth's efforts. There was simply "no material for the formation of a party." None of the suggestions put forth by his friends appeared to hold out any chance of success. He dismissed the fertile Schrader's idea that by offering positive proposals one could reconquer a respectable political position as an idea that he had heard many years ago. To another suggestion that the party's salvation lay in a vigorous campaign against the agricultural duties, he skeptically replied: "You have tried that once already. With what results you know." Equally without merit was Barth and Schrader's proposal to take up the cause of the eight-hour day. This notion he attributed to the influence of Schrader's "eccentric" wife. Toward the end of 1893, he even advised against trying to call a party convention which would turn out to be an "abortion," with no participation from the countryside or south Germany. Compounding this bleak picture was the hostility coming from Richter, who rejected any cooperation between the political half brothers. In spite of Richter's very flattering letter immediately after the split, Bamberger's hatred for the former Progressive greatly increased. It was the "accursed" Richter who, with his "mischief-making," was the "worst enemy of a healthy liberal movement" and threatened to ruin whatever limited possibilities the current situation offered. Therefore he had to be "discredited before German public opinion." For all his complaints Bamberger was too pessimistic to propose much. New legislative proposals or increased agitation were useless. "It is completely false to strengthen mankind in this delusion, as if legislation must be commanded once again to fabricate more belief." Only "keeping still" was appropriate for the liberal group.[61]

In spite of Bamberger's discouragement and the Radical Union's new disaster in the Prussian election, where they won only six seats, Barth and his friends went ahead with their efforts and held the Radical Union's initial national convention on December 2 and 3, 1893. But rather than formally organize a new party, they fell back on the device of the Secessionists and constituted themselves as an "electoral association of the liberals" whose purpose was to serve as a gathering point for liberal forces in Germany. No formal program was even proposed.[62]

The one hopeful sign Bamberger saw in 1893 and 1894 was the successful conclusion of Caprivi's commercial treaties with Serbia, Rumania, and Russia. This had not been an easy accomplishment. By 1893–94 German farmers, large and small, were convinced they were in the midst of an agricultural crisis and that the proposed trade treaties with Rumania and Russia would only increase their troubles. The world market price for wheat and rye had already dropped 25 percent below the average price for the 1880s, and the farmers feared that a new influx of cheap grain products from the two eastern European countries would only worsen the situation. Agricultural interests had organized in February 1893 into the Farmers' League, which had 170,000 members ten months after its organization. An "Economic Association" in the Reichstag which embraced some one hundred and fifty members was also formed. In December 1893, after extremely bitter debates over the Rumanian treaty, the conservative newspaper, *Kreuz Zeitung,* announced that it no longer had confidence in the German chancellor.[63] Moreover, Russia and Germany had engaged in a brief tariff war in 1893. Even when this was overcome by December and the signing of the treaty was certain, Bamberger still had doubts about the Russian treaty's finding a majority in the Reichstag. Only if William intervened to neutralize some Conservative opposition would the treaty have a chance. This the emperor did, helping to provide the government with a 200–146 victory in February 1894. The government pacified the opposition by eliminating certain restrictions on the importation and reexportation of Russian grain which would benefit the large landowners of the northeast. Both Radical parties, plus the Social Democrats, the Poles, most of the National Liberals, one half of the Center, and scattered Conservatives provided the majority. The victory signified, Bamberger wrote, that the supposedly outmoded free-trade approach still was in touch with economic realities. It also represented a recognition that the interests of industry and trade were not antithetical but rather complementary. If industry could be persuaded to continue on this path and resist agrarian attempts to lure them back into an alliance, then German economic policy might well be at a "turning point."[64]

Unfortunately the commercial treaties were Caprivi's last accomplishment, and they did not stave off his dismissal in October 1894. Bamberger characterized it as a "catastrophe" and regarded the fallen minister as a victim of the hostility of the "court and hunting society" because he was the "only one who dared to express an independent opinion."[65] Although favorably disposed to Caprivi's successor, Prince Chlodwig zu Hohenlohe, and convinced of his good will, Bamberger viewed the seventy-five-year-old as "completely worn out" and merely a fig leaf to cover a momentary embarrassment. He had visions of the cartel's being reorganized with Herbert Bismarck or General Alfred Waldersee at the helm, particularly after the emperor's cabinet purge of the summer of 1897 which brought in Alfred von Tirpitz, Bernhard von Bülow, and Arthur von Posadowsky. The driving force behind the new team, he maintained, was "fear of Social Democracy."[66]

The prospects for a resurgent liberalism did not improve during the 1890s as far as Bamberger was concerned. The scapegoat, at least in part, was still Eugen Richter, whose policy "for thirty years has been directed toward the high goal of remaining in the minority." Bamberger's anticolonialism weakened enough that he could applaud the Radical Union's support for the navy bill of 1898. He also saw some rays of hope coming from the smaller states whose existence he once disparaged. Württemberg was now "an oasis in

Germany" and men like Friedrich von Payer and Conrad Haussmann of the German People's party (Deutsche Volkspartei), "splendid persons."[67]

Although the political prospects for his friends continued to look poor, Bamberger's retirement gave him even more time to think and write about Germany. "That both of us . . . have been retired in the empire," he sadly wrote Stauffenberg, "has nothing to do with our respective ages. We are not done, but the empire is with us. . . . Our time is up. A new, completely different sort of breed has taken over the stage. For us there is still only room in the gallery."[68] In the last decade of his life, Bamberger took his seat in the gallery. But even though he claimed to have "correctly" anticipated so many things, it was "impossible for me to cast a prophetic look into the next decade of German development."[69] Nevertheless, he tried. The objects of his concern in the 1890s were the same as in previous years: the weakness of representative institutions, warding off state intervention, relations between liberals and workers, the weakness of the middle class, and the expanding anti-Semitic movement. His views on these subjects in part changed, in part grew more intense.

The second half of the 1890s viewed from the angle of government policy has been characterized as the Stumm era, after the industrialist Karl Ferdinand von Stumm, who was a member of the Free Conservative party. While he did not in any sense direct government policy in the mid-1890s, he was a favored adviser of William II's. He ruled his industrial complex at Neunkirchen in the Saar with an iron hand, hated the Social Democrats and unions, and advocated strict laws to deal with working-class organizational or political activities. He demanded a withdrawal of voting rights from socialists and the expulsion of their leaders. He also attacked university professors, particularly Socialists of the Chair, who dared to discuss social-political questions. The emperor, after a wave of anarchist activity in Europe and increased strike activity in Germany, went along with Stumm's suggestions to the extent of contemplating a coup d'état in 1894 whose aim was a change in the voting law. In Saxony the voting law was revised to make it similar to the Prussian three-class system. William also introduced a bill against "subversion" in 1894 that proposed to punish incitements to disobedience whether carried out or not, as well as attacks on monarchy, religion, marriage, family, or property. The bill was rejected in May 1895 because of determined liberal and socialist opposition. Another attempt in 1897 in Prussia to pass a miniature antisocialist law failed by four votes, 209–205, as did the so-called workhouse bill of 1899.[70]

With the mid-1890s dominated by an antilabor and antisocialist policy, it is not surprising that Bamberger would turn to this, for him, very old problem. What is unexpected is his changing attitude toward the old social problem. It was symbolized in one sense by his rapprochement with his old foes, Lujo Brentano and the Socialists of the Chair. It was his and Brentano's parallel struggle on behalf of Caprivi's commercial policy and against subsequent attempts to undo his work that brought the two men together. It began when Brentano wrote a letter to the editor of *Die Nation* outlining his reasons for the decline of liberalism. The liberals, he wrote, had not been able to exercise any influence on the worker because they had not permitted the worker to influence the liberals' view of the world. What killed liberalism was dogmatism. The liberals had originally based their ideas on critical observation which had yielded much that was positive and in agreement with the requirements of the time. But out of this teaching came orthodoxy, and when political power turned away from them they became a sect. Brentano denied the liberal claim that lack of character caused the decline of liberalism among German youth. Youth was simply finding more satisfaction for its ideals on the right or the left. What saved the English liberals, he went on, was the absence of rigidity and the presence of the ability to develop and absorb the workers' movement as liberalism's left wing. The German liberals should have attempted to satisfy the workers' demands instead of trying to frustrate them. Because of this, the liberals lost as well the allegiance of the youth who found no solution to social problems in liberalism and no outlet for their idealism.[71]

Bamberger was quick to respond to Brentano's accusation, but the tone of the essay was far less caustic than twenty years before. Bamberger confessed that the old quarrel between him and Brentano was buried. "In the scholars whom we called academic socialists we no longer see our enemies." But the old liberal still refused to accept Brentano's analysis of liberalism's failure. "I am very skeptical about all recipes that declare which way the liberals would have been able to prevent the masses from being ensnared by the siren calls of socialism. . . . All parallels to other lands, namely England," he wrote, apparently forgetting his own efforts in the 1870s, "float in the air of abstraction."[72]

From this first exchange, Bamberger and Brentano rapidly drew closer. Brentano contributed several articles to *Die Nation,* one of which (on agrarian reform in Prussia) Bamberger claimed was so "relevant and profound that it should be reprinted."[73] To Stauffenberg he confessed privately that of all the Socialists of the Chair, Brentano was the "most sympathetic," and the following year he called the scholar a man of "inner liberal and independent disposition."[74] The same year he paid Brentano the compliment of attending his lecture at the Economic Society (Volkswirtschaftliche Gesellschaft), which Brentano considered, perhaps with some injustice, "the most gracious way to make good the earlier sins which he committed against me."[75]

Not only Brentano but also the academic socialists were treated more gently by their once embittered opponent. Bamberger withdrew his charges against them of "cringing servility or place-seeking" before Bismarck and admitted that they were sincerely antiplutocratic. Even the spread of the academic socialists throughout the universities he no longer found sinister.[76] He claimed to detect a new spirit pervading political economy, which, he said, could earn the applause of the "individualists" as well.[77] Bamberger did lament the propensity of the scholars to bury themselves in specialized works to the detriment of general syntheses. In the 1870s, of course, he had been extremely critical of them for proposing grandiose schemes for the solution of social problems.[78] Again in contrast to his views in the 1870s, when he all but threatened the Socialists of the Chair with restrictions on academic freedom, Bamberger expressed concern when they were attacked by industrialists like Stumm. Still he could not help remarking that by attacking the scholars, the industrialist was trying to "seize the socialist idea at the roots."[79]

Bamberger's new sympathy for the academic socialists was part of his changing attitude toward socialism, an evolution which also affected many other liberals. In 1890 Theodor Barth reprinted an essay hostile to socialism and the Social Democrats which he had written in 1878. Proudly he noted that he had altered virtually nothing and had not added fifty words, since no essential changes had taken place in the intervening twelve years.[80] However, in the 1890s this view was increasingly rejected by left liberals, particularly in view of the evolution of the Social Democratic party. The repression of 1878–90 had strengthened the moderate elements in the labor movement as the party had to emphasize its reformist nature. During the debates on the various antisocialist laws, Bebel and Liebknecht never tired of telling the Reichstag that their party was reformist in the "strictest sense of the word" and denying that it aimed at the overthrow of the existing order. Strengthened by their addiction to economic determinism, they rationalized their political passivity. These beliefs were also instilled in the rank and file and resulted in the expulsion of several members who tended toward anarchism. The party leadership stressed that election propaganda and the use of the parliamentary regime were the most effective means of demonstrating the ineffectiveness of the ruling system.[81] There was still, of course, the danger of a reintroduced antisocialist measure, as the subversion and workhouse bills demonstrated, while the continuous increase in votes during the 1890s seemed to hold out the promise of a parliamentary majority. Strong reformist movements also grew up around the unions and within the state parliaments. Capping this development was Eduard Bernstein's open call for the party to free itself from the rhetoric of the past.[82]

These developments were not missed by the liberals. At the founding meeting of the Radical Union in 1893 one member could declare: "Somebody who is politically free must . . . also be socially free." Three years later *Die Nation* conceded that the maximum workday was consistent with liberal principles and maintained that the liberals should at least support the political aims of the Social Democrats, such as a change in the Prussian voting system and a reapportioning of election districts.[83] The idea of a maximum workday was still too much for Bamberger to accept.[84]

Bamberger nevertheless began to see the Social Democrats from a new perspective. In 1892 he found that the Social Democratic party since the lapsing of the Antisocialist Law had turned more and more from "revolutionary strivings," and he traced this development to the party's increasing Reichstag representation. It had meant growing respect and influence, and he believed the Social Democratic leaders had wisely decided not to jeopardize these gains through revolutionary actions. He estimated that half of the Social Democratic voters were not supporters of the party's program but merely dissatisfied people who did not want to overturn the present social system. He drew no conclusions from this about liberalism's future strategy. The thirty-five Social Democrats then in the Reichstag, he continued, played an altogether different role than the handful of twenty-five years before. Apparently forgetting his own views in the 1870s Bamberger wrote that the Social Democrats had been treated, especially by the conservatives, as a kind of expectoration from which one had to protect oneself in every way. But in 1892 they were represented on all committees, could bring proposals before the Reichstag in their own name, and were treated by the ministers on the same level as other parties. He was also pleased by their better mode of dress and milder speeches. Nevertheless, he still could warn that behind the socialist chiefs stood a class that had no reason to feel satisfied and which at a given moment could push aside its leaders.[85]

This one reservation receded into the background, and two years before his death he saw the peaceful trends continuing. The crucial question, he claimed, had been whether the worker's movement led by the Social Democrats would carry on the struggle via parliamentary means or by some form of direct action. It appeared to him that the proponents of parliamentary socialism had won the day. Bamberger pretended not to be surprised at this evolution since it confirmed his thesis that the Germans were at the same time the most socialistic and the least revolutionary people in the world. He seemed to agree with the criticism of anarchists and later the syndicalists that parliamentary participation at the national or local level was corrupting for a revolutionary because it required the discarding of extremes. "So it occurs that the supporters of Marx, who originally represented the revolutionary element, have become the proponents of the peaceful solution of the struggle at the political level." Moreover, he saw the belief in the peaceful approach to socialism extending beyond Germany's borders to France and other European countries. It indicated "that the future might be somewhat quieter."[86]

What was liberalism to make of this apparent evolution within the socialist movement? Barth argued that the liberals must not shrink from an alliance with the Social Democrats. He had visions of a liberal-socialist progressive party supported by the "million strong army of workers." Even Theodor Mommsen saw the merit of cooperating with the socialists.[87] Bamberger also saw the political possibilities of a new relationship with the Social Democrats, but given his still strongly held political beliefs, there was only one basis for cooperation. The chance to strengthen liberalism lay not in its "evolution to socialism, but rather the opposite, a reversion of socialism to radicalism," that is, to a radical democracy.[88] After a meeting with Bamberger in 1898, Brentano wrote: "He has become a different man, and I hear from him words which today sound prophetically for liberalism in all countries, that nothing further will remain for the liberals than to unite with the Social Democrats" to form a "great liberal party."[89] So had the eternal left liberal's dream been transformed by the 1890s.

The left liberals were thus still primarily concerned with emancipating the working class politically rather than taking on a "strong socialistic alloy." But even on this issue the Radical Union, not to mention Richter's group, hesitated somewhat, with opposition coming from coastal areas. Barth's biographer writes: "In the final analysis the left liberals were not ready for Barth's proposals for a common front against the right." On the other hand, the liberals were ready for a common front against the left, as the "Bülow block" election of 1907 proved.[90]

If liberals like Bamberger were attracted by the idea of cooperation with the Social Democrats, it was only because the other alternatives looked worse, and new enemies on the right appeared to overshadow the socialist menace. "When I read that . . . the crown is pregnant with a new plan for equalizing earthly justice, that is for new taxes," he joked, "I feel the sanctity of my private property more endangered than when . . . Bebel writes a new book or . . . Singer delivers an angry speech."[91] However, more serious than the government's plans were the challenges from the Junker agrarians. The differences between Manchesterites, Socialists of the Chair, and even Social Democrats receded into the background before what Bamberger considered to be the real danger to middle-class society.[92] In one of his last Reichstag speeches on the eve of the organization of the Farmers' League, Bamberger singled out the agrarians as more dangerous than the Social Democratic party. With prophetic accuracy he warned his listeners that the agrarians would never be satisfied but had made dissatisfaction into a system. What they had demanded until then was only a preface to the hostile propaganda that would be set in motion against the government and the parties that supported the government's commercial policy. The agrarians had become the great model for demagoguery in Germany.[93]

The emergence of the agrarians was merely another manifestation of the basic weakness in German society. In Bamberger's not entirely accurate words: "The imprint of the young German Empire, which originally was created in the spirit of civil freedom, has been transformed after the first decade of its existence into the imprint of a state ruled by the military and the landed aristocracy, and between the aristocracy on the one side and the increasing socialistic propaganda on the other stands the middle class as a weak ball which is pressed against these ever more opposite poles."[94] Here was the tragedy of nineteenth-century German history. The entire development of the German Empire from 1876 on he summed up in the phrase "The decline of middle-class influence." In his memoirs he looked back to the liberal decade of the 1860s, when the middle class, with the "masses behind it," showed itself imbued with the spirit of enlightenment.[95] The blame for the decline and fall of the middle-class ideology of liberalism he fastened primarily on the National Liberals. There was no trace of the old liberal fundamentals in the present National Liberal party. The leadership of Bennigsen and Miquel had contributed a good deal to the "demoralization which the Bismarckian regime systematically spread in order finally to bring Germany under a Junker domination as it never before existed."[96]

In a broader sense there was a failure of the middle class or at least a large part of it. Had the nation been "politically more mature," Bamberger maintained, or had Bismarck found in the liberal tradition of the middle class the same kind of powerful resistance with which the Catholics and Social Democrats opposed him, "he would have made his peace with liberalism." But in "wide ranks" of the middle class there was a turning away from liberalism as these elements succumbed to Bismarck's pressures. He could not help remarking while reviewing the publication of Lasker's letters from 1870–71 "that they demonstrated" to what degree Bismarck in his actions adapted himself to the influence of middle-class liberalism, "if it only showed itself strong." [97] When he reviewed a book dealing with the history of Florence in the early Renaissance and stressed what its middle class had been able to create, it was an indirect rebuke to the German middle class.[98] To Stauffenberg he expressed himself more bluntly, although ignoring his earlier views: "Now one claims the degeneration [of political life] comes from universal suffrage, but the true evil is the low standard of our bourgeoisie at every level. We ignored this from 1866 to 1876 because we, as its cream, ruled alone. Since it has entered the political arena in strength, the lack of culture has shown." The main feature of all German history," he complained to Stern, was the "domination of the Junkers and the wretchedness of the middle class." [99] Bamberger saw the low level of political life in many forms. The emperor's speeches, Bamberger sarcastically wrote, "give the title page to a book in which there is nothing." Even though they offended various groups inside and outside Germany, there was "nobody in the whole royal family who had even the understanding, not to mention the authority and the will, to intervene." [100] Besides the emperor, Bamberger found other evidence of degeneration. The new Reichstag building, over two decades in the making and finally completed shortly after Bamberger retired, struck him as a sign of the new order in Germany. Instead of pictures of people like Wilhelm Humboldt, Baron Karl von Stein, Friedrich Dahlmann, and Friedrich Schiller, "ornaments in the spirit of the 1870s," the new building was bedecked with "countless coats of arms; monsters with crowns, beaks, and claws... armored knights with opened and closed visors, lances, and swords; and names of princes and rulers. And various things occurred to me which are better left unsaid here." That ministers appeared in parliament in uniform leaning on their swords was a reflection of Germany's political and social realities. Appropriately a parliamentary occupation remained one of the "most thankless" and least honored pursuits in Germany. [101] In the political world Bamberger also missed the "social connection" between representatives of different political groups. The ability to ignore party differences in personal relations, he claimed, was the mark of a "politically cultured nation." The Germans, however, lacked a *politesse du coeur*." When the young Maximilian Harden complimented him on a recent article, Bamberger replied: "There is nothing more rewarding [than this] for one of us [writers], especially in Germany, where a person who is not an officer or professor so seldom experiences that he relates to others."[102]

Of all the problems which he saw plaguing Germany during the last decade of his life, none seemed to disturb him more than the burgeoning anti-Semitic movement. [103] Anti-Semitic groups had held several international congresses during the 1880s and were able to elect five members to the Reichstag in 1890. Two years later the German Conservative party inserted an anti-Semitic plank in its Tivoli program, and in 1893 the Anti-Semite party sent sixteen members to the Reichstag. Symptomatic of the growing popularity of the movement was the bizarre case of Hermann Ahlwardt. Dismissed from his position as a school principal in 1890 for embezzlement, he blamed his difficulties on Jews and made them the cause of everything evil in Germany. His first book included an attack on Bismarck's Jewish banker, Gerson Bleichröder, for allegedly perjuring himself in an alimony case, and he claimed that Caprivi was protecting the banker. Undeterred by a resulting prison sentence for libel and slander, he next charged in a pamphlet entitled *Judenflinten* (*Jew Rifles*) that a Jewish weapons manufacturer had delivered defective weapons to the army as part of a Franco-Jewish plot to destroy Germany. Again he was brought to court and convicted, but rather than being ruined he became enormously popular and in an 1892 by-election was elected to the Reichstag, where he continued his wild accusations. Even after the Reichstag investigated his charges and found them to be unsubstantiated, Ahlwardt was elected in two districts in 1893.[104] Ahlwardt's meteoric career left Bamberger with the uncomprehending remark: "Who after 1848, 1867, and 1870 would have said such a thing would be possible again!"[105]

Similar thoughts must have occurred to him as he reviewed the fourth volume of Treitschke's history of Germany. Ever since the clash in 1880, the two men had been bitter opponents. For Bamberger, Treitschke was "a genius of mendacity with his virtuous bombast in the service of the cynicism of a Bismarck," or simply a "phony . . . with a dose of vulgarity."[106] Bamberger singled out for special mention the historian's treatment of Jewish writers like Ludwig Börne and Heine, who supposedly had a negative influence on German history. It struck Bamberger as ironic that Treitschke had selected for his example people who had converted to Christianity. It proved, he claimed, that "anti-Semitism can only fall back upon racial theory and not religion." Half jokingly, but more prophetically than he imagined, he claimed that without an "Imperial Family Tree Office the great reform of the future will therefore not be realizable."[107]

Not merely Treitschke's literary efforts but also the new situation in the Reichstag after the 1890 election disturbed Bamberger. During the first session of the new Reichstag, Max Liebermann von Sonnenberg, an anti-Semitic deputy, warned Bamberger that a good deal would be heard about anti-Semitism in the course of the debates.[108] Ahlwardt's first appearance in the Reichstag in March 1893 was accompanied by accusations of Jewish-sponsored embezzlement of public funds, which a Reichstag commission found unsubstantiated. The Reichstag's debates on a bill to regulate usury often sounded like a debate on the "Jewish question." Even the wine regulation bill of 1892 was the occasion for an anti-Semitic speech. Petitions and bills came into the Reichstag demanding that Jews be made to pay for the costs caused by military increases and that the immigration of Jews into Germany be ended.[109]

Anti-Jewish attacks also came from unexpected sources. In one of the numerous colonial debates of Bamberger's last Reichstag, his old opponent Kardorff suggested that Bamberger, as a Jew, did not appreciate the general German desire to spread Christianity in pagan lands. The following month, replying to Bamberger's charge that the profit motive moved the world and explained why so few businessmen wanted to invest their money in African ventures, the German Conservative deputy Arnold Frege disagreed but pointedly stated that he knew only Christian businessmen. Frege also claimed that Bamberger, because he was childless, did not appreciate the need to secure an inheritance for Germany's future generations. Bamberger answered sarcastically that Frege ought to introduce legislation to forbid Jews and bachelors to sit in the Reichstag.[110]

Not only colonial but also currency debates provided the setting for anti-Jewish exchanges. Count Julius von Mirbach argued that as the controllers of the greatest part of liquid and international capital, the Jews were interested in the gold standard because it served their interests. Thus it was "no accident that Representative Bamberger was really the father of the gold standard." The count tried to soften his words by denying that Bamberger would find anything insulting in his expressions since his position on Bamberger's "nationality" was well known. Bamberger replied, probably more in sorrow than anger, that if someone had told him twenty-five years before that he would be so accused he would not have believed it. "I am glad that the disillusionment has come so late."[111] Before his parliamentary career was over he also had to listen to the eerie prophecy of Liebermann, who told his audience: "I am convinced that the next great . . . statesman of the future—he will come—will use anti-Semitism as a means of again pulling the ship of state out of the abyss."[112]

Proceedings such as these helped convince Bamberger to retire. Not merely the split of the Radical party drove him away, but also anti-Semitism. "If you had sat for the last four months in my seat," he wrote Hartwig, "you would have been seized with disgust and abomination, not only for [Otto] Böckel and Liebermann, but for the three-quarters of all my colleagues whom it does not disturb. Yet I do not say this loudly in order not to support the method."[113] The future of the Jews in Germany looked bleak. If a serious crisis occurred, he remarked, at "the worst the Jews will be beaten to death," and if a foreign war should go badly then "the first thing after a lost battle would be that one would probably kill all the Jews, for which the *Judenflinten* gives the best pretext." To one who had been in the vanguard of the drive for German unity, it was not easy to admit that recent developments indicated that "anti-Semitism and Germandom are identical," and thus by implication Judaism and Germandom were not and could not be.[114] No wonder he wrote to Stern, "The world may move forward, but it moves in a zigzag course."[115]

Time also moved forward for Bamberger. During the last few years of his life he continued to keep busy, as his extensive correspondence and his many articles in *Die Nation* attest. He also oversaw the publication of five volumes of his collected works and completed the manuscript of an autobiography which was published shortly after his death. As Barth wrote of him, "One paid attention to what he said," and he "found no joy in the passive taking note of events."[116] Even though he once remarked that he revenged himself on his enemies by keeping healthy, this too began to change.[117] The letters of his last years are filled with references to various ailments, mainly catarrh and eye problems. He suffered a severe stroke in the spring of 1898 from which he never completely recovered. To the end he remained pessimistic about Germany's future.[118]

He died on March 14, 1899, around noon. The ceremonies were kept brief and entirely secular. Mommsen spoke during the obsequies on March 17 at 10 A.M. Bamberger was buried at 11, and at 8 that evening Barth delivered the memorial address. The government was not officially represented, although former minister Delbrück and former Reichstag president Nikolaus von Ballestrem attended, while the widow of Frederick III sent a wreath. He was buried in the Jewish cemetery on Schönhauser Allee next to Lasker under a common headstone which read: "Here lie, united in death, who in life engaged in common effort for Germany's unity and freedom." The inscription offended Mommsen, who complained that he would not "dare to carve Germany's unity and freedom in stone under our pseudo-constitutional system." Eight months later Bamberger's bust was put in the library of the Reichsbank, where it remained until its disappearance in the 1930s. In 1923 there was a commemoration of Bamberger's birth by Interior Minister Rudolf Oeser.[119]

Besides an enormous literary estate, Bamberger left behind an impressive financial inheritance. Although he had worked only twenty years, he had accumulated enough by the 1860s to live off his income. He had continued to buy and sell stocks, and his income grew rapidly. His cash bequests totaled over 1.6 million marks and he seemed to remember everyone from close relatives to distant acquaintances.[120]

Of the many personal expressions of sympathy, only one need be mentioned, that of Anna von Helmholtz:

For almost thirty years he was our friend, . . . often my adviser in material things, in intellectual matters a constantly noble man, adhering to the highest standard and demanding it. There were not two more different persons than he and I in race and outlook and convictions . . . and still we were bound in the deepest sympathy. His radicalism in politics and religion, in opinion of artistic interests—nothing harmed the friendship. He was so eminently gifted in grace and refinement . . . in the amenities of social relations. No one can compare to him. He was a European and a kind and generous person who left far, far behind everything base."[121]

·12·
Conclusion

More significant than Bamberger's personal refinement were his political achievements and heritage. The *Berliner Tageblatt* printed a very friendly and favorable obituary hailing his accomplishments of the 1870s as well as his struggles of the 1880s. The *Kölnische Zeitung*, generally National Liberal in orientation, praised Bamberger as a writer in whom the "most charming and brilliant qualities of the Semitic race came to an artistic deployment." On the whole favorable, the obituary seemed almost sorry that Bamberger had not taken the right road in 1878 but instead returned to the "sterile philistinism" which he had overcome in the 1850s. The democratic *Frankfurter Zeitung* still regarded Bamberger as the turncoat of 1866, and nothing else over-shadowed this event.[1]

These three newspapers spanned the breadth of his political, economic, and social views at various stages of his life. But what of Bamberger's body of beliefs remained the irreducible core? Anna von Helmholtz once reported that she had received a "passionate political outpouring" from Bamberger which demonstrated that "everyone has his completely invisible core out of which everything develops."[2] She never revealed what that invisible core was; nevertheless what comprised the bedrock of Bamberger's convictions was an uncompromising individualism. He might talk about the need to cooperate with the Social Democrats or even the necessity of a liberal-socialist alliance, but these tendencies pale in comparison to his praise of a system of unre-stricted free enterprise and his criticism of the Bismarckian social legislation. Looking back on three decades of "struggle between individualistic and state socialistic ideas," he still regarded the individual as the driving force of the world. "An individual who on his own power has worked himself up one rung of the economic ladder is more valuable to the totality than hundreds who are supposedly pulled up by tutelary welfare institutions."[3] He continued to sing hymns of praise to the entrepreneurs. Krupp might make 7 million marks per year, Bamberger admitted, but think of the tremendous wealth spewed forth by his factories. "What the brain of the entrepreneur has created!" Revising Saint-Simon's famous parable, he asked what would happen if for a day those individual forces did not function. The most beautiful social and political institutions, he answered, "would go to the devil." On the contrary, no one would notice if all the welfare institutions disappeared.[4] Social legislation, dismissed as something designed to "pacify the conscience of the middle class," signified a "colossal dissipation of energy and money," and he still argued that the liability law of 1871 offered the best approach to the problem of social insurance.[5] He was, in his own words, a "hard-boiled Manchesterian," and he intended "to live and die as one."[6]

While his unabashed individualism was increasingly out of tune with events, his rabid antisocialism of the 1870s and 1880s shows Bamberger in the least attractive light. His views on socialism as well as government intervention were shaped by the central European institution of the police state, and the struggles of the last quarter of the nineteenth centruy were fought, it seems, against this old but still not imaginary enemy. New phenomena were judged largely in relation to this old picture. His total opposition to the police state made him see freedom and individualism as the hallmark of the good state.[7]

His liberalism was also clearly separate from democracy. Universal suffrage always seemed a dubious even if inevitable experiment to him, and he blamed Bismarck, who "serving the moment but obeying the eternal law . . . opened the portals through which the fateful question of the socialistic problem entered. . . . It stands written in the stars that we have entered upon a time of full democratic development and that this, by one or the other detour, by the republican, the constitutional, or the absolutist, pushes toward the socialistic experiment. But the stars . . . give . . . no answer to the question of how it will come out." That was reserved for the descendants "in a way and at a place which no one living suspects."[8] The above statement of the seventy-two-year-old epitomized his rather narrow view of liberalism and made him see any deviation as a form of collectivism, whether from the left or the right.

Rather than his theoretical musings about liberalism and democracy, although not unrelated to them, it is his parliamentary efforts that must provide the substance for a judgment of Bamberger. For this many-sided individual was above all a political animal. Although he was interested in increasing the power of parliament, he never regretted his acceptance of the accomplished fact in 1866.[9] Given the alternatives, he regarded the Bismarckian option as preferable to more years in the political wilderness, especially since at the time, as well as later, his opinion of the political maturity of the German people was low. Moreover, he should not be too strongly criticized for believing that the spirit of the age was on his side and that the political structures of 1867 and 1871, with all their admitted shortcomings, were merely initial installments. What Bismarck offered did represent progress, and even the chancellor, he believed, would have to realize what was "life-giving" to the nation. He never took seriously the constitutional conflict of the 1860s, and regarded its resolution as demonstrating that even out of such events progress must occur. It can be argued that as a non-Prussian and as an exile he did not know the Prussian system, but even those close to events, like Lasker and Twesten, made the same decision. His decision of 1866 seemed correct even eight or nine years later, as events appeared to lead Germany toward Bamberger's models in western Europe and he participated in this evolution. Gains had to be made by compromise. One had to settle for less than the ideal, but all this mattered little as long as each agreement signified a step forward.[10] He paid less attention to which side set the terms of the compromise.

He, as well as other parliamentarians, deserves recognition for his legislative achievements. Bamberger's key contribution to German unification, shaping the financial legislation of the 1870s, is enough to secure his reputation. It almost secured the reputation of the Reichstag, which appeared to be the government's equal during these deliberations. Most of his essays during his last years dealt with financial questions, and if there was any consolation for him in the twilight of his life, it came from financial developments. The gold standard seemed less threatened as India ended the minting of silver coins, the free silver challenge of Bryan was beaten back by McKinley, and new gold discoveries assured a sufficient supply. In his final essay on bimetallism he could write confidently that it was "dead." It was a fitting climax to his thirty years of dedication to monetary stability.[11]

More difficult to evaluate is his change of attitude toward Bismarckian policy after 1878. For Bamberger the question of tariffs was fundamental, going to the heart of a country's political and economic system, and it was a harbinger of the coming political reaction. He was not pacified by Bennigsen's claim that there was no necessary link between tariffs and political retrogression. In the context of 1878, a backward economic step would both encourage and symbolize political reaction. Thus it was not merely a technical question that could be considered open by a united party.[12] His opposition to protective tariffs was portrayed in epic dimensions, and in exculpation it must be admitted that Bismarck also viewed the question as a turning point in imperial policy. Moreover, the tariffs signified a strengthening of those groups, particularly the Junkers, who stood most directly in the way of parliamentarizing Germany.

Bamberger's move to the opposition after 1878 meant a return to the political wilderness. Like others before him, he chose the sterile path of opposition to Bismarck. In a country that made one's relationship to the chancellor the measure of right and wrong, this was a fateful step. For brilliant parliamentary figures like Richter, Windthorst, and Lasker, there has been little praise. They have been dismissed as merely good tacticians instead of being applauded for their fine work under unfavorable circumstances. Only Bennigsen, who usually managed to find a way or reason to go along with Bismarck, and Miquel, who eventually became a minister, have fared better. To compromise with the government in the 1880s meant, in Bamberger's mind, to cooperate in antiliberal legislation. Thus, with the exception of financial measures, he voted against virtually every major government bill.

He led the fight against and helped delay Germany's colonial policy. Perhaps, as Wehler suggests, in reality only the question of method separated Bamberger from his opponents, but this was the only serious question of the day. He continually pointed to foreign policy complications that would ensue from an aggressive overseas policy, particularly with regard to England, and he saw these fears confirmed before he died.[13] He also had the good sense and courage to recognize publicly what Bismarck confessed privately, that the colonial business was a swindle which offered profits to no one but a few entrepreneurs. Similarly the brandy and tobacco taxes and monopolies also seemed destined to aid not only the few at the cost of the many, but precisely those few whose decline Bamberger regarded as indispensable for the progress of Germany.

His stance was less firm on the questions of antisocialism and the army. His acceptance of the exceptional law in 1878 was a price he was willing to pay for party harmony and perhaps for the possibility that something might be salvaged from the tariff question. It is difficult to believe that he actually expected the government to strike at the nonsocialist critics of the free enterprise system. And the shabby arrangement in 1884 in order to avoid dissolution of the Reichstag did not do credit to his or progressive liberalism's belief in equality before the law. If the antisocialist laws embarassed both Bamberger and the left liberals, the army bills destroyed them. Again and again it revealed the true basis of the Prusso-German state and the powerlessness of the liberals to withstand, let alone attack, one of the real power bases of the Prussian ruling group. It also leads to the ultimate question that one must ask of Bamberger and German liberalism. Could its course and impact on German history have been different?

In one sense the answer is yes. Had there been no Bismarck, had he departed earlier from the scene, had William I passed away sooner, and had his son not been near death in 1888, the course of domestic developments might have been different. Looked at from the liberals' or Bamberger's vantage point, however, there was no profitable course of action. The left liberals tried everything between 1848 and the end of the century, and nothing seemed to make any difference. The most serious attempt to provide a new political structure for Germany, the 1848–49 uprising, failed because of the superiority of the Prussian army and the inadequate response of the population. This failure convinced Bamberger that the revolutionary road led to a mirage and helped push him to accept the Bismarckian solution to the German question. In addition, the Prussian constitutional conflict demonstrated that majorities alone would have no impact on political developments as long as the Prussian government did not lose its nerve. Bismarck repeatedly made clear both before and after 1870 that parliamentary majorities would have no effect on him or government policy. If revolution failed, if majorities were not enough, there remained the policy of progressive compromise. But since the government set the terms of the compromise, this policy could be productive only as long as it tolerated a forward-looking program. Perhaps, as Seeber suggests in reference to the military bill, there was a popular movement waiting to be tapped. The election of 1887, however, demonstrated that at least the untapped reservoir of voters was ready to be swept along by government propaganda. There may have been something to Bamberger's lament made both in the 1860s and the 1890s that the people were worse than the government.

Given Germany's political realities, Bamberger found himself stymied time and again in his search for a political breakthrough. Western European in orientation, he moved from revolutionary to Bismarckian to anti-Bismarckian, belonging to three political parties in his search for a group that knew how to walk the razor's edge between rigid adherence to doctrine and pliant acceptance of the accomplished fact. He never found it.

Notes

Bibliography

Index

𝔑𝔬𝔱𝔢𝔰

The following abbreviations for works frequently cited are used throughout the notes:

AZ   *Allgemeine Zeitung*
DLZB   Julius Heyderhoff and Paul Wentzcke, eds., *Deutscher Liberalismus im Zeitalter Bismarcks*
GS   Ludwig Bamberger, *Gesammelte Schriften*
GW   Otto von Bismarck, *Die gesammelten Werke*
HZ   *Historische Zeitschrift*
MZ   *Mainzer Zeitung*
PJ   *Preussische Jahrbücher*
SBR   *Stenographische Berichte über die Verhandlungen des deutschen Reichstags*
SBZP   *Stenographische Berichte über die Verhandlungen des Zollparlaments*

CHAPTER 1. EARLY LIFE AND EDUCATION

1. Otto Hartwig, *Ludwig Bamberger: Eine biographische Skizze* (Marburg, 1900), pp. 1–2; *Mainzer Adressbuch* (Mainz, 1800–); Sali Levi, ed., *Magenza* (Mainz, 1927), pp. 61–62.

2. Ludwig Bamberger, *Erinnerungen* (Berlin, 1899), pp. 1–5, 98–99; idem, "Fragen an die ewigen Sterne," *GS*, I:69–71.

3. Hartwig saw the report of Bamberger's grades (*Ludwig Bamberger,* pp. 3–4). See also Hans Blum, "Ludwig Bamberger, Jugend- und Mannesjahre," in his *Vorkämpfer der deutschen Einheit* (Berlin, 1899), pp. 198–99. Blum was the son of executed 1848er Robert Blum and a close friend of Bamberger's. His article is based on personal letters from Bamberger.

4. Bamberger, *Erinnerungen,* pp. 7–12; Hartwig, *Ludwig Bamberger,* pp. 4–5; Bamberger, "Karl Hillebrand," *GS,* II:145–46. An excellent description of student life at Giessen can be found in Carl Vogt, *Aus meinem Leben* (Stuttgart, 1896), pp. 22, 29–31, 114–19.

5. Bamberger, *Erinnerungen,* pp. 12–13, 236–39; Blum, "Ludwig Bamberger," p. 199; Bamberger, "Zur Erinnerung an Friedrich Kapp," *GS,* II:129–30. Bamberger to Anna Belmont, n.d. [April 1844], April 14, 1844, n.d. [April 1844], May 3, 1844; Bamberger to his aunt, Henriette Bischoffsheim, May 12, 1844; Anna to Bamberger, n.d.

[July 1844] ; all in Bamberger Nachlass, Handschriftenabteilung der Stiftung Preussischer Kulturbesitz, Staatsbibliothek, Berlin-Dahlem, hereafter cited as Bamberger Nachlass, Berlin-Dahlem. Bamberger to Franz Schenck von Stauffenberg, April 19, 1880, Stauffenberg Nachlass, Deutsches Zentralarchiv I, Potsdam; Hans Ulrich Wehler, ed., *Friedrich Kapp: von radikalen Frühsozialisten des Vormärz zum liberalen Parteipolitiker des Bismarckreichs: Briefe 1843–1884* (Frankfurt on the Main, 1969), pp. 9–10; Edith Lenel, *Friedrich Kapp, 1824–1884* (Leipzig, 1935), pp. 29–35.

6. Bamberger to Anna, n.d. [July 1844], December 4, 1844; Bamberger to his mother, July 28, 1844; Anna to Bamberger, n.d. [July 1844]; Bamberger to his aunt, May 26, 1844; all in Bamberger Nachlass, Berlin-Dahlem. Bamberger, *Erinnerungen*, pp. 14–16, 214–15; Blum, "Ludwig Bamberger," p. 200. Karl Braun describes Göttingen university life (*Bilder aus der deutschen Kleinstaaterei*, II [Berlin, 1870], pp. 271–83).

7. Bamberger, *Erinnerungen*, pp. 16–23; Hartwig, *Ludwig Bamberger*, p. 6; John R. Gillis, *The Prussian Bureaucracy in Crisis, 1840–1860: Origins of an Administrative Ethos* (Stanford, 1971), p. 39; Lenore O'Boyle, "The Problem of an Excess of Educated Men in Western Europe, 1800–1850," *Journal of Modern History*, XLII (December 1970):471–95.

8. Bamberger, *Erinnerungen*, pp. 34, 77, 439, 470; Blum, "Ludwig Bamberger," pp. 199–200; Bamberger to Anna, n.d. [April 1844], September 25, October 7, 1846, July 11, 1847, Bamberger Nachlass, Berlin-Dahlem; Wehler, *Friedrich Kapp,* pp. 11–12; Lenel, *Friedrich Kapp,* p. 49; Bamberger, "Des sympathies françaises aux bords du Rhin," *Revue moderne,* XXXIV (1865):503.

9. *MZ,* July 24, 1849.

10. Anton Maria Keim, "Die Judenfrage vor dem Hessischen Landtag in der Zeit von 1820–1849; ein Beitrag zur Geschichte der Juden im Vormärz" (Ph.D. dissertation, Gutenberg University, Mainz, 1953), pp. 48–49; Carlo Buckler, *Die politischen und religiösen Kämpfe in Mainz während der Revolutionsjahre 1848–1850* (Giessen, 1936), pp. 17–18; Hellmuth Rössler, "Mainz im Jahre 1848," *Mainzer Zeitschrift,* LVIII, (1963):91; Eduard Reis, *Mainzer Silhouetten und Genrebilder: Ein Panorama des heutigen Mainz* (Mainz, 1841), pp. 66–71; Levi, *Magenza,* pp. 89–90; K.A. Schaab, *Diplomatische Geschichte der Juden zu Mainz und dessen Umgebung* (Mainz, 1855), pp. 413, 425–29. On the relatively slight political activity of the Jews before 1848 see Jacob Toury, *Die politischen Orientierungen der Juden in Deutschland: von Jena bis Weimar,* Schriftenreihe wissenschaftlicher Abhandlungen des Leo Baeck Instituts, XV (Tubingen, 1966), pp. 1–14; Lenore O'Boyle, "The Democratic Left in Germany, 1848," *Journal of Modern History,* XXXIII (December 1961):374–83.

11. Gisbert Beyerhaus, "Die Krise des deutschen Liberalismus und das Problem der 99 Tage," *PJ,* CCXXXIX (1935):5; Bamberger to Anna, January 31, 1844, April 15, 1844, Ascension Day, 1844, n.d. [1844], Anna to Bamberger, n.d. [April 1844], n.d. [May 1844], May 7, 1844, Bamberger Nachlass, Berlin-Dahlem; Anna von Helmholtz to Ida Siemens, March 16, 1899, in Ellen von Siemens-Helmholtz, ed., *Anna von Helmholtz: Ein Lebensbild in Briefen,* 2 vols. (Berlin, 1929), II:183. Bamberger, "Wunsch an mein Testamentsvollstrecker," May 19, 1892, Bamberger Papers, Leo Baeck Institute, New York, hereafter cited as Bamberger Papers, New York. Toury claims that approximately seven hundred and fifty Jews took part in the events of 1848, while the rest were passive or disapproved (*Die politischen Orientierungen,* pp. 47, 67, 73, 85–86, 90–92). Alexander Meyer, "Ludwig Bamberger," *Biographisches Jahrbuch und Deutscher Nekrolog: 1899,* IV (Berlin, 1900), p. 130.

12. Karl-Georg Faber, *Die Rheinlande zwischen Restauration und Revolution: Probleme der rheinischen Geschichte von 1814 bis 1848 im Spiegel der zeitgenössischen Publizistik* (Wiesbaden, 1966), pp. 55–64, 305–12, and passim; Blum, "Ludwig Bamberger," p. 197; Bamberger, *Erinnerungen,* pp. 2–6; idem, "Fragen an die ewigen Sterne," pp. 69–71; idem, "Die Französelei am Rhein, wie sie kam, und wie sie ging (1790 bis heute)," *GS,* I:144, 176–84; Reis, *Mainzer Silhouetten,* pp. 124–27.

13. Bamberger, "Die Französelei," pp. 181–83; idem, "Arthur Chuquet," *GS,* II: 295–96.

14. Bamberger, *Erinnerungen,* pp. 6, 470. Recently an East German historian called this article "the best assessment the petty bourgeois democracy devoted to the Mainz republic in the nineteenth century" (Heinrich Scheel, "Die Mainzer Republik im Spiegel der deutschen Geschichtsschreibung," *Jahrbuch für Geschichte,* IV [1969], pp. 50–53). Bamberger, "Kandidatenrede," *GS,* IV:47; idem, "Heinrich von Treitschke," *GS,* II: 195–97; *MZ,* December 12, 1867, January 1, 3, 1868 (Bamberger's speech, "Deutschland vor 100 Jahren"); Toury, *Die politischen Orientierungen,* p. 32.

15. Walter Bussman, "Zwischen Revolution und Reichsgründung, die politische Vorstellungswelt von Ludwig Bamberger," in *Schicksalswege deutscher Vergangenheit,* ed. Walter Hubatsch (Dusseldorf, 1950), p. 204; Faber, *Rheinlande,* pp. 379–85, 405; Bamberger, *Erinnerungen,* p. 6.

16. Bamberger, *Erinnerungen,* pp. 4–5, 7–16; Bamberger to Anna, n.d. [May 4, 1844], July 3, 1844, September 10, 1846, September 26, 1846, October 7, 1846, n.d. [early 1847]; Anna to Bamberger, n.d. [July 1844], Bamberger Nachlass, Berlin-Dahlem.

17. Bamberger, *Erinnerungen,* pp. 6–8; idem, "Otto Gildemeister," *GS,* II:314–15; Leonard Krieger, "Liberal Ideas and Institutions in the German Era of Unification" (Ph.D. dissertation, Yale, 1949), pp. 21, 33; Lothar Gall, *Der Liberalismus als regierende Partei. Das Grossherzogtum Baden zwischen Restauration und Reichsgründung,* Veröffentlichungen des Instituts für Europäische Geschichte, XLVII (Wiesbaden, 1968), pp. 29, 32; Fritz Valjavec, *Die Entstehung der politischen Strömungen in Deutschland, 1770–1815* (Munich, 1951), passim, especially pp. 396–415; Bamberger to Anna, June 6, 1844, April 24, 1845, n.d. [1846 or 1847], Bamberger Nachlass, Berlin-Dahlem. For a description of a similar stage in Friedrich Kapp's development see Lenel, *Friedrich Kapp,* pp. 47–53.

18. Bamberger to Anna, n.d. [May 1844], n.d. [July or August, 1844], December 4, 28, 1844, n.d. [spring 1847, four letters], Bamberger Nachlass, Berlin-Dahlem.

19. Bamberger, *Erinnerungen,* pp. 22–23, 179–82; Bamberger to Anna, October 10, 1846, July 19, 1847, September 17, 1847, October 1, 1847, n.d. [spring 1847], Bamberger Nachlass, Berlin-Dahlem. Most of the correspondence between Anna and Bamberger from 1844 to 1847 concerns Anna's problems with her father. See also Rahel Liebeschütz, "The Wind of Change: Letters of Two Generations from the Biedermeier Period," *Leo Baeck Institute Yearbook,* XII (1967), pp. 227–56.

20. Bamberger, "Fragen an die ewigen Sterne," p. 71; idem, *Erinnerungen,* p. 25.

CHAPTER 2. REVOLUTION OF 1848

1. Bamberger, *Erinnerungen,* pp. 185–86, 190.

2. For the preceding two paragraphs see Siegfried Büttner, *Die Anfänge des Parla-*

mentarismus in Hessen-Darmstadt und das du Thilsche System (Darmstadt, 1969), pp. 1–3, 36–52, 185–220; Buckler, *Die politischen und religiösen Kämpfe,* pp. 1–16; Rössler, "Mainz im Jahre 1848," pp. 90–92; Karl Georg Bockenheimer, *Mainz in den Jahren 1848 und 1849* (Mainz, 1906), pp. 142–43; Mathilde Katz-Seibert, *Der politische Radikalismus in Hessen während der Revolution von 1848/49,* Quellen und Forschungen zur Hessischen Geschicte, IX (Darmstadt, 1929), pp. 1–12; Levi, *Magenza,* p. 89; Faber, *Die Rheinlande,* pp. 21, 107–10, 116–20, 180–83, 263–65; Hans Andres, *Die Einführung des konstitutionellen Systems in Grossherzogtum Hessen,* Historische Studien, LXIV (Berlin, 1908), p. 234; Reinhardt C. T. Eigenbrodt, *Meine Erinnerungen aus den Jahren 1848, 1849 und 1850,* ed. Ludwig Bergsträsser, Quellen und Forschungen zur Hessischen Geschichte, II (Darmstadt, 1914), pp. 4–6, 16–18; Keim, "Die Judenfrage," p. 206; Valmar Cramer, "Die katholische Bewegung im Vormärz und im Revolutionsjahr 1848–1849," in *Idee, Gestalt und Gestalter des ersten deutschen Katholikentages in Mainz 1848,* ed. Ludwig Lenhart (Mainz, 1948), pp. 24–36; Hans Döhn, "Eisenbahnpolitik und Eisenbahnbau in Rheinhessen 1835–1914" (Ph.D. dissertation, Gutenberg University, Mainz, 1957); Wolfgang Köllman, *Sozialgeschichte der Stadt Barmen im 19. Jahrhundert,* Soziale Forschung und Praxis, XXI (Tubingen, 1960), pp. 42–43; Theodore S. Hamerow, *Restoration, Revolution, Reaction: Economics and Politics in Germany, 1815 to 1871* (Princeton, 1958), pp. 75–93.

3. Bamberger, *Erinnerungen,* pp. 27–31; Anton Maria Keim, "Der politische Gehalt des Mainzer Karnevals im deutschen Vormärz," *Hambacher Gespräche* (Wiesbaden, 1964), pp. 87–88. Zitz had been succeeded as president of the Carnival Association by Müller-Melchiors, who also was a leader of the democratic opposition in Mainz in 1848. Bockenheimer, *Mainz in den Jahren 1848 und 1849,* pp. 12–14; *Der Demokrat,* April 16, 1848, p. 3; Bamberger to Anna, July 3, 1868, Bamberger Nachlass, Berlin-Dahlem; Buckler, *Die politischen und religiösen Kämpfe,* pp. 13–17; Rössler, "Mainz im Jahre 1848," p. 92; Wendelin Weiler, *Darstellung der Ereignisse in Mainz im ersten halben Jahre 1848* (Mainz, n.d. [1848]), pp. 10–19; Katz-Seibert, *Der politische Radikalismus,* pp. 12–15; Eigenbrodt, *Meine Erinnerungen,* pp. 24–26, 28; *Mainzer Flugblätter, 1846–1851,* nos. 19, 20, 27, 28, Stadtbibliothek, Mainz; *Grossherzoglich Hessisches Regierungsblatt auf das Jahr 1848* (Darmstadt, n.d.), pp. 61, 63, 65–66, 72–73.

4. Bamberger, *Erinnerungen,* pp. 24–27, 31–34, 182–83; Blum, "Ludwig Bamberger," pp. 201–03; Bamberger to his mother, March 6, 1881, Bamberger Nachlass, Berlin-Dahlem.

5. Bamberger, *Erinnerungen,* pp. 34–35; *MZ,* May 7, 1848. His editorials became so popular that they were reprinted in other newspapers, often without the source being given. *MZ,* April 5, 1849; Jacques Droz, *Les révolutions allemandes de 1848* (Paris, 1957), p. 241; Katz-Seibert, *Der politische Radikalismus,* pp. 18–20; Faber, *Die Rheinlande,* pp. 102–03; Alfred Börckel, "Karl Theodor von Zabern," *Hessische Biographien,* I (Darmstadt, 1918), pp. 229–31.

6. Bamberger, "Flitterwochen der Pressefreiheit," *GS,* III:5.

7. *MZ,* March 10, 16, April 4, May 7, 1848; Bamberger to Anna, March 24, 1848, cited in Bamberger, *Erinnerungen,* pp. 183–84; Bamberger, "Fragen an die ewigen Sterne," p. 73; speech of Baron Dalwigk in the Hessian Chamber, February 14, 1851, *Mainzer Flugblätter 1846–1851,* no. 60.

8. Bockenheimer, *Mainz in den Jahren 1848 und 1849,* pp. 32–33; Weiler, *Darstellung der Ereignisse,* pp. 70–72; Bamberger, *Erinnerungen,* pp. 48–50; *MZ,* April 17, 1848.

9. Bockenheimer, *Mainz in den Jahren 1848 und 1849*, pp. 33–34; Weiler, *Darstellung der Ereignisse*, p. 106; *MZ*, April 17, 1848; Buckler, *Die politischen und religiösen Kämpfe*, p. 30.

10. Bockenheimer, *Mainz in den Jahren 1848 und 1849*, p. 33; Bamberger, *Erinnerungen*, pp. 50–51. Bamberger never forgot the acts of Luddism, and his intolerance of them seems to have grown with the years (*SBR*, 5. Legislaturperiode, 2. Sitzung, March 4, 1883, p. 1909; hereafter cited as *SBR*, 5 LP, 2 S).

11. Bamberger, *Erinnerungen*, pp. 27, 35; *MZ*, March 13, 16, April 7, 1848. *Der Demokrat*, a democratic weekly, echoed Bamberger's comments (April 23, 1848, pp. 10–11).

12. Bamberger, *Erinnerungen*, pp. 35, 59, 65. Years later, Bamberger stressed the spontaneity, naturalness, and openness of his speeches in 1848. Bamberger, "Fragen an die ewigen Sterne," pp. 73–74.

13. *MZ*, June 19, 1848; Bockenheimer, *Mainz in den Jahren 1848 und 1849*, pp. 34–35; *Grossherzoglich Hessisches Regierungsblatt*, p. 235.

14. Bamberger, *Erinnerungen*, pp. 35–39; 46–48; 50–55, 184–85; *MZ*, March 16–19, 21, April 1, 2, 6, 1848; *Mainzer Flugblätter, 1846–1851*, nos. 12, 18.

15. *MZ*, April 3, 1848; Rössler, "Mainz im Jahre 1848," p. 93; Weiler, *Darstellung der Ereignisse*, p. 79; Bockenheimer, *Mainz in den Jahren 1848 und 1849*, pp. 58–59; *Mainzer Flugblätter, 1846–1851*, nos. 6, 16, 17.

16. Bamberger, *Erinnerungen*, pp. 65–66; *MZ*, April 11, 12, 14, 16, 1848; Bockenheimer, *Mainz in den Jahren 1848 und 1849*, pp. 59–60.

17. Bamberger, *Erinnerungen*, pp. 66–73, 76, 186; *MZ*, April 17, 18, 25, 1848.

18. Bamberger, *Erinnerungen*, pp. 185–86.

19. *MZ*, April 21, 23, 25, 1848; Weiler, *Darstellung der Ereignisse*, p. 88.

20. *MZ*, March 23, 1848; Hans Krause, *Die demokratische Partei von 1848 und die soziale Frage* (Frankfurt on the Main, 1923), pp. 18–23.

21. *MZ*, April 9, 1848.

22. *MZ*, March 23, 30, April 29, 1848; Buckler, *Die politischen und religiösen Kämpfe*, p. 43. The lower-class-oriented *Demokrat* was also interested in restoring business confidence. It proposed nationalization of the uncompleted state railway in order to save the railroad and reimburse investors (April 24, 1848, pp. 11–13).

23. *Mainzer Flugblätter, 1846–1851*, nos. 29, 30, 31; Stadtarchiv, Mainz, *Polizeiberichte 1847–1851*, sec. 131, XVIII, 5; Bamberger, *Erinnerungen*, p. 76.

24. Bamberger, *Erinnerungen*, pp. 76–78, 79, 187; *MZ*, May 6, 1848; Bamberger, "Flitterwochen der Pressefreiheit," pp. 4–5.

25. Franz Hildebrandt, *Reinhard Freiherr von Dalwigk zu Lichtenfels und die deutsche Revolution* (Rostock, 1931), pp. 20–37; Eigenbrodt, *Meine Erinnerungen*, pp. 49, 55–56; *Mainzer Flugblätter über 1848–1849*, nos. 1, 2, Stadtbibliothek, Mainz; Bamberger, *Erinnerungen*, pp. 98–100.

26. Bamberger, *Erinnerungen*, pp. 83–107, 113; his sketches of the participants at Frankfurt are excellent. Julius Fröbel, *Ein Lebenslauf*, 2 vols. (Stuttgart, 1890–91), 1:172.

27. Krause, *Die demokratische Partei*, pp. 117–26; Veit Valentin, *Frankfurt am Main und die Revolution von 1848–49* (Stuttgart and Berlin, 1908), p. 293; Heinz Günther Böse, "Ludwig Simon von Trier" (Ph.D. dissertation, Gutenberg University, Mainz, 1950), pp. 30–33; *Mainzer Flugblätter über 1848–1849*, no. 35; *MZ*, April 7, May 17, 20, 1848, January 4, 1849; *Der Demokrat*, May 14, 1848, p. 39.

28. *Der Demokrat,* May 14, 1848, p. 39; Bamberger, *Erinnerungen,* pp. 79–81; *Statuten des Demokratischen Vereins in Mainz* (Mainz, 1848).

29. *MZ,* January 4, 1849. The association survived the defeat of 1849 and became the basis of his support in 1868. Bamberger, *Erinnerungen,* p. 79; *MZ,* July 25, 1849, September 27, 1849.

30. Bamberger, *Erinnerungen,* pp. 80, 114, 131, 140, 145–46, 157; *MZ,* September 27, 1848; *Der Demokrat,* May 6, 1849; *Namensverzeichnis der Mitglieder des Demokratischen Vereins in Mainz (August 1848),* (n.p., n.d.).

31. Bamberger, *Erinnerungen,* pp. 89–90, 113–14, 127–29; *Der Demokrat,* August 27, September 10, 1848; *MZ,* June 7, July 17, 1848; Buckler, *Die politischen und religiösen Kämpfe,* pp. 47–63; Lenore O'Boyle, "The Democratic Left in Germany, 1848," pp. 374–83; idem, "The Problem of an Excess of Educated Men in Western Europe, 1800–1850," pp. 471–77; Hildebrandt, *Reinhard Freiherr von Dalwigk,* pp. 72–74. On the role of judicial officials during a later period see Eugene N. Anderson, *The Social and Political Conflict in Prussia, 1858–1864* (Lincoln, Nebr., 1954), pp. 289–90.

32. Buckler, *Die politischen und religiösen Kämpfe,* pp. 52–55; Hildebrandt, *Reinhard Freiherr von Dalwigk,* pp. 70–71; Eigenbrodt, *Meine Erinnerungen,* p. xxviii; *MZ,* June 17, 1848, November 3, 4, 1848.

33. Norbert Heise, "Demokratischer Turnerbund und Deutscher Turnerbund," in *Die bürgerlichen Parteien in Deutschland, 1830–1945,* I (Leipzig, 1968), pp. 274–77; *MZ,* July 9, August 17, November 28, 1848; Bamberger, *Erinnerungen,* pp. 114–22; Bamberger to Max Broemel, August 20, 1884, Broemel Nachlass, Deutsches Zentralarchiv I, Potsdam; Katz-Seibert, *Der politische Radikalismus,* p. 25.

34. *Der Bund der Kommunisten: Dokumente und Materialien,* I (Berlin, 1970), pp. 645, 751–52, 754–55, 755–56, 765–68, 770–71, 775–76, 776–77, 779–80, 785–86.

35. *MZ,* March 25, April 19, 24, May 3, 15, June 7, November 5, 1848; *Der Demokrat,* April 16, July 23, August 20, November 11, 1848; Keim, "Der politische Gehalt des Mainzer Karnevals," pp. 90–91; P. H. Noyes, *Organization and Revolution: Working Class Associations in the German Revolutions of 1848–49* (Princeton, 1966), pp. 117, 195–98; Roger Morgan, *The German Social Democrats and the First International, 1864–1872* (Cambridge, Mass., 1965), pp. 83, n. 2, 89; Hamerow, *Restoration, Revolution, Reaction,* pp. 143–47.

36. *MZ,* June 21, 26, July 31, August 1, 5, 1848, January 25, March 9, April 10, 1849; Katz-Seibert, *Der politische Radikalismus,* pp. 25, 32–34; Bamberger, *Erinnerungen,* p. 68; Bockenheimer, *Mainz in den Jahren 1848 und 1849,* pp. 109–10; Rössler, "Mainz," pp. 93–94.

37. Krause, *Die demokratische Partei,* pp. 37–55, 63–94, 98–108; *MZ,* June 22, 29, July 3, 5, 18, 23, August 30, September 3, 5, October 21, 29, November 3, 4, 1848; Noyes, *Organization and Revolution,* pp. 326–27.

38. *MZ,* September 7, October 20, 28, 1848; *Statuten des Demokratischen Vereins in Mainz; Namensverzeichnis;* Börckel, "Karl Theodor von Zabern," pp. 229–31; Richard Falck, *Germain Metternich* (Mainz, 1954), pp. 55–85.

39. Bamberger, *Erinnerungen,* pp. 43, 127; *MZ,* March 16, 1848.

40. Bamberger, "Flitterwochen der Pressefreiheit," p. 5; *MZ,* March 16, April 1, 12, 15, May 5, 1848, May 31, 1849.

41. *MZ,* April 17, October 3, 4, 5, December 2, 6, 8, 10, 1848, February 15, 1849; *Mainzer Flugblätter über 1848–1849,* no. 2; *Grossherzoglich Hessisches Regierungsblatt,* pp. 123–30.

42. Bamberger, "Die Nationalehre," *Der Demokrat*, August 16, 1848, pp. 123–25; *MZ*, June 13, 1848; Lewis B. Namier, *1848: The Revolution of the Intellectuals* (London, 1944), pp. 78–79; Eberhard Meier, *Die aussenpolitischen Ideen der Achtund-vierziger*, Historische Studien, CCCXXXVII (Berlin, 1938), pp. 103–33.

43. Bamberger, *Erinnerungen*, p. 112; *MZ*, July 15, 16, 20, August 3, September 3, 1848; Bamberger, "Flitterwochen der Pressefreiheit," p. 6; *Der Demokrat*, April 16, 20, 1848, pp. 1–2, 17.

44. Gustav Lüders, *Die demokratische Bewegung in Berlin im Oktober 1848*, Abhandlungen mittlerer und neuerer Geschichte, XI (Berlin and Leipzig, 1909), pp. 25–27, 135–36, 146; Karl Obermann, *Die deutschen Arbeiter in der Revolution von 1848*, 2nd ed. (Berlin, 1953), pp. 274–79; Police Report, no. 1, *Acta des königlichen Polizei-Praesidenten zu Berlin betreffend den Gerichtsass. Ludwig Bamberger aus Mainz, 1851–1899*, Staatsarchiv Potsdam, hereafter cited as Police Reports, Potsdam; Fröbel, *Ein Lebenslauf*, I:173, 174–77; Krause, *Die demokratische Partei*, pp. 129–30; Droz, *Les révolutions allemandes de 1848*, pp. 548–50.

45. *MZ*, June 16, 17, July 28, 1848; Jacques Droz, *Le libéralisme rhénan, 1815–1848* (Paris, 1940), p. 422. Gottschalk in fact was Marx's main competitor for support among the workers of Cologne (Noyes, *Organization and Revolution*, pp. 63–64, 115–18, 122–23, 284–89).

46. Bamberger, *Erinnerungen*, pp. 108–12.

47. Ibid., pp. 102–08.

48. *MZ*, July 11, 1848; *Der Demokrat*, July 16, 1848, pp. 97–98.

49. Bamberger, *Rede von Ludwig Bamberger gehalten bei der Gründung des demokratischen Vereins in Kostheim* (Kastel, n.d.); Friedrich C. Sell, *Die Tragödie des deutschen Liberalismus* (Stuttgart, 1953), p. 261.

50. Bamberger, *Erinnerungen*, p. 114; *MZ*, July 22, 25, 1848; Eigenbrodt, *Meine Erinnerungen*, p. xxviii; Katz-Seibert, *Der politische Radikalismus*, p. 30; Buckler, *Die politischen und religiösen Kämpfe*, pp. 56–57.

51. *Grossherzoglich Hessisches Regierungsblatt*, pp. 67, 72, 73, 217–30, 245; *MZ*, May 29, June 28, July 9, August 5, 1848; Bamberger, *Erinnerungen*, p. 82; *Flugblätter, 1848*, no. 14, Stadtbibliothek, Mainz; Eigenbrodt, *Meine Erinnerungen*, pp. 50–53; Bockenheimer, *Mainz in den Jähren 1848 und 1849*, pp. 139–40.

52. Hildebrandt, *Reinhard Freiherr von Dalwigk*, pp. 18, 38–40, 43–46, 56–59; Walter Vogel, *Die Tagebücher des Freiherrn Reinhard von Dalwigk zu Lichtenfels als Geschichtsquelle*, Historische Studien, CCXXXIV (Berlin, 1933), p. 15; Eigenbrodt, *Meine Erinnerungen*, pp. 158–60; Buckler, *Die politischen und religiösen Kämpfe*, pp. 40, 60; Katz-Seibert, *Der politische Radikalismus*, pp. 45–50; Bamberger, *Erinnerungen*, pp. 114, 123–26; *MZ*, August 5, 13, 1848; *Der Demokrat*, August 13, September 10, 17, November 5, 1848, pp. 136, 168, 176, 232.

53. Bamberger, *Erinnerungen*, pp. 77–78; Bamberger to Anna, May 28, 1844, Bamberger Nachlass, Berlin-Dahlem; *MZ*, July 24, 1848; *Mainzer Flugblätter, 1846–1851*, nos. 13, 16; *Mainzer Flugblätter über 1848–1849*, no. 16; Buckler, *Die politischen und religiösen Kämpfe*, pp. 43–45, 60; Rössler, "Mainz im Jahre 1848," p. 95.

54. August Schuchert, "Der erste Mainzer Katholikentag in seinem historisch-ideellen Verlauf," in *Idee, Gestalt und Gestalter*, ed. Ludwig Lenhart, p. 93; Cramer, "Die katholische Bewegung im Vormärz und im Revolutionsjahr 1848/49," pp. 39–43; Emil Ritter, *Die katholisch-soziale Bewegung Deutschlands im neunzehnten Jahrhundert und der Volksverein* (Cologne, 1954), pp. 16, 36, 95; Anton Diehl, *Zur Geschichte der katholischen Bewegung im 19. Jahrhundert: das Mainzer Journal im Jahre 1848* (Mainz,

1911), passim; Ludwig Bergsträsser, *Studien zur Vorgeschichte der Zentrumspartei* (Tubingen, 1910), pp. 132–54, 166–68; Franz Schnabel, *Der Zusammenschluss des politischen Katholizismus in Deutschland im Jahre 1848,* Heidelberger Abhandlungen zur mittleren und neueren Geschichte, XXIX (Heidelberg, 1910), pp. 40–50; *MZ,* April 30, May 11, December 15, 1848; Bamberger, *Erinnerungen,* pp. 118, 146; Bamberger, "Gibt es eine von der Religion unabhängige Moral?" *Der Demokrat,* September 28, 1848, pp. 177–79; Rudolf Stadelmann, *Soziale und politische Geschichte der Revolution von 1848* (Munich, 1948), pp. 96–97.

55. Valentin, *Frankfurt,* pp. 313, 354; Carl Vogt, *Der achtzehnte September in Frankfurt* (Frankfurt on the Main, 1848), passim; *MZ,* October 1, 1848; Bamberger, *Erinnerungen,* pp. 129–34; Bockenheimer, *Mainz in den Jahren 1848 und 1849,* p. 132; Noyes, *Organization and Revolution,* pp. 259–69.

56. Lüders, *Die demokratische Bewegung,* pp. 27, 84–89, 102; Krause, *Die demokratische Partei,* pp. 137–63; Obermann, *Die deutschen Arbeiter,* pp. 309–10; Noyes, *Organization and Revolution,* pp. 274–77; Bamberger, *Erinnerungen,* pp. 134–36; *MZ,* October 31, 1848.

57. Bamberger to Anna, October 22, November 6, 1848, as cited in Bamberger, *Erinnerungen,* pp. 189–190.

58. *MZ,* November 5, 7, 8, 1848.

59. *MZ,* November 9, 10, 11, 1848.

60. Bamberger, *Erinnerungen,* p. 137.

61. *MZ,* August 28, December 2, 6, 8, 10, 27, 30, 1848; January 21, February 15, April 24, May 31, June 4, 1849; Bamberger, *Erinnerungen,* pp. 65, 140, 157; Bamberger, *Trauerrede auf Robert Blum* (Mainz, 1848), pp. 12–13; *MZ,* April 5, 1849.

62. *Mainzer Flugblätter über 1848–1849,* no. 60; *MZ,* December 29, 30, 1848, February 20, March 2, 3, 4, 1849; *Demokratenfest in Mainz* (Frankfurt, 1849); Bamberger [A. Freimund], *Demokratischer Kalender für 1849* (Mainz, 1849), pp. 9, 22, 26, 30.

63. *MZ,* March 24, 25, 27, 28, 29, April 3, 5, 1849; Pierre-Joseph Proudhon, *Die Volksbank,* trans. and intro. by Ludwig Bamberger (Frankfurt on the Main, 1849), pp. 32, 42; Bamberger, *Erinnerungen,* p. 113; Mary Allen, "P.-J. Proudhon in the Revolution of 1848," *Journal of Modern History,* XXIV (March 1952):10–14; Alan Ritter, *The Political Thought of Pierre-Joseph Proudhon* (Princeton, 1969), pp. 168–72.

64. Bamberger, *Erinnerungen,* pp. 113, 163–64; idem, *Uber Rom und Paris nach Gotha oder die Wege des Herrn von Treitschke* (Stuttgart, 1866), p. 42.

65. For a Marxist analysis of this "petty bourgeois" radicalism see Fritz Gebauer, "Vom Steuerverweigerer zum Gehilfen Bismarcks. Zur politischen Entwicklung Lothar Buchers von 1848–49 bis 1864" in *Die grosspreussich-militaristische Reichsgründung 1871,* ed. Horst Bartel and Ernst Engelberg (Berlin, 1971), II:345–50.

66. *Der Demokrat,* April 22, May 6, 20, July 9, 12, 15, 1849; *MZ,* May 1, 7, June 23, 29, 1849; *Mainzer Flugblätter über 1848–1849,* nos. 4, 5, 45, 54, 61 62; *Anklage-Akte,* 2 vols. (Zweibrucken, 1850), I:17–18, 79, 98, 115; II:59–60, 97–102, 106, 226 (this was the official Bavarian investigation into the Palatinate uprising). Bamberger, *Erinnerungen,* pp. 156–57, 162; idem, *Erlebnisse aus der pfälzischen Erhebung im Mai und Juni 1849* (Frankfurt on the Main, 1849), passim; Otto Fleischmann, *Geschichte des pfälzischen Aufstandes im Jahre 1849* (Kaiserslautern, 1899), pp. 284–99.

67. *Mainzer Journal,* June 16, 1849; *MZ,* July 24–26, 1849, October 18, 1850; Bamberger, *Erinnerungen,* pp. 244–45.

68. Bamberger, *Erlebnisse,* pp. v–vii, 7, 22, 51, 83, 87; Bussmann, "Zwischen Revolution und Reichsgründung," pp. 207, 209–10; Theodor Barth, "Ludwig Bamberger," in his *Politische Porträts* (Berlin, 1904), p. 18. For other post-mortems see Carl Vogt, *Die Aufgabe der Opposition in unserer Zeit (Giessen, October 1849)*, und Heinrich Bernhard Oppenheim, "Zur Kritik der Demokratie," in his *Vermischte Schriften aus bewegter Zeit* (Stuttgart and Leipzig, 1866), pp. 1–36. Vogt argued that the only chance for the survival of freedom lay in the particularism of the individual states. Bamberger arrived at this conclusion only in the 1890s. Oppenheim's essay was typically Hegelian and thus typically ignored the realities of 1848 and 1849.

CHAPTER 3. EXILE AND UNIFICATION

1. Bamberger, *Erinnerungen,* pp. 91, 194–95, 197–211, 213, 216–23; Paul Neitzke, *Die deutschen politischen Flüchtlinge in der Schweiz, 1848–1849* (Charlottenburg, 1927), passim; Bamberger, "Zur Erinnerung an Friedrich Kapp," pp. 130–31; Fröbel, *Ein Lebenslauf,* I:271.

2. Bamberger to Anna, November 6, [1846], n.d. [winter 1846–47], n.d. [early 1847], Bamberger Nachlass, Berlin-Dahlem.

3. Bamberger, *Erinnerungen,* pp. 195, 228–32, 318; Blum, "Ludwig Bamberger," pp. 207–08.

4. Bamberger, *Erinnerungen,* pp. 234–44; Bamberger to his aunt, November 7, December 28, 1850, Bamberger Nachlass, Berlin-Dahlem.

5. Bamberger to his aunt, December 28, 1850, Bamberger Nachlass, Berlin-Dahlem; Bamberger, *Erinnerungen,* pp. 240–41, 245–46.

6. Bamberger, *Erinnerungen,* pp. 246–62.

7. Ibid., pp. 195–96; *SBR,* 7 LP, 2 S, February 17, 1888, p. 980; Bamberger, "Unsere Neuesten," *GS,* I:393–94; Karl Wippermann, "Ludwig Bamberger," *Allgemeine Deutsche Biographie,* XLVI (Leipzig, 1902), p. 194; *Berliner Tageblatt,* March 14, 1899.

8. Bamberger [Un Allemand], "Lettre sur l'unité allemande et la Parlement d'Erfurth," *La Voix du Peuple,* March 4, 11, 1850.

9. Böse, "Ludwig Simon," pp. 214, 218–24; Bamberger, *Erinnerungen,* pp. 105, 218–21; idem, "Monatskorrespondenz London," *Deutsche Monatsschrift für Politik, Wissenschaft, Kunst und Leben,* 1850, no. 1, pp. 170–71, no. 3, pp. 314–15, no. 4, pp. 128, 131–32, no. 6, p. 447, no. 7, pp. 154, 159–60.

10. Howard C. Payne and Henry Grosshans, "The Exiled Revolutionaries and the French Political Police in the 1850's," *American Historical Review,* LXVIII (July 1963): 954–73; Police Reports, Potsdam, nos. 1–6, 8, 15, 16, 20, 21; Bamberger, *Erinnerungen,* pp. 267–69.

11. Bamberger, *Erinnerungen,* p. 494.

12. Bamberger, *Erinnerungen,* pp. 358–87; Anna Bamberger to Babette Feist, December 18, 1857, January 10, 1860, originals in the possession of Mrs. Rahel Liebeschütz. Bamberger, *Erinnerungen,* p. 379.

13. Bamberger, *Erinnerungen,* pp. 366–67, 381–82, 385–87; Karl Helfferich, *Georg von Siemens,* 3 vols. (Berlin, 1923), I:213; 224–25.

14. Bamberger, *Erinnerungen,* p. 387.

15. Ibid., pp. 267–70, 355, 388, 484, 495, 519, 540–41. See Friedrich Kapp's similar complaint about feeling "alien" in America in spite of his monetary success

(Wehler, *Friedrich Kapp,* p. 21.) See also Heinrich Bernhard Oppenheim, "Die Deutschen im Auslande und das Ausland in den Deutschen," in his *Vermischte Schriften aus bewegter Zeit* (Stuttgart and Leipzig, 1866), pp. 190–204.

16. Bamberger, *Erinnerungen,* p. 388; idem, "Eine Stimme aus der Fremde," *MZ,* January 18, 1867.

17. Ernst Portner, *Die Einigung Italiens im Urteil liberaler deutscher Zeitgenossen: Studie zur inneren Geschichte des kleindeutschen Liberalismus,* Bonner Historische Forschungen, XIII (Bonn, 1959), passim; Bamberger, *Erinnerungen,* pp. 389–92; idem, "Juchhe nach Italia," *GS,* III:159–98; *Der Demokrat,* August 6, 1848, pp. 123–25; *MZ,* February 24, March 7, 1849; Bamberger, *Erlebnisse aus der pfälzischen Erhebung,* p. 3; idem, *Deutschlands Not und Ärzte* (Berlin, 1859); Julius Fröbel, *Deutschland und der Friede zu Villafranca* (Frankfurt on the Main, 1859), pp. 20–29; Carl Vogt, *Studien zur gegenwärtigen Lage Europas* (Geneva and Bern, 1859), pp. ix, 101–25, 132–33; Wilhelm Mommsen, *Johannes von Miquel* (Stuttgart, 1928), p. 172; Gall, *Der Liberalismus als regierende Partei,* p. 113; Bamberger to Broemel, August 5, 1884, Broemel Nachlass.

18. Bamberger describes the ups and downs of these two ventures (*Erinnerungen,* pp. 394–411). Bamberger to Carl Vogt, January 7, 1860, Bamberger Nachlass, Berlin-Dahlem; Anna Bamberger to Babette Feist, January 10, 1860, Liebeschütz collection; Otto Westphal, *Welt- und Staatsauffassung des deutschen Liberalismus, eine Untersuchung über die Preussischen Jahrbücher und die konstitutionellen Liberalismus in Deutschland von 1858–1863* (Munich and Berlin, 1919), pp. 167–68.

19. Bamberger, *Erinnerungen,* pp. 405–09. In 1880 he could mention in passing that he had placed 200,000 francs with his brothers, Rudolf and Heinrich, for investment (Bamberger to his mother, May 24, 1880, Bamberger Nachlass, Berlin-Dahlem).

20. Bamberger, *Erinnerungen,* pp. 505–06, 511–12; Johann Jacoby, *Heinrich Simon, ein Gedenkbuch für das deutsche Volk* (Berlin, 1865), pp. 384–85; Theodor Mommsen, "Ludwig Bamberger," in his *Reden und Aufsätze* (Berlin, 1905), pp. 469–71; Anna Bamberger to Babette Feist, December 10, 1862, Liebeschütz collection; Karl Mayer, "Eine Festfahrt zu Heinrich Simons Denkmal," *Deutsche Jahrbücher für Politik und Literatur,* IV (1863): 296–321.

21. Bamberger, *Erinnerungen,* pp. 503–04, 518–25.

22. Bamberger, "Vorwort" (from *Demokratische Studien*) *GS,* III:198–200; Wippermann, "Ludwig Bamberger," p. 197; Bussmann, "Zwischen Revolution und Reichsgründung," p. 218; Leonard Krieger, *The German Idea of Freedom* (Boston, 1957), pp. 348, 352.

23. Bamberger, "Über die Grenzen des Humors in der Politik," *Deutsche Jahrbücher für Politik und Literatur,* VI (1863):176–77, *GS,* III:269–71; idem, "Die Französelei am Rhein," pp. 151–54; idem, "Des Michael Pro Schriftenwechsel mit Thomas Contra aus dem Jahre 1859," *Demokratische Studien,* I (1860):183, 190; idem, *Rede gehalten am Schluss des ersten allgemeinen deutschen Turnfestes in Paris* (n.p., 1865), Ludwig Bamberger Nachlass, Deutsches Zentralarchiv I, Potsdam; hereafter cited as Bamberger Nachlass, Potsdam; idem, "Kandidatenrede," *GS,* IV:20–22.

24. Bamberger, *Erinnerungen,* p. 250; idem, "Des Michael Pro Schriftenwechsel," pp. 183–85; idem, "Ein Vademecum für deutsche Untertanen," *Deutsche Jahrbücher für Politik und Literature,* XIII (1864), 54–56.

25. Bamberger, "Die Französelei am Rhein," pp. 127, 189–90; idem, "Über die Grenze," p. 188; idem, "Ein Vademecum," pp. 66–69; idem, *Erinnerungen,* pp. 43, 530–35; idem, *Rede . . . Turnfestes;* idem, "Des sympathies françaises aux bords du Rhin," p. 524; Bussman, "Zwischen Revolution und Reichsgründung," pp. 207–08. It

took the subject of the pseudo-state Hesse-Darmstadt many years to admit the deep-rootedness of particularism and even to find something beneficial in it (Bamberger, *Erinnerungen*, p. 518).

26. Bamberger, "Juchhe noch Italia," pp. 161 89: idem, "Don Michael Pro Schriften wechsel," pp. 171–72, 198–200; idem, "Ein Vademecum," p. 67; idem, *Über Rom und Paris nach Gotha*, p. 7; idem, *Erinnerungen*, pp. 78, 286, 541.

27. Bamberger, "Berlin in Paris," *Deutsche Jahrbücher für Politik und Literatur*, V (1862):313–19; idem, *Rede . . . Turnfestes;* Werner Schunke, *Die preussischen Frei-händler und die Entstehung der Nationalliberalen Partei* (Erfurt, 1916), pp. 7–8; Bamberger to Oppenheim, November 21, 1869, Bamberger Nachlass, Potsdam; Bamberger, "Vertraulich Briefe aus dem Zollparlament, 1868, 1869, 1870," *GS*, IV:192.

28. Bamberger, *Über Rom und Paris nach Gotha*, pp. 25 26; *Frankfurter Zeitung*, March 15, 1899.

29. On the great conversion of 1866, see Karl Georg Faber, "Realpolitik als Ideo-logie: die Bedeutung des Jahres 1866 für das politische Denken in Deutschland," *HZ*, CCIII (1966):1–45; Gall, *Der Liberalismus als regierende Partei*, p. 383; Martin Spahn, "Zur Entstehung der nationalliberalen Partei," *Zeitschrift für Politik*, I (1907):402–413; Ludwig Dehio, "Die preussische Demokratie und der Kreig von 1866," *Forschungen zur brandenburgischen und preussischen Geschichte*, XXXIX (1927):229–59; Theodor Mommsen, "Ludwig Bamberger," p. 471; Walter Neher, *Arnold Ruge als Politiker und politischer Schriftsteller: Ein Beitrag zur Geschichte des 19. Jahrhunderts* (Heidelberg, 1933), p. 222; Heinrich A. Winkler, *Preussischer liberalismus und Deutscher National-staat: Studien zur Geschichte der Deutschen Fortschrittspartei, 1861–1866*, Tübinger Studien zur Geschichte und Politik, XVII (Tubingen, 1964), pp. 88–116.

30. Bamberger to Arnold Ruge, October 6, 1866, in *Arnold Ruges Briefwechsel und Tagebuchblätter aus den Jahren 1825–1880*, ed. Paul Nerrlich, 2 vols. (Berlin, 1886), II:279–80; Bamberger, "Alte Parteien und neue Zustände," *GS*, III:313; Wilhelm Löwe-Kalbe to Bamberger, January 30, 1867, Bamberger to Oppenheim, January 13, 1867, Bamberger Nachlass, Potsdam.

31. Bamberger, "Alte Parteien und neue Zustände," pp. 297–302; Bamberger to Oppenheim, October 5, 1866, Bamberger Nachlass, Potsdam; Bamberger to Ruge, October 6, 1866, *Arnold Ruges Briefwechsel*, II:280.

32. Bamberger, "Alte Parteien und neue Zustände," pp. 310–17. Bamberger's later political ally and friend, Max von Forckenbeck, also reasoned that the millions were gone and could not be gotten back. And "a conflict on account of an unalterable thing is very dangerous to freedom" (Max von Forckenbeck to his wife, January 2, 1867, in Martin Philippson, ed., [Forckenbeck's letters], *Deutsche Revue*, XXIII, no. 4 (1898): 143–45.

33. *Frankfurter Zeitung*, March 15, 1899; Bamberger, "Die Französelei am Rhein," pp. 133, 174, 186–89; idem, "Des sympathies françaises aux bords du Rhin," p. 524.

34. Bamberger, "Alte Parteien und neue Zustände," pp. 331–32; idem, "Kandidaten-rede," pp. 32, 34–36; idem, "An die Wähler Rheinhessens von einem alten Freunde," *MZ* (Extra Beilage), December 7, 1866; idem, "In Sachen Demokratie der Stadt Mainz contra Ludwig Bamberger und Genossen. Punkto: Hochverrath," *MZ*, January 18, 1867; idem, "Deutschland, Frankreich und die Revolution," in his *Herr von Bismarck*, trans. K.A. (Breslau, 1868), p. XLVI.

35. Bamberger, "Alte Parteien und neue Zustände," p. 307; Bamberger to Ruge, October 6, December 12, 1866, *Arnold Ruges Briefwechsel*, II:280, 281; Bamberger to Oppenheim, December 12, 1866, January 13, 27, 1867, Bamberger Nachlass, Potsdam;

A. Rapp, *Die Württemberger und die nationale Frage, 1863–1871* (Stuttgart, 1910), pp. 31, 80–85, 86–92; Böse, "Ludwig Simon," p. 254; Police Reports, Potsdam, nos. 29, 36; Bamberger, *Erinnerungen,* p. 508; Bamberger to Theodor Barth, August 23, 1893, Theodor Barth Nachlass, Deutsches Zentralarchiv I, Potsdam; *Frankfurter Zeitung,* March 15, 1899; *SBR,* 4 LP, 1 S, October 9, 11, 1878, pp. 122, 175.

36. Bamberger to Oppenheim, March 29, August 18, 1867, September 24, 1869, Löwe-Kalbe to Bamberger, January 30, 1867, Bamberger Nachlass, Potsdam; Bamberger to Ruge, October 6, 1866, October 10, 1867, *Arnold Ruges Briefwechsel,* II:280, 312–13; Bamberger, *Erinnerungen* pp. 95, 282–83; idem, *Bismarcks grosses Spiel; die geheimen Tagebücher Ludwig Bambergers,* ed. Ernst Feder (Frankfurt on the Main, 1932), pp. 89, 93; *MZ,* December 22, 1866; Bamberger to Anna, January 24, 1870, Bamberger Nachlass, Berlin-Dahlem.

37. Bamberger to Ruge, December 12, 1866, *Arnold Ruges Briefwechsel,* II:281. *MZ* (December 12, 1866 and January 23, 1867) commented on the favorable press reports about Bamberger's articles. *MZ,* January 16, 1867; Paul Lindau, *Elberfelder Zeitung,* to Bamberger, April 11, 1867, Bamberger Nachlass, Berlin-Dahlem; *Frankfurter Zeitung,* March 15, 1899; Spahn, "Zur Entstehung der nationalliberalen Partei," pp. 408–09; Heinrich Kruse, editor of the *Kölnische Zeitung,* to Bamberger, September 24, October 10, 1865, Bamberger Nachlass, Potsdam; see the newspaper clippings of Bamberger's articles in Police Reports, Potsdam, nos. 28, 30–35.

38. Bamberger to Ruge, October 10, December 12, 1866, *Arnold Ruges Briefwechsel,* II:280–81; Bamberger to Oppenheim October 5, 6, November 29, 1866, Bamberger Nachlass; Potsdam; Bamberger, "Eine Stimme aus der Fremde," *MZ,* January 18, 1867; "Demokraten und Diplomaten an der Mainlinie," *MZ,* June 16, 18, 1867; Bamberger to Johann Jacoby, July 9, 1860, April 20, June 26, 1867, Jacoby to Bamberger April 26, 1867, Bamberger Papers, Jewish National and University Library, Jerusalem, hereafter cited as Bamberger Papers, Jerusalem.

39. Karl Georg Bockenheimer, *Mainz im Jahre 1866* (Mainz, 1907), pp. 105–23; Gerhard Eisler, *Die Entstehung der liberalen Parteien in Deutschland 1858–1870* (Hanover, 1969), pp. 147–49; Ernst Götz, *Die Stellung Hessen-Darmstadts zur deutschen Einigungsfrage in den Jahren 1866–1871* (Darmstadt, 1914), pp. 12–16, 20–30; Bamberger to Ruge, April 4, December 12, 1866, *Arnold Ruges Briefwechsel,* II:266–67, 281; Bamberger to Carl Hellermann, publisher of the *Mainzer Zeitung,* April 4, 1867, Hellermann to Bamberger, April 14, 1867, Bamberger Nachlass, Berlin-Dahlem; Bamberger to Oppenheim, November 29, December 10, 1866, Bamberger Nachlass, Potsdam; Bamberger, "An die Wähler," *MZ,* December 7, 1866; *MZ,* December 2, 19, 21, 22, 29, 1866, March 20, 1867; *Frankfurter Zeitung,* January 12, November 11, 1867; George G. Windell, *The Catholics and German Unity, 1866–1871* (Minneapolis, Minn., 1954), pp. 24–27, 87, 108.

40. Bamberger to Oppenheim, October 5, 1866, May 2, August 10, December 31, 1867, January 14, 1868, Bamberger Nachlass, Potsdam; R. Bamberger to L. Bamberger, January 7, June 26, July 7, 16, December 3, 7, 14, 1867, January 10, 12, 14, 31, 1868, Hans Viktor von Unruh to Bamberger, October 2, 1867, Hermann Büttner to Bamberger, October 4, 1867, Bamberger Nachlass, Berlin-Dahlem; *Mainzer Abendblatt,* January 7, 23, February 4, 11, 1868; Bamberger, "Kandidatenrede," p. 14.

41. Windell, *Catholics,* pp. 24, 48, 100–02, 162–65; Morgan, *German Social Democrats,* pp. 83, 89, 109, 152; *Mainzer Anzeiger,* February 2, 27, March 3, 1868; Theodor Wacker, *Entwicklung der Sozialdemokratie in den zehn ersten Reichstagswahlen (1871–1898)* (Freiburg, 1903), pp. 335–36, 341–42; *Frankfurter Zeitung,* January 15, 1867;

Ernst Götz, "Konrad Alexis Dumont," *Hessische Biographien,* II (Darmstadt, 1927), pp. 430–35; Georg Eckert, *Zur Geschichte der "Sektionen" Wiesbaden und Mainz der Internationalen Arbeiter-Assoziation,* Archiv für Sozialgeschichte, VIII (Hanover, 1968), pp. 151–71.

42. *Mainzer Anzeiger,* January 2, 3, February 7, 8, 16, 18, 19, 22, 23, 27, 29, March 3, 1868; *MZ,* December 31, 1867, January 1, 19, 22, 23, February 18, 29, March 12, 13, 17, 1868; *Mainzer Abendblatt,* February 28, March 7, 12, 13, 14, 16, 17, 18, 1868; Bamberger to Ruge, March 3, 1868, Bamberger Papers, New York; Bamberger to Oppenheim, February 22, 1868, March 5, 1868, Bamberger Nachlass, Potsdam; Bamberger to Anna, March 14, 1868, Bamberger Nachlass, Berlin-Dahlem; Bamberger, "Kandidatenrede," pp. 14–15; Blum, "Ludwig Bamberger," p. 210; Götz, *Die Stellung Hessen-Darmstadts,* pp. 40–44; Eisler, *Die Entstehung der liberalen Parteien,* pp. 149–51; Bockenheimer, *Mainz im Jahre 1866,* pp. 133–36.

43. R. Bamberger to L. Bamberger, March 23, 1868, Bamberger Nachlass, Berlin-Dahlem; Bamberger to Oppenheim, March 29, 1868, Bamberger Nachlass, Potsdam; *Mainzer Abendblatt,* March 25, 1868.

44. On the attempt to organize a firm party organization throughout Hesse see *MZ,* July 7, 17, August 13, 18, September 30, 1868. *Mainzer Anzeiger,* June 24, 1868; R. Bamberger to L. Bamberger, April 8, June 8, 14, 16, 19, 1868, Bamberger Nachlass, Berlin-Dahlem; Bamberger to Eduard Lasker, June 10, 1868, Eduard Lasker Nachlass, Deutsches Zentralarchiv I, Potsdam; hereafter cited as Lasker Nachlass, Potsdam; Bamberger to Friedrich Dernburg, July 14, 1868, Bamberger Nachlass, Potsdam; Bamberger to Anna, January 1, 1869, Bamberger Nachlass, Berlin-Dahlem; Bamberger to Oppenheim, April 6, October 3, December 2, 10, 21, 1868, March 8, April 7, 1869, Bamberger Nachlass, Potsdam.

45. Bamberger, "Vertrauliche Briefe aus dem Zollparlament," p. 95; *MZ,* March 19, July 7, 22, November 14, 17, 18, 27, 28, December 13, 14, 1868; *Mainzer Anzeiger,* June 23, 1868; Bamberger to Lasker, June 22, 1868, Lasker Nachlass, Potsdam; Bamberger to Oppenheim, July 7, August 30, 1868, Bamberger Nachlass, Potsdam; Berthold Auerbach to Jakob Auerbach, November 13, 1868, Berthold Auerbach, *Briefe an seinen Freunde,* 2 vols. (Frankfurt on the Main, 1884), 1:383.

46. Bamberger to Lasker, December 15, 1868, April 19, 1869, Lasker Nachlass, Potsdam; Bamberger to Oppenheim, December 2, 10, 21, 1868, March 8, 1869, and the material in folder 227, nos. 158–74, 191–200, Bamberger Nachlass, Potsdam; *MZ,* August 7, November 17, 28, December 12, 19, 22, 1868, February 13, 14, 16, March 6, April 14, 1869; Bamberger to Anna, June 6, 1869, Bamberger Nachlass, Berlin-Dahlem.

47. Erich Eyck, *Bismarck,* 3 vols. (Erlenbach-Zurich, 1941–44), II:342–68; Johannes Ziekursch, *Politische Geschichte des neuen deutschen Kaiserreiches,* 3 vols. (Frankfurt on the Main, 1925–30), I:253–58; Erich Marcks, *Der Aufsteig des Reiches,* 2 vols. (Stuttgart and Berlin, 1936), II:292–304; E. Malcolm Carroll, *Germany and the Great Powers, 1866–1914* (New York, 1938), pp. 33–42; Erich Brandenburg, *Die Reichsgrundung,* 2nd ed., 2 vols. (Leipzig, 1916), II:247–58.

48. Bamberger, *Erinnerungen,* pp. 266–498; idem, *Bismarcks grosses Spiel,* pp. 77–87.

49. Bamberger, "Adam Lux," *GS,* II:3–40.

50. Bamberger, "Des sympathies françaises aux bords du Rhin," pp. 496–99, 503–23; idem, "Die Französelei am Rhein," p. 126.

51. Bamberger, "Alte Parteien und neue Zustände," p. 327; idem, "Eine Stimme aus der Fremde," *MZ,* January 18, 1867; *MZ,* January 31, 1867; Bamberger to Ruge, March

7, April 12, 13, middle of May, 1867, *Arnold Ruges Briefwechsel*, II:293–94, 296–99; Bamberger to Oppenheim, March 29, April 10, 27, May 3, May 29, June, 1867, Bamberger Nachlass, Potsdam; R. Bamberger to L. Bamberger, March 3, April 12, 24, 26, 1867, Bamberger Nachlass, Berlin-Dahlem; Bamberger, "Luxemburg oder die Logik der Tatsachen" and "Die Bedeutung des Friedenswerkes," *MZ*, April 10, May 16, 1867, Extra Beilage; *Rheinische Volkszeitung*, April 14, 21, 28, 1867; *Mainzer Anzeiger*, April 18, 1867; Bamberger et al. to Lasker, April 26, 1867, Lasker Nachlass, Potsdam; Böse, "Ludwig Simon," p. 260; Rapp, *Die Württemberger*, pp. 224–32; Eckert, *Zur Geschichte der "Sektionen,"* pp. 407–08.

52. Bamberger, "Kandidatenrede," pp. 20, 22, 43; Bamberger to Ruge, April 18, 1866, *Arnold Ruges Briefwechsel*, II:266–67.

53. Bamberger, *Erinnerungen*, pp. 499–501, 535–38.

54. Bamberger to Oppenheim, June 15, August 10, 1867, Bamberger Nachlass, Potsdam; Bamberger, *Erinnerungen*, p. 87; idem, *Bismarcks grosses Spiel*, pp. 97–98; Bamberger to Ruge, October 8, 1867, *Arnold Ruges Briefwechsel*, II:312; Hartwig is incorrect in stating that Bamberger joined the National Liberals in 1866 (*Ludwig Bamberger*, p. 44).

55. Bamberger to Oppenheim, April 10, June 15, August 18, 1867, Bamberger Nachlass, Potsdam; Bamberger to Ruge, December 12, 1866, October 8, 1867, Ruge to Bamberger, October 10, 1867, *Arnold Ruges Briefwechsel*, II:282, 312, 314; Bamberger, *Bismarcks grosses Spiel*, p. 90.

56. Bamberger to Ruge, middle of May, May 27, 1867, *Arnold Ruges Briefwechsel*, II:330; Löwe-Kalbe to Bamberger, January 30, 1867, Bamberger Nachlass, Potsdam; Bamberger, *Bismarcks grosses Spiel*, pp. 89–91; Bamberger to Oppenheim, November 14, 1867, March 29, April 6, 1868, Bamberger Nachlass, Potsdam, the emphasis is Bamberger's; Bamberger, "Kandidatenrede," pp. 22–23, 25–26; Oskar Klein-Hattingen, *Geschichte des deutschen Liberalismus*, 2 vols. (Berlin-Schoneberg, 1911), I:361–66; also see the correspondence in *DLZB*, I:392–99; Eyck, *Bismarck*, II:114–18, 371–73.

57. Bussmann, "Zwischen Revolution und Reichsgründung," pp. 218–21; R. Bamberger to L. Bamberger, March 15, 1867, Bamberger Nachlass, Berlin-Dahlem; Bamberger to Oppenheim, May 29, September 8, October 8, November 19, 1867, August 30, 1868, Bamberger Nachlass, Potsdam; Bamberger to Ruge, October 10, 1867, *Arnold Ruges Briefwechsel*, II:311; [Louis] Bamberger, "Monsieur de Bismarck," *Revue moderne*, XLV (February 25, March 10, 1868):8–49, 256–83.

58. Eyck, *Bismarck*, II:316; Faber documents the fact that 1866 did represent a revolution in the minds of many Germans ("Realpolitik," pp. 1–6). Mommsen, *Johannes von Miquel*, pp. 165, 312–16; Bussmann, "Zwischen Revolution und Reichsgründung," pp. 222, 227; Hajo Holborn, "Bismarck's Realpolitik," *Journal of the History of Ideas*, XXI, no..1 (1960):85; Bamberger, *Herr von Bismarck*, pp. 56, 61–62, 82, 88–90, 96–97, 108–18, 127–28; Bamberger to Oppenheim, September 8, 1867, Bamberger Nachlass, Potsdam; Hartwig, *Ludwig Bamberger*, pp. 36–37.

59. *Frankfurter Zeitung*, March 15, 1899; *Berliner Tageblatt*, March 14, 1899; Bamberger, *Herr von Bismarck*, pp. 118, 127; Bamberger to Ruge, May 27, 1868, *Arnold Ruges Briefwechsel*, II:330; Bamberger, "Kandidatenrede," pp. 37–39; Heinrich Poschinger, *Bismarck und die Parlamentarier*, 3 vols. (Breslau, 1896), II:127; Bamberger, "Vertrauliche Briefe aus dem Zollparlament," p. 150.

60. Gustav von Wilmowski, *Meine Erinnerungen an Bismarck* (Breslau, 1900), pp. 56–57; Bamberger to Lasker, April 19, 1869, Lasker Nachlass, Potsdam; Bamberger to Oppenheim, March 29, 1868, Lasker to Bamberger, December 23, 1868, Bamberger Nachlass, Potsdam; Lbt (*sic*) to Bamberger, April 29, 1869, Bamberger to Anna, June 6,

1869, March 31, 1873, Bamberger Nachlass, Berlin-Dahlem. Even after Bamberger and Bismarck had become political enemies, the chancellor admitted that he was still proud of Bamberger's study (*SBR*, 5 LP, 2 S, June 14, 1882, pp. 430–31).

61. Bamberger to Oppenheim, January 14, 1868, Bamberger Nachlass, Potsdam; Bamberger to Ruge, May 27, 1868, *Arnold Ruges Briefwechsel*, II:330; Bamberger, *Bismarcks grosses Spiel*, p. 102.

62. Ziekursch, *Politische Geschichte*, I:209, 247–48; *SBZP*, 1868, pp. 1, 7.

63. Bamberger to Oppenheim, March 29, 1868, April 25, 1869, Bamberger Nachlass, Potsdam; *SBZP*, 1868, pp. 30–52; *SBZP*, 1869, pp. 63–64, 242; *SBZP*, 1870, pp. 43, 185; Bamberger, "Vertrauliche Briefe aus dem Zollparlament," pp. 92–99; Walter Schübelin, *Das Zollparlament und die Politik von Baden, Bayern und Württemberg, 1866–1870*, Historische Studien, CCLXII (Berlin, 1935), pp. 71–72, 105, 107–15, 117–19, 125; Klein-Hattingen, *Geschichte des deutschen Liberalismus*, I:448–56; Windell, *Catholics*, pp. 137–38, 244; Heinrich Wehrenpfennig to Heinrich von Treitschke, May 8, 1868, in *DLZB*, I:419–20; Theodor Schieder, *Die kleindeutsche Partei in Bayern in den Kämpfen um die nationale Einheit 1863–1871* (Munich, 1936), pp. 181–83; Hermann Oncken, *Rudolf von Bennigsen*, 2 vols. (Stuttgart and Leipzig, 1910), II:156; Forckenbeck to his wife, May 17, 1868, in Philippson, *Deutsche Revue*, XXIII, no. 4 (1898):147–48; Bamberger to Anna, June 13, 17, 21, 1869, Bamberger Nachlass, Berlin-Dahlem.

64. Bamberger, "Vertrauliche Briefe aus dem Zollparlament," pp. 108–17; *SBZP*, 1868, pp. 151, 171–73, 258–59, 284; Heinrich von Gagern to Baron von Dalwigk, June 6, 1868, in *Die auswärtige Politik Preussens, 1858–1871*, ed. Historische Reichskommission 3. Sektion, X (Oldenburg, 1939), p. 60; Schieder, *Die kleindeutsche Partei*, pp. 185–88; Otto von Bismarck, *GW*, VIa: 397–98.

65. Bamberger, "Vertrauliche Briefe aus dem Zollparlament," pp. 71, 127–36, 154–55, 162–67, 181–92; Bamberger to Oppenheim, June 2, 1868, Bamberger Nachlass, Potsdam; R. Bamberger to L. Bamberger, June 8, 1868, Bamberger Nachlass, Berlin-Dahlem.

66. Bamberger to Lasker, April 19, 1869, in *DLZB*, I:442–43; Bamberger to Oppenheim, September 11, 24, November 5, 1869, February 20, April 11, 1870, Bamberger to Wilhelm Blum, October 10, 1869, Bamberger Nachlass, Potsdam; Eduard W. Mayer, "Aus der Geschichte der Nationalliberalen Partei in den Jahren 1868 bis 1871," in *Deutscher Staat und deutsche Parteien*, ed. Paul Wentzcke (Munich and Berlin, 1922), p. 137; Bismarck, *GW*, VIb:260–64, 277–78; Martin Philippson, *Max von Forckenbeck* (Dresden and Leipzig, 1898), pp. 205–06; Josef Becker, "Zum Problem der Bismarckschen Politik in der spanischen Thronfrage 1870," *HZ*, CCXII (June 1971):549.

67. Bamberger to Anna, June 19, 1869, Bamberger Nachlass, Berlin-Dahlem; Bamberger to Lasker, September 4, 1869, Lasker Nachlass, Potsdam; Bamberger to Oppenheim, January 11, April 25, September 11, 24, November 5, 21, December 26, 1869, January 13, February 20, March 15, 21, 29, June 9, 1870, Bamberger Nachlass, Potsdam; Bamberger to Lasker, April 19, 1869, in *DLZB*, I:442–43; Bamberger to Johann K. Bluntschli, December 9, 1868, Bluntschli Nachlass, Zentralbibliothek, Zurich; Bamberger, *Bismarcks grosses Spiel*, p. 144; Adalbert Delbrück to Bamberger, March 3, 1870; Bamberger Nachlass, Potsdam; Ernst Feder, "La valeur, comme source-historique, des papiers du député Louis Bamberger," *Societé d'histoire moderne, Bulletin*, series 7, vol. 32, no. 9, p. 76; Bamberger, "Vertrauliche Briefe aus dem Zollparlament," pp. 137–44; Becker, "Zum Problem der Bismarckschen Politik," pp. 536–43; Götz, *Die Stellung Hessen-Darmstadts*, pp. 45–51.

68. In jest, Bamberger wrote to Oppeheim in 1868 shortly after the Spanish

revolution which overthrew Isabella II: "Too bad that you or I have not learned Spanish. We could apply for the vacant throne" (Bamberger to Oppenheim, October 3, 1868, Bamberger Nachlass, Potsdam).

69. Bamberger, "Vor fünfundzwanzig Jahren," *GS*, I:420–22; idem, *Bismarcks grosses Spiel*, pp. 106–17, Bamberger to Oppenheim, July 14, 1870, Bamberger Nachlass, Potsdam. On the origins of the war, see the recent work of Becker, "Zum problem der Bismarckschen Politik," pp. 529–607.

70. Bamberger, *Bismarcks grosses Spiel*, pp. 117–19, 123–24, 127–28, 130, 132, 135–36, 140, 148; Wilhelm Blum to Bamberger, November 20, 1870, Bamberger to Oppenheim, July 23, August 6, 1870, Bamberger Nachlass, Potsdam.

71. Bamberger to Oppenheim, July 23, 1870, Bamberger Nachlass, Potsdam; *MZ*, September 9, 1871; Bamberger, "Vor fünfundzwanzig Jahren," p. 428.

72. Bamberger, *Bismarcks grosses Spiel*, pp. 140, 143–44, 147, 150, 153–56, 163, 178–79; idem, "Vor fünfundzwanzig Jahren," pp. 423–26. Robert Nöll von der Nahmer has discovered a payment of 600 thalers to Bamberger (*Bismarcks Reptilienfonds: aus den Geheimakten Preussens und des deutschen Reiches* [Mainz, 1968], pp. 82, 117, 200). Heinrich von Poschinger, ed., *Bismarck Portefeuille*, 5 vols. (Stuttgart and Leipzig, 1898–1900), III:38, V:50; Bamberger, "Einheit zur Einigkeit," *National Zeitung*, December 7, 1870; idem, "Material zur Völkerpsychologie," *Allgemeine Zeitung* (Beilage), November 1, 1870, pp. 4829–31. His articles in the Augsburg *Allgemeine Zeitung* were collected in idem, *Zur Naturgeschichte des französischen Krieges* (Leipzig, 1871). Editor of *Kolnische Zeitung* to Bamberger, August 10, 1870, Bamberger Nachlass, Potsdam. Treitschke proposed the establishment of a "completely independent" newspaper in Strassburg which would represent Germany's policy, but in the same breath he inquired of Bamberger whether the German government would lend its support.

73. Bamberger, *Bismarcks grosses Spiel*, pp. 127, 130–31, 181, 230, 231; idem, *Zur Naturgeschichte*, pp. 64–80; *Kölnische Zeitung*, August 21, 1870; Bamberger to Oppenheim, August 6, 1870, Bamberger Nachlass, Potsdam.

74. Bamberger, *Bismarcks grosses Spiel*, pp. 178, 184, 187–90; idem, *Erinnerungen*, pp. 414–16, 496; Moritz Busch, *Tagebuchblätter*, 3 vols. (Leipzig, 1899), I:75, 204; *Amtliche Nachrichten für das General Gouvernement Elsass*, September 1, 10, 15, 21, 1870; Moritz Busch to Bamberger, September 11, 16, 1870, Bamberger Nachlass, Potsdam; Bamberger to Robert von Keudell, September 24, 1870, Bamberger Papers, Jerusalem. On the role of the press in the annexation of Alsace and Lorraine, see Walter Lipgens, "Bismarck, die öffentliche Meinung und die Annexion von Elsass und Lothringen 1870," *HZ*, CXCIX (1964):32–112; idem, "Bismarck und die Frage der Annexion 1870: Eine Erwiderung," *HZ*, CCVI (1968):586–617; Lothar Gall, "Zur Frage der Annexion von Elsass und Lothringen 1870," *HZ*, CCVII (1968), 264–326. I find Gall's essay more persuasive.

75. Bamberger to Busch, September 13, 1870, Busch to Bamberger, n.d. [1870], September 29, 1870, Bamberger to Oppenheim, October 16, 1870, January 26, 1871, Bamberger Nachlass, Potsdam; Busch, *Tagebuchblätter*, I:241–42, 253–54; Carl Vogt, *Carl Vogts politische Briefe an Friedrich Kolb* (Biel, 1870), pp. 21, 23, 26–27; Bamberger, *Bismarcks grosses Spiel*, p. 234.

76. Busch, *Tagebuchblätter*, I:77; Robert Lucius von Ballhausen, *Bismarck Erinnerungen* (Stuttgart and Berlin, 1920), pp. 33–35; Bamberger, *Bismarcks grosses Spiel*, pp. 148, 150; idem, "Laskers Briefwechsel aus dem Kriegsjahre," *GS*, II:124–26; Oncken, *Rudolf von Bennigsen*, II:176, 178; idem, "Aus den Briefen Rudolf von Bennigsens," *Deutsche Revue*, XXXII, no. 1 (1907):39; "Aus Eduard Laskers Nachlass. Sein Briefwechsel aus den Jahren 1870–71," ed. W. Cahn, *Deutsche Revue*, XVII, no. 2

(1892):59; Götz, *Die Stellung Hessen-Darmstadts,* p. 78; Bamberger to Oppenheim, October 15, November 6, 18, 1870, Bamberger Nachlass, Potsdam.

77. Busch, *Tagebuchblätter,* I:299; Busch to Bamberger, October 16, 1870, Bamberger Nachlass, Potsdam; Bismarck, *GW,* VIII:372; Bamberger to Ruge, October 26, 1870, *Arnold Ruges Briefwechsel,* II:357; Bamberger, "Vor fünfundzwanzig Jahren," p. 442.

78. Bamberger, *Bismarcks grosses Spiel,* pp. 191–92, 200, 202, 206, 208, 221, 227, 234; Busch, *Tagebuchblätter,* I:341, 350, 419; "Aus Eduard Laskers Nachlass," pp. 287–90, 292–98; Bamberger to Oppenheim, November 10, 13, 21, 25, 1870, Bamberger Nachlass, Potsdam.

79. Busch, *Tagebuchblätter,* I:479; Bamberger, *Bismarcks grosses Spiel,* pp. 237–42; Oncken, "Aus den Briefen Rudolf von Bennigsens," *Deutsche Revue,* XXXII, no. 1 (1907):157–58; Heinrich Poschinger, ed., *Fürst Bismarck und der Bundesrat,* 4 vols. (Stuttgart and Leipzig, 1897–1901), III:74–76; Bismarck, *GW,* VIb:611, 615; Bamberger to Oppenheim, December 4, 1870, Bamberger Nachlass, Potsdam.

80. Gall, *Der Liberalismus als regierende Partei,* pp. 492–93.

81. Bamberger, *Erinnerungen,* p. 497; idem, *Bismarcks grosses Spiel,* pp. 248–54, 487–500; Busch, *Tagebuchblätter,* II:25; Bamberger to Lasker, February 19, 1871, Lasker Nachlass, Potsdam; Bamberger to Oppenheim, December 4, 1870, January 26, 1871, Bamberger Nachlass, Potsdam.

82. Bamberger, *Bericht über die Angelegenheit des Oktrois* (Mainz, 1870); Bamberger to Oppenheim, December 26, [1869], Bamberger Nachlass, Potsdam; Bamberger to Lasker, February 9, 1871; "Aus Eduard Laskers Nachlass," *Deutsche Revue,* XVII, no. 4 (1892):197–98; Moritz Busch to Bamberger, February 19, 1871, Bamberger Nachlass, Potsdam; Busch, *Tagebuchblätter,* II:155–61; Wilhelm Schüssler, ed., *Die Tagebücher des Freiherrn Reinhard von Dalwigk zu Lichtenfels aus den Jahren 1860–1871* (Stuttgart and Berlin, 1920), p. 483; Götz, *Die Stellung Hessen-Darmstadts,* pp. 94–95; Karl Georg Bockenheimer, *Mainz in den Jahren 1870 und 1871* (Mainz, 1909), pp. 14–17.

83. Bamberger to Lasker, February 19, 1871, Lasker Nachlass, Potsdam; Bamberger to Anna, February 25, March 5, 9, 10, 14, 1871, Bamberger Nachlass, Berlin-Dahlem; *MZ,* March 7, 1871; Götz, *Die Stellung Hessen-Darmstadts,* pp. 95–96.

84. Bamberger to Lasker, December 4, 1872, July 27, September 3, 1873, Lasker Nachlass, Potsdam; Bamberger to Anna, December 10, 1872, Bamberger Nachlass, Berlin-Dahlem.

85. Bamberger to Lasker, September 20, November 2, 6, December 2, 18, 1873, Lasker Nachlass, Potsdam; *MZ,* September 28, December 11, 1873.

86. A. Philipps, ed., *Die Reichstagswahlen von 1867 bis 1883* (Berlin, 1883), p. 165; Fritz Specht, *Die Reichstagswahlen von 1867 bis 1897* (Berlin, 1898), pp. 326–27; Wacker, *Entwicklung der Sozialdemokratie,* pp. 339–40; Helmut Neubach, "Die Mainzer Reichstagsabgeordneten von 1871 bis 1918," *Mainzer Almanach, 1969* (Mainz, 1969), pp. 9–15; Bamberger to his mother, December 25, 1876, June 13, 1878, Bamberger Nachlass, Berlin-Dahlem; Bamberger to Oppenheim, January 26, 1874, Bamberger Nachlass, Potsdam.

CHAPTER 4. FINANCIAL UNITY

1. Barth, "Ludwig Bamberger," p. 17; Karl Helfferich, *Ludwig Bamberger als Währungspolitiker* (Berlin, 1900), p. 32.

2. Bamberger to Anna, March 31, 1873, Bamberger Nachlass, Berlin-Dahlem; Bamberger, *Erinnerungen*, pp. 224–33, 246–50; Helfferich, *Ludwig Bamberger*, pp. 2–12.

3. Karl Helfferich, *Money*, trans. Louis Infield, 2 vols. (New York, 1927), I:121–38; Manfred Seeger, *Die Politik der Reichsbank von 1876–1914 im Lichte der Spielregeln der Goldwährung*, Volkswirtschaftliche Schriften, CXXV (Berlin, 1968), p. 71.

4. Helfferich, *Money*, I:138–39; Bamberger, "Die Gold und Silberfrage," *Deutsche Jahrbücher für Politik und Literatur*, I (1861):78–89; Helfferich, *Ludwig Bamberger*, pp. 22–25.

5. Helfferich, *Money*, I:137–46; Bamberger *Die Schicksale des Lateinischen Münzbundes* (Berlin, 1885), pp. 10–14.

6. Helfferich, *Ludwig Bamberger*, pp. 25, 30; idem, *Geschichte der deutschen Geldreform* (Leipzig, 1898), pp. 4–123; Bamberger, *Zur deutschen Münzgesetzgebung* (Berlin, 1872), p. 21; idem, "Adolph Soetbeer," *GS*, II:255–62; Ludolf Grambow, *Die deutsche Freihandelspartei zur Zeit ihrer Blüte* (Jena, 1903), pp. 215–24; Ernst Flotow, "The Congress of German Economists, 1858–1885: A Study in German Unification" (Ph.D. dissertation, American University, 1941), p. 21; Bamberger to Anna, December 13, 1872, Bamberger Nachlass, Berlin-Dahlem.

7. Helfferich, *Ludwig Bamberger*, pp. 28–30; Helfferich, *Money*, I:149–52; *SBZP*, June 21, 1869, pp. 242–43, May 5, 1870, pp. 180–88; Bamberger, "Vertrauliche Briefe aus dem Zollparlament," pp. 170–80.

8. Ziekursch, *Politische Geschichte*, II:287–89; Helfferich, *Money*, I:153–56.

9. *SBR*, 1 LP, 2 S, 1871, *Anlagen*, no. 50, pp. 123–24.

10. Bamberger, *Zur deutschen Münzgesetzgebung*, pp. 16–17; idem, "Die Entthronung eines Weltherrschers," *GS*, IV:317–18, 322, 332, 358, 376; idem, *Reichsgold* (Leipzig, 1876), pp. 29–40, 50; *SBR*, 1 LP, 2 S, November 18, 1871, p. 361; Helfferich, *Ludwig Bamberger*, pp. 30, 36.

11. *SBR*, 1 LP, 2 S, November 11, 1871, pp. 227–33; Bamberger to Anna, November 12, 1871, Bamberger Nachlass, Berlin-Dahlem.

12. *SBR*, 1 LP, 2 S, November 11, 13, 1871, pp. 233–62.

13. Helfferich, *Ludwig Bamberger*, pp. 32, 42; idem, *Geschichte der deutschen Geldreform*, pp. 157–77; Bamberger to Anna, October 17, November 8, 14, 1871, Bamberger Nachlass, Berlin-Dahlem.

14. *SBR*, 1 LP, 2 S, November 17, 1871, pp. 317–39.

15. *SBR*, 1 LP, 2 S, November 18, 1871, pp. 341–49, *Anlagen*, no. 89IV, p. 215.

16. *SBR*, 1 LP, 2 S, November 18, 1871, pp. 355–57, *Anlagen*, no. 91, p. 217.

17. *SBR*, 1 LP, 2 S, November 18, 1871, pp. 358–61, *Anlagen*, no. 89, p. 215, no. 91, p. 217.

18. Bamberger to Anna, November 18, 1871, Bamberger Nachlass, Berlin-Dahlem.

19. Bamberger to Anna, November 24, 1871, Bamberger Nachlass, Berlin-Dahlem.

20. *SBR*, 1 LP, 2 S, November 23, 1871, pp. 453–59; Helfferich, *Ludwig Bamberger*, pp. 39–47; idem, *Geschichte der deutschen Geldreform* pp. 177–92, 224; Walther Lotz, *Geschichte und Kritik des deutschen Bankgesetzes von 14 März 1875* (Leipzig, 1888), p. 147; Seeger, *Die Politik der Reichsbank*, p. 18.

21. *SBR*, 1 LP, 2 S, November 18, 23, 1871, pp. 361–62, 461; *SBR*, 1 LP, 3 S, June 13, 1872, pp. 962–66; Lotz, *Geschichte und Kritik*, pp. 141–42.

22. *SBR*, 1 LP, 4 S, 1873, *Anlagen*, no. 15, pp. 70–72.

23. *SBR*, 1 LP, 4 S, March 28, 1873, pp. 118–27; Bamberger to Anna, March 27, 31, 1873, Bamberger Nachlass, Berlin-Dahlem.

24. *SBR*, 1 LP, 4 S, March 28, 29, 1873, pp. 128–55.
25. *SBR*, 1 LP, 4 S, May 6, 1873, pp. 525–26, *Anlagen*, no. 90 Iab, p. 431.
26. *SBR*, 1 LP, 4 S, April 22, 24, 1873, pp. 241–305, *Anlagen*, nos. 40, 45, pp. 181, 234.
27. *SBR*, 1 LP, 4 S, April 24, May 8, 1873, pp. 305–11, 538–47, *Anlagen*, nos. 40, 89, pp. 181, 450; Helfferich, *Geschichte der deutschen Geldreform*, pp. 218–24; idem, *Ludwig Bamberger*, pp. 50–52.
28. Helfferich, *Geschichte der deutschen Geldreform*, pp. 237–40.
29. *SBR*, 1 LP, 4 S, 1873, *Anlagen*, nos. 32, 44, 49, pp. 160, 234, 235–36.
30. *SBR*, 1 LP, 4 S, April 25, 1873, pp. 324–39; Helfferich, *Geschichte der deutschen Geldreform*, pp. 240–41; Bamberger to Anna, April 27, 1873, Bamberger Nachlass, Berlin-Dahlem.
31. Helfferich, *Geschichte der deutschen Geldreform*, pp. 242–45; *SBR*, 1 LP, 4 S, May 8, 1873, pp. 560–66.
32. *SBR*, 1 LP, 4 S, May 8, 1873, pp. 566–69; Bamberger to Anna, May 10, 1873, Bamberger Nachlass, Berlin-Dahlem.
33. Helfferich, *Geschichte der deutschen Geldreform*, pp. 245–49.
34. Ibid., pp. 249–54.
35. Bamberger, *Bismarcks grosses Spiel*, pp. 305–08.
36. *SBR*, 1 LP, 4 S, June 23, 1873, pp. 1352–64, *Anlagen*, no. 220, p. 1026.
37. Helfferich, *Geschichte der deutschen Geldreform*, pp. 258–62.
38. Ibid., pp. 262–68.
39. Bamberger, "Die fünf Milliarden," *GS*, V:219–49; *SBR*, 1 LP, 4 S, April 24, 1873, pp. 334–55, *Anlagen*, no. 49, p. 236; *SBR*, 2 LP, 4 S, December 6, 1876, pp. 622–28; Helfferich, *Ludwig Bamberger*, pp. 77–87.
40. *SBR*, 2 LP, 1 S, March 26, 1874, pp. 557–68.
41. Ibid., pp. 568–75; Bamberger to Anna, March 26, 1874, Bamberger Nachlass, Berlin-Dahlem.
42. Helfferich, *Geschichte der deutschen Geldreform*, pp. 268–71.
43. *SBR*, 2 LP, 1 S, March 28, 1874, pp. 652–56.
44. *SBR*, 2 LP, 1 S, March 28, April 18, 1874, pp. 652–64, 923–42, *Anlagen*, nos. 130, 131, 132, 140, 142, pp. 415, 421; Bamberger to Anna, March 29, April 9, 1874, Bamberger Nachlass, Berlin-Dahlem.
45. *SBR*, 2 LP, 1 S, April 18, 1874, pp. 942–45.
46. Ibid., pp. 945–46; Helfferich, *Geschichte der deutschen Geldreform*, pp. 273–75.
47. Erich Achterberg, "Ludwig Bamberger," in his *Lebensbilder deutscher Bankiers aus fünf Jahrhunderten* (Frankfurt, 1963), pp. 208–09; Helfferich, *Ludwig Bamberger*, p. 10; Bamberger, *Erinnerungen*, pp. 224–65.
48. Bamberger to Anna, January 14, February 5, 1870, Bamberger Nachlass, Berlin-Dahlem; Adalbert Delbrück to Bamberger, June 19, 1870, Bamberger Nachlass, Potsdam; Hans Weber, *Der Bankplatz Berlin* (Cologne and Opladen, 1957), pp. 60–76; Helfferich, *Georg von Siemens*, I:212–25; Bamberger, *Erinnerungen*, p. 385.
49. *SBR*, 2 LP, 2 S, 1874–75, *Anlagen*, no. 27, pp. 652–90.
50. Bamberger, *Die Zettelbank vor dem Reichstag* (Leipzig, 1874), passim; Bamberger to his mother, November 26, 1875, Bamberger Nachlass, Berlin-Dahlem; Bamberger to Karl Hillebrand, November 19, 1874, Bamberger Nachlass, Potsdam; Achterberg, "Ludwig Bamberger," pp. 195–97; Helfferich, *Ludwig Bamberger*, pp. 63–65; idem, *Georg von Siemens*, III:163–64.

51. *SBR*, 1 LP, 2 S, June 13, 1872, pp. 962–66; Lotz, *Geschichte und Kritik*, pp. 141–43; Bamberger, "Zur Embryologie des Bankgesetzes," *GS*, IV:259–67; Ziekursch, *Politische Geschichte*, II:289.

52. Lotz, *Geschichte und Kritik*, pp. 156–61.

53. Ibid., p. 163; Bamberger, "Zur Embryologie," p. 253.

54. Bamberger to Oppenheim, September 3, 15, 23, October 16, 23, November 24, 29, 1874, Bamberger Nachlass, Potsdam.

55. *SBR*, 2 LP, 2 S, 1874–75, *Anlagen*, no. 27, pp. 648–52; Helfferich, *Geschichte der deutschen Geldreform*, pp. 276–88; Lotz, *Geschichte und Kritik*, pp. 165–80.

56. *SBR*, 2 LP, 2 S, November 16, 1874, pp. 149–53.

57. Ibid., pp. 154–64.

58. Ibid., pp. 164–72.

59. The rest of the long first reading can be followed in *SBR*, 2 LP, 2 S, November 17, 18, 1873, pp. 175–234; Lotz, *Geschichte und Kritik*, pp. 182–92.

60. *SBR*, 2 LP, 2 S, 1874-75, *Anlagen*, no. 195, pp. 1147–76. Between the first and second readings Bamberger wrote "On the Embryology of the Bank Law," which argued for an imperial bank and stressed the opposition from the Prussian minister of finance.

61. *SBR*, 2 LP, 2 S, January 25, 26, 1875, pp. 1268–1314; Bamberger, "Zur Geburt des Bankgesetzes," *GS*, IV:287–88, 291–92. Even Lasker opposed Bamberger.

62. Helfferich, *Geschichte der deutschen Geldreform*, pp. 296–97.

63. Ibid., pp. 297–99; *SBR*, 2 LP, 2 S, January 26, 1875, pp. 1319–27.

64. Helfferich, *Georg von Siemens*, III:163; *SBR*, 2 LP, 2 S, January 28, 1875, pp. 1371–89; *SBR*, 2 LP, 2 S, 1874–75, *Anlagen*, no. 217, pp. 1276–77; Bamberger, "Zur Geburt des Bankgesetzes," pp. 279–80, 295–302.

65. *SBR*, 2 LP, 2 S, January 30, 1875, pp. 1450–52; Bamberger to his mother, February 1, 1875, Bamberger Nachlass, Berlin-Dahlem.

66. Bamberger, "Zur Geburt des Bankgesetzes," pp. 305–06, and "Zur Embryologie des Bankgesetzes," pp. 275–76.

67. Lucius von Ballhausen, *Bismarck Erinnerungen*, p. 122.

68. Bamberger to Anna, November 3, 1871, Bamberger Nachlass, Berlin-Dahlem.

69. Helfferich, *Geschichte der deutschen Geldreform*, p. 175, and *Ludwig Bamberger*, pp. 53–54; Lotz, *Geschichte und Kritik*, pp. 139, 255, 258, 277–83; Achterberg, "Ludwig Bamberger," pp. 193, 198; Bamberger, *Reichsgold*, p. 81; Seeger, *Die Politik der Reichsbank*, pp. 12, 16, 20, 83; Karl Fürstenberg, *Lebensgeschichte eines deutschen Bankiers* (Berlin, 1931), pp. 74–76. Looking back fourteen years later, Bamberger was still pleased with the Reichsbank (Bamberger, "Die Reichsbank," *GS*, V:227–37).

70. Bamberger, "Die Entthronung eines Weltherrschers" and "Das Gold der Zukunft," *GS*, IV:311–438; idem, *Reichsgold*, pp. 198–99 and passim; idem, "Zur Geburt des Bankgesetzes," pp. 305–07.

71. Bamberger to Hillebrand, May 10, 1875, Bamberger Nachlass, Potsdam.

CHAPTER 5. THE 1870S: VICTORIES WITHOUT TRIUMPH

1. Ernst Fraenkel, "Historische Vorbelastungen des deutschen Parlamentarismus," *Vierteljahrshefte für Zeitgeschichte*, VIII, no. 4 (1960):323–40; Reinhard J. Lamer, *Der englische Parlamentarismus in der deutschen politischen Theorie im Zeitalter Bismarcks, 1857–1890,* Historische Studien, CCCLXXXVII (Lubeck and Hamburg, 1963), pp. 111–16; Gall, *Liberalismus als regierende Partei*, pp. 24–28.

2. Bamberger, "Des Michael Pro Schriftenwechsel," pp. 168–70.

3. Ibid., pp. 185–88; idem, "Vertrauliche Briefe aus dem Zollparlament," p. 83.

4. Bamberger, "Die soziale Frage," in *Berthold Auerbachs deutscher Volkskalender für 1868* (Berlin, n.d.), p. 38; idem, *Alte Parteien und neue Zustände*, pp. 42–43.

5. Bamberger, "Vertrauliche Briefe aus dem Zollparlament," pp. 141, 146, 198.

6. *SBR*, 1 LP, 4 S, March 24, 1873, p. 66; *SBR*, 2 LP, 2 S, November 16, 1874, p. 154.

7. *SBR*, 1 LP, 1 S, April 19, 26, May 17, 1871, pp. 295, 401–08, 762–70; *SBR*, 3 LP, 1 S, May 3, 1877, p. 1016; Peter Molt, *Der Reichstag vor der improvisierten Revolution* (Cologne, 1963), p. 38; Gerhard Stoltenberg, *Der deutsche Reichstag, 1871–1873*, Beiträge zur Geschichte des Parlamentarismus und der politischen Parteien, VII (Dusseldorf, 1955), p. 59; Bamberger, *Erinnerungen*, p. 306.

8. Bamberger, "Kandidatenrede," pp. 29–30; *SBR*, 2 LP, 4 S, November 7, 1876, pp. 63–64; Bamberger to Lasker, September 20, 1871, Lasker Nachlass, Potsdam.

9. Bamberger, *Alte Parteien und neue Zustände*, p. 43.

10. Cited in *Mainzer Abendblatt*, November 25, 1868.

11. Oncken, *Rudolf von Bennigsen*, II:59.

12. Lenore O'Boyle, "Liberal Political Leadership in Germany, 1867–1884," *Journal of Modern History*, XXVIII (December 1956):338–45; Ziekursch, *Politische Geschichte*, II:286; Molt, *Der Reichstag*, pp. 185–97; Willy Kremer, *Der soziale Aufbau der Parteien des deutschen Reichstags von 1871–1918* (Emsdetten, 1934), pp. 13–24; Hans Gabler, *Die Entwicklung der deutschen Parteien auf landschaftlicher Grundlage von 1871–1912* (Tubingen, 1934), pp. 33-35; Thomas Nipperdey, *Die Organisation der deutschen Parteien vor 1918,* Beiträge zur Geschichte des Parlamentarismus und der politischen Parteien, XVIII (Dusseldorf, 1961), pp. 119–20, 158–63; Joachim Knoll, "Die Elitebildung im Liberalismus des Kaiserreiches" (Ph.D dissertation, Erlangen University, Erlangen, 1956), p. 239. A good sample of notable politics is offered by a letter from Bamberger to Lasker in which the former relates that Friedrich Techow, a National Liberal deputy, was ready to sell his estate and retire. Bamberger writes: "The election of the successor to his estate is an easily arranged consequence" (Bamberger to Lasker, June 10, 1868, Lasker Nachlass, Potsdam).

13. Bamberger to Lasker, March 7, 1870, Lasker Nachlass, Potsdam; Philippson, *Max von Forckenbeck*, pp. 204–06; Nipperdey, *Organisation der deutschen Parteien*, p. 120; Bamberger to Anna, January 24, 1870, December 1, 1871, April 24, May 1, December 18, 24, 1872, January 14, 26, February 7, June 6, 1873, Bamberger Nachlass, Berlin-Dahlem; Julius Rodenberg, "Ludwig Bamberger," *Deutsche Rundschau*, XCIX (May 1899):302; Poschinger, *Fürst Bismarck und die Parlamentarier*, II:26, 167; Lucius von Ballhausen, *Bismarck Erinnerungen*, pp. 23, 33; Bamberger, *Bismarcks grosses Spiel*, pp. 297–300, 302–03.

14. Barth, "Ludwig Bamberger." pp. 23–24.

15. Bamberger, *Alte Parteien und neue Zustände*, p. 39; idem, "Vertrauliche Briefe aus dem Zollparlament," pp. 445–46.

16. *SBR*, 5 LP, 4 S, May 12, 1884, p. 544; Bamberger "Über Kompromisse," *GS*, V:310–13.

17. Bamberger to Hillebrand, March 6, 1876, Bamberger Nachlass, Potsdam; emphasis is Bamberger's.

18. Philippson, *Max von Forckenbeck*, p. 191; Wilhelm Wehrenpfennig to Heinrich von Treitschke, November 6, December 25, 1868, March 17, December 23, 1869, in *DLZB*, I:430, 433–34, 439, 447.

19. Bamberger to Oppenheim, July 4, 23, 1869, Bamberger Nachlass, Potsdam; emphasis is Bamberger's. The reference to the Gothaer is to those liberals who thought more could be gained by cooperation with the existing Prussian leadership. Their slogan was "Don't push" (the government). See Bamberger's letter to Lasker, September 13, 1869, Lasker Nachlass, Potsdam, about getting rid of the "feeble old liberal two-bit nationals."

20. Philippson, *Max von Forckenbeck*, p. 219; Ziekursch, *Politische Geschichte*, II:217; Hermann Block, *Die parlamentarische Krisis der Nationalliberalen Partei, 1879–1880* (Munster, 1930), p. 17.

21. J. C. G. Röhl, "The Disintegration of the *Kartell* and the Politics of Bismarck's Fall from Power 1887–1890," *Historical Journal*, IX, no. 1 (1966):64.

22. Ernst R. Huber, *Heer und Staat* (Hamburg, 1938), pp. 255–59; Philippson, *Max von Forckenbeck*, pp. 168–73.

23. *MZ*, March 4, 1849; Oskar Stillich, *Die politischen Parteien in Deutschland II: Der Liberalismus* (Leipzig, 1911), pp. 74–78; Bamberger, "Kandidatenrede," p. 50; idem, "Vertrauliche Briefe aus dem Zollparlament," pp. 183–84; idem, *Bismarcks grosses Spiel*, p. 218.

24. On military matters Forckenbeck tended to support the government (Philippson, *Max von Forckenbeck*, p. 113).

25. Philippson, *Max von Forckenbeck*, pp. 227–28; Forckenbeck to his wife, November 24, December 3, 1871, in Martin Philippson, *Deutsche Revue*, XXIV (May 1899):166–67; Friedrich Böttcher, *Eduard Stephani* (Leipzig, 1887), pp. 125–26; Ernst Rohmer to Heinrich Marquardsen, December 3, 1871, Otto Elben to Eduard Lasker, December 11, 1871, Heinrich von Sybel to Herman Baumgarten, November 29, 1871, all in *DLZB*, II:33, 34; Bamberger to Anna, November 28, 1871, Bamberger Nachlass, Berlin-Dahlem.

26. *SBR*, 1 LP, 2 S, November 30, 1871, pp. 630–32.

27. Bamberger to Anna, December 1, 1871, Bamberger Nachlass, Berlin-Dahlem; emphasis is Bamberger's.

28. Bamberger to Oppenheim, December 26, [1869], Bamberger Nachlass, Potsdam; Bamberger to Anna, December 12, 1872, February 7, 14, 21, May 4, 1873, Bamberger Nachlass, Berlin-Dahlem; [Deutsche Bank] to Bamberger, February 10, 1873, Bamberger to Berthold Auerbach, [1873], Berthold Auerbach Nachlass, Deutsches Literaturarchiv, Schiller Nationalmuseum, Marbach; Bamberger, *Erinnerungen*, pp. 282–83.

29. Stauffenberg to Bamberger, May 31, 1873, Bamberger Nachlass, Potsdam; Stauffenberg to Heinrich Marquardsen, July 16, 1873, Wehrenpfennig to Treitschke, December 28, 1873, in *DLZB*, II:84–86, 97.

30. *SBR*, 2 LP, 1 S, February 16, 1874, pp. 71–79, 86–90.

31. Stauffenberg to Lasker, April 1, 1874, Lasker to Stauffenberg, April 3, 1874, in *DLZB*, II:101–04; Oncken, *Rudolf von Bennigsen*, II:259.

32. Oncken, *Rudolf von Bennigsen*, II:258; Lasker to Stauffenberg, April 3, 1874, in *DLZB*, II:102–04.

33. Oncken, *Rudolf von Bennigsen*, II:260–61; Felix Rachfahl, "Eugen Richter und der Linksliberalismus im neuen Reiche," *Zeitschrift für Politik*, V (1912):281–83; Böttcher, *Eduard Stephani*, pp. 138–43.

34. *SBR*, 2 LP, 1 S, April 13, 14, 1874, pp. 753–58, 794–97.

35. Bamberger to Anna, April 11, 17, 1874, Bamberger Nachlass, Berlin-Dahlem; emphasis is Bamberger's.

36. *SBR*, 2 LP, 1 S, March 18, April 24, 1874, pp. 415–16, 1103, 1114–16, 1145–46.

37. Stauffenberg to Lasker, June 28, 1874, in *DLZB*, II:107.

38. Bamberger, "Zur Physiologie des Reichstags," *AZ*, July 21, 1874, p. 3151.

39. Bamberger, "Vertrauliche Briefe aus dem Zollparlament," pp. 184–88; Bamberger to Oppenheim, July 16, 1871, Bamberger Nachlass, Potsdam.

40. Bamberger to Anna, November 4, 1871, Bamberger Nachlass, Berlin-Dahlem.

41. Bamberger to Anna, February 15, 18, 1872, Bamberger Nachlass, Berlin-Dahlem.

42. Bamberger to Anna, February 23, 1872, Bamberger Nachlass, Berlin-Dahlem.

43. Erich Schmidt-Volkmar, *Der Kulturkampf in Deutschland 1871–1890* (Gottingen, 1962), pp. 106–11; *SBR*, 1 LP, 3 S, June 14, 17, 19, 1872, pp. 1001–28, 1059–95, 1123–50.

44. Busch, *Tagebuchblätter*, II:366.

45. *SBR*, 1 LP, 3 S, June 19, 1872, pp. 1123–26; Karl Biedermann to Lasker, June 12, 1872, Lasker to Oppenheim, July 1, 1872, in *DLZB*, II:53–54, 55.

46. Otto Georgi to Heinrich von Treitschke, May 10, 1872, in *DLZB*, II:50–51; *MZ*, July 1, 2, 1873; Bamberger, "Der Genius des Reichskanzlers und der Genius des Reichstags," and "Die Motive der liberalen Opposition gegen das Jesuitengesetz," *Die Gegenwart*, July 6, 1872, pp. 1–3, June 22, 1872, pp. 337–38; Oppenheim to Lasker, July 4, 1872, in *DLZB*, II:55–56.

47. Bamberger to Anna, May 28, 1873, Bamberger Nachlass, Berlin-Dahlem; Bamberger, "Zur Physiologie des Reichstags," *AZ*, July 21, 1874, p. 3151; Bamberger to Oppenheim, March 6, 1875, Bamberger Nachlass, Potsdam. The Center party won 23 percent of the seats in the 1874 election.

48. Karl Aegidi to Bamberger, March 22, 1875, Bamberger Nachlass, Potsdam.

49. Bamberger, *Bismarcks grosses Spiel*, pp. 313–14.

50. Konrad Listmann to Lasker, January 6, 1875, Oppenheim to Lasker, November 10, 1875, Karl Friedrich to August Lamey, February 1, 1876, Forckenbeck to Lasker, February 18, 1876, in *DLZB*, II:115–16, 137, 145; Bamberger, *Bismarcks grosses Spiel*, pp. 314–15; Lucius von Ballhausen, *Bismarck Erinnerungen*, p. 80; Bamberger to Oppenheim, July 6, 1876, Bamberger Nachlass, Potsdam; Bamberger to his mother, January 9, 1876, Bamberger Nachlass, Berlin-Dahlem; Bamberger to Hillebrand, March 6, 1876, Bamberger Nachlass, Potsdam. As with the military bill, Lasker regarded the December 1876 compromise over the judicial reform bill as a great liberal victory (Lasker's memorandum, December 24, 1876, Leopold von Winter to Lasker, December 27, 1876, in *DLZB*, II:163–65).

51. On Delbrück, see Rudolf Morsey, *Die oberste Reichsverwaltung unter Bismarck, 1867–1890* (Munster, 1957), pp. 40–84. Helmut Böhme treats Delbrück's activities on the commercial front *(Deutschlands Weg zur Grossmacht* [Cologne and Berlin, 1966], passim). Lucius von Ballhausen, *Bismarck Erinnerungen*, pp. 76–78, 86–88.

52. Bamberger, *Bismarcks grosses Spiel*, pp. 314, 317, 319.

53. The reference is to the crisis of 1875 with France which gave birth to the "Ist Krieg in Sicht?" ("Is War in Sight?") article in *Die Post*. Bamberger was extremely critical of the entire affair and viewed it as artificially stimulated in order to find an excuse for another round with France since she was recovering too quickly. He was even more upset by the outburst of German national sentiment which to him seemed to cry for war (Bamberger, *Bismarcks grosses Spiel*, pp. 310–13; Bamberger to Hillebrand, May 10, 1875, Bamberger Nachlass, Potsdam).

54. Bamberger to Oppenheim, May 5, 1876, Bamberger Nachlass, Potsdam; Morsey, *Die oberste Reichsverwaltung*, pp. 84–104.

55. *SBR*, 2 LP, 3 S, November 22, 1875, pp. 248–53.

56. For the background to the "candidacy" and Bismarck's plans, see Dietrich Sandberger, *"Die Ministerkandidatur Bennigsens,"* Historische Studien, CLXXXVII (Berlin, 1929), pp. 7–56.

57. Adalbert Wahl, *Deutsche Geschichte von der Reichsgründung bis zum Ausbruch des Weltkriegs (1871 bis 1914)*, 4 vols. (Stuttgart, 1926–36), I:74–82; Alfred von der Leiden, *Die Eisenbahnpolitik des Fürsten Bismarck* (Berlin, 1914), pp. 95–129.

58. Bamberger to Hillebrand, March 6, 1876, Bamberger Nachlass, Potsdam.

59. Heinrich von Poschinger, ed., *Erinnerungen aus dem Leben von Hans Viktor von Unruh* (Stuttgart, 1895), pp. 351–53; Bamberger to Oppenheim, May 5, 1876, Bamberger to Lasker, August 4, 1876, Bamberger Nachlass, Potsdam; Bamberger, "Ein Rundschreiben, welches der Präsident des Reichseisenbahnamtes an die deutschen Bahnverwaltungen erlassen sollte," *Die Gegenwart*, August 12, 1876, pp. 97–98.

60. *SBR*, 2 LP, 4 S, *Anlagen*, no. 95, pp. 781–82; *SBR*, 2 LP, 4 S, December 12, 1876, pp. 740–47, 847–48.

61. *SBR*, 2 LP, 4 S, December 12, 1876, p. 748.

62. *SBR*, 3 LP, 1 S, March 15, April 23, 27, 1877, pp. 182, 692–703, 831–33; Lucius von Ballhausen, *Bismarck Erinnerungen*, p. 99.

63. Bamberger, *Bismarcks grosses Spiel*, p. 326.

64. Ibid., pp. 320, 322.

65. Ibid., pp. 320–21; Sandberger, *"Die Ministerkandidatur Bennigsens,"* pp. 50–51.

66. Bamberger to Forckenbeck, February 19, 1877, Forckenbeck Nachlass, Deutsches Zentralarchiv, Merseburg; Forckenbeck to Bamberger, November 9, 15, 1877, Bamberger Nachlass, Potsdam; Philippson, *Max von Forckenbeck*, pp. 282–86; *MZ*, November 29, 1877.

67. Sandberger firmly believes in its reality.

68. Sandberger, *"Die Ministerkandidatur Bennigsens,"* pp. 79–88; Oncken, *Rudolf von Bennigsen*, II:317–21.

69. Bamberger, *Bismarcks grosses Spiel*, pp. 326–27; Bamberger to Forckenbeck, November 24, 1877, Forckenbeck Nachlass; Bennigsen to Bamberger, January 15, 1878, Bamberger Papers, New York. The emphasis is Bamberger's.

70. Böttcher, *Eduard Stephani*, pp. 260–61. Sandberger accepts this but places the date as February 29, 1881, by which time Forckenbeck had already left the party (*"Die Ministerkandidatur Bennigsens,"* pp. 107–08). Oncken believes this view to be exaggerated (*Rudolf von Bennigsen*, II:328–29).

71. Bamberger, *Bismarcks grosses Spiel*, pp. 327–28.

72. Bamberger to Stauffenberg, July 28, 1898, Stauffenberg Nachlass, Potsdam.

73. Stauffenberg to Bamberger, November 15–16, 1898, Bamberger Nachlass, Potsdam; Bamberger, *Bismarck posthumus* (Berlin, 1899), p. 8.

74. Oncken, *Rudolf von Bennigsen*, II:330–42, 346; Sandberger, *"Die Ministerkandidatur Bennigsens,"* pp. 115–26, 127–39.

75. Schmidt-Volkmar, *Der Kulturkampf*, pp. 219–25; Lucius von Ballhausen, *Bismarck Erinnerungen*, pp. 132–33; Erich Eyck, *Bismarck*, III:215–16.

76. Sandberger, *"Die Ministerkandidatur Bennigsens,"* pp. 151–59.

77. Bamberger, *Bismarcks grosses Spiel*, p. 328.

78. Poschinger, *Bismarck und die Parlamentarier*, II:268–70.

79. Morsey, *Die oberste Reichsverwaltung,* pp. 293–97, 302–08; Böttcher, *Eduard Stephani,* p. 201; *SBR,* 3 LP, 2 S, March 9, 1878, p. 418.

80. Bismarck to Arthur Hobrecht, Prussian finance minister, May 25, 1878, as cited in Böhme, *Deutschlands Weg zur Grossmacht,* p. 502; Lucius von Ballhausen, *Bismarck Erinnerungen,* p. 138; Philippson, *Max von Forckenbeck,* p. 297.

CHAPTER 6. ANTISOCIALISM

1. Bamberger, *Bismarcks grosses Spiel,* p. 319.

2. Bamberger, "Des Michael Pro Schriftenwechsel," pp. 188–89.

3. Ibid., p. 199; H. B. Oppenheim, "Zur Kritik der Demokratie," in his *Vermischte Schriften,* pp. 29–32.

4. H. B. Oppenheim, "Frankreich und England," in his *Vermischte Schriften,* pp. 74, 78.

5. H. B. Oppenheim, "Die Lassallesche Bewegung im Frühjahre 1863," in his *Vermischte Schriften,* pp. 207–09, 214.

6. Bamberger, "Die soziale Frage," pp. 21–25, 27–28.

7. Bamberger, "Kandidatenrede," pp. 47–49, *MZ,* February 29, March 13, 1868.

8. *Mainzer Abendblatt,* November 30, 1868; Bamberger to Oppenheim, November 19, 1867, Bamberger Nachlass, Potsdam.

9. Bamberger to Oppenheim, July 29, 1869, June 17, 1870, Bamberger Nachlass, Potsdam; Morgan, *German Social Democrats,* pp. 178–79, 199–203, 210.

10. Bamberger to Anna, March 20, 22, 1871, Bamberger Nachlass, Berlin-Dahlem; Bamberger, *Die erste Sitzungsperiode des ersten deutschen Reichstags* (Leipzig, 1871), pp. 33–34; *Mainzer Wochenblatt,* October 17, 1871.

11. Bamberger, "Zeitströmungen in der Wirtschaftslehre," *AZ* (Beilage), October 7, 8, 1872, December 27, 1873.

12. Bamberger, "Ein Deutscher Beitrag zur Geschichte der Commune," *Deutsche Rundschau,* XVIII (1879):477, 483.

13. For a more detailed treatment of the following section the reader is referred to Stanley Zucker, "Ludwig Bamberger and the Politics of the Cold Shoulder: German Liberalism's Response to Working Class Legislation in the 1870's," *European Studies Review,* II, no. 2 (1972):111–36.

14. Bamberger to Anna, April 24, 1872, Bamberger Nachlass, Berlin-Dahlem.

15. Bamberger, *Die Arbeiterfrage unter dem Gesichtspunkte des Vereinsrechtes* (Stuttgart, 1873).

16. On the success of his book see Bamberger to Anna, March 6, April 27, 1873, March 6, 1874, Bamberger Nachlass, Berlin-Dahlem.

17. Wolfgang Eras, "Der Kongress deutscher Volkswirte: seine Entstehung und seine IX Jahresversammlung," *Jahrbuch für Volkswirtschaft,* I (1868):138–64.

18. Gustav Schmoller, "Die Arbeiterfrage," *PJ,* XIV (1864):393–96, 412, 414–16, 423–24; Hans Gehrig, *Die Begründung des Prinzips der Sozialreform: eine literarhistorische Untersuchung über Manchestertum und Kathedersozialismus* (Jena, 1914), pp. 138, 143–49, 155–59; Fritz Völkerling, *Der deutsche Kathedersozialismus* (Berlin, 1959), p. 7; Abraham Ascher, "Professors as Propagandists: The Politics of the Kathedersozialisten," *Journal of Central European Affairs,* XXIII (October 1963):285; Else Conrad, *Der Verein für Sozialpolitik und seine Wirksamkeit auf dem Gebiet der gewer-*

blichen Arbeiterfrage (Jena, 1906), pp. 34–35; Gerhard Wittrock, *Der Kathedersozialisten bis zur Eisenacher Versammlung, 1872,* Historische Studien, CCCL (Berlin, 1939), pp. 19–31.

19. Conrad, *Verein für Sozialpolitik,* pp. 36–37; Evalyn A. Clark, "Adolf Wagner: From National Economist to National Socialist," *Political Science Quarterly,* LV (1940):395–97; Gehrig, *Begründung,* p. 174.

20. Conrad, *Verein für Sozialpolitik,* pp. 37–38, 39–41, 43–45; Grambow, *Deutsche Freihandelspartei,* pp. 68–71, 94–95; Gehrig, *Begründung,* pp. 165–69; Lujo Brentano to Gustav Schmoller, December 10, 31, 1870, January 31, 1871, January 12, August 1, 15, September 20, 28, 1872, in "Der Briefwechsel Gustav Schmollers mit Lujo Brentano," ed. Walter Goetz, *Archiv für Kulturgeschichte,* XXVIII (1938):340, 343–44, 346, 348, 350, XXIX (1939):150; hereafter cited as *AfK.*

21. Bamberger to Anna, May 1, 1872, Bamberger Nachlass, Berlin-Dahlem.

22. Franz Boese, *Geschichte des Vereins für Sozialpolitik 1872–1932* (Berlin, 1939), pp. 1–4; Gustav Schmoller to Heinrich von Sybel, July 29, 1872, Schmoller to Lasker, August 11, 1872, in *DLZB,* II:56–58.

23. Wittrock, *Die Kathedersozialisten,* pp. 198–99; Gustav Schmoller to Bamberger, August 11, 1872, Bamberger Nachlass, Potsdam.

24. Bamberger to Schmoller, draft, n.d., Bamberger Nachlass, Potsdam; Bamberger to Paul Lindau, September 12, 1872, Paul Lindau Nachlass, Bundesarchiv, Koblenz; Wittrock, *Die Kathedersozialisten,* p. 199.

25. Bamberger to Lasker, September 26, 1872, Lasker to Schmoller, n.d., in *DLZB,* II:60–61; Schmoller to Brentano, September 20, 1872, in "Briefwechsel," *AfK,* XXVIII (1938):351.

26. Boese, *Geschichte des Vereins,* pp. 6–12; Conrad, *Verein für Sozialpolitik,* pp. 58–67.

27. Bamberger, "Die Romantik auf dem Lehrstuhl der Volkswirtschaft," *Die Gegenwart,* October 5, 12, 1872, pp. 209–11, 228–30, and "Zeitströmungen," *AZ,* October 6–8, 1872.

28. Brentano to Schmoller, May 3, 1870, in "Briefwechsel," *AfK,* XXVIII (1938): 323; Lujo Brentano, "Die Gewerkvereine im Verhältnis zur Arbeitergesetzgebung," *PJ,* XXIX (1872):596–600; James J. Sheehan, *The Career of Lujo Brentano: A Study of Liberalism and Social Reform in Imperial Germany* (Chicago, 1966), pp. 25, 26–33, 35–36.

29. Bamberger, *Arbeiterfrage,* pp. 38–42, 56–60; idem, "Zeitströmungen," *AZ,* October 7, 8, 1872; idem, "Die Romantik auf dem Lehrstuhl der Volkswirtschaft," pp. 209–11, 228–30; Bamberger to Anna, April 27, 1873, Bamberger Nachlass, Berlin-Dahlem; Sheehan admits that Brentano allowed himself to be unduly influenced by the powerful and respectable Amalgamated Societies, which represented only a minority of the union movement, and that the unions were more militant than Brentano granted (*Career of Lujo Brentano,* pp. 43–45).

30. Brentano to Schmoller, August 5, 1871, January 4, August 10, 1877, October 27, 1878, in "Briefwechsel," *AfK,* XXVIII (1938):335, XXX (1940):170, 178, 200.

31. Brentano to Schmoller, August 1, 1872, Schmoller to Brentano, February 5, 1871, March 1, 1873, May 22, 1873, in "Briefwechsel," *AfK,* XXVIII (1938):329, 345, 346, XXIX (1939):167.

32. Brentano to Schmoller, February 14, 19, 21, March 8, 1873, in "Briefwechsel," *AfK,* XXIX (1939):162–64, 165; Lujo Brentano, *Mein Leben im Kampf um die soziale Entwicklung Deutschlands* (Jena, 1931), pp. 86–87.

33. Lujo Brentano, *Die wissenschaftliche Leistung des Herrn Ludwig Bamberger* (Leipzig, 1873); idem, *Mein Leben*, pp. 87–90; Sheehan, *Career of Lujo Brentano*, pp. 61–62; Brentano to Schmoller, May 22, November 17, 1873, in "Briefwechsel," *AfK*, XXIX (1939):167, 174.

34. Conrad, *Verein für Sozialpolitik*, pp. 47–49; Boese, *Geschichte des Vereins*, pp. 13–17.

35. Adalbert Hahn, *Die Berliner Revue: ein Beitrag zur Geschichte der konservativen Partei zwischen 1855 und 1875*, Historische Studien, CCXLI (Berlin 1934); Wolfgang Saile, *Hermann Wagener und sein Verhältnis zu Bismarck* (Tubingen, 1958); William O. Shanahan, *German Protestants Face the Social Question, 1815–1871* (Notre Dame, 1954), pp. 273–77, 377–78; Brentano to Schmoller, October 16, 1874, in "Briefwechsel," *AfK*, XXIX (1939):334.

36. Wittrock, *Die Kathedersozialisten*, pp. 121, 124–25, 151–57; Karl E. Born, *Staat und Sozialpolitik seit Bismarcks Sturz* (Wiesbaden, 1957), pp. 43–46; Brentano, *Mein Leben*, pp. 94–95; Sheehan, *Career of Lujo Brentano*, pp. 48–49, 63–64; Brentano to Schmoller, December 31, 1871, in "Briefwechsel," *AfK*, XXVIII (1938):343; Eugen Richter, *Im alten Reichstag*, 2 vols. in 1 (Berlin, 1894–96), I:100–01.

37. Bamberger, "Eisenach," *Die Gegenwart*, October 31, 1874, pp. 274–75; Bamberger to Oppenheim, August 9, September 15, 23, October 16, 19, 1874, Bamberger Nachlass, Potsdam; Isigrim *(sic)*, "Der Kathedersozialismus und Ludwig Bamberger," *Sozialistische Monatshefte*, I (1897):299–300; Bamberger, *Arbeiterfrage*, pp. 46–47.

38. *SBR*, 2 LP, 3 S, January 27, 1876, p. 964.

39. Brentano to Lasker, October 25, November 12, 21, 1875, January 30, 1876, in *DLZB*, II:137–39, 143–44; Brentano to Schmoller, January 30, 1876, in "Briefwechsel," *AfK*, XXX (1940):154–55.

40. Boese, *Geschichte des Vereins*, pp. 25–31; Brentano, *Mein Leben*, p. 96.

41. Sheehan, *Career of Lujo Brentano*, pp. 53–54, 75, 98–99.

42. A more detailed treatment of these factors can be found in Stanley Zucker, "Ludwig Bamberger and the Crisis of German Liberalism"(Ph.D. dissertation, University of Wisconsin, 1968), pp. 192–213; Bamberger, *Arbeiterfrage*, pp. 1–49.

43. Bamberger, *Arbeiterfrage*, pp. 47–49, and "Zeitströmungen," *AZ*, July 17, 1874.

44. Bamberger, "Die Motive der liberalen Opposition gegen das Jesuitengesetz," p. 338.

45. *SBR*, 2 LP, 3 S, 1875, *Anlagen*, pp. 468–69.

46. *SBR*, 2 LP, 3 S, December 3, 1875, pp. 385–87, 393–96.

47. *SBR*, 2 LP, 3 S, January 27, 1876, pp. 940–46.

48. Ibid., pp. 954–58.

49. *SBR*, 2 LP, 3 S, January 27, 1876, pp. 960–64; see also his speech in Ober Ingelheim, *MZ*, July 12, 1876. Lucius von Ballhausen reported that Bamberger's views harmonized with those of the right, although he did not dare to vote with them *(Bismarck Erinnerungen*, p. 82).

50. *SBR*, 2 LP, 3 S, February 9, 1876, p. 1331.

51. Bamberger, *Rede des Reichstagsabgeordneten Bamberger gehalten im Deutschen Reichsverein zu Dresden* (Berlin, 1876), pp. 9–10, 13–14.

52. Bamberger, *Rede . . . Reichsverein*, p. 16.

53. Speech in Sprendlingen, *MZ*, May 13, 1877.

54. Bamberger, *Deutschland und der Sozialismus* (Leipzig, 1878), p. vi. Bamberger's essay was reprinted in book form and quickly went through two editions.

55. Ibid., pp. 21–24, 34–36, 47–52.

56. Ibid., pp. 86–87.

57. Ibid., p. 18.

58. Ibid., pp. 26–29.

59. Ibid., p. 45.

60. Bamberger to his mother, April 13, 1878, Bamberger Nachlass, Berlin-Dahlem; Poschinger, *Fürst Bismarck und die Parlamentarier*, III:265, 268; Bamberger, "Fragen an die ewigen Sterne," pp. 82–83.

61. Bamberger, *Deutschland und der Sozialismus*, pp. v–vi.

62. For a recent treatment of Bismarck's motives during this period see Böhme, *Deutschlands Weg zur Grossmacht*, pp. 478–515.

63. Hans Rothfels, *Prinzipienfragen der Bismarckschen Sozialpolitik* (Konigsberg, 1929), p. 15; Wolfgang Pack, *Das parlamentarische Ringen um das Sozialistengesetz Bismarcks 1878–1890*, Beiträge zur Geschichte des Parlamentarismus und der politischen Parteien, XX (Dusseldorf, 1961), pp. 30–31; Poschinger, *Fürst Bismarck und die Parlamentarier*, II:278; Richter, *Im alten Reichstag*, II:61.

64. Lucius von Ballhausen, *Bismarck Erinnerungen*, p. 136.

65. Pack, *Das parlamentarische Ringen*, pp. 34–35.

66. *SBR*, 3 LP, 2 S, 1878, *Anlagen*, no. 274, pp. 1591–93.

67. Forckenbeck to Stauffenberg, May 17, 1878, in *DLZB*, II:193–94; Pack, *Das parlamentarische Ringen*, pp. 35–39.

68. Poschinger, *Fürst Bismarck und die Parlamentarier*, II:280; Otto Bähr to Friedrich Oetker, June 15, 1878, in *DLZB*, II:197–98.

69. *SBR*, 3 LP, 2 S, May 23, 24, 1878, pp. 1503–10, 1552–54.

70. Pack, *Das parlamentarische Ringen*, pp. 53–57; Paul Kampffmeyer and Bruno Altmann, *Vor dem Sozialistengesetz: Krisenjahre des Obrigkeitsstaates* (Berlin, 1928), pp. 167–76; Richard Lipinski, *Die Sozialdemokratie von ihren Anfängen bis zur Gegenwart*, 2 vols. (Berlin, 1928), II:27–34; Richter, *Im alten Reichstag*, II:70–73; Lucius von Ballhausen, *Bismarck Erinnerungen*, p. 140; Helmut Steinsdorfer, *Franz Freiherr Schenk von Stauffenberg als ein bayrischer und deutscher Politiker* (Munich, 1959), pp. 43–44; Robert von Benda to Rudolf von Bennigsen [mid-August 1878], in Hermann Oncken, "Aus den Briefen Rudolf von Bennigsens," *Deutsche Revue*, XXXII (August 1907): 150–51; Poschinger, *Fürst Bismarck und die Parlamentarier*, II:288.

71. Böhme, *Deutschlands Weg zur Grossmacht*, pp. 500, 533; Ivo Nikolai Lambi, *Free Trade and Protection in Germany, 1868–1879*, Vierteljahrschrift für Sozial- und Wirtschaftsgeschichte, XLIV (Wiesbaden, 1963), pp. 129–30; *SBR*, 4 LP, 2 S, June 11, 1879, pp. 2297–99. This election also provided the majority for Bismarck's protectionist program.

72. Böttcher, *Eduard Stephani*, pp. 217–18; the letters to Bennigsen are in Oncken, "Aus den Briefen," *Deutsche Revue*, XXXII (July–September, 1907):78–81, 147–48, and *DLZB*, II:196, 201–06, 207; Pack, *Das parlamentarische Ringen*, pp. 61–70.

73. Letter to the editor, *National Zeitung*, May 28, 1878.

74. Hajo Holborn, ed., *Aufzeichnungen und Erinnerungen aus dem Leben des Botschafters Joseph Maria von Radowitz*, 2 vols. (Berlin and Leipzig, 1925), II:15.

75. Bamberger to his mother, December 25, 1876, June 3, 1878, Bamberger Nachlass, Berlin-Dahlem; Bamberger to Oppenheim, October 2, 1876, June 4, 1878, Bamberger Nachlass, Potsdam.

76. *MZ*, June 20, 1878.

77. *MZ*, June 25, 1878; excerpts from his speech were printed in the *National Zeitung*, June 25, 1878.

78. *MZ*, July 27, 1878.

79. Bamberger to Oppenheim, July 16, 26, 1878, Bamberger Nachlass, Potsdam.
80. Bamberger to Oppenheim, July 26, 1878, Bamberger Nachlass, Potsdam.
81. *SBR*, 3 LP, 2 S, 1878, *Anlagen,* pp. 46–47, and *SBR,* 4 LP, 2 S, 1879, *Anlagen,* pp. 44–45, provide the election statistics.
82. Pack, *Das parlamentarische Ringen,* pp. 66–70, 74–76, 80. See Heinrich Rickert to Franz von Stauffenberg, July 15, 1878 (in *DLZB,* II:210–11) for a vivid description of National Liberal election problems.
83. Bamberger to Oppenheim, August 10, 1878, Bamberger Nachlass, Potsdam; Bamberger to Stauffenberg, August 13, 1878, Stauffenberg Nachlass.
84. *SBR,* 4 LP, 1 S, 1878, *Anlagen,* no. 4, pp. 2–3.
85. Bennigsen to Lasker, August 25, 1878, Bennigsen to his wife, September 15, 1878, in Oncken, "Aus den Briefen," *Deutsche Revue,* XXXII (August 1907) 151–55; Poschinger, *Fürst Bismarck und die Parlamentarier,* II:292–93; Johannes Miquel to Heinrich Rickert, September 3, 1878, in *DLZB,* II:222–23.
86. *SBR,* 4 LP, 1 S, September 16, 1878, pp. 38–50. Anna von Helmholtz, a spectator to the debate, wrote that "Bebel carried off the prize" (Siemens-Helmholtz, *Anna von Helmholtz,* I:226–27). Pack, *Das parlamentarische Ringen,* pp. 86–87.
87. *SBR,* 4 LP, 1 S, September 16, 1878, pp. 51–53.
88. Ibid., pp. 53–55.
89. Ibid., pp. 55–57.
90. *SBR,* 4 LP, 1 S, September 17, 1878, p. 60; Ferdinand Tönnies, *Der Kampf um das Sozialistengesetz 1878* (Berlin, 1929), pp. 21–23, 71.
91. *SBR,* 4 LP, 1 S, September 17, 1878, p. 90.
92. *SBR,* 4 LP, 1 S, 1878, *Anlagen,* no. 23, pp. 109–16.
93. Pack, *Das parlamentarische Ringen,* pp. 94–100; Richter, *Im alten Reichstag,* II:78–79; Lucius von Ballhausen, *Bismarck Erinnerungen,* pp. 143–45; Poschinger, *Fürst Bismarck und die Parlamentarier,* II:294, 297–301; Bennigsen to Bismarck, October 10, 1878, in Oncken, "Aus den Briefen," *Deutsche Revue,* XXXII (August 1907):155.
94. *SBR,* 4 LP, 1 S, October 9, 10, 1878, pp. 128–30, 169–70.
95. *SBR,* 4 LP, 1 S, October 12, 1878, pp. 207–23; Pack, *Das parlamentarische Ringen,* pp. 106–11.
96. *SBR,* 4 LP, 1 S, October 12, 1878, pp. 225–28.
97. Ibid., pp. 228–30.
98. Ernst Schraepler, *Quellen zur Geschichte der sozialen Fragen in Deutschland,* 2 vols. (Berlin, 1955, 1957), I:18, 74–82, II:3–4, 39–41; Roman Muziol, *Karl Rodbertus als Begründer der sozialrechtlichen Anschauungsweise* (Jena, 1927), pp. 68–97.
99. *SBR,* 4 LP, 1 S, October 12, 1878, pp. 230–32.
100. *SBR,* 4 LP, 1 S, October 18, 19, 1878, pp. 354–59, 387–89.
101. Brentano, *Mein Leben,* p. 122; Ziekursch, *Politische Geschichte,* II:345.
102. Bamberger to Auerbach, October 7, 1878, Auerbach Nachlass.
103. Bamberger, *Die kulturgeschichtliche Bedeutung des Sozialistengesetzes* (Leipzig, 1878), pp. 6, 7–8; see also his "Ein deutscher Beitrag zur Geschichte der Commune," pp. 477–78, 483.
104. Lipinski, *Die Sozialdemokratie,* II:39–44; Franz Osteroth and Dieter Schuster, *Chronik der deutschen Sozialdemokratie* (Hanover, 1963), pp. 59–62; Pack, *Das parlamentarische Ringen,* pp. 115, 116; Vernon L. Lidtke, *The Outlawed Party: Social Democracy in Germany, 1878–1890* (Princeton, 1966), p. 85.
105. *SBR,* 4 LP, 3 S, March 6, 1880, pp. 306–07; Pack, *Das parlamentarische Ringen,* pp. 122–29.

CHAPTER 7. PROTECTIVE TARIFFS AND SECESSION

1. Bamberger to Oppenheim, July 16, 1878, Bamberger Nachlass, Potsdam; Bamberger, *Bismarcks grosses Spiel*, p. 273; Bamberger [Epimetheus], "Fürst Bismarck und die Liberalen," *Deutsche Rundschau*, XXXVI (September 1883):421.

2. Bamberger, "Fürst Bismarck und die Liberalen," pp. 424–34.

3. This is the theme of Böhme, *Deutschlands Weg zur Grossmacht*. It had been expressed much earlier by Walther Lotz (*Die Ideen der deutschen Handelspolitik von 1860–1891*, Schriften des Vereins für Sozialpolitik, L [Leipzig, 1892], pp. 7–8, 27–30).

4. Werner Schuncke, *Die preussischen Freihändler und die Entstehung der Nationalliberalen Partei*, p. 2; Lambi, *Free Trade and Protection in Germany*, pp. 1–4.

5. Flotow, "The Congress of German Economists," pp. 31–40, 46–57, 135–53; Lotz, *Ideen der deutschen Handelspolitik*, pp. 13–26; Grambow, *Deutsche Freihandelspartei*, pp. 1–15; Julius Becker, *Das deutsche Manchestertum* (Karlsruhe, 1907), pp. 65–78.

6. Lambi, *Free Trade and Protection*, p. 35; Flotow, "Congress of German Economists," pp. 65–71.

7. Bamberger, *Erinnerungen*, pp. 214–15.

8. Busch, *Tagebuchblätter*, I:77, 175, 241–42.

9. Bamberger, "Die Sezession," *GS*, V:121; idem, "Der wunde Punkt," *GS*, V:275.

10. *SBR*, 2 LP, 2 S, January 28, 1875, p. 1385; Bamberger, *Die Geschäftswelt angesichts der Geschäftslage in Deutschland* (Mainz, 1875), pp. 8–22; idem, *Deutschland und der Sozialismus*, pp. 90–91; Grambow, *Deutsche Freihandelspartei*, pp. 60–62.

11. Bamberger, "Reminiscenzen an Napoleon III," p. 53.

12. Bamberger, "Deutsches Bürgertum," *Die Nation*, September 27, 1884, p. 707.

13. Lotz, *Ideen der deutschen Handelspolitik*, pp. 90–97; Lambi, *Free Trade and Protection*, pp. 43–54.

14. *SBZP*, June 14, 1869, p. 64; Bamberger, "Vertrauliche Briefe aus dem Zollparlament," pp. 153–61; idem, *Die Aufhebung der indirekten Gemeindeabgaben in Belgien, Holland und Frankreich* (Berlin, 1871).

15. Lotz, *Ideen der deutschen Handelspolitik*, p. 91

16. *SBZP*, April 29, 1870, p. 47.

17. Lambi, *Free Trade and Protection*, pp. 19–22, 56–64.

18. Lotz, *Ideen der deutschen Handelspolitik*, pp. 102–10; Lambi, *Free Trade and Protection*, pp. 64–71.

19. *SBR*, 1 LP, 4 S, June 24, 1873, pp. 1391–92, 1411–12.

20. Lambi, *Free Trade and Protection*, p. 23; Böhme, *Deutschlands Weg zur Grossmacht*, pp. 341–59; Hans Rosenberg, *Grosse Depression und Bismarckzeit: Wirtschaftsablauf, Gesellschaft und Politik in Mitteleuropa* (Berlin, 1967), pp. 25–30, 38–51, 62–78.

21. Lotz, *Ideen der deutschen Handelspolitik*, p. 129.

22. Lambi, *Free Trade and Protection*, pp. 76–79; Lotz, *Ideen der deutschen Handelspolitik*, pp. 129–33; Böhme, *Deutschlands Weg zur Grossmacht*, p. 534.

23. Siegfried von Kardorff, *Wilhelm von Kardorff, ein nationaler Parlamentarier im Zeitalter Bismarcks und Wilhelms II* (Berlin, 1936), pp. 123–32; Lambi, *Free Trade and Protection*, pp. 84–96; Lotz, *Ideen der deutschen Handelspolitik*, pp. 120–21.

24. Lotz, *Ideen der deutschen Handelspolitik*, pp. 122–29; Lambi, *Free Trade and Protection*, pp. 97–105, 114–19, 125–26; Böhme, *Deutschlands Weg zur Grossmacht*, pp. 457–459; Karl W. Hardach, *Die Bedeutung wirtschaftlicher Faktoren bei der Wieder-*

einführung der Eisen- und Getreidezölle in Deutschland 1879, Schriften zur Wirtschafts- und Sozialgeschichte, VII (Berlin, 1967), p. 192; Bamberger to Oppenheim, August 8, 1876, Bamberger Nachlass, Potsdam.

25. Bamberger, *Die Geheimschriften,* pp. 6–10, idem, speech at Würstadt, September 25, 1875, *MZ,* October 6, 1875; *MZ,* July 12, 1876.

26. *SBR,* 2 LP, 3 S, December 7, 1875, pp. 450–55.

27. *SBZP,* April 29, 1870, p. 47.

28. Bamberger to Oppenheim, September 9, October 2, 1876, Bamberger Nachlass, Potsdam.

29. Lambi, *Free Trade and Protection,* pp. 150–57.

30. *SBR,* 2 LP, 4 S, December 5, 12, 1876, pp. 591–92, 740–47; *Anlagen,* no. 95, pp. 781–82.

31. *SBR,* 2 LP, 4 S, December 12, 13, 1876, pp. 737–68, 772–93.

32. *SBR,* 3 LP, 1 S, March 15, 1877, pp. 179–92.

33. *SBR,* 3 LP, 1 S, 1877, *Anlagen,* no. 123, pp. 367–68.

34. *SBR,* 3 LP, 1 S, April 21, 1877, pp. 657–60.

35. *SBR,* 3 LP, 1 S, April 23, 27, 1877, pp. 692–703, 831–35.

36. *SBR,* 3 LP, 1 S, April 27, 1877, pp. 838–42.

37. Lambi, *Free Trade and Protection,* pp. 190–206; Bamberger to Stauffenberg, August 19, 1878, in *DLZB,* II:218.

38. *SBR,* 3 LP, 2 S, May 14, 1878, pp. 1321–22.

39. Lambi, *Free Trade and Protection,* pp. 132–36.

40. Lotz, *Ideen der deutschen Handelspolitik,* pp. 138–43; Böhme, *Deutschlands Weg zur Grossmacht,* pp. 446–49, 456–71; Lambi, *Free Trade and Protection,* pp. 137–41; Hardach, *Bedeutung wirtschaftlicher Faktoren,* pp. 181, 194–95.

41. Lambi, *Free Trade and Protection,* pp. 34, 162; Bismarck's talk with Busch, February 24, 1879, *GW,* VIII:303.

42. Böhme, *Deutschlands Weg zur Grossmacht,* pp. 378–79, 410, 538.

43. Böhme, *Deutschlands Weg zur Grossmacht,* p. 502; Lambi, *Free Trade and Protection,* pp. 172, 180, 216; Bismarck's talk with Busch, February 24, 1879, *GW,* VIII:304.

44. Böhme, *Deutschlands Weg zur Grossmacht,* pp. 423–24, 432–34, 436, 474–79; Lambi, *Free Trade and Protection,* pp. 164–65.

45. Lambi, *Free Trade and Protection,* pp. 177–84; Hardach, *Bedeutung wirtschaftlicher Faktoren,* p. 155; Lotz, *Ideen der deutschen Handelspolitik,* pp. 155–60; Böhme, *Deutschlands Weg zur Grossmacht,* p. 509; Ludwig Männer, *Deutschlands Wirtschaft und Liberalismus in der Krise von 1879* (Berlin, 1928), pp. 22–40.

46. Bamberger, *Bismarck posthumus,* pp. 26–27; idem, *Bismarcks grosses Spiel,* pp. 330–31, 335–36; Bamberger, "Deutsches Bürgertum," pp. 708–09.

47. Poschinger, *Fürst Bismarck und die Parlamentarier,* II:304–05.

48. Böttcher, *Eduard Stephani,* p. 226; Philippson, *Max von Forckenbeck,* pp. 302–03, 315; Nipperdey, *Organisation der deutschen Parteien,* p. 165; Poschinger, *Fürst Bismarck und die Parlamentarier,* II:338.

49. *DLZB,* II:201–03, 228.

50. Forckenbeck to Stauffenberg, January 19, 1878, in *DLZB,* II:230–31.

51. Lambi, *Free Trade and Protection,* p. 43; Hardach, *Bedeutung wirtschaftlicher Faktoren,* pp. 173–75; Böhme, *Deutschlands Weg zur Grossmacht,* p. 551; Lucius von Ballhausen, *Bismarck Erinnerungen,* pp. 149–50, 154.

52. Schauss to Stauffenberg, August 24, 1878, Miquel to Bennigsen, December 26,

1878, February 13, 1879, Miquel to Rickert, February 16, 1879, in *DLZB*, II:219–20, 227, 232, 232–33.

53. Forckenbeck to Stauffenberg, January 19, 1879, in *DLZB*, II:230–31.

54. Bamberger to his mother, October 28, [1878], Bamberger Nachlass, Berlin-Dahlem.

55. Bamberger to his mother, November 19, 1878, Bamberger Nachlass, Berlin-Dahlem.

56. Bamberger to his mother, December 5, 1878, Bamberger Nachlass, Berlin-Dahlem.

57. This appears to be a reference to "Fürst Bismarck und die Liberalen," cited in chap. 7, n. 1.

58. Bamberger to Hillebrand, March 12, 1879, Bamberger Nachlass, Potsdam.

59. Bamberger to Oppenheim, n.d. [early 1879], Bamberger Nachlass, Potsdam.

60. Bamberger, *Das Schreiben des Reichskanzlers an den Bundesrat von 15. Dezember 1878 betreffend die Revision des Zolltarifs* (Berlin, 1879), and *Was uns der Schutzzoll bringt: ein Schreiben an seine rheinischen Wähler* (Berlin, 1879).

61. Schauss to Stauffenberg, August 24, 1878, in *DLZB*, II:219–20.

62. Bamberger, *Das Schreiben des Reichskanzlers*, pp. 13–16, 20, 28, 29, 30–32, 38, and *Was uns der Schutzzoll bringt*, pp. 13–14, 21–23, 34–35, 39.

63. Bamberger to his mother, January 20, 1879, Bamberger Nachlass, Berlin-Dahlem.

64. *SBR*, 4 LP, 2 S, February 20, 21, 1879, pp. 39–66.

65. *SBR*, 4 LP, 2 S, February 21, 1879, pp. 66–71.

66. For Bamberger's speeches see *SBR*, 4 LP, 2 S, March 1, 17, 28, 1879, pp. 237–43, 458–63, 472, 674–78.

67. Bamberger to his mother, March 7, 1879, Bamberger Nachlass, Berlin-Dahlem; Böhme agrees with Bamberger's evaluation of the composition and procedure of the investigating commissions (*Deutschlands Weg zur Grossmacht*, pp. 510–16).

68. Böhme, *Deutschlands Weg zur Grossmacht*, pp. 516–24, 530–55, 563; Lambi, *Free Trade and Protection*, pp. 182–89; Ernst Feder, *Theodor Barth und der demokratische Gedanke* (Gotha, 1919), pp. 12–14; Bamberger, *Bismarcks grosses Spiel*, p. 130; Hardach, *Bedeutung wirtschaftlicher Faktoren*, pp. 193–95.

69. Lambi, *Free Trade and Protection*, pp. 189–90. The chart of proposed and previous tariffs as well as the bill can be found in *SBR*, 4 LP, 2 S, 1879, *Anlagen*, no. 132, pp. 758–59, no. 132(B), pp. 848–900.

70. Poschinger, *Fürst Bismarck und die Parlamentarier*, I:187.

71. *SBR*, 4 LP, 2 S, May 2, 1879, pp. 927–32.

72. *SBR*, 4 LP, 2 S, May 3, 1879, pp. 932–41.

73. Ibid., pp. 943–50.

74. Ibid., pp. 951–64.

75. Bamberger to his mother, May 9, 1879, Bamberger Nachlass, Berlin-Dahlem.

76. *SBR*, 4 LP, 2 S, May 6, 8, 1879, pp. 1026–37, 1043–57.

77. *SBR*, 4 LP, 2 S, May 8, 1879, p. 1060.

78. *SBR*, 4 LP, 2 S, May 15, 16, 1879, pp. 1221–30, 1240–50.

79. *SBR*, 4 LP, 2 S, May 16, 1879, pp. 1269–74; Lambi, *Free Trade and Protection*, pp. 217–19.

80. *SBR*, 4 LP, 2 S, May 21, 23, 1879, pp. 1370–79, 1419–24.

81. Bamberger to Stauffenberg, May 24, 1879, in *DLZB*, II:235–36.

82. Bamberger to Lasker, February 10, 1879, Lasker Nachlass, Potsdam; Böttcher, *Eduard Stephani*, p. 244.

83. Karl Hilty to Eduard Lasker, May 15, 1879, in *DLZB*, II:234–35.

84. Bamberger to Stauffenberg, May 21, [1879], Stauffenberg Nachlass, Potsdam, filed under 1884.

85. Franz Fischer to Heinrich Kruse, May 21, 1879, Forckenbeck to Stauffenberg, May 24, June 3, 1879, Stauffenberg to Lasker, June 4, 1879, Rickert to Stauffenberg, June 6, 1879, Forckenbeck to Lasker, June 9, 1879, Lasker to Stauffenberg, June 29, 1879, in *DLZB*, II:235, 239–40, 241–42, 242–43, 246, 248.

86. Bamberger to Stauffenberg, June 5, 1879, in *DLZB*, II:241–42.

87. *SBR*, 4 LP, 2 S, July 9, 1879, pp. 2177–2214.

88. Bamberger to Stauffenberg, June 17, 1879, in *DLZB*, II:244–45; *SBR*, 4 LP, 2 S, July 10, 1879, pp. 2241–45.

89. Lasker to Stauffenberg, July 15, 1879, in *DLZB*, II:252–53.

90. *SBR*, 4 LP, 2 S, July 11, 1879, pp. 2297–99; Poschinger, *Fürst Bismarck und die Parlamentarier*, II:356.

91. Böhme, *Deutschlands Weg zur Grossmacht*, pp. 564–65, 570–74; Walter Vogel, *Bismarcks Arbeiterversicherung* (Braunschweig, 1951), pp. 30–31; Bamberger to Oppenheim, October 4, 1879, Bamberger Nachlass, Potsdam.

92. *MZ*, May 30, 1880.

93. *SBR*, 4 LP, 3 S, April 15, 1880, p. 707.

94. Bamberger to Lasker, July 23, [1879], Lasker Nachlass, Potsdam; Bamberger to Oppenheim, July 29, [1879], Bamberger Nachlass, Potsdam.

95. Bamberger to Oppenheim, August 6, 1879, Bamberger Nachlass, Potsdam.

96. Bamberger to Oppenheim, September 14, 1879, Bamberger Nachlass, Potsdam.

97. Bamberger to Oppenheim, September 17, October 4, 1879, Bamberger Nachlass, Potsdam; Morsey, *Die oberste Reichsverwaltung*, pp. 156–57.

98. Bamberger to Oppenheim, October 4, 1879, Bamberger Nachlass, Potsdam; *DLZB*, II:272–73, n. 1; Oppenheim to Lasker, August 30, 1879, *DLZB*, II:273–74.

99. Bamberger to Oppenheim, October 15, 1879, Bamberger Nachlass, Potsdam. For other signs of liberal despair, see Stauffenberg to Lasker, October 29, 1879, and Unruh to Lasker, October 10, 1879, in *DLZB*, II:277, 280.

100. Miquel to Bennigsen, October 3, 1879, Miquel to Benda, October 15, 25, 1879, in *DLZB*, II:275, 278, 279–80.

101. Rickert to Stauffenberg, January 4, 1880, Bamberger to Lasker, January 22, [1880], Stauffenberg to Lasker, January 28, February 4, 1880, Gustav Lipke to Stauffenberg, February 5, 1880, in *DLZB*, II:286–87, 289, 290–91, 292, 293–94; Philippson, *Max von Forckenbeck*, pp. 328–31; Bamberger to Lasker, February 23, [1880], Lasker Nachlass, Potsdam; Böttcher, *Eduard Stephani*, pp. 260–61.

102. See chapter 9 for a detailed treatment of Bamberger and colonialism.

103. Helfferich, *Ludwig Bamberger*, pp. 97–102.

104. *SBR*, 4 LP, 2 S, June 19, 1879, pp. 1709–26; Bamberger, "Silber," *GS*, V:373–76.

105. Bamberger to Oppenheim, August 6, 1879, Bamberger Nachlass, Potsdam.

106. Bamberger to Stauffenberg, March 12, 1880, in *DLZB*, II:300.

107. Bamberger to his mother, March 23, 1880, Bamberger Nachlass, Berlin-Dahlem; Forckenbeck to Stauffenberg, March 14, [1880], in *DLZB*, II:301–02. Lasker left the party on March 15, 1880.

108. Bamberger to Stauffenberg, March 19, 1880, Bamberger to Lasker, March 31, 1880, in *DLZB*, II:307, 312; Bamberger to Lasker, April 16, 1880, Lasker Nachlass, Potsdam; Philippson, *Max von Forckenbeck*, pp. 331–32.

109. *SBR*, 4 LP, 3 S, April 15, 16, 1880, pp. 701–08, 718, 737–39. There were more than three, in spite of Bamberger's statement to Stauffenberg's wife (Bamberger to Baroness von Stauffenberg, April 19, 1880, Stauffenberg Nachlass).

110. Bamberger to his mother, May 4, 1880, Bamberger Nachlass, Berlin-Dahlem.

111. Schmidt-Volkmar, *Kulturkampf in Deutschland,* pp. 265–67; Wahl, *Deutsche Geschichte,* II:222–27.

112. Block, *Die parlamentarische Krisis,* pp. 87–93.

113. Forckenbeck to Stauffenberg, July 4, 1880, Stauffenberg to Lasker, n.d. [July 1880], in *DLZB,* II:323–24.

114. Bamberger to Lasker, July 8, 1880, Lasker Nachlass, Potsdam; Bamberger to Lasker, July 14, 1880, in *DLZB,* II:326–27.

115. Bamberger to his mother, July 26, 1880, Bamberger Nachlass, Berlin-Dahlem; Gustav Lipke to Theodor Barth, August 8, 1880, in Feder, *Theodor Barth,* p. 16; Forckenbeck to Rickert, August 11, 1880, in Oncken, "Aus den Briefen,"*Deutsche Revue,* XXXIII (March 1908):284–86.

116. Rickert to Bennigsen, September 16, 1880, in Oncken, "Aus den Briefen," *Deutsche Revue,* XXXIII (March 1908):293–94; see also pp. 284–86, 292.

117. Philippson, *Max von Forckenbeck,* p. 341; Bamberger to Lasker, July 14, 1880, in *DLZB,* II:326.

118. Rickert to Lasker, July 29, August 5, 12, 16, 1880, in *DLZB,* II:334–36, 338–40, 343–44, 347–48; Rickert to Theodor Barth, July 16, 1880, in Feder, *Theodor Barth,* p. 16.

119. Bamberger to Stauffenberg, August 13, 1880, in *DLZB,* II:344.

120. In *DLZB,* II:356–57; Block, *Die parlamentarische Krisis,* pp. 34–35.

121. Bamberger to Lasker, September 7, 1880, Lasker Nachlass, Potsdam.

122. Bamberger to Hillebrand, September 12, 1880, Bamberger Nachlass, Potsdam; Bamberger to Lasker, December 12, 1880, in *DLZB,* II:372.

123. Bamberger to Stauffenberg, August 31, 1880, Bamberger to Lasker, December 1, 4, 1880, in *DLZB,* II:358, 372–73; Bamberger to his mother, December 17, 1880, Bamberger Nachlass, Berlin-Dahlem; Busch, *Tagebuchblätter,* III:12; Lucius von Ballhausen, *Bismarck Erinnerungen,* p. 191; Eyck, *Bismarck,* III:352.

124. Bamberger, "Sezession," pp. 64, 98–104.

125. Ibid., pp. 77, 82, 83, 115, 128, 132.

126. Bamberger to Hillebrand, December 7, 1880, Bamberger Nachlass, Potsdam.

127. See chapter 8.

128. Bamberger to Lasker, November 15, December 12, 1880, in *DLZB,* II:371–72.

CHAPTER 8. IN OPPOSITION: THE EARLY 1880s

1. The very close and tender relationship between the two can be followed in their correspondence between 1844 and 1874, in the Handschriftenabteilung of the Staatsbibliothek in Berlin-Dahlem. See also Bamberger, *Bismarcks grosses Spiel,* pp. 255–69, and Rahel Liebeschütz, "The Wind of Change," pp. 227–56.

2. His diary, as well as his correspondence, gives an indication of the wide range of his acquaintances.

3. Stauffenberg to Lasker, February 10, 1881, in *DLZB,* II:375; Bamberger to Lasker, July 9, 1881, Lasker Nachlass, Potsdam.

4. Theodor Schieder, "Das Verhältnis von politischer und gesellschaftlicher Verfassung und die Krise des bürgerlichen Liberalismus," *HZ*, CLXXVII (1954):69–71; Nipperdey, *Organisation der deutschen Parteien*, pp. 182–83, 204–05; idem, "Die Organisation der bürgerlichen Parteien in Deutschland vor 1918," *HZ*, CLXXXV (1958):560–69; Stephani to Bennigsen, September 7, 1880, in Oncken, "Aus den Briefen," *Deutsche Revue*, XXXIII (March 1908):288–89.

5. Bamberger to Lasker, April 17, 1881, Lasker Nachlass, Potsdam; Bamberger to Mommsen, June 14, 1883, June 18, 1884, Mommsen Nachlass; Bamberger to Stauffenberg, March 9, 1883, Stauffenberg Nachlass; Philippson, *Max von Forckenbeck*, p. 350.

6. Nipperdey, *Organisation der deutschen Parteien*, pp. 205–06.

7. Oncken, "Aus den Briefen," *Deutsche Revue*, XXXIII (March 1908):294, (April 1908):54–59; Bottcher, *Eduard Stephani*, pp. 281, 285.

8. Bamberger to Lasker, October 3, 1881, Lasker Nachlass, Potsdam; Bamberger to Stauffenberg, n.d. [1883], August 2, 1884, Stauffenberg Nachlass; Bamberger to Theodor Barth, April 21, 1884, Theodor Barth Nachlass, Deutsches Zentralarchiv, Potsdam.

9. Rachfahl, "Eugen Richter und der Linksliberalismus," pp. 311–12; Richter to Lasker, September 7, 13, 1880, in *DLZB*, II:360, 362.

10. Bamberger to Oppenheim, August 6, 1879, Bamberger Nachlass, Potsdam; Bamberger to Lasker, July 14, 1880, Bamberger to Stauffenberg, August 31, 1880, in *DLZB*, II:326–27, 358; Bamberger to Lasker, September 6, 1882, Lasker Nachlass, Potsdam.

11. *Deutsche Parteichronik, 1866–1890* (Leipzig, 1892), pp. 93, 99; Philippson, *Max von Forckenbeck*, pp. 349–51.

12. Gustav Lipke to Stauffenberg, February 5, 1880, Bamberger to Lasker, July 14, December 14, 1880, in *DLZB*, II:294, 326–27, 372–73; Bamberger to Lasker, February 23, [1880], Lasker Nachlass, Potsdam; Bamberger to Mommsen, February 8, 1881, Mommsen Nachlass; Bamberger to Brömel, February 28, 1881, Brömel Nachlass; Gustav Seeber, *Zwischen Bebel und Bismarck: zur Geschichte des Linksliberalismus in Deutschland, 1871–1893* (Berlin, 1965), pp. 112–14.

13. Bamberger to Lasker, April 17, 1881, July 9, [1881], October 18, 1881, September 6, 1882, Lasker Nachlass, Potsdam; Bamberger to Hillebrand, December 6, 1881, Bamberger Nachlass, Potsdam; Bamberger to Stauffenberg, February 8, 1882, Stauffenberg Nachlass.

14. Bamberger's deposition, February 20, 1883, Bamberger Papers, Jerusalem; Bamberger to Stauffenberg, March 9, 1883, Stauffenberg Nachlass; Bamberger to Alfred Stern, April 7, 1883, Alfred Stern Nachlass, Bundesarchiv, Koblenz.

15. Emil Tetger to Bamberger, May 21, 24, 1883, Bamberger Nachlass, Potsdam. On Barth, see Konstanze Wegner, *Theodor Barth und die Freisinnige Vereinigung* (Tubingen, 1968), and Feder, *Theodor Barth*, pp. 17–18.

16. Barth to Bamberger, May 15, 1883, Bamberger Nachlass, Potsdam.

17. Barth to Bamberger, June 7, September 25, 1883, Bamberger Nachlass, Potsdam; Feder, *Theodor Barth*, p. 18; Bamberger to Stauffenberg, June 13, 1883, Stauffenberg Nachlass; Bamberger to Brömel, September 13, November 18, 1885, Brömel Nachlass; Bamberger, "Ein Weihnachtsbrief," *GS*, I:40; editorial statement, *Die Nation*, October 6, 1883, pp. 1–2; Bamberger, "Zum vierten Jahrgang der Nation," *Die Nation*, October 2, 1886, pp. 3–5.

18. Bamberger to Hillebrand, January 9, 1881, Bamberger Nachlass, Potsdam.

19. Helfferich, *Ludwig Bamberger*, pp. 110–25; SBR, 4 LP, 4 S, March 10, 1881, pp. 234–53; Bamberger, "Das Gold der Zukunft," *GS*, IV:385, 407–12, 424–32, 438.

20. *SBR,* 4 LP, 4 S, May 30, June 10, 1881, pp. 1388–92, 1429–31, 1614–15; Bamberger's speech in Ober Ingelheim, June 26, 1881, Lasker Nachlass, Brandeis University, Waltham, Mass.; hereafter cited as Lasker Nachlass, Brandeis.

21. For a detailed treatement of this issue, see Zucker, "Ludwig Bamberger and the Crisis of German Liberalism," pp. 302–44.

22. *SBR,* 3 LP, 2 S, May 4, 1878, pp. 1031–51.

23. *SBR,* 3 LP, 2 S, May 18, 1878, pp. 1398–1401.

24. *SBR,* 3 LP, 2 S, May 18, 1878, pp. 1401, 1406–08.

25. Bismarck to Minister of State Itzenplitz, January 17, 1871, cited in Otto Quandt, *Die Anfänge der Bismarckschen Sozialgesetzgebung und die Haltung der Parteien: das Unfallversicherungsgesetz 1881–1884,* Historische Studien, CCCXLIV (Berlin, 1938), p. 9.

26. Vogel, *Bismarcks Arbeiterversicherung,* pp. 131–32.

27. Quandt, *Die Anfänge der Bismarckschen Sozialgesetzgebung,* pp. 10–11.

28. Vogel, *Bismarcks Arbeiterversicherung,* pp. 23–25.

29. Hans Rothfels, *Theodor Lohmann und die Kampfjahre der staatlichen Sozialpolitik (1871–1905)* (Berlin, 1927), pp. 48–53; Vogel, *Bismarcks Arbeiterversicherung,* pp. 38–41, 97–100; Quandt, *Die Anfänge der Bismarckschen Sozialgesetzgebung,* pp. 12–13.

30. Vogel, *Bismarcks Arbeiterversicherung,* pp. 136–55; Hans Rothfels, "Bismarck's Social Policy and the Problem of State Socialism in Germany," *Sociological Review,* XXX (1938):87–94, 301; idem, *Prinzipienfragen,* pp. 8, 9, 14–15.

31. Rothfels, *Prinzipienfragen,* pp. 16–17; Vogel, *Bismarcks Arbeiterversicherung,* pp. 158–59.

32. Bamberger, "Die Invasion der sozialistischen Ideen," in *Gegen den Staatssozialismus: drei Abhandlungen von Ludwig Bamberger, Theodor Barth und Max Broemel* (Berlin, 1884), pp. 5, 6–8; idem, "Deutsches Bürgertum," p. 707; idem, "Fragen an die ewigen Sterne," p. 83; Hans Freyer, "Das soziale Ganze und die Freiheit des Einzelnen unter den Bedingungen des industriellen Zeitalters," *HZ,* CLXXXIII (1957):108.

33. Bamberger, *Die sozialistische Gefahr* (Berlin, 1886), pp. 16, 17, 22, 23–25.

34. *SBR,* 4 LP, 4 S, *Anlagen,* no. 41, pp. 222–27.

35. Quandt, *Die Anfänge der Bismarckschen Sozialgesetzgebung,* pp. 31–39. Quandt's book, written during the Nazi era, is extremely hostile to left liberalism and somewhat anti-Semitic in tone.

36. *SBR,* 4 LP, 4 S, April 1, 1881, pp. 674–75.

37. Seeber, *Zwischen Bebel und Bismarck,* pp. 118–19. See Bamberger to Mommsen, November 24, 1890, Mommsen Nachlass, about Barth's close friendship with the chairman of Lloyds.

38. Vogel, *Bismarcks Arbeiterversicherung,* pp. 47–50.

39. *SBR,* 4 LP, 4 S, April 1, 1881, pp. 675–77.

40. Ibid., pp. 691–95, 699, April 2, 1881, pp. 709, 711.

41. *SBR,* 4 LP, 4 S, April 1, 1881, pp. 681–91.

42. *SBR,* 4 LP, 4 S, April 2, 1881, pp. 712, 714–15, 718.

43. Quandt, *Anfänge der Bismarckschen Sozialgesetzgebung,* pp. 53–63; *SBR,* 4 LP, 4 S, 1881, *Anlagen,* no. 159, pp. 851–65.

44. To Quandt this signified the "narrowness and the fruitlessness of parliamentary life," and he approvingly quotes Bismarck's statements that he was dealing with "noisy idiots" (*Anfänge der Bismarckschen Sozialgesetzgebung,* p. 63).

45. *SBR,* 4 LP, 4 S, June 2, 1881, pp. 1524–29, 1531–39.

46. Ibid., pp. 1539–44. Bamberger defined Manchesterism as a political system based on morality and freedom that wished to maintain no dependent persons who could not rise up out of a lower rank to a higher one, and that issued from the belief that the only welfare, the only future for humanity, lay in each individual's self-determination and gradual liberation.

47. *SBR*, 4 LP, 4 S, June 15, 1881, pp. 1782–83.

48. *SBR*, 5 LP, 1 S, 1882–83, *Anlagen*, no. 19, pp. 173–86.

49. *SBR*, 5 LP, 2 S, May 5, 1883, pp. 2331–33.

50. *SBR*, 5 LP, 4 S, March 14, 1884, pp. 53–58; Quandt, *Anfänge der Bismarckschen Sozialgesetzgebung*, pp. 99–112; Heinz Edgar Matthes, "Die Spaltung der Nationalliberalen Partei und die Entwicklung des Linksliberalismus bis zur Auflösung der Deutsch-Freisinnigen Partei (1878–1893)" (Ph.D. dissertation, University of Kiel, 1953), pp. 188–89.

51. For a more detailed treatment of Bamberger's attitude toward this problem, see Stanley Zucker, "Ludwig Bamberger and the Rise of Anti-Semitism in Germany, 1848–1893," *Central European History*, III, no. 4 (December 1970):332–52.

52. Bamberger to Oppenheim, February 20, 1870, Bamberger Nachlass, Potsdam; *SBR*, 1 LP, 3 S, May 22, 1872, pp. 468–77.

53. Bamberger to his mother, December 19, 1879, January 10, 1880, Bamberger Nachlass, Berlin-Dahlem; Bamberger, "Deutschtum und Judentum," *Unsere Zeit*, 1880 (1):188–205.

54. Bamberger, "Deutschtum und Judentum," pp. 192, 198; Bamberger to his mother, December 19, 1879, Bamberger Nachlass, Berlin-Dahlem; Bamberger to Lasker, n.d. [1879], Lasker Nachlass, Potsdam; Bamberger to Oppenheim, n.d. [1879], Bamberger Nachlass, Potsdam.

55. Bamberger, "Deutschtum und Judentum," pp. 192–95.

56. Bamberger to Hillebrand, December 7, 1880, Bamberger Nachlass, Potsdam.

57. Kurt Wawrzinek, *Die Entstehung der deutschen Antisemitenparteien*, Historische Studien, CLXVIII (Berlin, 1927), pp. 33–36, 38; *SBR*, 4 LP, 4 S, April 2, 1881, p. 712.

58. Bamberger to his mother, April 4, 1881, Bamberger Nachlass, Berlin-Dahlem. In 1879 he had written Oppenheim that Schauss was "engaging in Jew-baiting" in Bamberger's district, "a certain proof that Bismarck secretly fosters this slogan" (Bamberger to Oppenheim, September 14, 1879, Bamberger Nachlass, Potsdam).

59. Bamberger, *Bismarck posthumus*, p. 38; Hans-Ulrich Wehler documents the political basis of Bismarck's acceptance of the anti-Semitic movement but holds the chancellor responsible for stimulating the more vulgar racial anti-Semitism (*Bismarck und der Imperialismus* [Cologne and Berlin, 1969], pp. 472–73).

60. *SBR*, 4 LP, 2 S, July 11, 1879, p. 2299; Lambi, *Free Trade and Protection*, pp. 144–45.

61. Bamberger to his mother, May 24, June 11, 1881, Bamberger Nachlass, Berlin-Dahlem; Böhme, *Deutschlands Weg zur Grossmacht*, p. 578.

62. Bamberger to his mother, June 27, 1881, Bamberger to colleague X, August 5, 1881, Bamberger Nachlass, Berlin-Dahlem; Bamberger to Broemel, June 20, 1881, Broemel Nachlass; Bamberger to Lasker, June 15, 1881, Lasker Nachlass, Potsdam; Bamberger's speech in Ober Ingelheim, June 26, 1881, Lasker Nachlass, Brandeis.

63. Bamberger to Hillebrand, September 30, 1881, Bamberger Nachlass, Potsdam; speeches in Wörrstadt and Ober Ingelheim, June 19, June 26, 1881, Lasker Nachlass, Brandeis.

64. Speech in Wörrstadt, June 19, 1881, Lasker Nachlass, Brandeis; Bamberger to Lasker, June 15, July 9, 1881, Lasker Nachlass, Potsdam.

65. Bamberger to Lasker, July 9, September 7, 22, October 3, 1881, Lasker Nachlass, Potsdam.

66. Bamberger to Lasker, October 18, 28, 1881, Lasker Nachlass, Potsdam.

67. Bamberger to Lasker, November 7, 1881, Lasker Nachlass, Potsdam; emphasis is Bamberger's. *Binger Anzeiger,* November 5, 9, 1881; Philipp Wasserburg to A. J. Pennrich, November 5, 1881, C. J. Preetorius to Wasserburg, November 1, 1881, Philipp Wasserburg Nachlass, Stadtarchiv, Mainz, Folder E 18/4.

68. Bamberger to Lasker, July 9, October 28, November 7, 1881, Lasker Nachlass, Potsdam; Bamberger to his mother, November 24, 1881, Bamberger Nachlass, Berlin-Dahlem.

69. Bamberger to colleague X, August 5, 1881, Bamberger Nachlass, Berlin-Dahlem; Philipps, *Reichstagswahlen,* chart opposite p. 287.

70. Cited in Böhme, *Deutschlands Weg zur Grossmacht,* p. 578; Philippson, *Max von Forckenbeck,* p. 348; Ziekursch, *Politische Geschichte,* II:355–56.

71. *SBR,* 5 LP, 1 S, November 28, 1881, pp. 62–63.

72. Bamberger to his mother, April 4, 1881, Bamberger Nachlass, Berlin-Dahlem.

73. Morsey, *Die oberste Reichsverwaltung,* p. 52.

74. Böhme, *Deutschlands Weg zur Grossmacht,* pp. 575–78; Ziekursch, *Politische Geschichte,* II:354–55, 361; *SBR,* 4 LP, 4 S, June 10, 1881, pp. 1609–11.

75. *SBR,* 5 LP, 1 S, December 1, 1881, pp. 129–33.

76. Ibid., pp. 134–39, 144–46.

77. Bamberger, *Erinnerungen,* pp. 386–87; *SBR,* 2 LP, 1 S, March 21, 1874, p. 452. None of his efforts in this direction seemed to help. He was accused of representing nickel interests during the currency debates and later charged with representing no interests and thus being incompetent to judge economic questions.

78. Bamberger, "Geburt des Bankgesetzes," p. 290; *SBR,* 1 LP, 4 S, March 27, 1873, pp. 98–100; *SBR,* 4 LP, 2 S, March 17, 1879, p. 459; *SBR,* 2 LP, 3 S, November 4, 1875, pp. 69–70.

79. Speech in Ober Ingelheim, June 26, 1881, Lasker Nachlass, Brandeis; speech in Bingen, March 4, 1882, *Mainzer Tagblatt,* March 12, 1882.

80. Bamberger, "Verdirbt die Politik," pp. 296, 298–99, 302.

81. *GS,* I:303–09.

82. Bamberger to Hillebrand, March 22, 1882, Bamberger Nachlass, Potsdam.

83. Bamberger to Hillebrand, October 26, 1882, January 22, 1883, Bamberger Nachlass, Potsdam; Bamberger, *Bismarcks grosses Spiel,* pp. 270–71, 273–75, 333–35.

84. Bamberger to Stauffenberg, August 2, 1884, Stauffenberg Nachlass.

85. Bamberger to Hillebrand, December 17, 1882, Bamberger Nachlass, Potsdam.

CHAPTER 9. COLONIALISM

1. *SBR,* 5 LP, 2 S, 1882–83, *Anlagen,* no. 7, pp. 48–68.

2. *SBR,* 5 LP, 2 S, 1882–83, *Anlagen,* no. 35, p. 294.

3. *SBR,* 5 LP, 2 S, June 12, 1882, pp. 353–64.

4. Bamberger to Hillebrand, March 22, 1882, Bamberger Nachlass, Potsdam.

5. Bamberger to Lasker, September 19, 1881, Lasker Nachlass, Brandeis.

6. *SBR,* 5 LP, 2 S, June 12, 13, 1882, pp. 370–73, 415.

7. *SBR,* 5 LP, 2 S, June 12, 1882, pp. 368–76.

8. *SBR,* 5 LP, 2 S, June 14, 1882, pp. 430–31.

9. Ibid., pp. 433–34, 437–38; Bamberger, *Erinnerungen*, p. 417.

10. Bamberger to his mother, June 21, [1882], Bamberger Nachlass, Berlin-Dahlem; the last sentence is in English in the original.

11. *SBR*, 5 LP, 3 S, June 14, 1882, pp. 454–57, June 15, 1882, pp. 460–508. See the factually rich, but unashamedly Bismarckian depiction of the tobacco struggle in Wahl, *Deutsche Geschichte*, II:126–39.

12. Bamberger to Hillebrand, January 22, 1883, Bamberger Nachlass, Potsdam.

13. Wehler, *Bismarck*, pp. 148–55, 168, 191, 421–25, 434–38, 445, 451–54, 467–74.

14. Helfferich, *Georg von Siemens*, II:273–89; Wehler, *Bismarck*, p. 230.

15. Bamberger, *Erinnerungen*, pp. 370–71; *SBR*, 2 LP, 3 S, December 18, 1875, p. 758.

16. *SBR*, 2 LP, 4 S, December 5, 1876, pp. 591–92.

17. *SBR*, 4 LP, 2 S, May 3, 1879, pp. 963–64.

18. *SBR*, 4 LP, 2 S, June 13, 1879, pp. 1601, 1605.

19. Ibid., pp. 1608–10.

20. Bamberger to Oppenheim, August 6, 1879, Bamberger Nachlass, Potsdam.

21. *SBR*, 4 LP, 3 S, 1880, *Anlagen*, no. 101, pp. 747–49; Wehler, *Bismarck*, pp. 210–17; Helmut Washausen, "Hamburg und die Kolonialpolitik des deutschen Reiches (1880 bis 1890)" (Ph.D. dissertation, Göttingen University, 1967), pp. 36–38, 83–94.

22. *SBR*, 4 LP, 3 S, April 22, 1880, pp. 857–61.

23. Ibid., pp. 861–69.

24. *SBR*, 4 LP, 3 S, April 23, 27, 1880, pp. 869–95, 946.

25. *SBR*, 4 LP, 3 S, April 27, 1880, pp. 953–58; Wehler, *Bismarck*, pp. 217–20; Maximilian Hagen, *Bismarcks Kolonialpolitik* (Stuttgart and Berlin, 1923), pp. 68–92. Hagen's detailed work suffers from at least one fundamental fault: It makes Bismarck's views the standard for right and wrong, good and evil. Bamberger, whose name appears frequently in the work, is variously described as "narrow-minded," "partisan," "a user of false information," "a philistine," "a slanderer," and "unscrupulous."

26. *SBR*, 4 LP, 3 S, April 27, 1880, pp. 960–62.

27. Bamberger to Hillebrand, n.d. (no. 96), Bamberger Nachlass, Potsdam.

28. Bamberger to his mother, May 4, 1880, Bamberger Nachlass, Berlin-Dahlem. In the same letter he noted that he got the "most beautiful anonymous insulting letters, but also enthusiastic epistles." Wehler, *Bismarck*, pp. 216, 396–97; Washausen, "Hamburg und die Kolonialpolitik," pp. 94–102.

29. Bamberger, "Köhlerglaube und Volkswirtschaft," *Die Nation*, November 10, 1883, pp. 76–78; Hagen, *Bismarcks Kolonialpolitik*, pp. 1–41, 114–212.

30. *SBR*, 5 LP, 4 S, 1884, *Anlagen*, no.111, pp. 826–30; Wehler, *Bismarck*, pp. 223, 239–44; Washausen, "Hamburg und die Kolonialpolitik," pp. 63–71.

31. *SBR*, 5 LP, 4 S, June 14, 1884, pp. 719–23.

32. Bamberger to Stauffenberg, May 16, 1884, Stauffenberg Nachlass.

33. *SBR*, June 14, 1884, 5 LP, 4 S, pp. 723–33.

34. *SBR*, 5 LP, 4 S, June 14, 1884, pp. 733–35, 736–43, 746–47; Wehler appears at times to make too much of his notion of an "ideological consensus" about export (*Bismarck*, pp. 244–46). Of course everyone was interested in furthering export, even Bamberger. How could one not be?

35. Wehler, *Bismarck*, pp. 246–47; Bamberger to Stauffenberg, August 1884, Stauffenberg Nachlass; Hagen refers to Bamberger's "calumny" and "a priori ad absurdum" argument. He is forced to admit, however, that although no one knew where the liberal

got his information, his "slander" was not "snatched from thin air," and that from a "national economic standpoint" Bamberger was correct (*Bismarcks Kolonialpolitik*, pp. 97–114; see in particular pp. 106, 112, n. 1).

36. Kusserow to Bamberger, June 28, 1884, Bamberger's statement and Kusserow's acceptance, June 28, 1884, Bamberger Nachlass, Potsdam; Bamberger to Broemel, August 5, 1884, Broemel Nachlass; Bamberger to Stauffenberg, August 2, 1884, Stauffenberg Nachlass.

37. For the passionate debate, see *SBR*, 5 LP, 4 S, June 26, 1884, pp. 1050–85.

38. Wehler, *Bismarck*, pp. 247–48; Wilhelm Wehrenpfennig, "Dampfliniensubvention," *PJ*, LIV (1884):97–99.

39. Bamberger to Stauffenberg, August 15, 1884, Stauffenberg Nachlass; Bamberger to Broemel, August 5, 20, 24, September 9, 1884, Broemel Nachlass; Bamberger, *Bismarcks grosses Spiel*, pp. 276–81.

40. Bamberger to Hillebrand, n.d. [August 1884], no. 91, n.d., no. 96, Bamberger Nachlass, Potsdam.

41. *SBR*, 5 LP, 4 S, March 14, 1884, p. 56; Bamberger to Stauffenberg, March 19, 24, 1884, Stauffenberg Nachlass; Rickert to Stauffenberg, March 22, 1884, in *DLZB*, II:402–03.

42. Wehler provides an interesting analysis of the campaign (*Bismarck*, pp. 247–48, 474–82). Schrader to Stauffenberg, August 21, 1884, in *DLZB*, II:417, 419; Bamberger to Stauffenberg, August 2, 15, 1884, Stauffenberg Nachlass.

43. Bamberger to Hillebrand, May 2, July 22, 1884, Bamberger Nachlass, Potsdam; Bamberger to Stauffenberg, August 15, October 5, 1884, Stauffenberg Nachlass; Bamberger to Broemel, August 12, [1884], September 9, 1884, Broemel Nachlass; *Mainzer Anzeiger*, October 7, 1884; *MZ*, June 20, July 23, 29, September 8, 24, October 2, 7, 16, 1884.

44. On the election see the broadsides and newspaper clippings in the Philipp Wasserburg Nachlass, Folder E 18/5.

45. Hagen, *Bismarcks Kolonialpolitik*, pp. 294–468, 510–52.

46. *SBR*, 6 LP, 1 S, 1884–85, *Anlagen*, no. 16, pp. 70–78; Wehler, *Bismarck*, pp. 247–50.

47. *SBR*, 6 LP, 1 S, December 1, 1884, pp. 136–42.

48. *SBR*, 6 LP, 1 S, 1884–85, *Anlagen*, no. 208, pp. 803–35; Wehler, *Bismarck*, pp. 250–52; Hans Spellmeyer, *Deutsche Kolonialpolitik im Reichstag* (Stuttgart, 1931), pp. 15–16.

49. *SBR*, 6 LP, 1 S, December 12, 1884, pp. 390–91, 396–405, March 4, 1885, pp. 1568–73.

50. *SBR*, 6 LP, 1 S, December 15, 1884, pp. 356–75.

51. Bamberger to Stauffenberg, December 18, 23, 31, 1884, Stauffenberg Nachlass; emphasis is Bamberger's.

52. Wehler, *Bismarck*, pp. 391–96; Bamberger to Stauffenberg, December 23, 1884, Stauffenberg Nachlass.

53. *SBR*, 6 LP, 1 S, March 4, 1885, pp. 1545–67.

54. *SBR*, 6 LP, 1 S, March 12, 14, 16, 17, 1885, pp. 1755–1892; Spellmeyer, *Deutsche Kolonialpolitik*, pp. 19–22; Wehler, *Bismarck*, pp. 252–53.

55. *SBR*, 6 LP, 1 S, March 23, 1885, pp. 2022–30, 2038–39. His prediction about the profitability of the East Asian line was accurate. Wehler is not entirely correct in claiming that in this speech Bamberger was willing to support export premiums (*Bismarck*, pp. 124–25). He was being sarcastic in suggesting that a better way to aid exports

would be to give the money directly to the exporters rather than to embark on a dubious experiment of subsidized steamers.

56. Wehler, *Bismarck,* pp. 253–57.

57. Bamberger to Stauffenberg, August 25, 1885, Stauffenberg Nachlass; Bamberger to Broemel, November 17, 20, 1885, December 26, 1886, n.d. [1886 or 1887], no. 237, Broemel Nachlass.

CHAPTER 10. NEW UNITY AND CONTINUED OPPOSITION: 1884–1890

1. Bamberger to Stauffenberg, August 2, 1884, Stauffenberg Nachlass; Bamberger, "Deutsches Bürgertum," pp. 706 07.

2. Rachfahl, "Eugen Richter," pp. 323–24; Bamberger, *Bismarcks grosses Spiel,* pp. 276–81, 331; Bamberger to Stauffenberg, December 26, 1886, Stauffenberg Nachlass.

3. Philippson, *Max von Forckenbeck,* p. 352.

4. *SBR,* 5 LP, 4 S, March 7, 13, 1884, pp. 9–11, 28–34.

5. Bamberger to Stauffenberg, January 14, 20, 1884, Stauffenberg Nachlass; Bamberger, *Bismarcks grosses Spiel,* pp. 276–77, 285–86; idem, "Eduard Lasker; Gedenkrede," *GS,* II:87–116.

6. Rachfahl, "Eugen Richter," pp. 321–23.

7. Seeber, *Zwischen Bebel und Bismarck,* pp. 78–91, 96.

8. Ibid., pp. 114–21. No material is available on the various local groups of the Liberal Union, so that Seeber had to concentrate on the major figures.

9. Bamberger to Hillebrand, August 21, 1883, Bamberger Nachlass, Potsdam; Bamberger to Lasker, October 18, 1881, Lasker Nachlass, Potsdam; Bamberger to Stauffenberg, October 23, 1886, Stauffenberg Nachlass.

10. Bamberger to Broemel, August 20, 1884, Broemel Nachlass; Stauffenberg to Bamberger, n.d. [1884], no. 15, Bamberger Nachlass, Potsdam.

11. Bamberger to Stauffenberg, February 9, 1884, in *DLZB,* II:400–01; Hänel to Bamberger, February 8, 1884, Bamberger Nachlass, Potsdam.

12. Stauffenberg to Bamberger, n.d. [February 1884], nos. 12–14; Bamberger, *Bismarcks grosses Spiel,* pp. 274–75.

13. Bamberger to Stauffenberg, February 25, 1884, in *DLZB,* II:401.

14. See the drafts in Bamberger Nachlass, Potsdam, File 232, nos. 1–9, and the final declaration in Gustav Seeber, "Deutsche Freisinnige Partei," *Die bürgerlichen Parteien in Deutschland,* I (Leipzig, 1968):358; Rachfahl, "Eugen Richter," pp. 324–31; Seeber, *Zwischen Bebel und Bismarck,* pp. 128–31.

15. Seeber, *Zwischen Bebel und Bismarck,* pp. 131–33.

16. Bamberger, *Bismarcks grosses Spiel,* p. 289; Seeber, *Zwischen Bebel und Bismarck,* pp. 130–32.

17. Rachfahl, "Eugen Richter," pp. 286–87, 311, 333–34; Matthes, "Spaltung der Nationalliberalen Partei," pp. 228–29; Leopold Ullstein, *Eugen Richter als Publizist und Herausgeber* (Leipzig, 1930), pp. 97–99.

18. Bamberger to Stauffenberg, March 13, 18, 19, 1884, Stauffenberg Nachlass.

19. Stauffenberg to Bamberger, n.d., nos. 12–14, Bamberger Nachlass, Potsdam.

20. Pack, *Das parlamentarische Ringen,* pp. 136–37.

21. Bamberger to Stauffenberg, March 18, 31, 1884, Stauffenberg Nachlass.

22. *SBR,* 5 LP, 2 S, May 5, 1883, p. 2331.

23. *SBR,* 5 LP, 4 S, May 12, 1884, pp. 545–47.

24. Bamberger to Stauffenberg, March 31, April 2, 1884, Stauffenberg Nachlass.

25. Seeber, *Zwischen Bebel und Bismarck*, p. 139; Alfred Heuss, *Theodor Mommsen und das 19. Jahrhundert* (Kiel, 1956), pp. 214–15; Bamberger to Mommsen, April 16, 1884, Mommsen Nachlass; Bamberger to Stauffenberg, April 13, 1884, Stauffenberg Nachlass.

26. Bamberger to Stauffenberg, April 13, 1884, Stauffenberg Nachlass; Bamberger, *Bismarcks grosses Spiel*, p. 291.

27. Bamberger, *Bismarcks grosses Spiel*, pp. 290–92; *SBR*, 5 LP, 4 S, 1884, *Anlagen*, no. 80, pp. 734–43; Pack, *Das parlamentarische Ringen*, pp. 148–51.

28. Bamberger, *Bismarcks grosses Spiel*, p. 293; Pack, *Das parlamentarische Ringen*, pp. 153–56.

29. Bamberger, *Bismarcks grosses Spiel*, pp. 293–94.

30. *SBR*, 5 LP, 4 S, May 8, 1884, pp. 443–48.

31. *SBR*, 5 LP, 4 S, May 9, 1884, pp. 478–83, 493–505.

32. *SBR*, 5 LP, 4 S, May 10, 1884, pp. 530–32; Pack, *Das parlamentarische Ringen*, p. 157.

33. Bamberger to Stauffenberg, March 18, April 13, May 16, 1884, Stauffenberg Nachlass.

34. Seeber, *Zwischen Bebel und Bismarck*, pp. 143–46.

35. Nipperdey, *Organisation der deutschen Parteien*, pp. 206–09.

36. Bamberger to Stauffenberg, October 5, 1884, Stauffenberg Nachlass; Rachfahl, "Eugen Richter," p. 322.

37. Bamberger to Stauffenberg, July 18, August 25, 1885, Stauffenberg Nachlass; Bamberger to Broemel, n.d., no. 220, Broemel Nachlass.

38. Bamberger to Stauffenberg, August 25, December 14, 1885, Stauffenberg Nachlass; Bamberger to Broemel, November 22, 29, 1885, Broemel Nachlass.

39. Pack, *Das parlamentarische Ringen*, pp. 165–73; *SBR*, 6 LP, 2 S, April 2, 1886, pp. 1827–37; Bamberger to Stauffenberg, February 16, September 12, 1886, Stauffenberg Nachlass.

40. Bamberger to Stauffenberg, February 16, April 29, May 12, 1886, Stauffenberg Nachlass; Schmidt-Volkmar, *Kulturkampf in Deutschland*, pp. 298–316.

41. Seeber, *Zwischen Bebel und Bismarck*, pp. 160–66.

42. Seeber, *Zwischen Bebel und Bismarck*, pp. 161–62; Wahl, *Deutsche Geschichte*, II:348–49; *SBR*, 6 LP, 4 S, 1886–87, *Anlagen* no. 11, pp. 74–77.

43. Seeber, *Zwischen Bebel und Bismarck*, pp. 167–68.

44. Bamberger to Stauffenberg, April 29, October 23, November 3, 19, 1886, Stauffenberg Nachlass; Bamberger to Broemel, November 17, 1886, Broemel Nachlass.

45. *SBR*, 6 LP, 4 S, December 3, 1886, pp. 71–81.

46. *SBR*, 6 LP, 4 S, 1886–87, *Anlagen*, no. 49, p. 350; Bamberger, "Parteipolitik und Patriotismus," *Die Nation*, December 25, 1886, p. 187; Bamberger to Stauffenberg, December 26, 1886, Stauffenberg Nachlass.

47. Bamberger to Stauffenberg, December 30, 1886, Stauffenberg Nachlass.

48. Seeber, *Zwischen Bebel und Bismarck*, pp. 177–78.

49. *SBR*, 6 LP, 4 S, January 11, 1887, pp. 350–51.

50. *Kölnische Zeitung* clippings of August 30 and September 13, 1886, in Barth's file 13, nos. 21–22, 24–25, Bamberger Nachlass, Potsdam; Bamberger's letter to *Die Nation*, September 11, 1886, p. 737; Barth to Bamberger, September 2, 1886, Bamberger Nachlass, Potsdam; Bamberger to Stauffenberg, September 7, 12, 1886, Stauffenberg Nachlass.

51. *SBR,* 6 LP, 4 S, January 13, 1887, pp. 419–24; see pp. 343–425 for the entire debate.

52. *SBR,* 6 LP, 4 S, January 14, 1887, pp. 427–31.

53. Bamberger to Stauffenberg, October 23, 1886, Stauffenberg Nachlass.

54. Seeber, although understandably concerned with the relationship of the Radical and Social Democratic parties, gives a stimulating view of the election (*Zwischen Bebel und Bismarck,* pp. 178–84).

55. Bamberger to Stauffenberg, February 25, 1887, in *DLZB,* II:429.

56. Bamberger to Stauffenberg, January 19, 24, 1887, Stauffenberg Nachlass; the emphasis is Bamberger's.

57. Anna von Helmholtz to Ida von Siemens-Helmholtz, January 26, 1887 in Siemens-Helmholtz, *Anna von Helmholtz,* I:305.

58. Bamberger to Stauffenberg, March 3, 1887, Stauffenberg Nachlass.

59. Bamberger to Stauffenberg, December 18, 1884, May 12, 1886, Stauffenberg Nachlass; Bamberger to Mommsen, June 17, 1886, Mommsen Nachlass; Bamberger to Stauffenberg, February 25, 1887, in *DLZB,* II:429–30.

60. *SBR,* 7 LP, 1 S, 1887, *Anlagen,* no. 73, pp. 615–79.

61. Bamberger to Stauffenberg, February 25, March 3, 1887, in *DLZB,* II:429, 432.

62. Bamberger, *Bismarcks grosses Spiel,* p. 339; Bamberger to Stauffenberg, March 24, 1887, Stauffenberg Nachlass; Matthes, "Spalting der Nationalliberalen Partei," p. 220.

63. Bamberger to Stauffenberg, March 3, 1887, Virchow to Stauffenberg, March 23, 1887, Schrader to Stauffenberg, April 9, 1887, in *DLZB,* II:431–34; Bamberger to Stauffenberg, March 24, 31, April 26, 1887, Stauffenberg Nachlass; Bamberger to Broemel, March 5, 1887, Broemel Nachlass; Rachfahl, "Eugen Richter," pp. 338–39; Seeber, *Zwischen Bebel und Bismarck,* pp. 188–90; Ullstein, *Eugen Richter,* pp. 142–47; Matthes, "Spaltung der Nationalliberalen Partei," pp. 232–43.

64. *SBR,* 7 LP, 1 S, March 7, 9, 11, 1887, pp. 16–22, 38–48, 72–93; Bamberger to Broemel, March 4, 5, 1887, Broemel Nachlass.

65. Bamberger to Stauffenberg, April 26, 1887, Stauffenberg Nachlass.

66. Bamberger to Stauffenberg, June 28, 1887, Stauffenberg Nachlass; Schrader to Stauffenberg, n.d. [early 1887], in *DLZB,* II:430–31; Rickert to Bamberger, July 2, 1887, Bamberger Nachlass, Potsdam; Bamberger to Stern, March 13, 1888, Stern Nachlass.

67. Bamberger, *Bismarcks grosses Spiel,* p. 339; Bamberger to Stauffenberg, June 28, 1887, Stauffenberg Nachlass.

68. Bamberger, "Die Bilanz der nationalen Mehrheit," *Die Nation,* March 19, 1887, pp. 367–68.

69. Bamberger to Stern, March 13, 1888, Stern Nachlass; Bamberger, "Die Aera der Toaste," *GS,* I:346; *SBR,* 7 LP, 2 S, February 1, 9, 1888, pp. 658–63, 787–90; *SBR* 7 LP, 4 S, January 15, 26, 1889, pp. 447, 636–38, 676–77. For the first and only time in his parliamentary career he was called to order.

70. For Bamberger's opposition to the brandy proposal, see his speeches in the previous year's debate (*SBR,* 6 LP, 2 S, March 6, 1886, pp. 1363–70), and Bamberger to Stauffenberg, March 31, April 10, 1887, Stauffenberg Nachlass.

71. Bamberger to Barth, October 16, 1879, Barth Nachlass.

72. See the material in the Staatsarchiv, Potsdam, "Der Verein zur Förderung der Handelsfreiheit, 1878–1892," and in the correspondence between Broemel and Bamberger in Broemel Nachlass.

73. *SBR,* 4 LP, 4 S, March 16, 21, 1881, pp. 355–58, 444; *SBR,* 5 LP, 1 S, December 16, 1881, January 13, 1882, pp. 436–40, 622–24; speeches in Wörrstadt and Ober Ingelheim, June 19, 26, 1881, Lasker Nachlass, Brandeis; Rolf Sonnemann, *Die Auswirkungen des Schutzzolls auf die Monopolisierung der deutschen Eisen- und Stahlindustrie, 1879–1892* (Berlin, 1960), pp. 19–21, 52–55, 65–67.

74. *SBR,* 6 LP, 1 S, February 12, 1885, pp. 1229–35.

75. *SBR,* 6 LP, 1 S, April 22, 1885, p. 2257.

76. Bamberger to Stauffenberg, November 30, December 29, 1887, Stauffenberg Nachlass.

77. *SBR,* 6 LP, 2 S, January 20, 1886, pp. 658–60; *SBR,* 7 LP, 4 S, December 14, 1888, p. 315.

78. Wehler, *Bismarck,* pp. 284–89.

79. *SBR,* 6 LP, 4 S, January 8, 1887, pp. 315–18.

80. *SBR,* 7 LP, 4 S, January 15, 1889, pp. 437–39; Bamberger, "Papiere und Kanonen," *Die Nation,* September 17, 1892, pp. 761–65.

81. *SBR,* 7 LP, 4 S, January 15, 1889, pp. 439–40.

82. Ibid., pp. 440–43.

83. *SBR,* 7 LP, 5 S, November 26, 27, December 2, 1889, pp. 507, 540, 544–45, 615.

84. Wehler, *Bismarck,* pp. 289–92.

85. Ibid., pp. 341–62.

86. *SBR,* 7 LP, 4 S, *Anlagen,* no. 71, pp. 491–93; Spellmeyer, *Deutsche Kolonialpolitik,* pp. 28–32.

87. *SBR,* 7 LP, 4 S, December 14, 1888, pp. 312–21.

88. *SBR,* 7 LP, 4 S, January 26, 1889, pp. 606–14.

89. Ibid., pp. 619–23; Spellmeyer, *Deutsche Kolonialpolitik,* pp. 332–38.

90. Wehler, *Bismarck,* pp. 363–67.

91. Bamberger to Stauffenberg, March 21, 1890, Stauffenberg Nachlass.

92. *SBR,* 8 LP, 1 S, May 12, June 9, 1890, pp. 31–38, 224–39; Bamberger, "Aera der Toaste," 351–52.

93. *SBR,* 7 LP, 5 S, November 27, 28, 1889, pp. 543–44, 557–60.

94. *SBR,* 8 LP, 1 S, May 12, 1890, p. 48.

95. *SBR,* 7 LP, 2 S, 1887–88, *Anlagen,* no. 29, p. 238.

96. Bamberger, "Zur Physiologie des Reichstags," *AZ,* May 29, 1874, p. 2186.

97. Bamberger, *Deutschland und der Sozialismus,* pp. 28–31, 34–36, 43–44.

98. *SBR,* 7 LP, 2 S, February 1, 9, 1888, pp. 658–61, 789–90; Walter Gagel, *Die Wahlrechtsfrage in der Geschichte der deutschen liberalen Parteien, 1848–1918* (Dusseldorf, 1958), p. 112.

99. *SBR,* 7 LP, 2 S, February 1, 9, 1888, pp. 661–66, 787–92; Bamberger, "Aera der Toaste," p. 352.

100. *SBR,* 7 LP, 2 S, February 1, 2, 1888, pp. 661, 663–72, 801.

101. *SBR,* 1 LP, 1 S, April 19, 1871, p. 295; Bamberger, *Deutschland und der Sozialismus,* pp. 31–34.

102. *SBR,* 7 LP, 2 S, February 7, 1888, pp. 752–58.

103. *Der Sozialdemokrat,* July 1, 1886.

104. Pack, *Das parlamentarische Ringen,* pp. 175–77; Lipinski, *Sozialdemokratie,* II:94–110; Osterroth and Schuster, *Chronik der deutschen Sozialdemokratie,* pp. 66–69; Dieter Fricke, *Bismarcks Prätorianer: die Berliner politische Polizei im Kampf gegen die deutsche Arbeiterbewegung 1871–1898* (Berlin, 1962), pp. 179–220, 338–40; Lidtke, *The Outlawed Party,* pp. 241–52.

105. *SBR*, 6 LP, 2 S, May 21, 1886, pp. 2098–2103.
106. Ibid., pp. 2108–09.
107. *SBR*, 6 LP, 2 S, May 21, 1886, pp. 2109–11, 2117–18. It is not correct to say, as Beeber claims, that Bamberger avoided a clear position on this issue (*Zwischen Bebel und Bismarck*, pp. 151–52). Also Puttkamer, the interior minister, did not praise Bamberger's speech but on the contrary criticized it strongly (*SBR*, 6 LP, 2 S, May 21, 1886, pp. 2111–13).
108. Pack, *Das parlamentarische Ringen*, pp. 177–81.
109. *SBR*, 7 LP, 2 S, January 27, 1888, pp. 537–57; Bamberger to Stauffenberg, January 2, 1888, Stauffenberg Nachlass; Fricke, *Bismarcks Prätorianer*, pp. 230–42.
110. *SBR*, 7 LP, 2 S, January 27, 1888, pp. 570–73. The reference to international relations was to Switzerland, which had drawn the wrath of the German government by providing a haven for socialists and not being more helpful to the German police.
111. This was done, giving Bebel a seat. Fourteen years before, the National Liberals had also made a seat available to the Social Democrats. At that time Bamberger wrote: "This mistake will not be repeated" ("Zur Physiologie des Reichstags," July 17, 1874).
112. *SBR*, 7 LP, 2 S, January 28, 1888, pp. 573, 578–80.
113. Ibid., pp. 580–89.
114. Pack, *Das parlamentarische Ringen*, pp. 205–23.
115. Osterröth and Schuster, *Chronik der deutschen Sozialdemokratie*, p. 73; Pack, *Das parlamentarische Ringen*, p. 239.
116. Bamberger, "Fragen an die ewigen Sterne," p. 83.
117. Wahl, *Deutsche Geschichte*, II:507–21; Bamberger to Stauffenberg, April 6, 1889, in *DLZB*, II:451–52; Bamberger to Stauffenberg, May 5, 14, 29, 1889, Stauffenberg Nachlass; Bamberger to Broemel, March 28, 1889, Broemel Nachlass; Bamberger, "Die Krisis in Deutschland und der deutsche Kaiser," *GS*, V:425–26; *SBR*, 7 LP, 4 S, May 18, 1889, pp. 1837–39. Bamberger did bestow the name "paste law" (*Klebegesetz)* on the measure, since workers were to receive stamps for every week's work which had to be pasted on a card and which served as proof of one's eligibility. The new rule of life, said Bamberger, would no longer be "live and let live, but paste and let paste."
118. Helfferich, *Ludwig Bamberger*, pp. 128–29, 141; Bamberger, *Die Schicksale des Lateinischen Münzbundes* (Berlin, 1885), pp. 4–9, 18–24, 34, 36, 86, 120; Bamberger to Broemel, December 6, 1885, Broemel Nachlass.
119. Bamberger, *Die Stichworte der Silberleute* (Berlin, 1893), passim; Achterberg, "Ludwig Bamberger," p. 203; Bamberger, "Das Reich und die Wissenschaft," *GS*, I:256–57; idem, "Die neueste Aera der Spekulation," *GS*, I:406, 416. In the 1870s he had also complained of the Reichstag's suspicion of the business world ("Zur Geburt des Bankgesetzes," *GS*, IV:287–88, 291–92).
120. Helfferich, *Ludwig Bamberger*, pp. 126, 128, 155; Bamberger to Broemel, December 24, 1885, December 29, 1893, July 9, 19, August 6, 1895, Broemel Nachlass; Otto Braun, *Allgemeine Zeitung*, Munich, to Bamberger, July 11, 1888, Bamberger Nachlass, Potsdam; Bamberger, *Die Verschleppung der deutschen Münzreform* (Cologne, 1882), passim.
121. Cited in Helfferich, *Ludwig Bamberger*, p. 133.
122. Ibid., pp. 134, 139.
123. Bismarck to Scholz, November 24, 1886, in Bismarck, *GW*, XIV/2:970–71.
124. Bamberger to Soetbeer, February 11, 1884, in Helfferich, *Ludwig Bamberger*, p. 134.
125. *SBR*, 6 LP, 1 S, March 6, 1885, pp. 1613–43; Helfferich, *Ludwig Bamberger*, pp. 137–41.

126. Bamberger to Soetbeer, December 19, 1885, cited in Helfferich, *Ludwig Bamberger*, pp. 142–44; Bamberger to Broemel, December 6, 1885, Broemel Nachlass.

127. *SBR*, 6 LP, 2 S, January 22, February 10, 1886, pp. 711–14, 720–21, 984–91, 1000–02; Helfferich, *Ludwig Bamberger*, pp. 144–46; Bamberger, *Bismarcks grosses Spiel*, pp. 353–54.

128. Helfferich, *Ludwig Bamberger*, pp. 152–56; Bamberger, "Silber," *GS*, V:378–92; Bamberger to Stauffenberg, May 30, 1893, May 16, 1894, February 17, 1895, Stauffenberg Nachlass; Bamberger to Broemel, April 29, 1894, Broemel Nachlass.

129. Speeches of Stolberg-Wernigerode and Gamp, *SBR*, 7 LP, 5 S, November 8, 29, 1889, pp. 191–93, 196, 581.

130. *SBR*, 7 LP, 5 S, November 8, 1889, p. 207.

131. *SBR*, 7 LP, 5 S, November 8, 29, December 6, 1889, pp. 191–213, 577–98, 599–630, 713–30; Bamberger, "Die Reichsbank," *GS*, V:227–37; idem, "Jupiter und Merkur," *Die Nation*, November 19, 1887, p. 100. The latter essay criticized the Reichsbank's policy against selling Russian bonds on the German market as an unhealthy use of the bank for foreign policy purposes. Privately, however, Bamberger wrote that the "campaign against the Russian bonds was entirely sound" (Bamberger to Stauffenberg, August 14, 1887, in *DLZB*, II:435).

132. According to Rachfahl, even Richter believed that only under a liberal emperor could Germany become liberal ("Eugen Richter," pp. 340–41).

133. Andreas Dorpalen, "Emperor Frederick III and the German Liberal Movement," *American Historical Review*, LIV, no. 1 (October 1948):6–7.

134. Bamberger to Stern, March 13, 1888, Stern Nachlass; Bamberger to Stauffenberg, April 29, 1888, Stauffenberg Nachlass; Bamberger, *Bismarcks grosses Spiel*, p. 342.

135. Bamberger's role in the ninety-nine-day reign is documented and discussed in his *Bismarcks grosses Spiel*, pp. 49–58, 340–406; Bamberger to Stern, March 13, 1888, Stern Nachlass; Bamberger to Stauffenberg, May 13, 1888, Karl Schrader Nachlass, Niedersächsisches Staatsarchiv, Wolfenbüttel; Michael Freund, *Das Drama der 99 Tage: Krankheit und Tod Friedrichs III* (Cologne and Berlin, 1966), pp. 351–93.

136. Schrader to Stauffenberg, June 21, August 11, 1888, in *DLZB*, II:443–44, 445–48.

137. Wegner, *Theodor Barth und die Freisinnige Vereinigung*, p. 4.

138. Bamberger to Stern, March 13, 1888, Stern Nachlass; Bamberger to Stauffenberg, February 3, [1888], Stauffenberg Nachlass.

139. Bamberger to Stauffenberg, April 6, 1889, Stauffenberg Nachlass. The last sentence is in English in the original.

140. Bamberger to Stauffenberg, April 6, 1889, Stauffenberg Nachlass.

141. Bamberger, "Aera der Toaste," p. 349.

142. Bamberger to Stauffenberg, April 6, 1889, Stauffenberg Nachlass.

143. Bamberger to Stauffenberg, October 2, 1889, February 23, 1889, Stauffenberg Nachlass; Bamberger to Broemel, July 15, 1889, Broemel Nachlass; Seeber, *Zwischen Bebel und Bismarck*, pp. 188–96.

144. Schrader to Stauffenberg, April 9, 1887, in *DLZB*, II:434.

CHAPTER 11. THE 1890s: A NEW BEGINNING?

1. Bamberger, *Die Nachfolge Bismarcks* (Berlin, 1889), pp. 4–6, 17–18, 26–27.
2. Bamberger to Stauffenberg, February 23, 1889, Stauffenberg Nachlass.

3. J. C. G. Röhl, "The Disintegration of the *Kartell* and the Politics of Bismarck's Fall from Power," pp. 60–89, and *Germany without Bismarck* (London, 1967), pp. 27–55; Wilhelm Mommsen, *Bismarcks Sturz und die Parteien* (Berlin, 1924), pp. 147–49.

4. Reichstagsbureau, ed., *Generalregister zu den stenographischen Berichten* . . . *Deutschen Reichstages*, III, Session 1894–95 (Berlin, 1896), pp. 350–51.

5. Bamberger to Stauffenberg, January 26, 1890, Stauffenberg Nachlass.

6. Bamberger, "Zum Jahrestag der Entlassung Bismarcks," *GS*, V:323.

7. Bamberger to Stauffenberg, January 3, 26, 1890, Stauffenberg Nachlass; Bamberger to Broemel, February 13, 1890, Broemel Nachlass.

8. Bamberger to Stauffenberg, March 21, 1890, Stauffenberg Nachlass; Mommsen, *Bismarcks Sturz*, pp. 147–49, 153, 159.

9. Bamberger to Broemel, n.d., no. 220, Broemel Nachlass.

10. Bamberger, "Über Kompromisse," *GS*, V:305; idem, "Die wahre Militärpartei," *GS*, I:328; idem, "Frankreich und Russland," *GS*, I:455; idem, "Fragen an die ewigen Sterne," p. 77.

11. Bamberger to Stauffenberg, August 14, 1887, in *DLZB*, II:435.

12. Bamberger, "Über Kompromisse," p. 305; idem, "Etwas über das Briefschreiben," *GS*, I:28; idem, "Der staatserhaltende Beruf der Hölle," *GS*, I:375; idem, "Zum Jahrestag der Entlassung Bismarcks," pp. 320, 329–30, 335–36, 339–40; idem, "Vor fünfundzwanzig Jahren," p. 439; idem, *Bismarck posthumus*, pp. 3, 5, 6, 14, 18, 20, 22, 59–60, 63–64; Bamberger to Broemel, June 14, 1891, Broemel Nachlass; Bamberger to Stauffenberg, August 3, 1893, Stauffenberg Nachlass; Adolf Rubinstein, *Die Deutsch-Freisinnige Partei bis zu ihrem Auseinanderbruch (1884–1893)* (Basel, 1935), pp. 47–48.

13. Cited in Hartwig, *Ludwig Bamberger*, pp. 73–74.

14. On the Caprivi era, see J. Alden Nichols, *Germany After Bismarck: The Caprivi Era, 1890–1894* (Cambridge, Mass., 1958); Heinrich O. Meisner, "Der Reichskanzler Caprivi," *Zeitschrift für die gesamte Staatswissenschaft*, CXI, no. 4 (1955):669–752; Röhl, *Germany without Bismarck*, pp. 56–117.

15. Rubinstein, *Deutsch-Freisinnige Partei*, pp. 63, 65–71; Meisner, "Der Reichskanzler Caprivi," pp. 695–707; Bamberger to Stauffenberg, March 26, April 5, 1891, August 18, 1892, Stauffenberg Nachlass; Bamberger to Broemel, July 7, August 16, 1892, Broemel Nachlass; Leo von Caprivi to Bamberger, March 28, 1898, Bamberger Nachlass, Potsdam; Schrader to Bamberger, April 6, 1891, Stauffenberg Nachlass; Theodor Barth, *Liberalismus und Sozialdemokratie* (Berlin, n.d. [1908]), p. 31.

16. From the *Berliner Börsenzeitung*, April 17, 1890, cited by Seeber, *Zwischen Bebel und Bismarck*, pp. 197–98.

17. Caprivi complained about Richter's "animosity" (Bamberger to Stauffenberg, April 5, 1891, Stauffenberg Nachlass).

18. Bamberger to Stauffenberg, March 21, 1890, Stauffenberg Nachlass.

19. Rachfahl, "Eugen Richter," pp. 343–46; Rubinstein, *Deutsch-Freisinnige Partei*, pp. 76–77; Nipperdey, *Organisation der deutschen Parteien*, p. 213.

20. Bamberger to Stauffenberg, April 11, 17, 1890, Stauffenberg Nachlass.

21. Bamberger to Rudolf Virchow, April 29, 1890, Bamberger Nachlass, Potsdam, Stauffenberg to Bamberger, April 25, 1890, Bamberger Nachlass, Potsdam; the emphasis is Bamberger's.

22. Bamberger to Stauffenberg, May 14, 1890, May 15, [1890], Stauffenberg Nachlass.

23. Bamberger to Stauffenberg, May 20, 1890, Stauffenberg Nachlass; the emphasis is Bamberger's.

24. Virchow to Hänel, May 21, 1890, Hänel to Virchow, May 21, 1890, Bamberger Nachlass, Potsdam.

25. Nipperdey, *Organisation der deutschen Parteien,* pp. 213–15; Rachfahl, "Eugen Richter," pp. 346–48; Seeber, *Zwischen Bebel und Bismarck,* pp. 198–99; Matthes, "Die Spaltung der Nationalliberalen Partei," pp. 258–60; Ullstein, *Eugen Richter als Publizist,* pp. 145–58.

26. Bamberger to Stauffenberg, May 22, 1890, Stauffenberg Nachlass; the emphasis is Bamberger's.

27. Schrader to Bamberger, May 24, 1890, Bamberger Nachlass, Potsdam.

28. Bamberger to Stauffenberg, May 26, 1890, Stauffenberg Nachlass.

29. Seeber, *Zwischen Bebel und Bismarck,* pp. 198–201; Nipperdey correctly sees the military question as incidental to the quarrel (*Organisation der deutschen Parteien,* p. 215). Bamberger to Stauffenberg, April 11, 17, May 14, 1890, Stauffenberg Nachlass.

30. Bamberger to Stauffenberg, May 22, 1890, Stauffenberg Nachlass. The last sentence is in English in the original.

31. Bamberger to Stauffenberg, May 26, 1890, Stauffenberg Nachlass; *SBR,* 8 LP, 1 S, June 26, 1890, pp. 611–13, 613–15; Bamberger, *Bismarcks grosses Spiel,* pp. 446–48, 468–69.

32. Bamberger to Stauffenberg, May 26, 29, 30, 1890, Stauffenberg Nachlass; Bamberger to Mommsen, May 28, 1890, Mommsen Nachlass.

33. See the statements of Barth and Richter in the *Freisinnige Zeitung,* June 1, 1890, File 209, Bamberger Nachlass, Potsdam. Richter made it clear that he would accept nothing less than restoration to his former position (Bamberger to Stauffenberg, June 3, 1890, Stauffenberg Nachlass).

34. Bamberger to Stauffenberg, June 9, 1890, Stauffenberg Nachlass; Seeber, *Zwischen Bebel und Bismarck,* pp. 199–200; Rachfahl, "Eugen Richter," pp. 348–53.

35. Seeber, *Zwischen Bebel und Bismarck,* p. 200; Matthes, "Die Spaltung der Nationalliberalen Partei," pp. 282–85.

36. Bamberger to Stauffenberg, April 7, 18, 1891, Stauffenberg Nachlass; Bamberger, *Bismarcks grosses Spiel,* p. 468; *SBR,* 8 LP, 1 S, December 5, 1891, pp. 3259–63.

37. Bamberger's arguments can be sampled in *SBR,* 8 LP, 1 S, December 1, 1891, January 14, March 4, 5, 7, 28, 1892, pp. 3171–85, 3627–35, 4564–66, 4579–83, 4607–11, 4618–29, 5065–66; *SBR,* 8 LP, 2 S, February 25, 28, March 1, 2, 1893, pp. 1261–66, 1316, 1350–52, 1375–79; Spellmeyer, *Deutsche Kolonialpolitik,* pp. 42–62; Bamberger to Broemel, August 16, 1892, Broemel Nachlass. For suggestions of the army's opposition to the colonial policy, see Alfred Waldersee, *Denkwürdigkeiten,* 3 vols. (Stuttgart, 1923), II:33; Bamberger, *Bismarcks grosses Spiel,* p. 473.

38. Bamberger to Stauffenberg, March 26, April 5, 1891, Schrader to Bamberger, April 6, 1891, Stauffenberg Nachlass.

39. Nichols, *Germany after Bismarck,* pp. 138–44; Bamberger to Stauffenberg, January 7, 1891, Stauffenberg Nachlass; Walther Lotz, *Die Handelspolitik des Deutschen Reiches unter Graf Caprivi und Fürst Hohenlohe (1890–1900),* Schriften des Vereins für Sozialpolitik, XCII (Leipzig, 1901), pp. 51–78; Kenneth D. Barkin, *The Controversy over German Industrialization, 1890–1902* (Chicago, 1970), pp. 37–40.

40. Bamberger to Stauffenberg, March 26, April 5, 18, 1891, Stauffenberg Nachlass; Bamberger to Broemel, June 2, 1892, Broemel Nachlass; Bamberger, *Bismarcks grosses Spiel,* pp. 468–69.

41. Nichols, *Germany after Bismarck,* pp. 144–53; *SBR,* 8 LP, 1 S, December 16, 1891, January 22, 1892, pp. 3482–84, 3807–10; *Schulthess' Europäischer Geschichtskalender,* 1891 (Munich, 1892), pp. 161–81; Lotz, *Handelspolitik des Deutschen Reiches,* pp. 80–97; Daikin, *Controversy over German Industrialization,* pp. 50–60.

42. Nichols, *Germany after Bismarck,* pp. 157–204.

43. Bamberger to Broemel, July 7, August 16, 1892, Broemel Nachlass; Bamberger to Stauffenberg, August 18, November 9, 1892, Stauffenberg Nachlass; Bamberger to Barth, July 27, 1892, Barth Nachlass; *Schulthess' Europäischer Geschichtskalender,* 1892 (Munich, 1893), pp. 99–103.

44. Nichols, *Germany after Bismarck,* pp. 204–15; Ludwig Rüdt von Collenberg, *Die deutsche Armee von 1871 bis 1914, Forschungen und Darstellungen aus dem Reichsarchiv,* IV (Berlin, 1922), pp. 43–49.

45. Nichols, *Germany after Bismarck,* pp. 216–28; Bamberger to Stauffenberg, April 18, 1891, Stauffenberg Nachlass.

46. Nichols, *Germany after Bismarck,* pp. 215–16, 229–38; Bamberger to Stauffenberg, November 9, 1892, Stauffenberg Nachlass; *SBR,* 8 LP, 2 S, December 12, 1892, p. 327; Bamberger to Otto Hartwig, December 11, 1892, Otto Hartwig Nachlass, Hessische Landesbibliothek, Wiesbaden; *Schulthess' Europäischer Geschichtskalender,* 1892 (Munich, 1893), pp. 187–91.

47. Bamberger to Stauffenberg. January 15, 20, 1893, Stauffenberg Nachlass; Nichols, *Germany after Bismarck,* pp. 243–45; Seeber, *Zwischen Bebel und Bismarck,* pp. 202–03.

48. Caprivi to Bamberger, April 23, 1893, and Bamberger's description of the meeting with the chancellor written on Caprivi's letter, Bamberger Nachlass, Potsdam; Bamberger, *Bismarcks grosses Spiel,* pp. 472–79; Bamberger to Stauffenberg, March 30, April 24, 1893, Stauffenberg Nachlass; Nichols, *Germany after Bismarck,* pp. 245–52.

49. Nichols, *Germany after Bismarck,* pp. 252–53; Bamberger to Stauffenberg, May 6, 1893, Stauffenberg Nachlass; *Schulthess' Europäischer Geschichtskalender,* 1893 (Munich, 1894), pp. 51–52.

50. Bamberger to Stauffenberg, May 6, 1893, Stauffenberg Nachlass; Helfferich, *Georg von Siemens,* II:192–93.

51. Bamberger to Stauffenberg, May 7, 1893, Stauffenberg Nachlass; Seeber, *Zwischen Bebel und Bismarck,* p. 205. Nipperdey, *Organisation der deutschen Parteien,* pp. 216–24; Rachfahl, "Eugen Richter," pp. 354–74. On the subsequent evolution of the two groups see Wegner, *Theodor Barth;* Peter Gilg, *Die Erneuerung des demokratischen Denkens im wilhelminischen Deutschland* (Wiesbaden, 1965); Ludwig Elm, *Zwischen Fortschritt und Reaktion: Geschichte der Parteien der liberalen Bourgeoisie in Deutschland, 1893–1918* (Berlin, 1968).

52. Seeber, *Zwischen Bebel und Bismarck,* pp. 205–06; Ziekursch, *Politische Geschichte,* III:66–68; Rubinstein, *Deutsch-Freisinnige Partei,* pp. 85–86.

53. Bamberger, "Einige Wahlbetrachtungen," *Die Nation,* X, June 24, 1893, p. 585.

54. Bamberger to Stauffenberg, May 11, 1893, Stauffenberg Nachlass.

55. Bamberger to Stauffenberg, June 15, September 14, 1893, Stauffenberg Nachlass; Bamberger to Barth, June 30, 1893, Barth Nachlass.

56. Bamberger to Stauffenberg, July 3, 1898, Stauffenberg Nachlass.

57. Bamberger to Stern, April 7, 1893, Stern Nachlass; Bamberger to Otto Hartwig, April 9, 1893, cited in Hartwig, *Ludwig Bamberger,* p. 75.

58. Bamberger to Hartwig, May 1893, cited in Hartwig, *Ludwig Bamberger,* p. 75; Bamberger to Stauffenberg, May 7, June 15, 1893, Stauffenberg Nachlass.

59. Broemel to Bamberger, May 8, 1893, Richter to Notary Public Wolf (Mainz), May 10, 1893, Richter to Bamberger, May 12, 1893, Bamberger Nachlass, Potsdam.

60. Bamberger to Stauffenberg, May 7, June 15, 1893, Stauffenberg Nachlass; Bamberger to Barth, June 30, July 2, 1893, Barth Nachlass; Wegner, *Theodor Barth*, pp. 68–70.

61. Wegner, *Theodor Barth*, pp. 19–20, 60, 104–07; Bamberger to Stauffenberg, May 7, August 13, September 14, November 5, December 29, 1893, Stauffenberg Nachlass; Bamberger to Barth, August 5, 23, 1893, Barth Nachlass; Bamberger to Broemel, September 13, December 4, 1893, Broemel Nachlass; Bamberger to Stern, October 29, 1893, Stern Nachlass.

62. Ludwig Elm, "Freisinnige Vereinigung," in *Die bürgerlichen Parteien in Deutschland*, II (Leipzig, 1970), p. 70; Bamberger to Stauffenberg, November 5, 1893, Stauffenberg Nachlass; Wegner, *Theodor Barth*, pp. 94–99; Nipperdey, *Organisation der deutschen Parteien*, pp. 224–30.

63. On the agrarian movement and its impact on German politics see Sarah R. Tirrell, *German Agrarian Politics After Bismarck's Fall* (New York, 1951); Hans-Jürgen Puhle, *Agrarische Interessenpolitik und preussischer Konservatismus im wilhelminischen Reich (1893–1914)* (Hanover, 1967); Johannes Croner, *Die Geschichte der agrarischen Bewegung in Deutschland* (Berlin, 1909). Over half the membership of the Bund der Landwirte came from outside Prussia and were small farmers (Puhle, *Agrarische Interessenpolitik*, pp. 39, 309). Nevertheless, its leadership and policies were Junker-oriented.

64. Barkin, *Controversy over German Industrialization*, pp. 62–89; Lotz, *Handelspolitik des Deutschen Reiches*, pp. 107–33; Nichols, *Germany after Bismarck*, pp. 287–307; Wegner, *Theodor Barth*, pp. 29–31; Bamberger to Stauffenberg, August 3, December 29, 1893, Stauffenberg Nachlass; Bamberger to Barth, August 5, 23, 1893, Barth Nachlass; Bamberger, "Und sie bewegt sich doch," *Die Nation*, March 24, 1894, pp. 375–77; idem, "Ein Wendepunkt," *Die Nation*, September 5, 1896, pp. 730–31.

65. Nichols, *Germany after Bismarck*, pp. 340–77; Bamberger to Stauffenberg, November 1, 1894, Stauffenberg Nachlass.

66. Bamberger to Stauffenberg, November 1, 1894, January 2, March 22, 1896, Stauffenberg Nachlass; Bamberger to Stern, Good Friday, 1897, Stern Nachlass; Bamberger to Broemel, June 30, July 22, 1897, October 6, 1898, Broemel Nachlass; Ziekursch, *Politische Geschichte*, III:78–87, 107–12; Röhl, *Germany without Bismarck*, pp. 210–40, 246–48.

67. Bamberger to Stauffenberg, January 2, 1896, September 13, 1897, Stauffenberg Nachlass; Bamberger to Broemel, June 30, July 22, 1897, Broemel Nachlass; Wegner, *Theodor Barth*, pp. 68–70; Elm, *Zwischen Fortschritt und Reaktion*, pp. 73–75.

68. Bamberger to Stauffenberg, July 31, 1894, Stauffenberg Nachlass.

69. Bamberger to Stern, April 16, 1893, Stern Nachlass.

70. Abraham Ascher, "Baron von Stumm: Advocate of Feudal Capitalism," *Journal of Central European Affairs*, XXII (October 1962):271–78; Shanahan, *German Protestants*, pp. 394–97; Sheehan, *Career of Lujo Brentano*, p. 141; Born, *Staat und Sozialpolitik*, pp. 42–43, 47, 59, 66–69, 113–16, 124–26, 135–39; Ziekursch, *Politische Geschichte*, II:73–84; Wahl, *Deutsche Geschichte*, III:569–86, 625–34; Ernst Engelberg, *Deutschland von 1871 bis 1897* (Berlin, 1965), pp. 370, 378–83; Dieter Fricke, "Zur Militärisierung des deutschen Geisteslebens in wilhelminischen Kaiserreich: der Fall Leo Arons," *Zeitschrift für Geschichtswissenschaft*, VII, no. 5 (1960):1097–98.

71. Sheehan, *Career of Lujo Brentano*, 104–12, 124–27, 129, 134–38; *Die Nation*, July 25, 1896, p. 641.

72. Bamberger, "Liberalismus und Sozialismus," *Die Nation*, August 1, 1896, pp. 653–54.

73. Bamberger to Barth, March 31, 1897, Brentano Nachlass, cited in Sheehan, *Career of Lujo Brentano*, p. 134; Lujo Brentano, "Die Agrarreform in Preussen," *Die Nation*, March 13, 20, 27, April 3, 1897, pp. 359–62, 374–79, 392–96, 406–10.

74. Bamberger to Stauffenberg, September 13, 1897, Stauffenberg Nachlass; Bamberger, "Wandlungen und Wanderungen in der Sozialpolitik," *Die Nation*, March 12, 1898, p. 344.

75. Brentano, *Mein Leben*, pp. 206–07.

76. Bamberger, "Wandlungen und Wanderungen," March 5, 1898, 326–27.

77. Bamberger, "Wandlungen und Wanderungen," March 19, 1898, pp. 360–61; Dieter Lindenlaub, *Richtungskämpfe im Verein für Sozialpolitik im Kaiserreich*, 2 vols. (Wiesbaden, 1967), II:83.

78. Bamberger, "Wandlungen und Wanderungen," March 5, 12, 1898, pp. 327–28, 343–44.

79. Bamberger, "Wandlungen und Wanderungen," March 12, 1898, pp. 344–45.

80. Theodor Barth, *Die sozialdemokratische Gedankenwelt*, Volkswirtschaftliche Zeitfragen, XII, nos. 95–96 (Berlin, 1890), pp. 1–3, 68.

81. Roth, *The Social Democrats in Imperial Germany*, pp. 179–83; Lipinski, *Die Sozialdemokratie*, II:142–45; Lidtke, *The Outlawed Party*, pp. 115–28, 176–78, 191–96, 200–40, 256, 275–78.

82. Roth, *Social Democrats in Imperial Germany*, pp. 183–85; Peter Gay, *The Dilemma of Democratic Socialism: Eduard Bernstein's Challenge to Karl Marx* (New York, 1952), pp. 141–252.

83. Walter Gagel, *Die Wahlrechtsfrage in der Geschichte der deutschen liberalen Parteien, 1848–1918* (Dusseldorf, 1958), pp. 147–48; Barth, *Liberalismus und Sozialdemokratie*, pp. 12–15, 23, 32–33; Sheehan, *Career of Lujo Brentano*, pp. 137–38; Born, *Staat und Sozialpolitik*, pp. 72, 104, 106–07; Ernst Cahn, "Die Stellung des Liberalismus zu den wirtschaftlichen und sozialen Problemen," in Leonard Nelson et al., *Was ist liberal?* (Munich, 1910), pp. 56, 60, 62.

84. Bamberger, "Zur Philosophie des Bäckerstreites," *Die Nation*, July 11, 1896, pp. 611–12.

85. Bamberger to Stern, May 31, 1890, Stern Nachlass; Bamberger, "Die Krisis in Deutschland," pp. 420–23.

86. Bamberger, "Die sozialistische Bewegung in Frankreich," *Die Nation*, March 6, 1897, pp. 343–44, 346; idem, "Fragen an die ewigen Sterne," p. 81; idem, "Wandlungen und Wanderungen," March 19, 1898, p. 361.

87. Barth, *Liberalismus und Sozialdemokratie*, pp. 23, 32–33, 39; Heuss, *Theodor Mommsen*, p. 217.

88. Bamberger, "Liberalismus und Sozialismus," p. 654.

89. Brentano, *Mein Leben*, pp. 206–07, 239.

90. *Die Nation*, July 25, 1896, p. 640; Wegner, *Theodor Barth*, pp. 17–26, 102, 131; Elm, *Zwischen Fortschritt und Reaktion*, pp. 39–45, 103–39.

91. Bamberger, "Aera der Toaste," 349–52; idem, "Fragen an die ewigen Sterne," pp. 74–75.

92. Bamberger, "Wandlungen und Wanderungen," March 19, 1898, pp. 360–62; Bamberger to Stern, July [June] 5, 1898, Stern Nachlass.

93. *SBR*, 8 LP, 2 S, February 15, 1893, pp. 1062–65, 1067. This indeed is Puhle's thesis.

94. Bamberger, "Die Krisis in Deutschland," pp. 428–30.

95. Bamberger, "Laskers Briefwechsel," pp. 119–20; idem, *Erinnerungen,* p. 519.

96. Bamberger, *Erinnerungen,* p. 501.

97. Bamberger, *"Über Kompromisse,"* pp. 306–07; idem, "Laskers Briefwechsel," pp. 120, 121, 126.

98. Bamberger, "Die ersten zwei Jahrhunderte der Geschichte von Florenz," *Die Nation,* November 11, 1895, pp. 87–89.

99. Bamberger to Stauffenberg, July 3, 1898, Stauffenberg Nachlass; Bamberger to Stern, January 12, 1892, Stern Nachlass.

100. Bamberger to Stauffenberg, March 6, 1892, Stauffenberg Nachlass.

101. Bamberger, "Fragen an die ewigen Sterne," pp. 85–86; idem, "Arthur Chuquet," *GS,* II:272; idem, "In Ferienstimmung," *GS,* II:224; Bamberger to Stauffenberg, July 31, 1894, Stauffenberg Nachlass.

102. Bamberger, "Über einige Formen des geselligen Verkehrs," *GS,* I:95–96; idem, *Erinnerungen,* p. 213; Bamberger to Maximilian Harden, December 22, 1889, Maximilian Harden Nachlass, Bundesarchiv, Koblenz.

103. Zucker, "Ludwig Bamberger and the Rise of Anti-Semitism in Germany, 1848–1893," pp. 348–52.

104. Peter Pulzer, *The Rise of Political Anti-Semitism in Germany and Austria* (New York, 1964), pp. 112–17; Richard Massing, *Rehearsal for Destruction* (New York, 1949), pp. 92–96.

105. Bamberger to Stern, December 24, 1892, Stern Nachlass; Bamberger to Stauffenberg, May 18, 1892, March 30, 1893, Stauffenberg Nachlass.

106. Bamberger to Oppenheim, n.d., no. 306, Bamberger Nachlass, Potsdam; Bamberger to Stauffenberg, n.d., no. 68, Stauffenberg Nachlass; Bamberger to Stern, January 12, 1892, Stern Nachlass.

107. Bamberger, "Heinrich von Treitschke," pp. 202–03.

108. *SBR,* 8 LP, 1 S, June 12, 1890, p. 300.

109. *Schulthess' Europäischer Geschichtskalender,* 1893, pp. 30–31, 32–33; *SBR,* 8 LP, 2 S, April 27, 28, 1893, pp. 2042–48, May 6, 1893, p. 2214; *SBR,* 8 LP, 1 S, March 24, 1892, pp. 5134–36; *SBR,* 8 LP, 2 S, 1892–93, *Anlagen,* no. 163, p. 879.

110. *SBR,* 8 LP, 1 S, May 12, June 9, 12, 1890, pp. 35–38, 47, 235–39, 285–86, 298–99.

111. *SBR,* 8 LP, 2 S, March 14, 1893, pp. 1642–43, 1648–49.

112. *SBR,* 8 LP, 2 S, December 12, 1892, p. 284.

113. Hartwig, *Ludwig Bamberger,* p. 75; Bamberger to Stauffenberg, May 7, 1893, Stauffenberg Nachlass.

114. Bamberger to Stern, July 8, 1889, April 16, 1893, Stern Nachlass; Bamberger to Barth, August 23, 1893, Barth Nachlass.

115. Bamberger to Stern, December 24, 1892, Stern Nachlass.

116. Barth, "Ludwig Bamberger," p. 17; Bamberger to Stauffenberg, July 31, 1894, Stauffenberg Nachlass.

117. Bamberger to Stern, April 3, 1887, Stern Nachlass.

118. Ernst Feder, *Paul Nathan: Politik und Humanität* (Berlin, 1929), pp. 59–60; Julius Rodenberg, "Ludwig Bamberger," p. 296; Bamberger to Stauffenberg, July 3, 15, November 15, 1898, Stauffenberg Nachlass; Bamberger to Mommsen, June 28, 1898, Mommsen Nachlass.

119. Anna von Helmholtz to Ida Siemens-Helmholtz, March 16, [1899], in Siemens-Helmholtz, *Anna von Helmholtz,* II:183; Feder, *Paul Nathan,* pp. 62–63; Bamberger,

"Wunsch an mein Testamentsvollstrecker," May 19, 1892, Bamberger Papers, New York; *National Zeitung,* March 18, 1899; *Neuste Anzeiger* (Mainz), January 28, 1916; Schrader to Rudolf Bamberger, November 6, 1899, Schrader Nachlass; Hartwig, *Ludwig Bamberger,* p. 85.

120. It is impossible to estimate the value of Bamberger's estate. Some idea of its enormous size can be gained from his will of December 24, 1874, plus the codicils of November 8, 1897, April 4 and October 28, 1898, found in his papers at the Leo Baeck Institute in New York.

121. Anna von Helmholtz to Ida Siemens-Helmholtz, March 16, [1899], in Siemens-Helmholtz, *Anna von Helmholtz,* II:183. See also Johannes von Miquel to Rudolf Bamberger, March 16, 1899, Bamberger Nachlass, Potsdam; Feder, *Paul Nathan,* pp. 61–62.

CHAPTER 12. CONCLUSION

1. *Berliner Tageblatt,* March 14, 1899; *Kölnische Zeitung,* March 15, 1899; *Frankfurter Zeitung,* March 15, 1899.

2. Anna von Helmholtz to Ida Siemens-Helmholtz, September 7, 1896, in Siemens-Helmholtz, *Anna von Helmholtz,* II:127.

3. Bamberger, "Wandlungen und Wanderungen," March 19, 1898, p. 361; idem, *Erinnerungen,* p. 97.

4. Bamberger, "Wandlungen und Wanderungen," March 19, 1898, p. 361; idem, *Erinnerungen,* pp. 381–82.

5. Bamberger, "Wandlungen und Wanderungen," March 5, 1898, pp. 328–29.

6. *SBR,* 7 LP, 2 S, January 28, 1888, p. 578.

7. Heuss, *Theodor Mommsen,* pp. 197–98; Bamberger's speech in Wörrstadt, June 19, 1881, Lasker Nachlass, Brandeis.

8. Bamberger, "Fragen an die ewigen Sterne," pp. 79, 84–85.

9. Bamberger, "Lieber schwäbisch als preussisch," *Die Nation,* October 2, 1897, p. 4.

10. Bamberger, "Zum Jahrestag der Entlassung Bismarcks," pp. 349–50.

11. Bamberger, "Die Ehrenrettung der hinkenden Währung," *Die Nation,* July 15, 1893, pp. 629–32; idem, "So reden die Tatsachen," *Die Nation,* November 7, 1896, pp. 82–84; idem, "Das Ende vom Lied," *Die Nation,* October 30, 1897, pp. 65–67; idem, "Zur Erneuerung des Bankgesetzes," *Die Nation,* December 24, 1898, January 28, 1899, pp. 181–82, 252–53.

12. Bamberger, "Politik und Wirtschaft," *Die Nation,* March 23, 1895, pp. 349–51.

13. Bamberger to Stauffenberg, January 2, 1896, Stauffenberg Nachlass; Bamberger, "Der Fall Rommel," *Die Nation,* March 26, 1898, pp. 376–78.

𝔅𝔦𝔟𝔩𝔦𝔬𝔤𝔯𝔞𝔭𝔥𝔶

UNPUBLISHED SOURCES

Berthold Auerbach Nachlass, Deutsches Literaturarchiv, Schiller Nationalmuseum, Marbach.

Ludwig Bamberger Nachlass, 90 Ba 3, Deutsches Zentralarchiv, Potsdam. The most useful material came from the following files:

File	3	Ludwig Aegidi
	7	Berthold Auerbach
	13	Theodor Barth
	26	Wilhelm Blum
	31	Otto Braun
	33	Max Broemel
	36	Moritz Busch
	37	Leo von Caprivi
	45	Hermann von Dechend
	46	Adalbert Delbrück
	48	Ludwig Dietz
	52	Franz Duncker
	59	Max von Forckenbeck
	78	Otto Hartwig
	80	Albert Hänel
	91	Karl Hillebrand
	103	Friedrich Kapp
	113	Heinrich Kruse
	114	Heinrich von Kusserow
	118	Eduard Lasker
	137	Wilhelm Löwe-Kalb
	151	Theodor Mommsen
	153	Paul Nathan
	155	Heinrich Bernhard Oppenheim
	166	Eugen Richter
	167	Heinrich Rickert
	186	Gustav Schmoller
	188	Karl Schrader
	192	Franz Freiherr Schenk von Stauffenberg
	202	Heinrich von Treitschke

209   Rudolf Virchow
226   Mainz, Hesse-Darmstadt, 1867–1884
232   Fusion
236   Franco-Prussian War
238   Currency matters

Ludwig Bamberger Nachlass, Stadtarchiv, Mainz, Packets 277, 278, 286, 296.

Ludwig Bamberger Nachlass, Handschriftenabteilung, Staatsbibliothek, Stiftung Preussischer Kulturbesitz, Berlin-Dahlem. Contains over five-hundred letters, mostly from Bamberger to his wife, mother, and mother-in-law from 1844–47 and 1867–82. The material is not catalogued.

Ludwig Bamberger Papers, Leo Baeck Institute, New York. A few letters, plus Bamberger's last will and testament.

Ludwig Bamberger Papers, Jewish National and University Library, Jerusalem. A handful of letters.

Theodor Barth Nachlass, 90 Ba 4, Deutsches Zentralarchiv, Potsdam. File 4 contains eleven letters from Bamberger.

Johann K. Bluntschli Nachlass, Zentralbibliothek, Zurich.

Max Broemel Nachlass, 90 Br 3, Deutsches Zentralarchiv, Potsdam. File 4 contains 190 letters from Bamberger.

Max von Forckenbeck Nachlass, rep. 92, Deutsches Zentralarchiv, Merseburg. Files 9 and 10 contain a few letters from Bamberger.

Maximilian Harden Nachlass, heft 1–6, no. 8, Bundesarchiv, Koblenz.

Otto Hartwig Nachlass, Hessische Landesbibliothek, Wiesbaden. Only one of Bamberger's

Eduard Lasker Nachlass, 90 La 6, Deutsches Zentralarchiv, Potsdam. File 8 contains seventy-five letters from Bamberger.

Rahel Liebeschütz Collection, Liverpool.

Paul Lindau Nachlass, Kl. Erw., no. 310, Bundesarchiv, Koblenz.

Theodor Mommsen Nachlass, Handschriftenabteilung, Deutsche Staatsbibliothek, Berlin.

Karl Schrader Nachlass, 240 N IV, 1, 8, Niedersächsisches Staatsarchiv, Wolfenbüttel.

Franz Freiherr Schenk von Stauffenberg Nachlass, Deutsches Zentralarchiv, Potsdam. Contains approximately one-hundred fifty letters from Bamberger in three files: File 1 (March 1877–December 1884), File 2 (April 1885–June 1890), File 3 (January 1891–January 1899).

Alfred Stern Nachlass, Kl. Erw., no. 314, Bundesarchiv, Koblenz.

Philipp Wasserburg Nachlass, Stadtarchiv, Mainz.

Polizei Berichte, 1847–1851, Abt. 131, XVIII, 5, Stadtarchiv, Mainz.

Polizei Berichte, Pr. Br. Rep. 30 Berlin C, Staatsarchiv Potsdam.

    Tit. 94, Lit. B, no. 382 (8921) Ludwig Bamberger
    Tit. 94, Lit. S, no. 1431 (13143) Die Sezessionistische Partei, 1883–1884.
    Tit. 95, Sekt. 5, Lit. 4, no. 72 (15131) Die Fortschrittspartei
    Tit. 95, Sekt. 5, Lit. F, no. 54 (15179) Verein zur Förderung der Handelsfreiheit
    Tit. 95, Sekt. 5, Lit. L, no. 53 (15278) Bestrebungen der Partei "Liberale Vereinigung" (Sezessionisten), 1882–1884

WORKS BY LUDWIG BAMBERGER

As in the notes, Bamberger's *Gesammelte Schriften* (5 vols., Berlin, 1894–98), is abbreviated as *GS*.

"Adam Lux." *GS*, II:3–40.
"Adolph Soetbeer." *GS*, II:251–62.
"Die Aera der Toaste." *GS*, I:342–52.
Alte Parteien und neue Zustände. Berlin, 1867. *GS*, III.291–336.
"An die Wähler Rheinhessens von einem alten Freunde." *Mainzer Zeitung* (Extra Beilage), December 7, 1866.
Die Arbeiterfrage unter dem Gesichtspunkte des Vereinsrechtes. Stuttgart, 1873.
"Arthur Chuquet." *GS*, II:263–308.
Die Aufhebung der indirekten Gemeindeabgaben in Belgien, Holland und Frankreich. Berlin, 1871.
"Aus der Praxis des Redens." *Die Nation*, September 22, 1894, pp. 752–55.
"Aus grünen Tagen." *Salon*, 1869, pp. 169–71.
"Auszug aus der Volkszeitung vom März 1860." *GS*, IV:58–67.
"Bedenken gegen die Freigebigkeit auf Staatskosten." *Mainzer Zeitung* (Extra Beilage), March 7, 1868.
Bericht über die Angelegenheit des Oktrois. Mainz, 1870.
"Berlin in Paris." *Deutsche Jahrbücher für Politik und Literatur*, V (1862):313–19. *GS*, III:255–66.
Bismarck posthumus. Berlin, 1899.
Bismarcks grosses Spiel: die geheimen Tagebücher Ludwig Bambergers. Edited by Ernst Feder. Frankfurt on the Main, 1932.
"Der Bürger zweier Welten." *Gartenlaube*, 1869, pp. 341–44.
"Demokraten und Diplomaten an der Mainlinie." *Mainzer Zeitung*, June 16, 18, 1867.
[A. Freimund, pseud.] *Demokratischer Kalender für 1849*. Mainz, 1849.
"Die deutsche Kolonie in Paris." *GS*, I:213–55.
"Ein deutscher Beitrag zur Geschichte der Commune." *Deutsche Rundschau*, XVIII (1879):477–83.
"Deutsches Bürgertum." *Die Nation*, September 27, 1884, pp. 706–09.
"Die deutsche Tagespresse." *GS*, V:277–99.
"Deutschland, Frankreich und die Revolution." In his *Herr von Bismarck*, pp. iii–lvi. Berlin, 1868.
Deutschlands Not und Aerzte. Berlin, 1859.
Deutschland und der Sozialismus. Leipzig, 1878.
"Deutschtum und Judentum." *Unsere Zeit*, 1880(1):188–205. *GS*, V:3–37.
"Dr. Wilhelm Cahns Pariser Gedenkblätter." *Deutsche Rundschau*, XCIV (1898):477–80.
"Dunkle Vorstellungen." *GS*, I:335–41.
"Eduard Lasker: Gedenkrede." *GS*, II:87–116.
"Die Ehre gerettet." *Die Nation*, March 2, 1895, pp. 307–09.
"Die Ehrenrettung der hinkenden Währung." *Die Nation*, July 15, 1893, pp. 629–32.
"Einheit zur Einigkeit." *National Zeitung*, December 7, 1870.
"Einige Wahlbetrachtungen." *Die Nation*, June 24, 1893, pp. 584–85.
"Eisenach." *Die Gegenwart*, October 31, 1874, pp. 273–75.
"Das Ende vom Lied." *Die Nation*, October 30, 1897, pp. 65–67.
"Die Entscheidungsschlacht vom 3. November 1896." *Cosmopolis*, V, no. 13 (January 1897):227–49.
"Die Entthronung eines Weltherrschers." (1876). *GS*, IV:311–81.
"Die Entthronung eines Weltherrschers." *Die Nation*, July 8, 1893, pp. 612–14.
Erinnerungen. Berlin, 1899.

Erlebnisse aus der pfälzischen Erhebung im Mai und Juni 1849. Frankfurt on the Main, 1849. *GS,* III:59–158.

"Ernst Renan." *GS,* II:237–50.

Die erste Sitzungsperiode des ersten deutschen Reichstags. Leipzig, 1871.

"Die ersten zwei Jahrhunderte der Geschichte von Florenz." *Die Nation,* November 11, 1893, pp. 87–89.

"Etwas über das Briefschreiben." *GS,* I:18–31.

"Der Fall Rommel." *Die Nation,* March 26, 1898, pp. 376–78.

"Fleisch und Brot–oder Papier?" *GS,* I:353–60.

"Die Flitterwochen der Pressefreiheit." *GS,* III:1–58.

"Die Folgen des deutsch-österreichischen Münzvertrages von 1857." *Die Nation,* December 17, 1894, pp. 99–100.

Foreword to *Gegen den Währungsumsturz,* by Karl Helfferich. Berlin, 1895.

Foreword to *Reimchronik des Pfaffen Maurizius,* by Moritz Hartmann. Stuttgart, 1874.

"Fragen an die ewigen Sterne." *GS,* I:69–86.

"Frankreich und Russland." *GS,* I:453–63.

"Die Französelei am Rhein. Wie sie kam, und wie sie ging (1790 bis heute)." *GS,* I:126–91.

"Die Frauenfrage." *Die Nation,* February 29, 1896, pp. 331–32.

"Die Friedensbedingung." *Amtliche Nachrichten für das General-Gouvernement Elsass* (Beilage), September 15, 1870.

"Die fünf Milliarden." *GS,* IV:219–49.

"Gedankenbann." *Die Nation,* September 17, 1887, pp. 741–44.

"Geht die Welt besseren Zeiten entgegen?" *GS,* V:159–72.

"Der Genius des Reichskanzlers und der Genius des Reichstags." *Die Gegenwart,* July 6, 1872, pp. 1–3.

"The German Daily Press." *Nineteenth Century.* XXVII (1890):24–37.

Die Geschäftswelt angesichts der Geschäftslage in Deutschland. Mainz, 1875.

"Das Gold der Zukunft." *GS,* IV:383–438.

"Die Goldklausel." *Die Nation,* July 28, 1894, pp. 635–37.

"Die Gold- und Silberfrage." *Deutsche Jahrbücher für Politik und Literatur,* I(1861):78–89.

"Gründer, Banken und Redner." *Die Gegenwart,* January 4, 1873, pp. 1–3.

"Heinrich Hombergers Essays." *GS,* II:229–36.

"Heinrich von Treitschke." *GS,* II:171–211.

Herr von Bismarck. Translated by K. A. Breslau, 1868.

"Der Herzog von Wellington über Doppelwährung." *Die Nation,* May 8, 1897, pp. 478–82.

"Das Idol der nationalen Arbeit." *Die Nation,* April 30, 1887, pp. 457–59.

"In Ferienstimmung." *GS,* II:213–25.

"In Sachen Demokratie der Stadt Mainz contra Ludwig Bamberger und Genossen. Punkto: Hochverrath." *Mainzer Zeitung* (Beilage), January 10, 27, 1867.

"In Sachen Gold gegen Silber." *Die Nation,* May 12, 1888, pp. 458–61.

Introduction to *Die Volksbank,* by Pierre-Joseph Proudhon, translated by Ludwig Bamberger. Frankfurt on the Main, 1849.

"Die Invasion der sozialistischen Ideen." In *Gegen den Staatssozialismus: drei Abhandlungen von Ludwig Bamberger, Theodor Barth und Max Broemel.* Berlin, 1884.

"Juchhe nach Italia." *GS,* III:159–92.

"Jupiter und Merkur." *Die Nation,* November 19, 1887, pp. 97–100.

"Kaisertum und Reichstag." *Die Nation,* March 21, 1888, pp. 371–73. *GS,* V:187–202.
"Der Kampf mit der Dummheit." *Die Nation,* August 21, 1897, pp. 707–09.
"Kandidatenrede." *GS,* IV:11–57.
"Eine Karikatur der Wissenschaft." *Die Nation,* May 12, 1091, pp. 473–77.
"Karl Hillebrand." *GS,* II:137–70.
"Die Krisis in Deutschland und der deutsche Kaiser." *GS,* V:417–39.
Die kulturgeschichtliche Bedeutung des Sozialistengesetzes. Leipzig, 1878.
"Die Kunst, sein Glück beim Zoll zu machen." *GS,* V:135–58.
"Kunst zu schencken, Die." *GS,* I:5–17.
"Laskers Briefwechsel aus dem Kriegsjahre." *GS,* II:117–26.
Letter to the Editor. *National Zeitung,* May 29, 1878.
[Un Allemand, pseud.] "Lettre sur l'unité allemande et le Parlement d'Erfurth." *La Voix du Peuple,* March 4, 11, 1850.
"Lieber schwäbisch als preussisch." *Die Nation,* October 2, 1897, pp. 3–5.
"Marseillaise und Afrikalotterie." *GS,* V:355–70.
"Material zur Völkerpsychologie." *Allgemeine Zeitung* (Beilage), November 1, 1870.
"Mein Freund Chenavard." *Die Nation,* June 29, 1895, pp. 556–59.
"Des Michael Pro Schriftenwechsel mit Thomas Contra, aus dem Jahre 1859." *Demokratische Studien,* I(1860):145–202. *GS,* III:204–54.
"Monatskorrespondenz London." *Deutsche Monatsschrift für Politik, Wissenschaft, Kunst und Leben,* I, nos. 1, 2 (1850):155–71, 311–25, II, nos. 4–6 (1850):123–35, 302–07, 443–49, III, nos. 7–8 (1850):153–61, 335–38.
"Monsieur de Bismarck." *Revue Moderne,* XLV (1868):8–49, 256–83. *GS,* III:337–443.
"Moritz Hartmann." *GS,* II:41–48.
"Die Motive der liberalen Opposition gegen das Jesuitengesetz." *Die Gegenwart,* June 22, 1872, pp. 337–38.
Die Nachfolge Bismarcks. Berlin, 1889.
"Nachträgliches gegen eine Berliner Weltausstellung." *Die Nation,* August 27, 1892, pp. 717–19.
"National." *GS,* V:203–25.
"Die Nationalehre." *Der Demokrat,* August 16, 1848, pp. 123–25.
"Ein neues französisches Werk über den Krieg von 1870." *Die Nation,* February 2, 1895, pp. 253–55.
"Die neue Silberkommission." *Die Nation,* January 13, 20, 27, 1894, pp. 218–20, 235–37, 251–55.
"Die neueste Aera der Spekulation." *GS,* I:401–16.
"Otto Gildemeister." *GS,* II:309–28.
"Papiere und Kanonen." *Die Nation,* September 17, 1892, pp. 761–65.
"Parteipolitik und Patriotismus." *Die Nation,* December 25, 1886, pp. 284–87.
Pessimistisches. Berlin, 1888.
"Politik und Wirtschaft." *Die Nation,* March 23, 1895, pp. 349–51.
Rede des Reichstagsabgeordneten Bamberger gehalten im Deutschen Reichsverein zu Dresden. Berlin, 1876.
Rede gehalten am Schluss des ersten allgemeinen deutschen Turnfestes in Paris. n.p., n.d. [1865].
Rede von Ludwig Bamberger gehalten bei der Gründung des demokratischen Vereins in Kostheim. Kastel, n.d.
"Die Reichsbank." *GS,* V:227–37.
Reichsgold. Leipzig, 1876.

"Reichskassenscheine, Münzreform und Reichsbank." In *Annalen des Deutschen Reiches,* edited by Georg Hirth, pp. 1602–11. Berlin, 1874.

"Das Reich und die Wissenschaft." *GS,* I:256–92.

"Reminiscenzen an Napoleon III." *GS,* II:49–86.

Reportorium des deutschen Reichstages. Berlin, 1872.

"Die Romantik auf dem Lehrstuhl der Volkswirtschaft." *Die Gegenwart,* October 5, 12, 1872, pp. 209–11, 228–30.

"Rudolf von Delbrück." *Die Nation,* April 17, 1897, pp. 433–35.

"Ein Rundschreiben, welches der Präsident des Reichseisenbahnamtes an die deutschen Bahnverwaltungen erlassen sollte." *Die Gegenwart,* August 12, 1876, pp. 97–98.

"Die russische Münzreform." *Die Nation,* January 22, 1898, pp. 239–40.

Die Schicksale des Lateinischen Münzbundes. Berlin, 1885.

Das Schreiben des Reichskanzlers an den Bundesrat vom 15. Dezember 1878 betreffend die Revision des Zolltarifs. Berlin, 1879.

"Die Sezession." *GS,* V:39–134.

"Silber." *GS,* V:371–416.

"So reden die Tatsachen." *Die Nation,* November 7, 1896, pp. 82–84.

"Die soziale Frage." In *Berthold Auerbachs Deutscher Volkskalender für 1868,* edited by Berthold Auerbach, pp. 21–37. Berlin, n.d.

Die sozialistische Gefahr. Berlin, 1886.

Speech, June 19, 1881, Wörrstadt. Lasker Nachlass, Brandeis University, Waltham, Mass.

Speech, June 26, 1881, Ober Ingelheim. Lasker Nachlass, Brandeis University, Waltham, Mass.

"Der staatserhaltende Beruf der Hölle." *GS,* I:361–86.

"Staatsmännische Indiskretionen." *GS,* I:316–25.

Die Stichworte der Silberleute. Berlin, 1893.

"Eine Stimme aus der Fremde." *Mainzer Zeitung,* January 18, 1867. *GS,* IV:1–9.

"Ein Stückchen Reminiscenz." *Die Nation,* September 23, 1893, pp. 780–82.

"Des sympathies françaises aux bords du Rhin." *Revue moderne,* XXXIV (1865):496–525.

Trauerrede auf Robert Blum. Mainz, 1848.

"Ueber das Alter." *GS,* I:108–25.

"Ueber die Gemütlichkeit in Geldsachen." *Die Nation,* November 7, 1891, pp. 79–81.

"Ueber die Grenzen des Humors in der Politik." *Deutsche Jahrbücher für Politik und Literatur,* VI(1863):175–90. *GS,* III:267–89.

"Ueber einige Formen des geselligen Verkehrs." *GS,* I:87–107.

"Ueber falsches Geld aus echtem Silber." *Die Nation,* September 2, 1893, pp. 734–36.

"Ueber Freundschaft." *Die Nation,* December 25, 1897, January 1, 1898, pp. 181–83, 197–200.

"Ueber Kompromisse." *GS,* V:301–16.

Ueber Rom und Paris nach Gotha oder die Wege des Herrn von Treitschke. Stuttgart, 1866.

"Ueber Toaste." *GS,* I:45–68.

"Und sie bewegt sich doch." *Die Nation,* March 24, 1894, pp. 375–77.

"Unsere Neuesten." *GS,* I:387–400.

"Ein Vademecum für deutsche Untertanen." *Deutsche Jahrbücher für Politik und Literatur,* XIII (1864):54–70. *GS,* I:192–212.

"Verdirbt die Politik den Charakter?" *GS,* I:293–315.

Die Verschleppung der deutschen Münzreform. Cologne, 1882.
"Ein Versuch im kleinen." *Die Nation,* February 11, 1893, pp. 301–03.
"Vertrauliche Briefe aus dem Zollparlament 1868, 1869, 1870." *GS,* IV:69–217.
"Der Vizekanitz." *Die Nation,* February 16, 1895, pp. 277–78.
"Vor fünfundzwanzig Jahren."*GS,* I:417–52.
"Vorwort." *Demokratische Studien* I(1860):1–6. *GS,* III:198–203.
"Die wahre Militärpartei." *GS,* I:326–34.
"Die Währungsfrage vor dem nationalliberalen Parteitag." *Die Nation,* October 10, 1896, pp. 20–21.
"Wandlungen und Wanderungen in der Sozialpolitik." *Die Nation,* March 5, 12, 19, 1898, pp. 326–28, 343–46, 360–62.
"Warum esse ich?" *GS,* V:173–86.
Was uns der Schutzzoll bringt: ein Schreiben an seine rheinischen Wähler. Berlin, 1879.
"Ein Weihnachtsbrief." *GS,* I:32–44.
"Ein Wendepunkt." *Die Nation,* September 5, 1896, pp. 730–31.
"Der wunde Punkt." *GS,* V:239–75.
"Zeitströmungen in der Wirtschaftslehre." *Allgemeine Zeitung* (Beilage), October 6–8, 1872, December 27, 28, 30, 31, 1873, February 12, 13, 1874.
Die Zettelbank vor dem Reichstag. Leipzig, 1874.
Die Zukunft des Zollparlaments. Mainz, n.d.
"Zum Jahrestag der Entlassung Bismarcks." *GS,* V:317–53.
Zur deutschen Münzgesetzgebung. Berlin, 1872.
"Zur Embryologie des Bankgesetzes." *GS,* IV:251–76.
Zur Entwicklung der internationalen Sozialdemokratie. Volkswirtschaftliche Zeitfragen, XIX, nos. 1–2. Berlin, 1897.
"Zur Erinnerung an Friedrich Kapp." *GS,* II:127–36.
"Zur Erneuerung des Bankgesetzes." *Die Nation,* December 24, 1898, January 28, 1899, pp. 181–82, 252–53.
"Zur Geburt des Bankgesetzes." *GS,* IV:277–310.
Zur Naturgeschichte des französischen Krieges. Leipzig, 1871.
"Zur Physiologie des Reichstags." *Allgemeine Zeitung,* May 29, June 3, 17, July 17, 21, 1874.

OTHER SOURCES

Achterberg, Erich. "Ludwig Bamberger." In his *Lebensbilder deutscher Bankiers aus fünf Jahrhunderten.* Frankfurt, 1963.
Allen, Mary. "P.-J. Proudhon in the Revolution of 1848." *Journal of Modern History,* XXIV (1952):1–14.
Ambreit, Paul. *Die gegnerischen Gewerkschaften in Deutschland.* Berlin, 1907.
Amtliche Nachrichten für das General-Gouvernement Elsass. Hagenau.
Anderson, Eugene N. *The Social and Political Conflict in Prussia, 1858–1864.* Lincoln: University of Nebraska Press, 1954.
Andres, Hans. *Die Einführung des konstitutionellen Systems in Grossherzogtum Hessen.* Historische Studien, LXIV. Berlin, 1908.
Anklag-Akte. 2 vols. Zweibrücken, 1850.
Ascher, Abraham. "Baron von Stumm: Advocate of Feudal Capitalism." *Journal of Central European Affairs,* XXII (October 1962):271–85.

——. "Professors as Propagandists: The Politics of the Kathedersozialisten." *Journal of Central European Affairs,* XXIII (October 1963):282–302.

Auerbach, Berthold. *Briefe an seinen Freund.* 2 vols. Frankfurt on the Main, 1884.

Barkin, Kenneth D. *The Controversy Over German Industrialization, 1890–1902.* Chicago: University of Chicago Press, 1970.

Barth, Theodor. *Liberalismus und Sozialdemokratie.* Berlin, n.d. [1908].

——. "Ludwig Bamberger." In his *Politische Porträts.* Berlin, 1904.

——. *Die sozialdemokratische Gedankenwelt.* Volkswirtschaftliche Zeitfragen, XII, nos. 95–96. Berlin, 1890.

Becker, Josef. "Zum Problem der Bismarckschen Politik in der spanischen Thronfrage 1870." *Historische Zeitschrift,* CCXII (June 1971):529–607.

Becker, Julius. *Das deutsche Manchestertum.* Karlsruhe, 1907.

Bergsträsser, Ludwig. *Geschichte der politischen Parteien in Deutschland.* 7th ed. Munich, 1952.

——. *Studien zur Vorgeschichte der Zentrumspartei.* Tubingen, 1910.

Bernstein, Eduard. *Die Geschichte der Berliner Arbeiterbewegung.* 2 vols. Berlin, 1907.

Beutin, Ludwig. "Das Bürgertum als Gesellschaftsstand im 19. Jahrhundert." In his *Gesammelte Schriften zur Wirtschafts- und Sozialgeschichte.* Cologne and Graz, 1963.

Beyerhaus, Gisbert. "Die Krise des deutschen Liberalismus und das Problem der 99 Tage." *Preussische Jahrbücher,* CCXXXIX (1935):1–19.

Binger Anzeiger.

Bismarck, Otto von. *Die gesammelten Werke.* 15 vols. in 19. Berlin, 1923–35.

Block, Hermann. *Die parlamentarische Krisis der Nationalliberalen Partei, 1879–1880.* Munster, 1930.

Blum, Hans. "Ludwig Bambergers Jugend- und Mannesjahre." In his *Vorkämpfer der deutschen Einheit.* Berlin, 1899.

Bockenheimer, Karl Georg. *Mainz im Jahre 1866.* Mainz, 1907.

——. *Mainz in den Jahren 1848 und 1849.* Mainz, 1906.

——. *Mainz in den Jahren 1870 und 1871.* Mainz, 1909.

Boehlich, Walter. "Der Berliner Antisemitismusstreit." *Der Monat,* XVII (September 1965):40–54.

Boese, Franz. *Geschichte des Vereins für Sozialpolitik, 1872–1932.* Berlin, 1939.

Böhme, Helmut. *Deutschlands Weg zur Grossmacht.* Cologne and Berlin, 1966.

Booms, Hans. *Die Deutschkonservative Partei: preussischer Charakter, Reichsauffassung, Nationalbegriff.* Dusseldorf, 1954.

Börckel, Alfred. "Karl Theodor von Zabern." *Hessische Biographien,* I. Darmstadt, 1918.

Born, Karl Erich. "Sozialpolitische Probleme und Bestrebungen in Deutschland von 1848 bis zur Bismarckschen Sozialgesetzgebung." *Vierteljahrschrift fur Sozial- und Wirtschaftsgeschichte,* XLVI (1959):29–44.

——. *Staat und Sozialpolitik seit Bismarcks Sturz.* Wiesbaden, 1957.

Böse, Heinz Günther. "Ludwig Simon von Trier." Ph.D. Dissertation, Gutenberg University, Mainz, 1950.

Böttcher, Friedrich. *Eduard Stephani.* Leipzig, 1887.

Brandenburg, Erich. *50 Jahre Nationalliberale Partei 1867–1917.* Berlin, 1917.

——. *Die Reichsgründung.* 2nd ed., 2 vols. Leipzig, 1923.

——. "Zum älteren deutschen Parteiwesen: eine Erwiderung." *Historische Zeitschrift,* CXIX (1919):62–84.

Braun, Karl. *Bilder aus der deutschen Kleinstaaterei.* Vol. II. Berlin, 1870.

Brentano, Lujo. "DieAgrarreform in Preussen." *Die Nation,* March 13, 20, 27, April 3, 1897, pp. 359–62, 374–79, 392–96, 406–10.

——. "Die Gewerbvereine im verhältnis zur Arbeitergesetzgebung. *Preussische Jahrbücher,* XXIX (1872):586–600.

——. "Die liberale Partei und die Arbeiter." *Preussische Jahrbücher,* XL (1877):112–23.

——. *Mein Leben im Kampf um die soziale Entwicklung Deutschlands.* Jena, 1931.

——. *Die wissenschaftliche Leistung des Herrn Ludwig Bamberger.* Leipzig, 1873.

Buckler, Carlo. *Die politischen und religiösen Kämpfe in Mainz während der Revolutionsjahre 1848–1850.* Giessen, 1936.

Der Bund der Kommunisten: Dokumente und Materialien. Vol. I. Berlin, 1970.

Busch, Moritz. *Tagebuchblätter.* 3 vols. Leipzig, 1899.

——. *Unser Reichskanzler.* 2 vols. Leipzig, 1884.

Bussmann, Walter. "Zur Geschichte des deutschen Liberalismus im 19. Jahrhundert." *Historische Zeitschrift,* CLXXXVI (1958):527–57.

——. "Zwischen Revolution und Reichsgründung, die politische Vorstellungswelt von Ludwig Bamberger." In *Schicksalswege deutscher Vergangenheit,* edited by Walter Hubatsch. Dusseldorf, 1950.

Büttner Siegfried. *Die Anfänge des Parlamentarismus in Hessen-Darmstadt und das du Thilsche System.* Darmstadt, 1969.

Cahn, Enrst. "Die Stellung des Liberalismus zu den wirtschaftlichen und sozialen Problemen." In *Was ist Liberal?* by Leonard Nelson et al. Munich, 1910.

Cahn, W., ed. "Aus Eduard Laskers Nachlass: sein Briefwechsel aus den Jahren 1870–71." *Deutsche Revue,* XVII, no. 2 (1892):46–64, 166–86, 296–317, no. 3 (1892):59–82, 157–77, 283–301, no. 4 (1892):60–76, 190–203, 352–66.

Clark, Evalyn A. "Adolf Wagner: From National Economist to National Socialist." *Political Science Quarterly,* LV (1940):378–411.

Conrad, Else. *Der Verein für Sozialpolitik und seine Wirksamkeit auf dem Gebiet der gewerblichen Arbeiterfrage.* Jena, 1906.

Conze, Werner. "Möglichkeiten und Grenzen der liberalen Arbeiterbewegung in Deutschland: das Beispiel Schulze-Delitzschs." *Sitzungsbericht der Heidelberger Akademie der Wissenschaften. Philosophisch-historische Klasse,* 1965, 2 Abhandlung, pp. 1–28.

——. "Vom 'Pöbel' zun 'Proletariat,' sozialgeschichtliche Voraussetzung für den Sozialismus in Deutschland." *Vierteljahrschrift für Sozial- und Wirtschaftsgeschichte,* XLI (1954):333–64.

Corti, E. C. *Alexander von Battenberg: sein kampf mit den Zaren und Bismarck.* Vienna, 1920.

Cramer, Valmar. "Die katholische Bewegung im Vormärz und im Revolutionsjahr 1848–49." In *Idee, Gestalt und Gestalter des ersten deutschen Katholikentages in Mainz 1848,* edited by Ludwig Lenhart. Mainz, 1948.

Croner, Johannes. *Die Geschichte der agrarischen Bewegung in Deutschland.* Berlin, 1909.

Dehio, Ludwig. "Die preussische Demokratie und der Krieg von 1866." *Forschungen zur brandenburgischen und preussischen Geschichte,* XXXIX (1927):229–59.

Der Demokrat. Mainz.

Demokratenfest in Mainz. Frankfurt, 1849.

Deutsche Parteichronik 1866 bis 1890. Leipzig, 1892.

Diehl, Anton. *Zur Geschichte der katholischen Bewegung im 19. Jahrhundert: das Mainzer Journal im Jahre 1848*. Mainz, 1911.

Dix, Arthur. *Die deutschen Reichstagswahlen 1871–1930 und die Wandlungen der Volksgliederung*. Tubingen, 1930.

Döhn, Hans. "Eisenbahnpolitik und Eisenbahnbau in Rheinhessen, 1835–1914." Ph.D. dissertation, Gutenberg University, Mainz, 1957.

Dorpalen Andreas, "Emperor Frederick III and the German Liberal Movement." *American Historical Review,* LIV, no. 1 (October 1948):1–31.

Droz, Jacques. *Le libéralisme rhénan, 1815–1848*. Paris, 1940.

——. *Les révolutions allemandes de 1848*. Paris, 1957.

Eckert, Georg. *Zur Geschichte der "Sektionen" Wiesbaden und Mainz der Internationalen Arbeiter-Assoziation*. Archiv für Sozialgeschichte, VIII. Hanover, 1968.

Eger, Georg. *Das Reichshaftpflichtgesetz*. Breslau, 1879.

Eigenbrodt, Reinhardt C. T. *Meine Erinnerungen aus den Jahren 1848, 1849 und 1850*. Edited by Ludwig Bergsträsser. Quellen und Forschungen zur Hessischen Geschichte, II. Darmstadt, 1914.

Eisfeld, Gerhard. *Die Entstehung der liberalen Parteien in Deutschland, 1858–1870*. Hanover, 1969.

Elm, Ludwig. "Freisinnige Vereinigung." In *Die bürgerlichen Parteien in Deutschland*. Vol. II. Leipzig, 1970.

——. *Zwischen Fortschritt und Reaktion: Geschichte der Parteien der liberalen Bourgeoisie in Deutschland, 1893–1918*. Berlin, 1968.

Engelberg, Ernst. *Deutschland von 1871 bis 1897*. Berlin, 1965.

Eras, Wolfgang. "Der Kongress deutscher Volkswirte: seine Entstehung und seine IX Jahresversammlung." *Jahrbuch für Volkswirtschaft,* I (1868):138–64.

Eyck, Erich. *Bismarck*. 3 vols. Erlenbach-Zurich, 1941–44.

——. "Ludwig Bamberger." In his *Auf Deutschlands politischem Forum*. Erlenbach-Zurich, 1963.

——. *Der Vereinstag deutscher Arbeitervereine, 1863–1868*. Berlin, 1904.

Faber, Karl Georg. "Realpolitik als Ideologie: die Bedeutung des Jahres 1866 für das politische Denken in Deutschland." *Historische Zeitschrift,* CCIII (1966):1–45.

——. *Die Rheinlande zwischen Restauration und Revolution: Probleme der rheinischen Geschichte von 1814 bis 1848 im Spiegel der zeitgenössischen Publizistik*. Wiesbaden, 1966.

Falck, Richard. *Germain Metternich*. Mainz, 1954.

Feder, Ernst. *Paul Nathan: Politik und Humanität*. Berlin, 1929.

——. *Theodor Barth und der demokratische Gedanke*. Gotha, 1919.

——. "La valeur, comme source-historique, des papiers due député Louis Bamberger." *Société d'histoire moderne, Bulletin,* ser. 7, vol. 32, no. 9.

Fleischmann, Otto. *Geschichte des pfälzischen Aufstandes im Jahre 1849*. Kaiserslautern, 1899.

Flotow, Ernst. "The Congress of German Economists, 1858–1885: A Study in German Unification." Ph.D. dissertation, American University, Washington, D.C., 1941.

Flugblätter, 1848. Stadtbibliothek, Mainz.

Fraenkel, Ernst. "Historische Vorbelastungen des deutschen Parlamentarismus." *Vierteljahrshefte für Zeitgeschichte,* VIII (1960):323–40.

Frank, Walter. *Hofprediger Adolf Stoecker und die christlich-soziale Bewegung*. Berlin, 1928.

Frankfurter Zeitung.

Freund, Michael. *Das Drama der 99 Tage: Krankheit und Tod Friedrichs III.* Cologne and Berlin, 1966.

Freyer, Hans. "Das soziale Ganze und die Freiheit des Einzelnen unter den Bedingungen des industriellen Zeitalters." *Historische Zeitschrift,* CLXXXIII (1957):97–115.

Fricke, Dieter. *Bismarcks Prätorianer: die Berliner politische Polizei im Kampf gegen die deutsche Arbeiterbewegung, 1871–1898.* Berlin, 1962.

——. "Zur Militarisierung des deutschen Geisteslebens im wilhelminischen Kaiserreich: der Fall Leo Arons." *Zeitschrift für Geschichtswissenschaft,* VII (1960):1069–1107.

Fröbel, Julius. *Deutschland und die Friede zu Villafranca.* Frankfurt on the Main, 1859.

——. *Ein Lebenslauf.* 2 vols. Stuttgart, 1890–91.

Fürstenberg, Karl. *Lebensgeschichte eines deutschen Bankiers.* Berlin, 1931.

Gabler, Hans. *Die Entwicklung der deutschen Parteien auf landschaftlicher Grundlage von 1871–1912.* Tubingen, 1934.

Gagel, Walter. *Die Wahlrechtsfrage in der Geschichte der deutschen liberalen Parteien, 1848–1918.* Dusseldorf, 1958.

Gall, Lothar. *Der Liberalismus als regierende Partei. Das Grossherzogtum Baden zwischen Restauration und Reichsgründung.* Veröffentlichungen des Instituts für Europäische Geschichte, XLVII. Wiesbaden, 1968.

——. "Zur Frage der Annexion von Elsass und Lothringen 1870." *Historische Zeitschrift,* CCVII(1968):264–326.

Gebauer, Fritz. "Vom Steuerverweigerer zum Gehilfen Bismarcks. Zur politischen Entwicklung Lothar Buchers von 1848/49 bis 1864." In *Die Grosspreussischmilitarische Reichsgründung 1871.* Edited by Horst Bartel and Ernst Engelberg. Vol. I. Berlin, 1871.

Gehrig, Hans. *Die Begründung des Prinzips der Sozialreform: eine Literar-historische Untersuchung über Manchestertum und Kathedersozialismus.* Jena, 1914.

Geschichte der Frankfurter Zeitung, 1856–1906. Frankfurt on the Main, 1906.

Gilg, Peter. *Die Erneuerung des demokratischen Denkens im wilhelminischen Deutschland.* Wiesbaden, 1965.

Gillis, John R. *The Prussian Bureaucracy in Crisis, 1840–1860: Origins of an Administrative Ethos.* Stanford: Stanford University Press, 1971.

Glagau, Otto. *Des Reiches Not und der neue Kulturkampf.* Osnabruck, 1879.

Gleichauf, W. *Geschichte des Verbandes der deutschen Gewerkvereine (Hirsch-Duncker).* Berlin, 1907.

Goetz, Walter, ed. "Der Briefwechsel Gustav Schmollers mit Lujo Brentano." *Archiv für Kulturgeschichte,* XXVIII (1938):316–54, XXIX (1939):147–83, 331–47, XXX (1940):142–207.

Götz, Ernst. "Konrad Alexis Dumont." In *Hessische Biographien,* vol. II. Darmstadt, 1927.

——. *Die Stellung Hessen-Darmstadts zur deutschen Einigungsfrage in den Jahren 1866–1871.* Darmstadt, 1914.

Grambow, Ludwig. *Die deutsche Freihandelspartei zur Zeit ihrer Blüte.* Jena, 1903.

Grossherzoglich Hessisches Regierungsblatt auf das Jahr 1848. Darmstadt, n.d.

Hagen, Maximilian. *Bismarcks Kolonialpolitik.* Stuttgart and Berlin, 1923.

Hahn, Adalbert. *Die Berliner Revue: ein Beitrag zur Geschichte der konservativen Partei zwischen 1855 und 1875.* Historische Studien, CCXLI. Berlin, 1934.

Hamburger, Ernest. *Juden im öffentlichen Leben Deutschlands: Regierungsmitglieder, Beamte und Parlamentarier in der monarchischen Zeit 1848–1918.* Schriftenreihe wissenschaftlicher Abhandlungen des Leo Baeck Instituts, XIX. Tubingen, 1968.

Hamerow, Theodore S. *Restoration, Revolution, Reaction: Economics and Politics in Germany, 1815–1871.* Princeton: Princeton University Press, 1958.

Hardach, Karl W. *Die Bedeutung wirtschaftlicher Faktoren bei der Wiedereinführung der Eisen- und Getreidezölle in Deutschland 1879.* Schriften zur Wirtschafts- und Sozialgeschichte, VII. Berlin, 1967.

Hartwig, Otto. *Ludwig Bamberger: eine biographische Skizze.* Marburg, 1900.

Heise, Norbert. "Demokratischer Turnerbund und Deutscher Turnerbund." In *Die bürgerlichen Parteien in Deutschland, 1830–1945.* Vol. I. Leipzig, 1968.

Held, Adolf. "Der Verein fur Sozialpolitik." *Die Gegenwart,* January 3, 1874, pp. 3–6.

Helfferich, Karl. *Georg von Siemens.* 3 vols. Berlin, 1921–23.

——. *Geschichte der deutschen Geldreform.* Leipzig, 1898.

——. *Ludwig Bamberger als Währungspolitiker.* Schriften des Vereins zum Schutz der deutschen Goldwährung, I. Berlin, 1900.

——. *Money.* Translated by Louis Infield. 2 vols. New York: The Adelphi Company, 1927.

Hess, Adalbert. *Das Parlament das Bismarck widerstrebte: zur Politik und sozialen Zusammensetzung des preussischen Abgeordnetenhauses der Konflitszeit (1862–1866).* Cologne, 1964.

Heuss, Alfred. *Theodor Mommsen und das 19. Jahrhundert.* Kiel, 1956.

Heyderhoff, Julius, and Wentzcke, Paul, eds. *Deutscher Liberalismus im Zeitalter Bismarcks.* 2 vols. Bonn and Leipzig, 1925–26.

Heyel, Ludwig. *Abriss der Sozialpolitik.* Heidelberg, 1959.

Hildebrandt, Franz. *Reinhard Freiherr von Dalwigk zu Lichtenfels und die deutsche Revolution.* Rostock, 1931.

Hirsch, Max. *Die Arbeiterbewegung und Organisation in Deutschland.* Berlin, 1892.

——. *Die gegenseitigen Hülfskassen und die Gesetzgebung.* Berlin, 1875.

Historische Reichskommission, ed. *Die auswärtige Politik Preussens 1858–1871.* Oldenburg, 1939.

Holborn, Hajo. "Bismarck's Realpolitik." *Journal of the History of Ideas,* XXI (1960): 84–98.

——. "Der deutsche Idealismus in sozialgeschichtlicher Beleuchtung." *Historische Zeitschrift,* CLXXIV (1952): 359–84.

——, ed. *Aufzeichnungen und Erinnerungen aus dem Leben des Botschafters Joseph Maria von Radowitz.* 2 vols. Berlin and Leipzig, 1925.

Huber, Ernst Rudolf. *Heer und Staat.* Hamburg, 1938.

Isegrim [pseud.]. "Der Kathedersozialismus und Ludwig Bamberger." *Sozialistische Monatshefte,* I. Berlin, 1897.

Jacoby, Johann. *Heinrich Simon, ein Gedenkbuch für das deutsche Volk.* Berlin, 1865.

Jöhlinger, Otto. *Bismarck und die Juden.* Berlin, 1921.

Kampffmeyer, Paul, and Altmann, Bruno. *Vor dem Sozialistengesetz: Krisenjahre des Obrigkeitsstaates.* Berlin, 1928.

Kardorff, Siegfried von. *Wilhelm von Kardorff, ein nationaler Parlamentarier im Zeitalter Bismarcks und Wilhelms II.* Berlin, 1936.

Katz-Seibert, Mathilde. *Der politische Radikalismus in Hessen während der Revolution von 1848/49.* Quellen und Forschungen zur Hessischen Geschichte, IX. Darmstadt, 1929.

Keim, Anton Maria. "Die Judenfrage vor dem Hessischen Landtag in der Zeit von 1820–1849: ein Beitrag zur Geschichte der Juden im Vormärz." Ph.D. dissertation, Gutenberg University, Mainz, 1953.

———. "Der politische Gehalt des Mainzer Karnevals im deutschen Vormärz." *Hambacher Gespräche, 1962.* Wiesbaden, 1964.

Kelsch, Wolfgang. *Ludwig Bamberger als Politiker.* Berlin, 1933.

Klein-Hattingen, Oskar. *Geschichte des deutschen Liberalismus.* 2 Vols. Berlin-Schoneberg, 1911 12.

Knoll, Joachim. "Die Elitebildung im Liberalismus des Kaiserreiches." Ph.D. dissertation, Erlangen University, Erlangen, 1956.

———. *Führungsauslese in Liberalismus und Demokratie.* Stuttgart, 1957.

Kolb, Eberhard. "Bismarck und das Aufkommen der Annexionsforderung 1870." *Historische Zeitschrift,* CCIX (1969):318–56.

Köllmann, Wolfgang. *Sozialgeschichte der Stadt Barmen im 19. Jahrhundert.* Soziale Forschung und Praxis, XXI. Tubingen, 1960.

Kranenberg, Ernst. *Die Stellung Ludwig Bambergers zur Sozialpolitik Bismarcks.* Bielefeld, 1935.

Krause, Hans. *Die demokratische Partei von 1848 und die soziale Frage.* Frankfurt on the Main, 1923.

Kremer, Willy. *Der soziale Aufbau der Parteien des deutschen Reichtags von 1871–1918.* Emsdetten, 1934.

Krieger, Leonard. *The German Idea of Freedom.* Boston: Beacon Press, 1957.

———. "Liberal Ideas and Institutions in the German Era of Unification." Ph. D. dissertation, Yale University, New Haven, 1949.

Lambi, Ivo Nikolai. *Free Trade and Protection in Germany, 1868–1879.* Vierteljahrschrift für Sozial- und Wirtschaftsgeschichte, XLIV. Wiesbaden, 1963.

Lamer, Reinhard J. *Der englische Parlamentarismus in der deutschen politischen Theorie im Zeitalter Bismarcks (1857–1890).* Historische Studien, CCCLXXXVII. Lubeck and Hamburg, 1963.

Leiden, Alfred von der. *Die Eisenbahnpolitik des Fürsten Bismarck.* Berlin, 1914.

Lenel, Edith. *Friedrich Kapp: 1824–1884.* Leipzig, 1935.

Leppla, Ruprecht. *Carl Justi/Otto Hartwig: Briefwechsel 1858–1903.* Veröffentlichungen des Stadtarchivs Bonn, V. Bonn, 1968.

Levi, Sali, ed. *Magenza.* Mainz, 1927.

Lidtke, Vernon L. *The Outlawed Party: Social Democracy in Germany, 1878–1890.* Princeton: Princeton University Press, 1966.

Liebeschütz, Hans. "Treitschke and Mommsen on Jewry and Judaism." *Leo Baeck Institute Year Book,* VII. London, 1962.

Liebeschütz, Rahel. "The Wind of Change: Letters of Two Generations from the Biedermeier Period." *Leo Baeck Institute Year Book,* XII. London, 1967.

Lindenlaub, Dieter. *Richtungskämpfe im Verein für Sozialpolitik: Wissenschaft und Sozialpolitik im Kaiserreich.* 2 vols. Wiesbaden.

Lipgens, Walter, "Bismarck, die öffentliche Meinung und die Annexion von Elsass und Lothringen 1870." *Historische Zeitschrift,* CXCIX (1964):31–112.

———. "Bismarck und die Frage der Annexion 1870: eine Erwiderung." *Historische Zeitschrift,* CCVI (1968):586–617.

Lipinski, Richard. *Die Sozialdemokratie von ihren Anfängen bis zur Gegenwart.* 2 vols. Berlin, 1928.

Lotz, Walther. *Geschichte und Kritik des deutschen Bankgesetzes von 14. März 1875.* Leipzig, 1888.

———. *Die Handelspolitik des Deutschen Reiches unter Graf Caprivi und Fürst Hohenlohe (1890-1900).* Schriften des Vereins für Sozialpolitik, XCII. Leipzig, 1901.

———. *Die Ideen der deutschen Handelspolitik von 1860-1891.* Schriften des Vereins für Sozialpolitik, L. Leipzig, 1892.

Lucius von Ballhausen, Robert. *Bismarck Erinnerungen.* Stuttgart and Berlin, 1920.

Lüders, Gustav. *Die demokratische Bewegung in Berlin im Oktober 1848.* Abhandlungen mittlerer und neuerer Geschichte, XI. Berlin and Leipzig, 1909.

Ludwig Bamberger und die Demokraten. Mainz, n.d.

Mainzer Abendblatt.

Mainzer Anzeiger.

Mainzer Flugblätter über 1848-1849. Stadtbibliothek, Mainz.

Mainzer Flugblätter, 1846-1851. Stadtbibliothek, Mainz.

Mainzer Tagblatt.

Mainzer Wochenblatt.

Mainzer Zeitung.

Männer, Ludwig. *Deutschlands Wirtschaft und Liberalismus in der Krise von 1879.* Berlin, 1928.

Massing, Richard. *Rehearsal for Destruction.* New York: Harper, 1949.

Matthes, Heinz Edgar. "Die Spaltung der Nationalliberalen Partei und die Entwicklung des Linksliberalismus bis zur Auflösung der Deutsch-Freisinnigen Partei (1878-1893.)" Ph.D. dissertation, University of Kiel, 1953.

Mayer, Eduard Wilhelm. "Aus der Geschichte der Nationalliberalen Partei in den Jahren 1868 bis 1871." In *Deutscher Staat und deutsche Parteien,* edited by Paul Wentzcke. Munich and Berlin, 1922.

Mayer, Georg. *Die Freihandelslehre in Deutschland.* Jena, 1927.

McCready, H. W. "British Labor and the Royal Commission on Trade Unions 1867–1869." *University of Toronto Quarterly,* XXIV, no. 4 (1955):390–409.

Meier, Eberhard. *Die aussenpolitischen Ideen der Achtundvierziger.* Historische Studien, CCCXXXVII. Berlin, 1938.

Meinecke, Friedrich. "Zur Geschichte des älteren deutschen Parteiwesens." *Historische Zeitschrift,* CXVIII (1917):46–62.

Meisner, Heinrich O. "Der Reichskanzler Caprivi." *Zeitschrift für die gesamte Staatswissenschaft,* CXI, no. 4 (1955):669–752.

Meyer, Alexander. "Ludwig Bamberger." *Biographisches Jahrbuch und Deutscher Nekrolog: 1899,* VI. Berlin, 1900.

Meyer, Michael A. "Great Debate on Antisemitism: Jewish Reaction to New Hostility in Germany 1879–1881." *Leo Baeck Institute Year Book,* XI. London, 1966.

Molt, Peter, *Der Reichstag vor der improvisierten Revolution.* Cologne, 1963.

Mommsen, Theodor. "Ludwig Bamberger." In his *Reden und Aufsätze.* Berlin, 1905.

Mommsen, Wilhelm. *Bismarcks Sturz und die Parteien.* Berlin, 1924.

———. *Johannes von Miquel.* Stuttgart, 1928.

Morgan, Roger. *The German Social Democrats and the First International, 1864–1872.* Cambridge: Cambridge University Press, 1965.

Morsey, Rudolf. *Die oberste Reichsverwaltung unter Bismarck, 1867–1890.* Munster, 1957.

Müller, Josef. *Die Entwicklung des Rassenantisemitismus in den letzten Jahrzehnten des 19. Jahrhunderts.* Historische Studien CCCLXXII. Berlin, 1940.

Muziol, Roman. *Karl Rodbertus als Begründer der sozialrechtlichen Anschauungsweise.* Jena. 1927.

Namier, Lewis B. *1848: The Revolution of the Intellectuals.* London, 1944.

Nathan, Paul. "Ludwig Bamberger, ein Sohn der Stadt Mainz." *Volkszeitung* (Mainz), July 27, 1923.

National Zeitung. Berlin.

Neher, Walter. *Arnold Ruge als Politiker und politischer Schriftsteller: Ein Beitrag zur Geschichte des 19. Jahrhunderts.* Heidelberg, 1933.

Neitzke, Paul. *Die deutschen politischen Flüchtlinge in der Schweiz 1848/49.* Charlottenburg, 1927.

Nerrlich, Paul, ed. *Arnold Ruges Briefwechsel und Tagebuchblätter aus den Jahren 1825–1880.* Vol. II. Berlin, 1886.

Neubach, Helmut. *Die Ausweisungen von Polen und Juden aus Preussen 1885/86.* Wiesbaden, 1967.

———. "Die Mainzer Reichstagsabgeordneten von 1871 bis 1918." *Mainzer Almanach 1969.* Mainz, 1969.

Neues ABC Buch für freisinnige Wähler. Vols. III, IV. Berlin, 1884, 1885.

Nichols, J. Alden. *Germany After Bismarck: The Caprivi Era, 1890-94.* Cambridge: Harvard University Press, 1958.

Nipperdey, Thomas. "Die Organisation der bürgerlichen Parteien in Deutschland vor 1918." *Historische Zeitschrift,* CLXXXV (1958):550–602.

———. *Die Organisation der deutschen Parteien vor 1918.* Beiträge zur Geschichte des Parlamentarismus und der politischen Parteien, XVIII. Dusseldorf, 1961.

Nöll von der Nahmer, Robert. *Bismarcks Reptilienfonds: aus den Geheimakten Preussens und des deutschen Reiches.* Mainz, 1968.

Noyes, P. H. *Organization and Revolution: Working-Class Associations in the German Revolutions of 1848–1849.* Princeton: Princeton University Press, 1966.

Obermann, Karl. *Die deutschen Arbeiter in der Revolution von 1848.* 2d ed. Berlin, 1953.

O'Boyle, Lenore. "The Democratic Left in Germany, 1848." *Journal of Modern History,* XXXIII (December 1961):374–83.

———. "Liberal Political Leadership in Germany, 1867–1884." *Journal of Modern History,* XXVIII (December 1956):338–52.

———. "The Problem of an Excess of Educated Men in Western Europe, 1800–1850." *Journal of Modern History,* XLII (December 1970):471–95.

Oncken, Hermann. "Bennigsen und die Epochen des parlamentarischen Liberalismus in Deutschland und Preussen." *Historische Zeitschrift,* CIV (1910):52–79.

———. "Ludwig Bamberger." In his *Historisch-politische Aufsätze und Reden.* Vol. II. Munich and Berlin, 1914.

———. *Rudolf von Bennigsen.* 2 vols. Stuttgart and Leipzig, 1910.

———, ed. "Aus den Briefen Rudolf von Bennigsens." *Deutsche Revue,* XXIX–XXXIII (1904–08).

Oppenheim, Heinrich Bernhard. "Eine persönliche Bemerkung in Sachen des 'Volkswirtschaftlichen Verirrungen.' " *Die Gegenwart,* April 6, 1872, p. 175.

———. "Ein ernstes Wort über scurrile Angriffe." *Die Gegenwart,* April 27, 1872, p. 223.

———. *Vermischte Schriften aus bewegter Zeit.* Stuttgart and Leipzig, 1866.

———. "Volkswirtschaftliche Verirrungen." *Die Gegenwart,* March 30, 1872, pp. 145–47.

———. "Die Wohnungsnot und der Kommunismus." *Die Gegenwart,* May 4, 1872, pp. 224–27.

Osterroth, Franz, and Schuster, Dieter. *Chronik der deutschen Sozialdemokratie.* Hanover, 1963.

Pachnicke, Hermann. "Ludwig Bamberger." In his *Führende Manner.* Mainz, 1890.

Pack, Wolfgang. *Das parlamentarische Ringen um das Sozialistengesetz Bismarcks 1878–1890.* Beiträge zur Geschichte des Parlamentarismus und der politischen Parteien, XX. Dusseldorf, 1961.

Parisius, Ludolf. *Deutschlands politische Parteien und das Ministerium Bismarck.* Vol. I. Berlin, 1878.

Pflanze, Otto. *Bismarck and the Development of Germany: The Period of Unification, 1815–1871.* Princeton: Princeton Unversity Press, 1963.

Philippson, Martin. *Max von Forckenbeck.* Dresden and Leipzig, 1898.

——, ed. [Forckenbeck's letters]. *Deutsche Revue,* XXIII, no. 4 (1898):1–16, 141–58, XXIV, no. 1 (1899):129–46, XXIV, no. 2 (1899):164–73.

Phillips, A., ed. *Die Reichstagswahlen von 1867 bis 1883.* Berlin, 1883.

Portner, Ernst. *Die Einigung Italiens im Urteil liberaler deutscher Zeitgenossen: Studie zur inneren Geschichte des kleindeutschen Liberalismus.* Bonner Historische Forschungen, XIII. Bonn, 1959.

Poschinger, Heinrich von. *Fürst Bismarck und der Bundesrat.* Vols. II–IV. Stuttgart and Leipzig, 1897, 1898, 1901.

——. *Fürst Bismarck und die Parlamentarier.* 3 vols. Breslau, 1896.

——, ed. *Bismarck Portefeuille.* 5 vols. Stuttgart and Leipzig, 1898–1900.

——, ed. *Erinnerungen aus dem Leben von Hans Viktor von Unruh.* Stuttgart, 1895.

Puhle, Hans-Jürgen. *Agrarische Interessenpolitik und preussischer Konservatismus im wilhelminischen Reich (1893–1914).* Hanover, 1967.

Pulzer, Peter. *The Rise of Political Anti-Semitism in Germany and Austria.* New York: Wiley, 1964.

Quandt, Otto. *Die Anfänge der Bismarckschen Sozialgesetzgebung und die Haltung der Parteien: das Unfallversicherungsgesetz, 1881–1884.* Historische Studien, CCCXLIV. Berlin, 1938.

Rachfahl, Felix. "Eugen Richter und der Linksliberalismus im neuen Reiche." *Zeitschrift für Politik,* V (1912):261–374.

——. "Windthorst und der Kulturkampf." *Preussische Jahrbücher,* CXXXV (1909): 213–52, 460–90, CXXXVI (1909):56–73.

Rapp, A. *Die Württemberger und die nationale Frage, 1863–1871.* Stuttgart, 1910.

Reichstagsbureau, ed. *Generalregister zu den stenographischen Berichten . . . des Deutschen Reichstages,* III, Session 1894–95. Berlin, 1896.

Die Reichstagswahlen seit 1871. Berlin, 1903.

Reis, Eduard. *Mainzer Silhouetten und Genrebilder.* Mainz, 1841.

Rheinische Volkszeitung. Mainz.

Richter, Eugen. *Im alten Reichstag.* 2 vols. in 1. Berlin, 1894–96.

Ritter, Alan. *The Political Thought of Pierre-Joseph Proudhon.* Princeton: Princeton University Press, 1969.

Robolsky, Hermann. "Ludwig Bamberger." In his *Der Deutsche Reichstag.* Vol. I. Leipzig, 1884.

Rodenberg, Julius. "Ludwig Bamberger." *Deutsche Rundschau,* XCIX (May 1899):296–303.

Röhl, J. C. G. "The Disintegration of the *Kartell* and the Politics of Bismarck's Fall from Power, 1887–90." *Historical Journal,* IX, no. 1 (1966):60–89.

——. *Germany Without Bismarck.* London, 1967.

Rosenberg, Hans. *Grosse Depression und Bismarckzeit: Wirtschaftsablauf, Gesellschaft und Politik in Mitteleuropa.* Berlin, 1967.

Rössler, Hellmuth. "Mainz im Jahre 1848." *Mainzer Zeitschrift,* LVIII (1963):89–99.

Roth, Guenther. *The Social Democrats in Imperial Germany.* Totowa, N.J.: Bedminster Press, 1963.

Rothfels, Hans. "Bismarck's Social Policy and the Problem of State Socialism in Germany." *Sociological Review,* XXX(1938):81–94, 288 302.

———. "Bismarck und Johann Jacoby." *Königsberger Beiträge.* Konigsberg, 1929.

———. *Prinzipienfragen der Bismarckschen Sozialpolitik.* Konigsberg, 1929.

———. *Theodor Lohmann und die Kampfjahre der staatlichen Sozialpolitik. (1871–1905).* Berlin, 1927.

Rubinstein, Adolf. *Die Deutsch-Freisinnige Partei bis zu ihrem Auseinanderbruch (1884–1893).* Basel, 1935.

Rüdt von Collenberg, Ludwig. *Die deutsche Armee von 1871 bis 1914.* Forschungen und Darstellungen aus dem Reichsarchiv, IV. Berlin, 1922.

Saile, Wolfgang. *Hermann Wagener und sein Verhältnis zu Bismarck.* Tubingen, 1958.

Salomon, Felix. *Die deutschen Parteiprogramme.* 2 vols. Leipzig, 1907.

Sandberger, Dietrich. *"Die Ministerkandidatur Bennigsens."* Historische Studien, CLXXXVII. Berlin, 1929.

Schaab, K. A. *Diplomatische Geschichte der Juden zu Mainz und dessen Umgebung.* Mainz, 1855.

Scheel, Heinrich. "Die Mainzer Republik im Spiegel der deutschen Geschichtsschreibung." *Jahrbuch für Geschichte,* IV. Berlin, 1969.

Schieder, Theodor. *Die kleindeutsche Partei in Bayern in den Kämpfen um die nationale Einheit 1863–1871.* Munich, 1936.

———. "Das Verhältnis von politischer und gesellschaftlicher Verfassung und die Krise des bürgerlichen Liberalismus." *Historische Zeitschrift,* CLXXVII (1954):49–74.

Schmidt-Volkmar, Erich. *Der Kulturkampf in Deutschland 1871–1890.* Gottingen, 1962.

Schmoller, Gustav. "Die Arbeiterfrage." *Preussische Jahrbücher,* XIV (1864):393–424, 523–47.

———. "Die soziale Frage und der preussische Staat." *Preussische Jahrbücher,* XXXIII (1874):323–42.

Schnabel, Franz. *Der Zusammenschluss des politischen Katholizismus in Deutschland im Jahre 1848.* Heidelberger Abhandlungen zur mittleren und neueren Geschichte, XXIX. Heidelberg, 1910.

Schraepler, Ernst. "Linksliberalismus und Arbeiterschaft in der preussischen Konfliktszeit." In *Forschungen zu Staat und Verfassung,* edited by Richard Dietrich. Berlin, 1958.

Schroth, Hans-Georg. *Welt- und Staatsideen des deutschen Liberalismus in der Zeit der Einheits- und Freiheitskämpfe, 1859–1866.* Historische Studien, CCI. Berlin, 1931.

Schübelin, Walter. *Das Zollparlament und die Politik von Baden, Bayern und Württemberg, 1866–1870.* Historische Studien, CCLXII. Berlin, 1935.

Schuchert, August. "Der erste Mainzer Katholikentag in seinem historisch-ideellen Verlauf." In *Idee, Gestalt und Gestalter des ersten deutschen Katholikentages in Mainz, 1848,* edited by Ludwig Lenhart. Mainz, 1948.

Schulthess' Europäischer Geschichtskalender, 1891, 1892, 1893. Munich, 1892, 1893, 1894.

Schunke, Werner. *Die preussischen Freihändler und die Entstehung der Nationalliberalen Partei.* Erfurt, 1916.

Schüssler, Wilhelm, ed. *Die Tagebücher des Freiherrn Reinhard v. Dalwigk zu Lichtenfels aus den Jahren 1860–1871.* Stuttgart and Berlin, 1920.

Seeber, Gustav. "Deutsche Freisinnige Partei." In *Die bürgerlichen Parteien in Deutschland.* Vol. I. Leipzig, 1968.

——. *Zwischen Bebel und Bismarck: zur Geschichte des Linksliberalismus in Deutschland, 1871–1893.* Berlin, 1965.

Seeger, Manfred. *Die Politik der Reichsbank von 1876–1914 im Lichte der Spielregeln der Goldwährung.* Volkswirtschaftliche Schriften, CXXV. Berlin, 1968.

Sell, Friedrich C. *Die Tragödie des deutschen Liberalismus.* Stuttgart, 1953.

Shanahan, William O. *German Protestants Face the Social Question, 1815–1871.* Notre Dame, Ind.: University of Notre Dame Press, 1954.

Sheehan, James J. *The Career of Lujo Brentano: A Study of Liberalism and Social Reform in Imperial Germany.* Chicago: University of Chicago Press, 1966.

Siemens-Helmholtz, Ellen von, ed. *Anna von Helmholtz: Ein Lebensbild in Briefen.* 2 vols. Berlin, 1929.

Sonnemann, Rolf. *Die Auswirkungen des Schutzzolls auf die Monopolisierung der deutschen Eisen- und Stahlindustrie, 1879–1892.* Berlin, 1960.

Der Sozialdemokrat. Zurich.

Spahn, Martin. "Zur Entstehung der nationalliberalen Partei." *Zeitschrift für Politik,* I (1907):346–470.

Specht, Fritz, ed. *Die Reichstagswahlen von 1867 bis 1897.* Berlin, 1898.

Spellmeyer, Hans. *Deutsche Kolonialpolitik im Reichstag.* Stuttgart, 1931.

Stadelmann, Rudolf. *Soziale und politische Geschichte der Revolution von 1848.* Munich, 1948.

Steinbrecher, Ursula. *Liberale Parteiorganisation unter besonderer Berücksichtigung des Linksliberalismus, 1871–1893.* Cologne, 1960.

Steinsdorfer, Helmut. *Franz Freiherr Schenk von Stauffenberg als ein bayrischer und deutscher Politiker.* Munich, 1959.

Stenographische Berichte über die Verhandlungen des deutschen Reichstags. Berlin, 1871–93.

Stenographische Berichte über die Verhandlungen des Reichstags des Norddeutschen Bundes, 1869. Berlin, 1869.

Stenographische Berichte über die Verhandlungen des Zollparlaments. Berlin, 1868–70.

Stillich, Oskar. *Die politischen Parteien in Deutschland.* Vol. II, *Der Liberalismus.* Leipzig, 1911.

Stürmer, Michael. "Staatsstreichgedanken im Bismarckreich." *Historische Zeitschrift,* CCIX (1969):566–617.

Tirrell, Sarah R. *German Agrarian Politics after Bismarck's Fall.* New York: Columbia University Press, 1951.

Tönnies, Ferdinand. *Der Kampf um das Sozialistengesetz, 1878.* Berlin, 1929.

Toury, Jacob. *Die politischen Orientierungen der Juden in Deutschland: von Jena bis Weimar.* Schriftenreihe wissenschaftlicher Abhandlungen des Leo Baeck Instituts, XV. Tubingen, 1966.

Treitschke, Heinrich. "Der Sozialismus und seine Gönner." *Preussische Jahrbücher,* XXXIV (1874):67–110, 248–301.

——. *Ein Wort über unser Judentum.* Berlin, 1880.

Ullstein, Leopold. *Eugen Richter als Publizist und Herausgeber.* Leipzig, 1930.

Valentin, Veit. *Frankfurt am Main und die Revolution von 1848–1849.* Stuttgart and Berlin, 1908.

_____.*Geschichte der deutschen Revolution von 1848–1849.* 2 vols. Berlin, 1930–31.

Valjavec, Fritz. *Die Entstehung der politischen Strömungen in Deutschland, 1770–1815.* Munich, 1951.

Vogel, Walter. *Bismarcks Arbeiterversicherung.* Braunschweig, 1931.

———. *Die Tagebücher des Freiherrn Reinhard von Dalwigk zu Lichtenfels als Geschichtsquelle.* Historische Studien, CCXXXIV. Berlin, 1933.

Vogt, Carl. *Das achtzehnte September in Frankfurt.* Frankfurt on the Main, 1848.

———. *Aus meinem Leben.* Stuttgart, 1896.

———. *Carl Vogts politische Briefe an Friedrich Kolb.* Biel, 1870.

———. *Studien zur gegenwärtigen Lage Europas.* Geneva and Bern, 1859.

Völkerling, Fritz. *Der deutsche Kathedersozialismus.* Berlin, 1959.

Wacker, Theodor. *Entwicklung der Sozialdemokratie in den zehn ersten Reichstagswahlen (1871–1898).* Freiburg, 1903.

Wahl, Adalbert. *Deutsche Geschichte von der Reichsgründung bis zum Ausbruch des Weltkriegs (1871 bis 1914).* 4 vols. Stuttgart, 1926–36.

Waldersee, Alfred. *Denkwürdigkeiten des General Feldmarschall Alfred Grafen von Waldersee.* 3 vols. Stuttgart and Berlin, 1923.

Washausen, Helmut. "Hamburg und die Kolonialpolitik des Deutschen Reiches (1880 bis 1890)." Ph.D. dissertation, Gottingen University, 1967.

Wawrzinek, Kurt. *Die Entstehung der deutschen Antisemitenparteien.* Historische Studien, CXLVIII. Berlin, 1927.

Weber, Hans. *Der Bankplatz Berlin.* Cologne and Opladen, 1957.

Wegner, Konstanze. *Theodor Barth und die Freisinnige Vereinigung.* Tubingen, 1968.

Wehler, Hans-Ulrich. *Bismarck und der Imperialismus.* Cologne and Berlin, 1969.

———, ed. *Freidrich Kapp: vom radikalen Frühsozialisten des Vormärz zum liberalen Parteipolitiker des Bismarckreichs: Briefe 1843–1884.* Frankfurt on the Main, 1969.

Weiler, Wendelin. *Darstellung der Ereignisse in Mainz im ersten halben Jahre 1848.* Mainz, n.d. [1848].

Westphal, Otto. *Welt- und Staatsauffassung des deutschen Liberalismus, eine Untersuchung über die Preussischen Jahrbücher und die konstitutionellen Liberalismus in Deutschland von 1858–1863.* Munich and Berlin, 1919.

Williamson, John G. *Karl Helfferich, 1872–1924.* Princeton: Princeton University Press, 1971.

Wilmowski, Gustav von. *Meine Erinnerungen an Bismarck.* Breslau, 1900.

Windell, George G. *The Catholics and German Unity, 1866–1871.* Minneapolis: University of Minnesota Press, 1954.

Winkler, Heinrich A. *Preussischer Liberalismus und deutscher Nationalstaat: Studien zur Geschichte der Deutschen Fortschrittspartei 1861–1866.* Tübinger Studien zur Geschichte und Politik, XVII. Tubingen, 1964.

Wippermann, Karl. "Ludwig Bamberger." In *Allgemeine Deutsche Biographie,* XLVI. Leipzig, 1902.

Wittrock, Gerhard. *Die Kathedersozialisten bis zur Eisenacher Versammlung 1872.* Historische Studien, CCCL. Berlin, 1939.

Zechlin, Egmont. *Staatsstreichpläne Bismarcks und Wilhelms II, 1890, 1894.* Stuttgart and Berlin, 1929.

Ziekursch, Johannes. *Politische Geschichte des neuen deutschen Kaissereiches.* 3 vols. Frankfurt on the Main, 1925–30.

Zorn, Wolfgang. "Wirtschafts- und sozialgeschichtliche Zusammenhänge der Deutschen

Reichsgründungszeit (1850–1879)." *Historische Zeitschrift,* CXCVII (1963): 318–42.

Zucker, Stanley. "Ludwig Bamberger and the Crisis of German Liberalism." Ph.D. dissertation, University of Wisconsin, 1968.

———. "Ludwig Bamberger and the Politics of the Cold Shoulder: German Liberalism's Response to Working Class Legislation in the 1870's." *European Studies Review,* II, no. 3 (1972):201–26.

———. "Ludwig Bamberger and the Rise of Anti-Semitism in Germany, 1848–1893." *Central European History,* III, no. 4 (December 1970):332–52.

Index